Male Envy

Male Envy

The Logic of Malice in Literature and Culture

MERVYN NICHOLSON

LEXINGTON BOOKS
Lanham • Boulder • New York • Oxford

LEXINGTON BOOKS

Published in the United States of America
by Lexington Books
4720 Boston Way, Lanham, Maryland 20706

12 Hid's Copse Road
Cumnor Hill, Oxford OX2 9JJ, England

Copyright © 1999 by Lexington Books

All rights reserved. No part of this publication may be reproduced,
stored in a retrieval system, or transmitted in any form or by any
means, electronic, mechanical, photocopying, recording, or otherwise,
without the prior permission of the publisher.

British Library Cataloguing in Publication Information Available

Library of Congress Cataloging-in-Publication Data

Nicholson, Mervyn, 1951–
   Male envy : the logic of malice in literature and culture / Mervyn
Nicholson
     p.   cm.
   Includes bibliographical references and index.
   ISBN 0-7391-0062-9 (alk. paper)
   1. Envy in literature. 2. Evil eye in literature. 3. Literature—
History and criticism.   I. Title.
PN56.E64N53 1999
809'.93353—dc21   99–10347
                                                                     CIP

Printed in the United States of America

♾™ The paper used in this publication meets the minimum requirements of American
National Standard for Information Sciences—Permanence of Paper for Printed Library
Materials, ANSI/NISO Z39.48–1992.

to Susan and Christian

Tomorrow to fresh woods, and pastures new.

CONTENTS

Acknowledgments	ix
1. The Scene of Male Envy	1
2. The Tricky Female	49
3. Object Thinking	83
4. Holy Murder	131
5. The Academy of Envy	171
6. Transform	215
Index	247
About the Author	261

Acknowledgments

An earlier version of Chapter 2, "The Tricky Female," appeared as *"L'Homme fatal* in *Hedda Gabler"* in *Modern Drama* 35 (1992): 365-77.

Excerpt from Edward Albee, *Who's Afraid of Virginia Woolf?* (Scribner, 1962), reprinted by permission of Simon & Schuster.

Excerpt from E. J. Dijksterhuis, *The Mechanization of the World Picture*, trans. C. Dikshoorn (Princeton University Press, 1986), reprinted by permission of Princeton University Press.

Excerpts from Sigmund Freud, *Totem and Taboo*, *New Introductory Lectures on Psychoanalysis* (W. W. Norton, 1966), reprinted by permission of W. W. Norton.

Excerpts from Henrik Ibsen, *Ibsen: Four Major Plays*, trans. James McFarlane and Jens Arup (Oxford University Press, 1962), reprinted by permission of Oxford University Press.

Excerpts from C. S. Lewis, *The Screwtape Letters* (HarperCollins, 1955), reprinted by permission of HarperCollins Publishers, Ltd.

Excerpts from Friedrich Nietzsche, *The Birth of Tragedy and The Genealogy of Morals*, trans. Francis Golffing (Doubleday, 1956), reprinted by permission of Doubleday.

Excerpt from Jean-Jacques Rousseau, *The Social Contract*, trans. Maurice Cranston (Penguin, 1968), reprinted by permission of The Peters, Fraser & Dunlop Group, Ltd.

Excerpts from Klaus Theweleit, *Male Fantasies, Vol 1: Women, Floods, Bodies, History*, trans. Stephen Conway (University of Minnesota Press, 1987), reprinted by permission of University of Minnesota Press.

1

The Scene of Male Envy

To be weak / Is miserable, doing or suffering.
Satan, *Paradise Lost*

Man is projected on a scene where he has to be a warrior among warriors. He is assigned to the scene of castration. He must defend his phallus; if not, it is death.
Hélène Cixous

It is a curious fact that there is a kind of taboo on envy. One must not speak of it, especially male envy, the hostility that males feel for other males. By "envy," I do not mean the momentary flash of resentment when someone else gets a gift or a lucky break, but instead something more continuous, something that is not easy to define but that has the power to motivate action and to condition consciousness. The emblem of this envy is the "evil eye," a superstition that is surprisingly common around the world and that expresses the ominous feeling that surrounds envy, its intensity, indeed its supernatural aura.

Envy and the malice that undergirds it are difficult to discuss, but male envy is especially difficult; the taboo is doubly strong. Male envy raises profound and fundamental questions and directs our attention to aspects of experience that are either neglected or threatening. The envy of males toward other males is a powerful force; its effects are subtle, intricate, and deep. It also has many bizarre and strange features. But the basic point of departure is simple enough, and that is that male-male relationships are constituted in our culture as hostile.

In part, the taboo expresses the fact that men are not supposed to be envious, and if they are, if they admit it, then there is something "wrong" with them—they are defective. To envy is to fail a kind of test. One is not supposed to be envious, because envy is weakness, and weakness is something a man never admits, even to himself. Despite this silence about envy—this silencing—male envy is pervasive. It is silent, but it is everywhere.

The silence of male envy actually proves to be a complex problem in itself, at the center of an already complicated subject, with ramifications extending in all directions. Envy is close to jealousy—the feeling of anger and hostility toward someone of preferred status or quality, but it is also close to malice—an unmotivated hatred that seeks to damage another person, and that enjoys the suffering of others: a hatred of what is good *because* it is good. Thus, unavoidably, envy takes us deep into the mystery of evil, in a way that few topics can. The silence of envy is ultimately the silence of evil itself.

The mysterious potency of envy is a recurring motif in folklore. Belief in the evil eye is not only common, it is also a focus for many other superstitions and practices. And it is *old*. It dates back at least to the ancient Egyptians and was very common among the Romans. The feeling that envy is to be avoided because it evokes dangerous supernatural powers indicates the instinctive respect, even awe, that this emotion, this state of mind, elicits. It is interesting that the evil eye has been subjected to much academic processing, but envy as such is practically untouched. It is perhaps no coincidence that extensive discussion of the evil eye has followed a loss of belief in it, as if it were now safe to talk about. By contrast, what discussion there is of envy as such is typically fragmentary, casual, unhelpful. Or it simply repeats commonplaces without analyzing them. This absence of discussion is curiously consistent with the taboo around envy.

One reason why this study deals with literature, with stories, is that literature is subtly at odds with the culture of male envy. It breaks the taboo. It shows envy with an unmatched precision. Furthermore, literature is the expression of imagination; it depends on a richness of sensory experience that is closed to envy, because of envy's obsessiveness: envy cannot permit the openness and receptivity that imagination requires. Literature not only illuminates male envy, but the reverse is also true: studying male envy yields many insights into literature. In fact, it discloses an aspect of literature that has been neglected, as if to conform with the taboo noted earlier.

Envy is one of the traditional seven deadly sins, but it has none of the glamor or *frisson* associated with sin (lust for example), or even with wrongdoing. "Envy is the hardest sin to acknowledge," says René Girard,[1] whereas it is practically meritorious to admit to other sins. One may admit to lust in one's heart, but hardly to envy in one's heart. Nobody boasts about being envious: a fact that has been noted for centuries. "No one claims to be envious," says Plutarch in antiquity—envy always is "masked and hidden"[2]; envy is shameful. One keeps it quiet, as indeed the whole subject of male envy is kept quiet. Speaking about it is somehow wrong, or perhaps threatening, or worse, in bad taste. "Malicious hatred is all pervasive, yet it is curiously unfashionable," says Joseph Berke.[3] Ultimately, male envy is a horror.

The silence of envy is a recurring theme in discussions of the subject: "Human kind has reacted towards envy with more ignorance and concealment than towards sex," notes Gonzalo Fernàndez de la Mora in *Egalitarian Envy: The Political Foundations of Social Justice*. Other students of envy, Joseph Berke and Helmut Schoeck, argue similarly,[4] following Max Scheler's study *Ressentiment* and its Nietzschean inspiration. Envy is seen to be inseparable from memory and repetition, and is in effect a perversion of imagination (as it is for example in David Hume's analysis of envy in his *Treatise of Human Nature*).[5] "Ressentiment" renews, in the self, perceived wrongs from the past: "This form of envy strips the opponent of his very existence, for this existence as such is felt to be a 'pressure,' a 'reproach,' and unbearable humiliation."[6] To speak this kind of humiliation, even to oneself, is to risk renewing it; hence its speech is silence. In turn, envy is a form of tribute, and the one envied may take gratification from it, as a kind of offering to his ego, even if it is socially unacceptable to speak this gratification. Thus, envy remains doubly unspoken.

But the unspoken has meaning of other kinds. For the unspoken is that which is taken for granted; it is so much a part of reality that it operates unconsciously, like breathing or blinking. But then, the most important things are always unspoken. Male envy occupies the fringes of awareness: it is something that is known, and not known, at the same time; understood, and denied understanding. Merely to assert something implies its opposite, as in some Hegelian dialectic. The silence is a communication, a sharing without speaking.

In this respect, male envy oddly links up with a notion that is very popular now, the notion that repressing something actually draws attention to it and even (in Foucault) brings it into being. In computer jargon, to delete is to insert. Ignoring something is actually a way of acknowledging it. Hence the fascination with various forms of paralysis, or what literary theorists term "aporia," a point in a text where contradictory meanings are present in the same words: a cancelling out of the possibility of meaning, where erasing merely reinscribes.[7] Variations on this paradigm are everywhere. It is especially popular in that curious but common assumption that when others disagree with one's argument, their disagreement proves that one is right. Negative criticism or disagreement—Freud would have called it "resistance"—actually *demonstrates* one's correctness.

Whatever its validity, this assumption generates a convoluted type of arguing that is characteristic of male envy. Because it is usually implied rather than expressed openly, this type of argument inevitably has a predilection for obscurity. Obscurity of expression and irrationality of thinking are in fact instinctive to male envy. Since winning is everything for male envy, confusion can be a useful tactic. Given its instinctive predilection for convoluted and opaque rhetoric, it is in turn imperative to discuss male envy in the plainest, most direct terms possible.

Despite its immense influence, the "resistance" paradigm (disagreement proves one is right) is not really so mysterious: paying attention to something is paying attention to it, whether one approves or disapproves, whether one represses or emphasizes it. Thus, while male envy is also unspoken, it is not something esoteric or textual; it is powerful and immediate. The silence that surrounds it is its *modus operandi*, its way of working, and not a paralysis or ironic paradox—male envy is not an intellectual game. On the contrary, intellectuals engage in it very seriously, and for keeps. The silence of envy is not simply the hiding of envy, but a kind of fear, or perhaps awe, as in the complex superstitions of the evil eye: it suggests some primal power, which might get out of control if acknowledged openly. It is as if envy were access to a large but evil force, like the power the witches represent in *Macbeth*, a play much concerned with our topic—and the object of intense superstition on the part of theatre people. So potent is envy that merely to speak of it is to risk untold dangers.

In Shakespeare, the real target of Macbeth's "ambition" seems to be the life-force itself, the sexual power of reproduction, fertility in nature and humanity, as Macbeth's preoccupation with killing children and progeny and the boasted childlessness of his wife imply. It is hardly an accident that the traditional amulet used against the evil eye is a representation of the sex organs: a fertility symbol to ward off the principle that kills fertility. In *Envy and Gratitude*, the psychoanalyst Melanie Klein argues that envy "is unconsciously felt to be *the greatest sin of all*, because it spoils and harms the good object which is *the source of life*."[8] The silence of envy, in the manner of the silence of the mafiosi, is actually part of a language, or what is in practice a *code* of male envy.[9]

Women envy, too, of course, but it seems acceptable to discuss women's envy in a way that it does not seem acceptable to discuss the envy of men. Male envy has, however, constant relevance to women, because it has shaped women's roles and relations with men in countless forms. Men's dominance has made their envy more potent—but also less accessible to scrutiny, and for that very reason, extremely important to probe. Because of the power of men in society generally, male envy has been a structuring force in social and individual experience and is therefore qualitatively different from the envy of women. Unremitting, intense competitive struggle is the context of that envy—male power over other men, not simply as a kind of monolithic power over women. This is a force both social and psychological at the same time, at once intricate and brutal, with effects that sometimes surprise and sometimes shock.

Finally, because the presence of male envy is so extensive, and so subtle, I may seem to exaggerate its power. But this is to be expected: as soon as one discusses openly what is done silently, the openness itself appears to exaggerate, simply by speaking.

* * *

To begin, a kind of précis of the way male envy works is helpful. For this purpose, a useful beer commercial displays the essentials rather neatly; in this particular beer commercial, there are three young men drinking their brew at a table in a bar. Enter two beautiful women, laughing. They sit down—and eye the boys. After much judicious ogling, they beckon one boy over. This fellow, while not ugly, is not handsome: he is a kind of everymale, one of the guys—someone that the male target audience can identify with. What does distinguish him is that he is paying attention, whereas his friends are not (the full significance of this point will be clearer later). Nevertheless, at first, he cannot believe his good luck —they want *him* to come over—and not one of his better-looking buddies? Unlikely as it seems, the young women pick *him*.

"Pick" / "pickup." The point of this commercial is *de te fabula narratur*: drink this beer, and you, too . . . ! But all is done silently, by gesture, without words. In the scene of envy, no words are necessary. Communication is silent. The last frame in the commercial, always a crucial one, displays our young man with the two women beside him, happily possessing what is a standard male fantasy—*two* beautiful women at a time, not just one. The Beach Boys give us the definitive encapsulation of this theme in "Surf City," possibly their best-known song, when they rhapsodize ecstatically of having two girls for each boy. But ironically, this final display shows our friend looking not at the beautiful women, but back at his male friends—and at the male viewing audience, mutely saying: Look at me, guys. Getta load of what *I* got! And what you *don't*!

This commercial identifies beer with sex power—in this case, access by a young man of average looks to women of exceptional beauty. Beer is thus the proverbial elixir of love. Sex, as advertisers remind us with the tireless patience of machines, sells. Yet the real point of this drama is something else altogether— male envy: a force that permeates patriarchal culture. In the code of male envy, sex is regarded as a reward for winning: it is something that winning males get, and losing males don't. This way of understanding of sex, as a reward for winning, cannot be overemphasized.

Beer, the commercial reveals, allows a male to attract beautiful women. But these women are semiotic—not sexual—in nature. They mediate something more basic than sex, as it were, for by possessing a gorgeous woman—in this case, *two* women—the man wins ego points in a male competition. Males who do not have this desideratum envy those who do, envy being a tribute that losers pay to winners. Thus the climactic last scene shows the man enjoying the envy of his "friends"—and presumably of male viewers who do not drink this beer (an obviously ridiculous folly).

The final point of the commercial is thus not sex, but male competition. Pleasure is all right—but pleasure is a sensation of power, a byproduct of power, something made available by power. And to have power is by definition to have the envy of other males. Part of the buoyant merriment of the closing scene is, in turn, laughter at those who fail to get what the protagonist-winner gets. In fact, ridicule and sarcasm directed at losers—*Schadenfreude*—is a standard feature of the scene of male envy. "Invidious comparison," observed Thorstein Veblen, is "the conventional end of action. The currently accepted legitimate end of effort becomes *the achievement of a favorable comparison with other men*."[10] However, this "comparison" is not a linking but a dividing: it is what Veblen calls an "invidious distinction," a differentiation which simultaneously exalts one man and empties another. It is hostile and aggressive and has nothing to do with connecting, still less with equalizing. Note the boasting implicit here: the need to boast, especially to announce sexual supremacy, is compulsive in the scene of male envy, a kind of delicious enjoyment that absorbs and supplants sexual pleasure; indeed it makes sexual pleasure subsidiary, even unnecessary.

Above all, notions of "male bonding" or of "homosocial" society, as this commercial suggests, are suspect in view of the fundamental point: *the primacy of hostility between men.*

* * *

I cite Veblen here because his seminal study, *The Theory of the Leisure Class*, remains constantly useful in exploring male envy. Veblen emphasizes in particular a distinction between production and control, between human creative activity and the social disposition of that creative activity. This distinction, in various forms, is a continuing point of reference throughout this study. Veblen's insight that this controlling/disposition of human productive power is exhibited most dramatically in the form of waste has a disturbing applicability to male envy and its logic. The characteristic image implicit in male envy is that of emptiness, a void or lack, of which the wasting of resources is only one of several variants.

In this respect, male envy is a kind of parody of literature: it spins out fantasies of its own making that fulfill its wishes and fears. It can control, but it cannot create, and literature is the created object *par excellence*: unlike other arts, it is made out of words, not sounds or sights; its sounds and sights are imagined sights and sounds. Envy's fascination with manipulating others is a perversion of the artist's or entertainer's wish to communicate with an audience. Writers and critics can certainly be envious, and literature displays envy with remarkable power. But literature in itself is a kind of counter to envy. Envy is peculiarly complex in that it fuses emotion, intellect, character, perception, and action: it is not abstract or capable of being abstracted or converted into an abstract system. Literature is phenomenologically rich—literature, that is, in terms of what the Germans call *Gedankenexperimente*: "thought experiments," more completely, "imagination experiments," ways of identifying and posing possibilities.

In general, values, practices, modes of perceiving, the academy—and the roles of women—all have been to a significant extent constituted by the envy of males for other males. This subject is fascinating partly because of its importance; almost every aspect of culture bears on it, and therefore many disciplines have been drawn on here for insights. The approach to it has to be comparative and synthetic, and literature, with its synthetic energy—its logic of "condensation," in Freud's term—is a powerful means of illumination.[11] In this study, therefore, literature is treated in terms of the logic of imaginable forms, and not as a collection of separate text-objects to analyze and argue about. Approached in this way, as "imagination experiments," literature becomes a reservoir of social power, a significant resource.

The problems involved in male envy are difficult to approach directly. The assumptions of male envy are so built into our perceiving and thinking that we do not recognize its presence even when it is the determining factor. The value of literature is that it poses the forms of male envy in a detached manner, so that these forms are clarified and have more impact, without the threatening immediacy of real life. It also preserves the extremely important *image* content of consciousness, instead of draining that image content off into abstractions. For images have a logic, as Freud found in his study of dreams, a metaphoric logic of unfoldment and transformation, that is at least as important in the texture of human life as abstract reasoning is, and that is not inferior to abstraction. Some mastery of this metaphoric logic is essential for coming to grips with male envy. At the same time, literary texts also begin to look very different as one becomes aware of the code of male envy, its cues and preoccupations: familiar features acquire new meaning. Indeed, some features become noticeable for the first time.

Before exploring how male envy functions, certain basic motifs need to be identified, in effect an intellectual tool-kit. The code of male envy is not so much a "code" in the sense of a set of rules as it is an ethos, an encompassing current of values and assumptions. Still, a number of configurations are identifiable, even predictable, in its scene. At the center is the compete/control hierarchy, as it may be termed. This is a scale of power; on it, individual males compete with one another for control of objects and domination of other competitors, hence "compete/control." There are different versions of the compete/control hierarchy, depending on specific context, but they operate on similar lines, and to that extent are the same. Thus, one rises on the compete/control hierarchy by gaining power points—markers—for example: victories over competitors, displays of prestige, monopoly over power objects (i.e., objects that facilitate power over others or enhance ego, especially money and weapons, sometimes sacred arcana or technological artifacts), and other emblems of control, including desirable women, or the bodies of defeated enemies, whether metaphoric or actual.

Grouped around the compete/control hierarchy, then, are a number of interrelated motifs:

- Male Display; boasting
- command of attention
- Intimidation Rituals
- public humiliation; casual insults as a means of ego inflation
- invidious distinction, invidious comparison (Thorstein Veblen)
- disaster fantasies
- fascination with death as mystic agency or universal ruler
- language of convolution (corresponding to bizarre reasoning)
- obsession with ideology
- power-over relationships
- *Schadenfreude* (malicious joy: pleasure at the pain of others)
- face-saving compulsions (damage others to compensate for humiliation)
- convoluted rationalizing: reason pressed into the service of hate
- motifs relating to gaze, especially evil eye
- hallucinations: distorted perception
- the Doctrine of Good Suffering
- magic fluids

Each of these motifs will require attention in this exploration. The term "Doctrine of Good Suffering" refers to the belief that hurting people solves problems; the conviction that inflicting pain is a powerful elixir, a kind of magically effective resource. This strange notion is deeply ingrained in our culture; according to the Doctrine of Good Suffering, the way to solve problems is to make someone suffer—someone else, of course, though masochistic elements are certainly present in the code of male envy. If hurting someone solves problems, then *killing* must be especially efficacious. The sacrificial logic —killing other beings placates anxiety and deflects threats—is as primitive (in the negative sense) as it is common; though, once again, it circulates silently and is not normally expressed in the open. Indeed, the Doctrine of Good Suffering is endlessly rationalized, disguised, and projected as a panacea. Its logical culmination is the belief that killing or inflicting pain is a sacred duty: "the sacred act of blood-sacrifice," in Walter Burkert's term.[12]

The reference to blood is not fortuitous. A curious feature of the scene of male envy that may be noted here is the motif of the *magic fluid*, often a special drink, which turns up surprisingly frequently, as in the beer commercial cited earlier. Psychologically, the motif suggests some primal life-substance or condensation of the lifecycle, as in Melanie Klein's emphasis on milk and the breast. Klein concludes that envy is in essence an assault on the breast, the source of life and growth (it is interesting to note that the motif of the drink is conspicuous in *Macbeth* in a way that is far out of proportion in terms of realism or common sense, but that is consistent with the play as an exploration of envy).

Because male envy has a central location in societal relations—and in individual consciousness and perception—it connects to many unexpected places and has unexpected ramifications. Male envy reconstitutes a number of fundamentals, generating its own subtextual version, so to speak. For example, male envy reconstitutes good and evil, and also love. Beneath good and evil, in the code of male envy, lie winning and losing. Winning and losing are keystone concepts and have such complexity and resonance that they can only be approached cumulatively, through exploring other features of male envy. That is why this study focuses on illustrations, on plots and recurring character types; at bottom, this is because male envy is not a matter of abstraction. Male envy actually values and prizes hostile emotion, for instance, and cannot be approached abstractly, by way of some High Theoretical system.

Like most social constructs, male envy manipulates and uses mental images and emotions, not just abstract ideas. Its reasoning is not the reasoning of abstraction, of logic strictly speaking, but the kind of reasoning that power and control over others thinks with. And this kind of reasoning is neither rational in the strict sense of logical, nor rational in the looser sense of being reasonable. It is a logic of manipulation. It works with forms of reasoning as *forms* rather than as content. Its logic is a directed one of controlling a target, hence its obsession with ideology, with the rationalizing of power. It perceives everything in ideological terms, and ideology, at least in the sense in which Marx coined the term, refers to false reasoning; or more precisely, reasoning that rationalizes what is done on other grounds, in effect pseudo-reasoning. Because it is impossible to differentiate male envy from its motivation, the wish to hurt and defeat others, its logic is that of self-deception and lying.

Emotion can be articulated by means of character and narrative, but it cannot be simply transposed to an abstract matrix or all-explanatory construct. Male envy *uses* abstract systems for its own aims: to control and deceive. For male envy, abstract ideas are the cover for intensely experienced struggles of attack and defense. For example, in the university, intellectual life coexists with a peculiarly vicious exercise of envy. As Liam Hudson and Bernadine Jacot put it, "delicately poised abstraction is surrounded, apparently as a matter of course, by personal feuds, political finagling, bullying and abuse."[13] Whereas male envy hides, literature discloses and is self-disclosing in its emphasis on image, character, and emotion: the non-abstract.

One of the most important features in the scene of male envy is what might be called "Male Display": a dramatic exhibition of the signifiers of individual male control—not over women (who don't count)—but over other *males*, to impress strong ones especially. The male erects a display made up of women and other power objects for spectators to view.[14] In the context of Male Display, the woman is a position-marker on the compete/control hierarchy. This is what I mean by "Male Display": a dramatic tableau designed to exhibit objects that show how powerful a man is: "The spectacle of masculinity," as Steven Cohan says[15]—in common parlance, "showing off." It may not include the display of women, but frequently does. Thorstein Veblen's comment about "barbaric society" will be recalled:

> Tangible evidences of prowess—trophies—find a place in men's habits of thoughts as an essential feature of the paraphernalia of life. Booty, trophies of the chase or of the raid, come to be prized as evidence of preeminent force. Aggression becomes the accredited form of action, and booty serves as *prima facie* evidence of successful aggression. . . . the accredited, worthy form of self-assertion is contest. (30)

The imperative that underlies Male Display, that pushes it forward, is the need to keep attention; to attract and focus the attention of others on the self. This process necessarily means withdrawing attention from others, and so implies monopoly. That is, it is a need not simply to gain attention—more attention than others—but to have *all* the attention. In the dictum of that impressive winner, Rupert Murdoch: "Monopoly is a terrible thing until you have it." In male envy, there is not enough for everybody—and shouldn't be: the normal way to gain is by the failure of others. Humiliating rivals and exposing weaknesses in them has an honored place in male envy. Nor does the attention drawn to the winner have to be favorable; what matters is that the awareness of others be magnetized by the self. Attention is a kind of tribute or ego-supply that inflates the sense of self, or that even, more disturbingly, *creates* the sense of self. Hence, without it, feelings of impaired identity, or even panic, threaten to take control. Fear is a powerful enforcer in the code of male envy, as we shall see.

Male Display is aggressive, not aesthetic, in intent, though there is a certain artistry involved in showing off and in putting others down. The fundamental relation between males is constituted as hostile. Hence Male Display is related to what sociologist Rory O'Day terms an "intimidation ritual": an "intimidation ritual" is used to frighten weaker males and to challenge rivals.[16] Male Display, as opposed to an intimidation ritual, properly speaking, is intended more to impress males who are equal (or greater) in power; and, in the manner of our friend in the commercial, Male Display often involves the control of women.

The notion that women were the first form of "private property" is a longstanding theme in the social sciences (found in Engels, Veblen, and Lévi-Strauss, for example). Whether true or not, this idea about the role of women is consistent with the logic of male envy and possibly even derives from it. In any case, women are traditionally not on the compete/control hierarchy at all, but exist off to the side of it—as a means of male power. There is, of course, a female compete/control hierarchy, too, but it has in practice had the kind of interest that Little League has, compared to the World Series.

In this respect, the oppression of women is a complex function, the expression of a system by which males do not form a simple unity, but are distributed over a hierarchy based on competing for control. Male power is always *differential* power: that is, it is power defined in relation to superior and inferior in comparison to one another. This differential quality cannot be overemphasized. Sociologist Michael A. Messner's analysis of sport is illuminating generally here:

> The meaning that most men give to their athletic strivings has more to do with competing for status among men than with proving superiority over women . . . Hegemonic masculinity (that definition of masculinity which is culturally ascendent) is constructed in relation to various subordinated masculinities as well as in relation to femininities. The project of men's domination of women may tie all men together, but *men share very unequally in the fruits* of this domination.[17]

In the competitive struggle for control, men traditionally use women as matériel, and as a marker to display winning over other males. The transfer of a woman from one male to another is a traditional marker of victory over the other male, a process already illustrated with complete clarity in *The Iliad* (c. 750 B.C.). Likewise, it is an unspoken rule between men that a man never criticizes another man's woman—unless he wants a fight, that is. (It is interesting that the reverse does not seem to hold true: women seem free to criticize their men to one another.) In the context of male envy, even a bond of genuine love between a man and a woman must be used as a subsidy for the male's struggle against other males. Competition between the man and his spouse is therefore *a priori* ruled out and taboo. Under patriarchy in its capitalist phase, women thus have been indirectly, as well as directly, an object of exploitation.

Curiously, women are culturally associated with envy, not men. That is, women have a reputation for being envious and hostile to one another; numerous expressions, such as "catty," attest to this association. But this reputation may be seen as a displacement, a way of distracting attention from *male* envy, which is the real issue and which has far greater priority and potency than female envy. It is interesting that feminists have pondered *female* envy, whereas men, as if silenced by the contingencies of male envy, avoid the subject.[18] It is clear, however, that the logic of male envy is inseparable from the logic of oppression in general. Notions of "homosocial desire," in Eve K. Sedgwick's familiar phrase, which merge males in solidarity against women, are thus misleading. "Masculinity," as Peter Lehman notes, is not "an ahistoric, powerfully secure, monolithic position," but "one riddled with cracks," "a constant contradictory struggle"—and not "just the privileged position within a power disequilibrium."[19] In Susan Jeffords's words, men need "to disguise social hierarchies through the presentation of images of collectivity."[20] Happy scenes of male camaraderie thus conceal hostility behind their cliché images of boyish fun and togetherness. The scrutiny of male-male relations complements feminist analysis—but is also an essential part of the process of emancipation itself, for male as well as for female. The full impact and range of male envy as a constituting force on plot (and on literary studies)—indeed on culture itself—has yet to be determined. But there can be no doubt that it has deep and pervasive consequences, for women as well as for men. Female emancipation is in fundamental and unavoidable conflict with the whole ideology of male envy.

The use of women to mark control—i.e., as a means of marking rank on a hierarchy of control—is one of the factors that informs rape. Feminists argue that "sexual violence is used by men as a way of securing and maintaining the relations of male dominance and female subordination, which are central to the patriarchal social order," as Jill Radford and Elizabeth Stanko put it.[21] But rape is understood, traditionally, not as an assault on women but on the males to whom the woman "belongs." That is, it is a means of inflicting damage on the males who "own" her, where the woman embodies wealth and power:

> The male rapist embodies the envious penis. He deploys his organ like an evil eye, to pry and invade, to inflict fear and instill pain. The Beast of Belgravia [a notorious rapist] terrorized women throughout a prosperous part of London . . . because he was "jealous" (envious) of the women's wealth and boasted: "They have everything and I have nothing. They are not so good now they have been raped!" (Berke 137).

Rape = an assault on wealth and prestige: now the women are "not so good," not just in and for themselves—but for the wealthy men that they represent. Nietzsche's comment in *The Genealogy of Morals* comes to mind:

> That pleasure is induced by his being able to exercise his power freely upon one who is powerless, by the pleasure of *faire le mal pour le plaisir de le faire*, the pleasure of rape. That pleasure will be increased in proportion to the *lowliness* of the [rapist]; it will appear to him as a delicious morsel, a foretaste of a *higher rank*.[22]

The motif of *higher* and *lower* here should be noted, because it indicates the pervasive presence of the compete/control hierarchy.

The multiple murder of women appears to be psychologically related to this traditional paradigm of rape. By murdering women, a killer wins power points against the stratum of social power that the women represent—that is, against the males that enclose the woman: the murder is a kind of social theft.[23] The males fight for the woman, not just because they want the woman (or because they want to attack women in general); but because possessing the woman represents male power over other males; represents power.

The compete/control hierarchy is internalized by males, to an extent that the compete hierarchy becomes identity itself: the field of identity. Conflict *is* identity, as for example in the familiar belief in "War as an educator in manliness," as George Mose puts it.[24] To a large degree, then, a man's placement on the compete/control hierarchy constitutes his sense of self. Male envy is like gravity, as a result: a force that affects everything that passes through it. The plot of male war, the use of women as power points for parlaying status to higher rank, is, to adapt Lyotard's familiar term, a "master narrative." But it is mainly a subtextual narrative: it is so taken for granted as to operate silently, in places and ways where it is unexpected, and under many guises—as love, as work, as belief—even as creativity. In literature, male envy is a sustaining tension that informs much of Romantic/post-Romantic narrative: a force field in which plot is enacted. Hence much of what is presented as being of genuine value—love, ambition, honour, creative endeavour, etc.—in practice is the masking structure for the working out of male envy. The forms of love, ambition, honour, etc., mask an actual content of male hostility.

The exploration of the code of male envy—"Male Envy," for short—inevitably leads one to ponder origins: this is the subject of Chapter 3, "Object Thinking," which deals with the worldview that underlies Male Envy, that generates and even necessitates it. In other words, the "origins" of Male Envy are not a matter of myth or primeval speculation, or neolithic ritual, or testosterone; but *a way of thinking rooted in a social system*, one that has a specific history as well as specific social dynamics. Hence René Girard's theorem of primal violence and scapegoating/substitution is not needed, still less Freud's theorem of male hordes killing neolithic patriarchs so as to enact on a social scale the personal and private dynamic of Oedipal guilt.[25] If these theories were correct—if Male Envy were totally in control—society could not function, and probably would not have survived. These theorems have the air of mystifications: they are *myths*, in the sense of stories about divine or semi-divine beings in some "eternal dream time."

In fact, when one becomes familiar with the logic of Male Envy, Freud's theorem looks strangely different. For example, in the Oedipus complex, one is struck by the curious absence of the *father's* viewpoint—and even in Freud's writing generally: how a father feels about his son. Genuine love of one male for another male, in accord with the primacy of male hostility, has to be silenced, including even that of father for son. Indeed, the father-son relationship becomes a metaphor for more powerful male-less powerful male, a relationship, in other words, that has nothing to do with family connection. Other, related theories, those of Melanie Klein and Eve Sedgwick, despite their value, are misleading about Male Envy (or perhaps they lead in other directions). What one notices about such theories is that they themselves illustrate the code of Male Envy, rather than explaining it. They take the primacy of male hostility for granted, as though it were a given rather than something in need of explanation, or at least observation, in itself.

Freud's direct intellectual ancestor, in this context, is "Population" Malthus, who gets us closer to the root of Male Envy as we know it than attempts to reconstruct infantile consciousness (Klein), or generalizations about male-male relations (Sedgwick). The consciousness of infants has always been a matter of obsessive fascination to psychoanalysts, perhaps because it is inherently unknowable[26]; and the notion that male-male relations are subtextually homosexual is misleading, for both heterosexual and gay men. More useful is Klaus Theweleit's disturbing study of the psychology of fascism, *Male Fantasies*. But, again, the chief influence on this study has been Thorstein Veblen, who, for his originality—for his sheer intellectual size—is probably the most neglected thinker of his time.[27]

The logic of Male Envy is horrifying enough, but its fascination with the suffering of others results in true horrors: this is the subject of Chapter 4, "Holy Murder." It is difficult to ponder Male Envy without considering, however briefly, its role in the production and control of knowledge—in short, the impact of Male Envy on the academy, with its obsessive invidious distinctions, its preoccupation with prestige, fashion, competition, and related insignia of Male Envy. Academics are practically trained in the cutting use of language, where verbal hostility is an art-form, and where a subservient fascination with prestige is obsessive. Chapter 5, "The Academy of Envy," explores the logic of Male Envy in Freud, Malthus, and a number of influential theorists in a variety of fields, including cultural and literary theory. Finally, since a study of Male Envy would be incomplete without some consideration of resistance to it, the final chapter, "Transform," ponders the way literature has attempted to find alternatives to Male Envy, and not merely act out its contingencies.

To study literature is to study the logic of imaginable forms, a thinking-in-images that is the emphasis of the present exploration. Of particular interest are the *plots* that display Male Envy and the recurring *character types* that demonstrate its logic. The logic of imaginable forms discloses clusters or complexes of motifs that operate as groupings, and periodically throughout this exploration, I present these clusters or complexes precisely in that form, as an inter-related ensemble. Inevitably, the subsidiary argument of this study is that literature has a social function, and an important one. It is not simply a pile of discrete texts to do things to, but an intellectual power in its own right. It constitutes a coherent body of imagination-experiments that are, in their own fashion, an important mode of knowing. As such, literature also insists that the code of Male Envy, with its obsessions and cruelties, is only one of many possible ways of perceiving. Literature is itself the exercise of a type of thinking that conflicts with Male Envy. And this in turn is a reason for studying literature, as a mode of resistance.[28]

* * *

Male Envy crystallizes in its modern form in the eighteenth and early nineteenth centuries. The critical phase is 1780-1830, what in literature and culture is known as the Romantic period. Many of the most important Romantic narratives provide fascinating expositions of the way Male Envy functions.

For our purposes, one of the most lucid of these expositions is John Keats's narrative poem *Lamia* (1820), which gives us a paradigm of the plot of Male Envy. *Lamia* has been extensively processed by academic commentators; typically, interpretation is preoccupied with deconstructing something called "imagination" and ignores the crucial role of Male Envy in the action. *Lamia* is not about reason or about imagination as much as it is about male hatred, which in every respect takes priority.

A "lamia" is a mythological being, a supernatural female who can take the form of a serpent. The character in the story named "Lamia" thus has a generic —not a personal—name, as if specific personality did not matter. What does matter is that Lamia has magic powers and so constitutes a significant resource; her serpent aspect manifests semi-divine identity with the occult forces of nature. Lamia wants to love and to be loved: the freedom to love and be loved. The tale begins when, aided by the trickster god Hermes, she sheds her serpent form and sets out to find a student named Lycius with whom she has fallen in love, thanks to her extrasensory and clairvoyant powers. She quickly finds him and offers the young man her passionate devotion and—again, thanks to her remarkable magic powers—ease, liberty, riches.

But this opulence hardly satisfies. For Lamia refuses to do what Lycius really wants, and that is to let him *show her off* to his friends and rivals. It is not love or beauty—or wealth—that matters; it is the *envy of other men*. Here the plot of Male Envy absorbs the action: what Lycius needs is to accumulate ego points on the control hierarchy. To possess this beauty is nice—but without the acknowledgement of other males, Lamia is like an uncashed cheque. Lycius himself is clear about his need, though it takes a while for him to articulate it openly. The fact that he finally spells it out—instead of leaving it in silence, as the code of Male Envy prefers—is a noteworthy sign of the intensity of his need: the anxiety of losing that permeates his character. He should not have to speak; he should get his way by sheer force of personality.

Thus he reveals his need—she has, after all, been willing to give him everything else: why not this?

"My thoughts! shall I unveil them? Listen then!
What mortal hath a prize, that other men
May be confounded and abash'd withal,
But lets it sometimes pace abroad majestical,
And triumph, as in thee I should rejoice
Amid the hoarse alarm of Corinth's voice.
Let my foes choke, and my friends shout afar,

> While through the thronged streets your bridal car
> Wheels round its dazzling spokes." (2.65-64)

He says "My thoughts" here, but they are hardly "thoughts" in the technical sense of reasons and perceptions: it is simply his weakness—and his social conditioning—speaking. "That other men / May be confounded and abash'd withal": the principle of Male Envy could hardly be more precisely articulated. Foes and friends alike—is there really a difference in Male Envy?—will "be confounded and abash'd" by his Male Display. To gain maximum advantage, Lycius wants an elaborate public wedding, complete with parade and banquet. The "dazzling spokes" here are emblematic: visual display that magnetizes and even paralyzes the attention of others.[29]

Lycius wants to show off his prize, but he also wants to enclose that prize within the social-legal ownership of marriage. Thus, he will rise on the compete/control hierarchy and will at the same time consolidate his control over Lamia: "to entangle, trammel up and snare / Your soul in mine, and labyrinth you there," as he puts it (2.52-53). He expresses his need for control with remarkable frankness. Lycius is also lying, of course. It is obvious that there is no need to consolidate his grip on her in this way, unless he has no real love for her or only a shallow love. Lamia does not wish to be displayed to other men and resists his plan with the intensity of prophetic understanding, as well as a conviction that to be valued as part of a Male Display is wrong. But she loves; and, in the manner of lovers, she wishes to please. Hence, after some arm-twisting, Lamia submits to the display that Lycius's vanity demands. She even provides food, gifts, and servants for a lavish party.

Meanwhile, Lycius's philosopher-professor-mentor, Apollonius, has seen him with Lamia. Apollonius is an old man, allegorized by collaborating critics as "Reason" (as Lamia is allegorized as "imagination"). He crashes the party, in order to denounce her publicly as a monster. He is honor-bound to do this, for, he says, he has to "protect" his student, who is so obviously suffering. His interest in Lycius has a peculiar, almost irrational intensity. One thing is clear, though: Keats does not present Lamia as an incubus feeding on men, which is the fantasy of Apollonius. On the contrary, she is a seeker of emancipation, however groping or confused. But this is the point: Lamia is not an evil monster, despite Apollonius's disaster fantasy to this effect (the monster motif turns up surprisingly frequently in the scene of Male Envy). And her evil or lack of evil, her deceitfulness or honesty, are not the issue—in fact, they hardly matter. By destroying Lamia, Apollonius is attacking the younger man's power base; he collapses his student's status on the compete/control hierarchy.[30]

It is difficult to rationalize the philosopher's actions. Perhaps Apollonius is jealous. Perhaps he is in love with the young man. More obviously, he was not invited to the party—Lamia did not want him there. Enacting the folklore role of the uninvited guest, Apollonius disrupts the celebration and destroys its stars.

He denounces her as a monster and him as a fool. The use of vicious language is an important technique in Male Display; indeed, it is implicit in all Male Display, for Male Display is aggressive in intent. Denunciation is of course also a key method of gaining attention from others. Furthermore, such language is not merely an intimidation ritual, but a weapon in its own right, for hate-filled words have power to penetrate the weakness of others. Language is power, after all—it is not merely a collection of empty signifiers, but a social, intrapsychic force.

As soon as Apollonius speaks, the party stops. "And not a man but felt the terror in his hair": he seizes control over the scene, displaying his power by intimidating every male who is present. He hardly needs to speak, in fact. What he does say is directed less at "exposing" Lamia, so much as at his student:

> "Fool!" said the sophist, in an under-tone
> Gruff with contempt; which a death-nighing moan
> From Lycius answer'd, as heart-struck and lost,
> He sank supine beside the aching ghost.
> "Fool! Fool!" repeated he, while his eyes still
> Relented not, nor mov'd; "from every ill
> Of life have I preserv'd thee to this day,
> And shall I see thee made a serpent's prey?"
> Then Lamia breath'd death breath; the sophist's eye,
> Like a sharp spear, went through her utterly,
> Keen, cruel, perceant, stinging.   (2.291-301)

Apollonius explicitly claims to be responsible for Lycius's continuing existence, even as he is in fact destroying him. It is as if destroying life, in the code of Male Envy, were the same as creating it; as if, indeed, destroying were the same as creating. This kind of confusion is common in the convoluted thinking that is characteristic of Male Envy, where the motivation for malice has to be carefully concealed and justified to others, as well as screened from the competitor's own self-awareness. In the scene of Male Envy, the motif of bizarre reasoning is a recurring feature. But Apollonius's speech identifies a number of motifs in the code of Male Envy:

- stinging contempt for another man
- public expression of this contempt, as a mode of triumph
- assertion of personal power; boasting
- the evacuation of love as a power worthy of respect
- the insistence that hurting Lycius is actually protecting him
- the motif of the serpent, which in Apollonius's speech symbolizes betrayal, and which really refers to Apollonius himself (not Lamia)
- the contemptuous, hate-filled rejection of what deviates from accepted norms in the compete/control culture (Lamia; love *per se*)
- above all, the motif of the killing eye, which Keats emphasizes

The image of the "evil eye" is a recurring motif in envy. Indeed, it seems inseparable from the topic, so that references to envy are regularly accompanied by the image of the evil eye (compare the emphasis on gaze in the commercial cited at the beginning of our exploration; in the crucial final frame, the hero gazes at the male audience with a look of triumph, the famous "look of triumph" being nothing but the look of successful aggression). The penetrating force of the hostile eye is proverbial ("looks that kill"), as is the *hardness* of the hostile stare ("steely looks"). Anyone familiar with the techniques of "anger management" courses will recall the hate-filled look that men regularly give each other before they physically attack each other. This kind of gaze is a weapon in its own right. In Keats, "the sophist's eye, / Like *a sharp spear*, went through her utterly, / Keen, cruel, *perceant*, stinging." In fact, the word "envy" is derived from the Latin *invidere*, for which the closest equivalent in English is probably "to look askance at." Wrong use of the eyes is a curiously persistent motif with envy.

So is the motif of the casual insult: to insult another man when he is unable to retaliate is not only a basic pleasure in Male Envy, but a standard means of self-inflation. For Male Envy, it is like free money, invidious and delightful.

Apollonius's denunciation is so effective that it kills Lamia. Or rather, it makes her disappear—vanish, as if she never existed. The theme of annihilation is conspicuous: this is what envy does when it wins absolutely. It makes its target turn into nothing. Apollonius's assault on Lamia, however, is really an assault on the student that he professes to care about. When Lamia dies—or vanishes—Lycius's power position dies. A standard method for attacking another man is to attack not him but his woman. To insult the woman associated with a man is to insult the man. It is a threat to destroy his marker on the compete/control hierarchy (as Iago cleverly saps Othello in Shakespeare's play. Othello's absorption of Desdemona in the first place is an assault on the established control hierarchy and treated as a theft). Direct attack on a competitor/rival is not as cost-effective. What Apollonius does is to nullify Lycius on the compete/control hierarchy; he abolishes the young man's ego. Having nothing left, Lycius dies. Failure on that hierarchy kills. Envy wishes not simply to kill but to annihilate: to make into nothing, so that even the memory of a hated enemy is erased.

If Apollonius truly cared about Lycius, as he claims—or even if he was worried about Lamia's snaky background, for that matter—he would try something else than a public assault. This public assault inflicts maximum humiliation on his pupil and does far more than merely expose the supposedly evil Lamia and her female/animal/super/natural power. The banquet was to be the locale of the young man's public exhibition of power—his Male Display, with its riches, varied sensory pleasures, abundance—and female beauty—all possessed by the young man.

Deftly, Apollonius converts the banquet into the site of the old man's triumph. He "wins."

* * *

Keats attempted to write a vast epic poem modeled upon Dante's *Divine Comedy* (1321) and on Milton's *Paradise Lost* (1667), but abandoned the project, leaving behind the two *Hyperion* fragments (1820). The way the plot of these fragments is constructed, with the titan Hyperion falling from power and the young god Apollo rising up to take his place, could hardly avoid probing the code of Male Envy as a central theme. This would be far more direct than is the case in *Lamia*, where the mystic female figure Lamia attracts so much attention to herself that she obscures or represses the prior theme of male competition. *The Fall of Hyperion*, the revision of the original *Hyperion* fragment, would have to confront the anxieties aroused by Male Envy, which block out the overarching themes Keats chose for his epic—the themes of expanded awareness, the social function of literature, and the meaning of suffering and of evil in the world. One reason why Keats abandoned the *Hyperion* project was that he could not resolve the difficult prior theme of Male Envy—a theme that would appear more difficult to deal with than expanded awareness, the social function of literature, suffering, and evil. Male Envy is a profoundly threatening and anxiety-arousing subject.

The dynamics of Male Envy give a different cast to texts. Features come forward that are otherwise invisible or acquire a very different meaning. Motifs that seem random, insignificant, or unaccountable fall into place in a logic. As a force, Male Envy becomes conspicuous in the eighteenth century, particularly in Romantic narrative, but "Romantic narrative" is really a generic term and not something confined to the writers of the 1780-1830 period. It refers to a body of narrative texts, in prose and in verse, that tell stories of the exotic, the extreme, the alien, the marvelous. It is a form in which inhibitions are loosened; what has been silenced can be, however cautiously, allowed to speak. That is one reason why it is such a useful resource for investigating the present topic.

As a generic formation, Romantic narrative shares common conventions and motifs. It appears at the start of the Romantic period, most notably in the Gothic fiction popular in the 1790s, though the "oriental" romances that evolve earlier in the eighteenth century (such as Samuel Johnson's *Rasselas* [1759]) are related. The generic roots of Romantic narrative reach back, in fact, to the beginnings of prose fiction proper, in Hellenistic Greece. In Roman culture, Apuleius's *The Golden Ass* (c. 180 A.D.) is perhaps the best-known example of the genre, which later re-emerges in the Romantic period, using essentially the same conventions and plot-motifs—in spite of totally different social conditions.[31] Romantic narrative flourishes in the Romantic period itself, migrates to the United States, where it modulates into the "American romance" tradition of James Fenimore Cooper, Poe, Stowe, and Hawthorne, then re-emerges in England toward the end of the nineteenth century in writers such as William Morris, George Macdonald, Robert Louis Stevenson, Rider Haggard, Bram Stoker, Wilde, Kipling, Arthur

Conan Doyle, W. H. Hudson, H. G. Wells. It coincides with the rise of science fiction, detective fiction, and the efflorescence of children's literature that starts with Lewis Carroll but develops on both sides of the Atlantic (children's literature is surprisingly concerned with Male Envy themes). In England, Dickens is the major link between earlier and later phases of Romantic narrative.

Romantic narrative illustrates forces that still operate in our own society and does so with a specific kind of insight. Writers at the beginning of a cultural development often probe its meaning with a clarity and openness of perception that later writers, who are immersed in it, cannot; hence they see further, at times with prophetic clarity. It works both ways: focusing on Male Envy reveals elements in these texts that have been ignored and underestimated. Romantic narrative also contains a complex protest against Male Envy, just as Romanticism includes a complex critique of the worldview that underwrites Male Envy.

For the logic of Male Envy, Hawthorne is especially helpful. Like other important American writers of his time, Hawthorne is directly in the line of English Romanticism, a fact that explains why he (and other Americans) could in turn influence the Victorian writers in England who followed the Romantics: they were working out of a shared body of experiment and plot configurations. One of Hawthorne's most fascinating texts is "Rappaccini's Daughter" (1844), a short story that explores the logic of Male Envy in a manner very similar to Keats's *Lamia*, but yields further insights.

The title, "Rappaccini's Daughter," recalls *Lamia* in that it presents the title character again in a generic form, as if the "daughter," like Lamia, did not have a name—an identity—of her own. Like Lamia, she attracts an eager but naive young student. Also, like Lamia, the "daughter" can be interpreted as a tricky female whose beauty lures men to disaster: a standard male nightmare and an obsessive anxiety in Male Envy. This view of her as *femme fatale* is shallow, but it is not exactly superficial; rather, it reflects the code of Male Envy itself, which is scarcely able to perceive the personality of women apart from their function in the code of Male Envy.

Like Lamia, Hawthorne's heroine cannot escape the enclosing compulsions of male competition and dies as a consequence of them. Beatrice—Hawthorne does give her a name, one of the sainted names of western culture—is carefully presented as a decent, open-minded, intelligent person who is seeking experience and, more broadly, emancipation. Unfortunately for Beatrice, she is entrapped in male competition—not a good predicament for a woman in the régime of Envy. Her father is a mad scientist type whose experiment has made her poisonous, like the plants he appears to be genetically engineering in his garden so as to be lethal. Meanwhile, Giovanni, a student who lodges next door, is attracted to her. But this attraction is not just on account of her beauty (or personality): it has to do with who her father is. The father's importance gives her ("*Rappaccini*'s daughter") special appeal. Professor Rappaccini tops the particular compete/

control hierarchy that Giovanni aspires to climb—the scientific one. Affiliation with the daughter of an important man is a standard means of rising on that hierarchy, of stealing a march on one's competitors.

Unlike the many young men who have heard about Rappaccini's daughter but who lack access to her, Giovanni discovers her—as if by luck—in the next door garden; then, unexpectedly, again as if by luck, he finds out that there is a private entrance to it—and to her. His landlady informs him of this convenience, and he is eager to take advantage of it, not only because he has been able to watch her from his window, but because his father's friend, Professor Baglioni, has warned him to keep away. Baglioni has told him about Rappaccini and the beautiful Beatrice and warned him to stay clear of both of them. The warning is a recurring motif in stories where Male Envy is a significant factor. The warning is a simple form of Intimidation Ritual and typically incites the threatened male to do precisely what he is told not to do, as in so many crime stories, where the warning motif is practically built into the genre.

The second-rate Baglioni lets slip that he deeply resents the eminent Dr. Rappaccini, whose success has eclipsed his own. He has "the poisonous eye of resentment," in Nietzsche's phrase. He resents Rappaccini's daughter and fears that she may succeed to her father's position. This would eclipse him for yet another generation, thus permanently foreclosing his ambitions. Baglioni may find the naive Giovanni useful in damaging his rival; Giovanni, meanwhile, is less interested in the loser Baglioni than in the winner Rappaccini. He naturally ignores the advice of an older man who has failed to reach the top of the compete/control hierarchy that matters to him, the medico-scientific one. Who listens to a loser (except another loser)? Baglioni's warning appears to backfire, for it only whets Giovanni's appetite to penetrate the garden, meet Beatrice, and make contact with the reclusive great scientist-male.

Other young men are eager for the access that only Giovanni acquires: his enjoyment is partly the delight of getting what his peers want—but fail to obtain. The motif of the *numerous competitors* is conspicuous. Given her father's status (and the difficulty of access), Beatrice is a prize worth substantial power points on the control hierarchy. Giovanni may love her, but Other Factors are involved. As Martha bluntly tells the young male professor in Edward Albee's *Who's Afraid of Virginia Woolf?* (1962): "You didn't chase me . . . out of mad, driven passion, did you now? You were thinking a little bit about your career, weren't you?"[32] Martha ought to know, for she is another daughter of an important man, in her case the President of the University. The same *topos* of Male Envy is found in a university drama of the 1960s as in a tale of 1844—a tale of an academic scene set hundreds of years earlier. The association of the academy with Male Envy is hardly gratuitous.

Giovanni visits Beatrice in her garden; her deep interest in him is tempered by fear that he may be harmed by her father's poisons. Ironically, Rappaccini has planned it all: he is in fact engaged in creating a tricky female—his daughter herself—as a potent weapon. He needs a young man to test her—his experiment—out on. Hence he requires just such a young man as Giovanni. He even arranges for Giovanni's landlady to give him access to the exclusive Rappaccini garden. With the type of irony so dear to Hawthorne, the antidote Giovanni brings to save Beatrice kills her; an antidote given by none other than the envious Baglioni. (Notice the motif of the special drink.)

In the terrible climax of this story, Giovanni viciously attacks Beatrice, denouncing her as a tricky female who has made him poisonous, like her. Compare the similar denunciation of Lamia by Apollonius.

> "Accursed one!" cried he, with venomous scorn and anger. "And, finding thy solitude wearisome, thou hast severed me likewise from all the warmth of life and enticed me into thy region of unspeakable horror! . . . Yes, poisonous thing!" repeated Giovanni, beside himself with passion. "Thou hast filled my veins with poison! Thou hast made me as hateful, as ugly, as loathsome and deadly a creature as thyself—a world's wonder of hideous monstrosity! . . . Thy very prayers, as they come from thy lips, taint the atmosphere with death."[33]

And on he goes, losing control, like Hamlet verbally assaulting Ophelia in Shakespeare's play. Giovanni's attempt to wield the weapon of hate-language is premature; it suggests weakness rather than strength on the control hierarchy. Indeed, it is a measure of his loss of control, since he does not realize that he is performing for other, more powerful males, who are secretly observing him: the motif of being watched by more powerful males is an index of the anxieties of Male Envy. Beatrice is deeply shocked by her lover's hate-filled words: "what is death after such words as thine?" she asks (208), and she drinks the antidote that Giovanni has brought from Baglioni, insisting she drink first, in case it is actually poisonous.

Now old Dr. Rappaccini appears from out of a dark doorway—he has a predilection for watching voyeuristically from the shadows, as the narrator carefully notes. Watching without being affected by what one watches is basic training in Male Envy, a technique necessary for the successful manipulation of others: it is a technique that "Young Goodman Brown," in Hawthorne's story of that name, fails to master, despite his wish to enjoy vicarious midnight thrills at the witches' sabbath. In Rappaccini's case, it is related to the motif of the evil eye, and to hostile or calculating gaze generally. "The pale man of science seemed to gaze with a triumphant expression at the beautiful youth and maiden, as might an artist who should spend his life in achieving a picture or a group of statuary and finally be satisfied with his success. He paused; his bent form grew erect with conscious power" (208). This is Dr. Rappaccini's Male Display: his crowning achievement. He has turned living beings, by his own power, into objects that are, unlike people, totally manipulable: a goal highly coveted and prized. The intensity of his satisfaction is indicated by the transparent sexual symbolism: "his bent form grew erect with conscious power." In the code of Male Envy that is what sexual feeling is: the sensation of control over others: the implication of incest should also be noted; for Male Envy, nothing is sacred, except Male Envy. Sexual violation is a recurring motif in the scene of Male Envy, as we shall see.

When his daughter protests against what he has done to her, her father is genuinely surprised. He insists he has "endowed [her] with marvelous gifts against which no power nor strength could avail an enemy" (209). He assumes as a matter of course that the greatest good is to have absolute power over others: to control relationships at will, and this power—this poison, literally—is what he has given his daughter. What more could one ask for? Kill-power is the ultimate gift. If you have untrammeled kill-power at your disposal, you can make others do whatever you wish—no concessions, no parlaying, no waiting. Do it, or else. A fascination with any force or instrument that has the power to hurt others is characteristic of Male Envy. Rappaccini has also, it goes without saying, destroyed the cocky young man who has so foolishly crept into his trap.

In a matter of only a few moments, Beatrice has a series of terrible recognitions, as she realizes what her father has done to her ("I see it! I see it!"); and what her lover's shallow love amounts to—not much ("was there not, from the first, more poison in thy nature than in mine?"), and she dies. With his daughter, Rappaccini's experiment dies. Beatrice Cenci, in Percy Shelley's radical drama *The Cenci* (1820), may lie behind Hawthorne's Beatrice Rappaccini: the patriarch-father of *The Cenci* rapes his daughter Beatrice: a cruel treatment very parallel to the scientist's use of his daughter in Hawthorne.

Hence the real winner turns out to be plodding Dr. Baglioni, Rappaccini's envious rival at the university. Baglioni incited Giovanni's interest in Beatrice and provided the "antidote"; he also monitored the naive youth's progress in wooing her. Baglioni pits one male against another to engineer the final scene: a tableau of real impact. Thus in the story's last words, he mysteriously pops up in the window of Giovanni's room overlooking the scene, to crow over the defeat of his hated rival, the famous Rappaccini, who had (crime of crimes!) outshone him in the academic world. Note that Hawthorne depicts the academy, even in Renaissance Italy, as a byword for jealousy, hate, and pettiness. With the death of Beatrice, Baglioni has destroyed Rappaccini's most prized possession— his scientific life's work, as it were; using Giovanni as "his tool for destroying the Rappaccinis,"[34] he has also deftly annihilated the cocksure young man, in a manner perhaps not unpleasing to an older man's ego. Baglioni may be unattractive—he may be impotent. But he is not weak.

A similar configuration crystallizes at the end of *The Scarlet Letter* (1850).[35] However, unlike Giovanni in "Rappaccini's Daughter," the young man in this case (Dimmesdale) beats the old man (Chillingworth). Significantly, both here and in *Lamia*, the crucial backdrop is *public display*—a large public occasion where all the important people are assembled. Dimmesdale's famous guilt and anguish amounts, in practice, to anxiety about his position on the male control grid. His adultery with Hester before the novel starts cost him power points as a violation of the patriarchal code, threatening his rank as preacher on the local male hierarchy—not to mention in the eyes of a jealous male God preoccupied with His own power position. Yet adultery also *paid* power points in the form of possession of another male's woman.

That is why, in turn, Dimmesdale's opponent, Chillingworth, cannot be satisfied merely to hurt (or even kill) Dimmesdale; he must *gut* Dimmesdale, annihilate his personal power and sense of identity, to make up the power points he lost. His quarrel is not with his wife, Hester, as one might expect, but with the man who damaged him by possessing his wife sexually. This is especially hateful, because, it seems, Chillingworth is impotent himself and unable to love Hester, possibly was unable to consummate the marriage in the first place. (Their marriage thus resembles Dorothea Brooke's to old Casaubon in George Eliot's novel *Middlemarch* [1872]—Eliot was deeply influenced by Hawthorne.) The further implication is that Chillingworth's fearful hate of Dimmesdale—his *Ressentiment*—is actually hatred of his own weakness, self-hate.

Dimmesdale carefully stages his confession speech at the end. First there is a big parade, in which he participates conspicuously, so as to gain maximum attention from the male hierarchy. All eyes are upon him. With remarkably effective timing (it suggests the skill of a professional actor), he then dies, but not until he has publicly confessed, in such a way as to win points on the ultimate male hierarchy—the one presided over by God the Father Almighty Himself. No confession = no heaven, after all. Chillingworth acknowledges in the climactic scene that Dimmesdale "won," beating him in the contest—a big win indeed; so big that Chillingworth dies shortly afterward (male identity being constituted, again, as placement in Male Envy). The final public scene is not about morality or spirituality; it is about Male Envy. What is striking about Dimmesdale's confession is that overtly he acknowledges his sexuality and its failings; implicitly, however, his confession renounces eros altogether.

Like Lamia in Keats's poem, Hester is motivated by love—the desire to love and to be loved. She wants to talk to her lover Dimmesdale; the last she knew was that they had agreed on a plan to escape Boston. Like Lamia with Lycius, she tries but fails to dissuade him from his need for Male Display: Male Display is a priority that few needs can match—certainly not the needs of family or subordinates. Dimmesdale's reaction to Hester's words is significant. Irritatedly, he pushes her aside. He is emphatic: he does not see relation with her—now, or hereafter. Dimmesdale needs Hester on stage essentially as a prop, not because he in any sense loves her; she is like Pat Nixon standing by her sorrowing man in his famous Checkers speech, or Tammy Bakker stationed beside her chastened, heroically pious husband, the famous evangelist, in TV confessions.

It is interesting that Hester, right to the end, loves Dimmesdale. Note that he does not inform her of his plan to confess publicly to adultery with her—giving her some advance warning would seem to be a requirement of mere politeness, if not of love. His public confession once again reminds everyone of Hester's sin, years after her humiliation had been put to rest. He whispers to her that this public confession is better than her plan to escape Boston altogether, which he had earlier agreed with her to do. She is not convinced by his change of plan ("I know not! I know not!": compare Beatrice's similarly impassioned "I see it! I see it!"). Unlike Dimmesdale, she is concerned with their daughter's future. When it is obvious Dimmesdale is about to expire, Hester hopes that he can see into eternity, since he is on its threshold: "Shall we not spend our immortal life together? Surely, surely, we have ransomed one another, with all this woe! Thou lookest far into eternity, with those bright dying eyes! Then tell me what thou seest?" (304). Dimmesdale responds with "Hush, Hester, hush!" Shut up!

To Hester, the suffering has been pointless and dreadful—to Dimmesdale, by contrast, it has been a complex means of gaining the attention of God as the personification of male hierarchy. In this context, one notes also the "sign" in the sky earlier in the narrative, associated with the death of a more powerful man in the hierarchy (the governor); the self-flagellation; the cat-and-mouse torments of Chillingworth; the amazing mark on the body, like the stigmata of Christ; and so on: all suggest attention control. The suffering has also served as a means of deluding and finally destroying Chillingworth. What concerns Dimmesdale exclusively, in the final analysis, is status on the male power grid. It is worth dying to gain mastery on it, because, really, there is nothing else. That is what life is. A man's identity is not mere anatomy (or biological existence): it is placement in Male Envy. Male Envy is sacred.

Dimmesdale is a kind of Girardian *vaniteux*; he shows no spiritual boldness, no originality: he is wholly enclosed, intellectually, within the values of the male hierarchy that controls his society.[36] His conformism becomes conspicuous when one compares him with Hester, an original thinker: "radicalism sets her apart."[37] The respect that the community gives to her is spontaneous—it is not socially enforced, as it is for Dimmesdale, who must be respected and obeyed simply by virtue of the position he occupies. Hester in fact embodies desire, the sanctity of desire, which in its genuine form is free and freeing: "le désir est toujours spontané," as René Girard puts it.[38] Hester may be an outcast; nevertheless, she lives by her art. She is independent; the community willingly supports her, a community that does not have to deal with her at all. Dimmesdale's livelihood, by contrast, is simply servicing the male hierarchy.

Since she is off the compete/control ladder altogether, Hester has nothing to lose by being who she truly is. Dimmesdale never ventures beyond the hierarchy and its repressive mentality. In the context of that hierarchy, to fall for physical love is absurd (unless it consolidates power, weakens other males, or wins envy). Love as such—as affection, mutual trust, and enjoyment—is impossible: more important, it is undesirable, for it costs points on the hierarchy, as Antony finds in Shakespeare's *Antony and Cleopatra*. Since genuine love equalizes—how can one be lover to an inferior?—it is ruled out by the hierarchic war of males against males. One may not treat inferiors, here females, as equals, without becoming in a degree the equal of one's inferiors—that is, without dropping on the hierarchy. And to do that would be to lose identity and enter the sort of alienation reserved for losers.

This brings us back to our commercial: in competitive male war, the value of females is as markers on the hierarchy, to incite envy or acquire advantage, not for their own sake. The locus of interest is male competition. Dimmesdale hardly knows Hester as who she really is—still less Pearl, his own daughter—an independent personality with traits specific to her. Personality would distract from the assigned female function of marking gradations of male control and supplying/servicing male competitors. To leave Boston, as Hester urges Dimmesdale, would be to throw away his investment in male power—an unthinkable notion for someone of his position and conditioning.

It is a curious feature of Male Envy that it is persistently associated with religion and religious themes. It seems that this subject, unavoidably, raises spiritual questions—spiritual in the conventional sense of institutional religion, but also in the larger sense of that which gives meaning: what expresses identity in its most comprehensive level. It is simply not possible to explore Male Envy without respecting its spiritual dimension (most obviously, for example, when it touches on the nature of evil). The contrast between Dimmesdale and Hester, then, is also a contrast between institutional religion, on one hand, and spirituality in the primary sense of that which gives meaning to life, of what theologian Paul Tillich called "ultimate concern," on the other hand.

Hester's mistake was to love *Dimmesdale* in the first place, instead of a man equal to her remarkable personality. But that is the real point: there are no males equal to Hester in her environment. Genuine love, it seems, requires abandoning the compete/control hierarchy and its values altogether.

* * *

Male Envy is pervasive, but it is one of those forces that are so taken for granted as to be invisible. Dickens's *Great Expectations* (1860) is another canonic text (close to *The Scarlet Letter* in time) that also uses Male Envy as organizing paradigm. This is emblematized in the grotesque scene of the young men showing off their muscles at Jaggers's dinner party. Jaggers, a successful lawyer, sits back and enjoys the spectacle of the naive young men competing with one another in this absurdly un-self-aware and revealing manner. It is a naive exercise of the competitive struggle: practice for measuring, so that, to borrow the expression of football veteran Don Sabo, "elite men can have a clear sense of where they stand in the inter-male pecking order."[39]

The relation of Pip, the protagonist and narrator, to other males is hostile/competitive—till he is forced to accept identity with his spiritual father, Magwitch. It is significant that Pip's friend, Herbert Pocket, is introduced into the story as a boy-combatant, someone that Pip has physically to fight; Pip beats him (Herbert later remembers it as a win for *him*). The assumption is that only after openly fighting can two males establish, in Veblen's term, a non-invidious relation. What the fight shows is the priority of male competition, even as explicitly it renounces it. This boyhood fight is a play version of the fight to the death with Orlick later in the novel, which is anything but play. Pip's link with the saintly Joe, the blacksmith, is one of Blakean Innocence—a child-like dependency. It is only after Pip has been collapsed on the male compete/control hierarchy that he can achieve genuine relation with others, male or female.

The primary axis of *Great Expectations* is the compete/control hierarchy, with all its tensions—indeed, the title is a metaphor for that hierarchy, with its climbing imperative. The figure of Estella, and Pip's feeling for her, must be read carefully in terms of that axis. Pip's obsession with Estella is not really love; it is inseparable from property anxiety—that is, the need to rise on the male hierarchy. Pip insists that he loves her, and his feeling for her may include love. But the mainspring of his attraction is her semiotic function, which is consistent with Male Envy: her beauty is a metaphor for class status. She constitutes the ego points that Pip needs in order to free himself from the criminal underclass to which psychologically—almost phylogenetically—he belongs: the condemned, *les damnés de la terre*, in Frantz Fanon's expression, to which he feels such primal affiliation, the human detritus at the bottom of the compete/control hierarchy. Hence the obsessive quality of Pip's fascination with her. This obsessive quality draws attention to itself: it recalls the intensity of the male "stalker," who wishes to enclose a woman entirely within his will, so as to establish or shore up his identity to himself.

The break with Estella coincides with the collapse of his "expectations" and with imminent proletarianization, which Pip comes painfully to accept. The scene of Magwitch's reappearance, when Pip least suspects that Magwitch is his "benefactor," is the novel's supreme achievement: it recalls the uninvited guest motif in *Lamia*, the interruption of festivity by one who denounces, merely by being present (like the ghost of Banquo at Macbeth's feast). The emphasis on the eye and the gaze in this scene is striking. "He put a foot up to the bars, to dry and warm it, and the wet boot began to steam; but, he neither looked at it, nor at the fire, but steadily looked at me."[40] This is the trick of another uninvited guest, the ghost of Marley in Dickens's *A Christmas Carol*: he sees any object without dropping his fearful gaze at Scrooge. Pip is to be knocked off the compete/control hierarchy by Magwitch, even if Magwitch does not know that that is what he is doing. In fact, Magwitch is using Pip to rise on that hierarchy himself. As he explains to his "son" Pip, he is "buying" a gentleman—Pip, that is. And Magwitch is doing so in order to get even for his own crushing demotion, in particular for the wrenching public humiliation of his trial. At that trial, the man who had used him (his "friend," Compeyson) was effectively exonerated, because of his higher class status. *Great Expectations* is permeated by Male-envious themes and motifs, which are repeated, varied, and counterposed in a complex manner.

Pip's reaction to Magwitch's sudden appearance and revelation that he is the one who has provided Pip's "great expectations" needs to be observed carefully, for this reaction is a paradigm of defeat on the control hierarchy, what it is like to be awarded the status of loser. The whole scene suggests a rape. Thus, Pip feels himself "to be suffocating" and faints; he is overcome by nausea—"dread," "abhorrence"—and an ego-shattering evaporation of self, like the collapse of Lycius in *Lamia* or of Chillingworth at the end of *The Scarlet Letter*, who effectively shrivels up and dies. "The repugnance with which I shrank from him, could not have been exceeded if he had been some terrible beast" (337): "I recoiled from him as if he had been a snake." When Magwitch touches him, "my blood ran cold" (338). Magwitch, meanwhile, is triumphant: "In his heat and triumph, and in his knowledge that I had been nearly fainting, he did not remark on my reception of all this" (338). Magwitch feels his triumph—he has been waiting for this moment for years—and he observes Pip's weakness, as the younger man actually faints. Pip is "stunned" (339), experiencing "a half-formed terror that it might not be safe to be shut up there with him in the dead of the wild solitary night" (341; out of fear of Magwitch, he locks the door between him and his "benefactor"), and he sinks to the ground, as if literally crushed. Even there, he does not find relief; sleep does not let him escape "the perception of my wretchedness" (342). This is what a man feels like when he is defeated, when he is pushed off the compete/control hierarchy.

Pip's identity collapses. Every aspect of his life up to this point changes its meaning—or rather, everything till now *loses* its meaning. He is not who he thought he was: heir to a respectable pile of cash and the hand of Estella, the favored of fortune. It is only after Pip is demoted, and thoroughly absorbs that demotion, that Estella—also demoted in social status—reappears. The evil of the male compete/control hierarchy pervades *Great Expectations* (and is not just, in Charles Rzepka's words, "the harrowing tensions generated by false self-representations"[41]). It is an evil expressed, in paradigmatic form, in the fight to the death with Pip's apprentice-rival Orlick, a fight that is appropriately silenced and hidden, yet utterly desperate, utterly terrifying. This fight is conspicuously not necessary to the plot, but it is crucial to the symbolism of Male Envy which forms the matrix of the novel, where the motif of *losing* and *humiliation* is fundamental to the novel. The hopelessly vulnerable Pip is rescued from Orlick's deadly attack by his friend Herbert Pocket: the motif of friendship based on love, not competition, stands out in dramatic contrast.

Magwitch, in turn, thinks he loves Pip when he returns to him, and perhaps he does. The problem is that in the code of Male Envy, emotions such as love cannot be separated from winning and humiliating, displaying and accumulating; and, like Pip with Estella, Magwitch's happiness at meeting Pip is really delight in rising on the compete/control hierarchy, a delight, in turn, inseparable from revenge, the humiliation of others, and the treatment of people as objects. Without humiliation and control, success is not fully demonstrated, not fully substantial or proved. Or enjoyed. In the force field of Male Envy, real emotions are withered and mutated into ego-inflation or ego-deflation, and lose authenticity as genuine emotions. It must be this way; otherwise, emotions would divert resources or distract attention from the struggle, thus threatening a slippage in control. Real emotions pose a serious threat to identity—identity constituted, it goes without saying, as placement in Male Envy. Perhaps what is most remarkable about *Great Expectations* is the way that the novel *purges* Male Envy and allows the emergence of genuine feeling, and genuine love, when Herbert Pocket saves Pip, when Pip comforts the dying Magwitch at the end of the novel, and when Joe saves Pip, allowing the reunion of Pip and Estella—on very different terms from their earlier relation.

Not only does Male Envy structure Pip's love for Estella earlier; it subtly warps the narration itself. Pip is an "unreliable narrator"—not to us, but to himself, for he must conceal the real issue, which is his compete/control anxieties; that is, his place in Male Envy: how he will be measured—appraised— by the hierarchy. And hence his life within it—his survival. It is too painful to face this obsession directly; it must be disguised or filtered, or associated with love or some other distraction (like religion for Dimmesdale in *The Scarlet Letter*, or science for Giovanni in "Rappaccini's Daughter").

The inability to disentangle "love" from the compulsion to rise on the control hierarchy needs to be observed carefully. What this compulsion makes clear is that, in the code of Male Envy, nothing is more prized than power over others. "Love" and other apparent goods—or things that have a reputation for being good, at any rate—are tacitly understood as euphemisms for control power, or else as byproducts of success in control struggles, epiphenomena, booty.

* * *

In terms of Male Envy, the Estella-Miss Havisham complex in *Great Expectations* takes on new meaning, as a female war against the compete/control hierarchy, not just against men. Actually, it is an attempt to seize control of it, to win on the opponent's ground, and so, like Blake's fiery youth Orc turning into the ultraconservative old man Urizen, it ends up becoming more of what the rebellion was against, in the first place: the use of people as objects. Willful Miss Havisham was jilted by Compeyson at the altar in a spectacular act of (remote) control—a splendid Male Display, by which Compeyson publicly asserted his power, exposing his target to ridicule and humiliation. By it, Miss Havisham was not merely robbed, but deftly, publicly collapsed. She could never show her face again and withdrew, like a nun, into a sex-hostile realm of lost identity, where time has ceased, and with time, life itself.

Miss Havisham is, like Hester, a withdrawn (technically defeated) woman with an alternative vision. But unlike Hester, she tries to win by accumulating ego points, by in effect winning on the compete/control hierarchy itself, instead of seeking to escape its tyranny. Thus Miss Havisham creates Estella, crafting her to be a secret weapon (somewhat like Rappaccini with his daughter or Victor Frankenstein with his creature/son), and so wage war against male "winners" on the compete hierarchy. Estella achieves some success in this war. Estella herself tries vainly to escape her role as proxy warrior by marrying (the motif of the numerous competitors is emphasized by Pip's jealousy). But ultimately she fails disastrously. She is *physically* attacked. The husband who assaults her abuses animals: a significant motif in itself, for as Mary Wollstonecraft notes in *The Wrongs of Woman* (1798), the abuse of animals is basic training for male children. The pleasure of hurting those who are weaker is not something casual, but a major value, and a necessity of the code of Male Envy, something that has to be inculcated and not experienced as merely incidental. The sanctity of aggression is one of the most deeply felt and observed pieties in Male Envy.

A more complex example, Hedda Gabler in Henrik Ibsen's play of that name, is treated in the next chapter, "The Tricky Female." Hedda Gabler, Miss Havisham, and, in a different way, Hester all struggle with male domination. Hester withdraws from the arena of male war; Miss Havisham fights; Hedda, true to her traditional aristocratic provenance, manipulates males as proxies for her own control ambitions. What gives these texts their sharpness and complexity is the way they cast a struggling woman within and against the male compete/ control hierarchy. An ongoing function of that hierarchy is to police females, to exclude them altogether from control-power.[42] But this policing is not, as Eve K. Sedgwick argues, a means of male bonding—of uniting all males against all females—but of accumulating ego points. (Similarly, Male Envy is not, or not only, a dread of female reproductive power, as Bruno Bettelheim or Julia Kristeva and other feminist-psychoanalysts hold.) The function of policing women is an exercise of *differential* value, depending on the man's competitive position vis-à-vis other males.

For in the code of Male Envy, male bonding as friendship is undesirable, except in so far as it underwrites competition: that is, except in so far as it is a means of subordination of males to males, and the draining of power from weaker men to stronger men.[43] Michael Messner's incisive words again come to mind: "The project of men's domination of women may tie all men together, but men share very unequally in the fruits of this domination."[44] "The imperatives of masculinity disallow intimacy"; hence "brotherhoods," argues Heather Formaini, "present no threat of emotional entanglement or intimacy."[45] As William Doty puts it, "male friendships are tainted by the suspicion that the person making the initial overtures must be seeking to gain something or to take some advantage."[46] Doty quotes Perry Garfinkel: "This dominant competitive theme in men's relationships is clearly the reason that men fear and avoid intimacy with one another. After all, men reason, what fool would open up to one's potential rival?" It is interesting that the comedian Jerry Seinfeld, a figure millions have watched, observes that any arrangements between two men, however important, are suspended if a chance for one of them at pursuing a woman comes up, as if the men had never known each other. "Friends" in this view are really rivals, not friends in any meaningful sense.[47]

Friendship for its own sake may not be impossible: the point is that it *conflicts with the needs of competition/control*. More broadly, the *denial* of male friendship is a prime directive of the code of Male Envy. Betraying affection or denying affiliation with another male is a standard requirement of Male Envy, almost a *rite de passage*. For it demonstrates that one is a true competitor, an aspiring winner determined not to be a loser. Thus, the denial of connection with another male is a kind of Male Display in itself, a proof of one's strength.

In fact, this is a crucial point: male bonding is not simply a unifying of males in the face of female power, a unifying that is potentially or covertly homosexual. Male bonding is a process of domination of other males, by which some gain benefits from subordinating others. In this way male bonding is paradoxically a function of competitive struggle and requires the destruction of close male relationship for its own sake. Even in a context of war, male bonding is a weapon for unifying one side, in order to attack, overcome, and destroy the other side. It is not a unity for its own sake. These unities of men, moreover, arise only in a context of strict subordination by rank: they express control-power over others. Freud—ever sensitive to issues of aggression—makes the shrewd observation that "What appears later on in society in the shape of *Gemeingeist, esprit de corps*, 'group spirit,' etc., does not belie its derivation from what was originally envy."[48]

Male bonding, in this sense, is inseparable from competitive struggle; indeed it is constituted by that struggle, for without it the male bonding would not exist. It is a testament to the strength of human beings that even in these circumstances, genuine friendship can appear and grow alongside the competitive unities formed by conflict. "Male bonding," as Ben Greenstein argues, "is probably one of the most important phenomena responsible for the traditional suppression of women,"[49] but such "bonding" is not designed to enhance male privilege at the expense of females, but to enhance some males at the expense of other males, to drain power and resources away from weak males toward strong ones, from "losers" to "winners."

It follows, therefore, that fictions of female rebellion must inevitably involve decapitating or disrupting the compete/control hierarchy. An example of such "decapitation" appears in Margaret Atwood's important novel *Surfacing* (1972), an example I return to in the last chapter. The emancipation of women means confronting and overturning the male compete/control hierarchy that requires female subordination as its instrument.[50]

* * *

In Hemingway's *The Sun Also Rises* (1926), the "wound" that disables the protagonist-narrator Jake Barnes—the male wound—pushes him off the compete/control hierarchy altogether. The problem that this wound poses is not loss of sexual love: the "problem" is total defeat in male competition—"the experience of vulnerability, helplessness, loss of control, uncertainty, and threat to life," as Henry Holloway and Carol Fullerton put it.[51] The sexual aspect is semiotic, again: the substance is a matter of competitive power. It is significant that this wound is never named; it is the most important thing in the novel, but it is silenced, as if a metaphor for Male Envy itself. One does not talk about it. Now permanently off the hierarchy, Jake is exposed to withering sensations of meaninglessness that even numbing doses of alcohol cannot relieve. (One may compare the horror of the impotent Popeye in Faulkner's *Sanctuary*, who rapes a young woman named "Temple" with a corncob.)

Such feelings of alienation are not a matter of personal psychology (still less existential angst)—but a normal consequence of defeat or demotion on the compete/control hierarchy: what losers get. Pip's reaction to Magwitch's evisceration of his status in *Great Expectations* needs to be kept in mind. He bears the "full brunt of humiliation in the competitive environment," as Alex J. Tuss puts it.[52]

This then raises a difficult point: angst and related feelings of alienation often have nothing to do with metaphysical perceptions or nihilistic terrors or confrontations with a void of meaninglessness. On the contrary, angst and related emotions of alienation often express feelings of weakness; that is, feelings of *defeat* in the competitive struggle: to be an object of ridicule and contempt by stronger males, and so by the compete/control hierarchy itself. And since the compete/control hierarchy shapes identity, failure or defeat on that hierarchy means loss of essence, a catastrophic self-separation that cannot be articulated—a feeling that haunts the modernist male novelists in the United States, such as Dreiser, Hemingway, Fitzgerald, Nathanael West, and Faulkner, with their disturbing and claustrophobic ironies. Thorstein Veblen articulates the context of this struggle: "Under the régime of emulation the members of a modern industrial community are rivals, each of whom will best attain his individual and immediate advantage if, through an exceptional exemption from scruple, he is able serenely to overreach and injure his fellows when the chance offers" (154). This is what the male protagonist of the modernist novel faces.

In *The Sun Also Rises*, Jake doesn't need to compete for women or other ego points: he cannot win. Ironically, this collapse explains the curious subtextual satisfaction that is palpable in this novel. Liberated from the stresses of Male Envy, Jake can now turn to fishing—away from the horrifying anxieties of the control struggle. He can even pursue male bonding in the sense of mutual affection and equality.[53] Friendship based on *interest*, as in a business deal or contract—that is, friendship as a form of alliance, as a means of warring more effectively against others—is, of course, different. This latter kind of "friendship," is rational and acceptable in Male Envy, indeed a potent means of sustaining acquisition or aggression. Male bonding of this type is better understood as a line of credit than as the pleasurable mutuality usually understood by the term "friendship"—at least, if friendship is understood as a relationship that exists for its own sake and not for purposes of attacking or defending against others.

As Victor J. Seidler expresses it, "The thinness of men's relationships with each other and the ways that they seem to be constantly undermined through competition and jealousy are distinctive features of modern society"[54]—the "thinness of men's relationships" is a standard theme in discussions of the subject. Hence male bonding as an equalizing love between friends (apart from relations based on homosexual love) tends to be a myth of innocence—a condition realized by Tom Sawyer and his prepubescent buddies whooping it up naked on the beach of Jackson Island, the last bit of unlogged wilderness in the neighborhood. The fact that Tom Sawyer's refuge is an island is symbolic: it is not part of reality. In the code of Male Envy, that is what reality is: Male Envy.

Likewise, the genuine companionship of Huck and Jim in *Huckleberry Finn* (1884) takes place on a raft, where no one can see: what is forbidden here is not about race (or sex, as has been claimed) but about deep male friendship. By contrast, the con-artists known as the "King" and the "Duke" are together because they are allies in competition, not because of friendship, and their primary activity is to sap, exploit, and ultimately destroy the genuine link between Huck and Jim. In the régime of Male Envy, genuine friendship, for its own sake, is a crime.

One reason why male homosexuality is so taboo is that love between males attacks the compete/control hierarchy itself; in a sense it commits the ultimate sin: denying the authority of winning.[55] According to Richard Mohr, the gay man threatens the notion that only "straight men" are "fully real persons," as if gay men "have betrayed their socially assigned gender-status"; this "betrayal is a willful action."[56] The "panic" posed by this threat (Sedgwick's term) is intense; the whole weight of the compete/control hierarchy is behind it. For by attacking the compete/control hierarchy, the "homosexual panic" undermines identity itself. In fact, the hostility to love between men is almost a definition of Male Envy. I will return to this theme in the final chapter. Sedgwick's influential studies *Between Men* and *The Epistemology of the Closet* have limited value, however, for understanding the code of Male Envy. The difficulty with her approach is epitomized by her term "homosocial desire." This is a key term, but it is never defined and acquires an arbitrary force.[57] On one hand, it is used to cover all male-male relations; on the other, it continuously implies that all such relations are really homosexual in nature—"homosocial" is practically a homonym of "homosexual." The result is a certain confusion, even apart from a writing style that itself makes the argument difficult to follow.

"Homosociality" implies bonding and friendship among males as the primary human identification for men, but in post-Romantic literature the "natural" relation between males is understood to be hostile. Friendship becomes a liability, love—as love—a burdensome problem. Or a quixotic fantasy, as in F. Scott Fitzgerald's *The Great Gatsby* (1925), where Gatsby's love for Daisy—and the narrator's equally intense love for Gatsby—are both crushed. Fitzgerald's more ambitious novel, *Tender Is the Night* (1934; rev. 1939), demonstrates what happens when a man puts love ahead of competition: he loses love *and* competition, both. "Love" is a byproduct of successful competition—one of the spoils of winning. The cultural assumptions involved here crystallize in sociobiology, which constitutes males as competitors warring against one another. For a male to behave otherwise than as a competitor-warrior is an aberration, one that requires special explanation (such as Jake's "wound" in *The Sun Also Rises*).

Sometimes, male bonding functions as an accepting submission to the existing compete/control relations. That is, one male accepts or even seeks a stronger male to affiliate with. The prototype for this kind of relationship in American culture is Hawkeye and Chingachgook in James Fenimore Cooper's *The Last of the Mohicans* (1826). It is true that their relation is not competitive—but neither is it equal. Chingachgook and his son Uncas are *subordinates*. Hawkeye refers continually to his racial purity; in Cooper as in much of earlier American culture, racial purity functions as metaphorically a magic power like chastity in medieval romance. It is a power that enables Hawkeye to kill and escape—to use the wilderness as a source of supply, instead of finding it an impediment to winning or a even a threat to survival.

Thus, the Indians resemble "familiars," who function as magic servants, daemons of the forest that Hawkeye, thanks to his magic racial purity, has caught. They are "good" Indians, for they are the *last* Mohicans. Wisely accepting extinction, they have joined the winning whites. "Finally, the Indian is . . . another species altogether. What is left after this last removal [the death of Chingachgook in *The Pioneers*] is indeed a fantastic frontier, the white male world figured as all that is human."[58] Cooper's Indians are a topic that has consumed an immense amount of critical paper: what makes *The Last of the Mohicans* so odd is that aside from the two last Mohicans, it has no "good" Indians; i.e., no Indians allied with the whites—*American* whites, that is. Hawkeye seems to identify the Hurons with their ancestral enemies, the Iroquois, when the Hurons were allies of the French/Canadians, the Iroquois of the English. But from Hawkeye's point of view, it does not perhaps matter much. They are in any case doomed.

The male bond of Hawkeye/Chingachgook is vertical; not a horizontal one of equals. Nor is this relation (homo)sexual in nature. Especially in *Mohicans*, Hawkeye is asexual ("Probably he dies virgin," says D. H. Lawrence). Thus his cultural heirs—his fictional sons—are anything but lovers. They are characters of the Bronson, Eastwood, Stallone, Willis style in popular movies, with numerous clones (the figure is popular!); or the males in detective fiction of the Mike Hammer school, or "action" fiction of the Mac Bolan genre. As a prototype for all such figures, Hawkeye is (1) middle-aged—not a young man (when he wrote *Mohicans*, Cooper was significantly younger than the age he assigned to Hawkeye); (2) he is not a lover (a point so critical that it has to be explored at length in *The Pathfinder* [1840]—as well as in *The Deerslayer* [1841]); (3) he is a professional hunter, a hardened tracker trained to kill; the killing he claims to hate is subtextually what gives his life meaning; (4) his instinct is for solitude, for independence of social structure; he is the prototypical vigilante.

His penis—his male signifier—is projected as a gun (Hawkeye's nickname *La longue carabine* is semiotically plain enough. He has a big one, clearly). Male identity is constituted not sexually but exclusively, as *ranking* on the compete hierarchy. Hawkeye has achieved that perfect sublimation of sex energy which Freud hailed as the highest task of civilization. Neutralizing his sexuality yields a competitive advantage in the control struggle. He is not susceptible to love as an equalizing (hence degrading) force. In this respect the model, as in so many other ways, is the Satan created by John Milton for his epic *Paradise Lost*; Satan is technically male (it seems), but is oddly sexless, as if he had transcended sex altogether and were an independent substance without any need of others; that is, he is complete in and of himself and does not require another being, either to "complete" him, or, in a kind of Frankenstein fantasy, to generate him.

He is self-made, independent and isolated, so that he owes nothing to anybody; he is constituted as a solitary, alone in an antagonistic universe. And he likes it that way.

* * *

Cooper brings us to a key point about Male Envy: its historical conditioning. The compete/control hierarchy is a hierarchy, but it is a fluid or emergent hierarchy, not a fixed one. It assumes a class structure where social mobility is possible, and competition extends throughout the range of society. It assumes, in short, a market-based, commercial society, as opposed to a social order where the ruling stratum is a fixed, landowning nobility, and status and power are determined, for life, before one is even born, simply by the identity of one's parents. In feudal and precapitalist societies the notion of social mobility is, with few exceptions, a meaningless notion. Romantic narrative lies at the cusp of the shift from an earlier tradition of a fixed, pre-established hierarchy, to a society where universal competition has become a meaningful and active condition, indeed the dominant force.

Thus, Cooper illustrates a defining shift in the history of Male Envy: from a social structure with a pre-fixed ruling class to a universal competition that pits each (male) individual against potentially all other (male) individualnys. Equally important: it installs no limit to ambition. Power becomes simply force, not a function of any antecedent order, with its impeding rules and customs.

The independent male controller/competitor/winner sublimates sexual dependency on women, converting it to control-power that is then displayed in tricking or killing. The bodies of enemies—competitors—form prized units in Male Display, notches on the proverbial gun. This figure becomes (1) the ideal of Male Envy; and also (2) a cultural norm—a male paragon/paradigm generally. As winner, he excites the envy of other men; his power base is in himself— hence he is invulnerable. He doesn't need anybody else, and he doesn't depend on anybody. While not depending on others, he controls others, so that he has no obligations. Rank is won not by subordination to a fixed code of rules, but by throwing off the old-style hierarchy.

Mohicans thus contrasts lethal Hawkeye with bumbling Major Heywood: unlike Hawkeye, Heywood is committed to rising in the ranks—and so to obeying commanding officers. As far as obeying orders is concerned, the fate of Colonel Munro, after he surrenders his power object, Fort William Henry, is instructive: Munro is psychologically crushed and never recovers from his collapse on the control hierarchy—a hierarchy based, for him, on established, inherited rules—not on the preferred method of raw force. A similar difficulty appears with the gallant Montcalm (the French general who later died defending Québec), whom Cooper praises—and vilifies: Montcalm is a believer in chivalry but is unable to live up to his own code, because of his trust in the "savages," who do not live by rules but by force. By contrast, Hawkeye wins by personal force, not by obeying the established control hierarchy, which Cooper identifies with the obscenely incompetent rule of England and its king.

To be precise, Hawkeye's hierarchy is the elemental one of male force—raw "nature" itself—not a social grid built upon the fossilized male force of previous ages. Wilderness—in modern jargon "the jungle"—is a standard metaphor for the site of this universal competition, justifying and encouraging its ghastly atrocities —and conveniently hiding them.[59]

In this respect, the archetype is, again, the Satan of Milton's *Paradise Lost*: the figure of competitive war against the established Father-authority. Satan is a prototype of the competitor-warrior who is to become the cultural norm of commercial society. It is significant that Milton's fallen angel is a presiding figure in *The Last of the Mohicans* (which frequently alludes to *Paradise Lost*), for Milton's Satan is a model for the deracinated enemy-competitor Magua, who has the same revenge-obsession. Satan thinks about only one thing in *Paradise Lost*: power: who controls whom, how. Everything he says, even in asides and even down to matters of small detail, concerns using, controlling, competing— the insignia and emotional paraphernalia of Male Envy. A particularly important example, one that repays scrutiny, is Satan's address to the sun in Book 4 of *Paradise Lost*, especially its opening lines:

"O thou that with surpassing glory crowned
Look'st from thy sole dominion like the god
Of this new world—at whose sight all the stars
Hide their diminished heads—to thee I call,
But with no friendly voice, and add thy name,
O sun, to tell thee how I hate thy beams,
That bring to my remembrance from what state
I fell, how glorious once above thy sphere,
Till pride and worse ambition threw me down,
Warring in Heaven against Heaven's matchless King!" (4.32-41)

Notice (1) the overarching theme of invidious distinction in Satan's speech; also (2) the words of hate, (3) the motif of the power gaze, (4) the obsession, (5) Male Display (the dazzling, god-like sun), (6) the cosmic scale—there is no limit to Male Envy, (7) the motif of the numerous competitors ("at whose sight all the stars / Hide their diminished heads"), with its interesting allusion to Joseph's dream of power over his competitor-brothers in Genesis. One reason why this speech is so significant is that it was the first part of Milton's poem to be written. It is the kernel out of which the epic as a whole grew: the logical starting point of the poem and indication of the fact that the classic epic in the English language, *Paradise Lost*, is fundamentally concerned with Male Envy.

The feeling that he has been utterly collapsed on the compete/control hierarchy energizes the hate in Satan's speech and gives a fearful motivation to his words and acts. More exactly, the speech indicates the *creation* of the compete/control hierarchy, which had not existed before Satan. The sensation of imploded identity, of humiliation/demotion is something so appalling that it must at all costs be withdrawn from the self and passed on to others, whether Eve and Adam, or Satan's subordinate devils in Hell. Thus Satan boasts to his #2 man, the devil Beelzebub, and condenses his compete/control obsessions to a phrase: "to be weak / Is miserable, doing or suffering" (1.157-58: "suffering" in the old sense, of course: "doing or suffering" = "whether one is acting, or being acted upon"). Evil is *weakness*. For Satan, evil is simply vulnerability to others' control. Significantly, he targets his second-in-command for this dictum, for like everything he says, it has a practical point as an intimidation message, a reminder to Beelzebub of his place: #1 is already taken.

Paradise Lost deals extensively with the motif of competition and envy. The Romantic writers were fascinated by Milton, partly because his central motifs are so applicable to their own imaginative situation. When Byron wrote *Cain* (1821) —he termed it a "metaphysical" drama—he closely replicated Milton's Satan as one of the principal actors. *Cain* is set after the fall of humanity from Paradise, with Adam, Eve, Cain and Abel, and their wives and (in Cain's case) children. Cain is alienated from his family because he does not understand what was so dreadful about his parents' crime, and why their children and all their descendants are to be punished for what his parents did—he has many questions. The crucial one, however, is: what is death?

As if this anxious questioning was a cue, Lucifer appears, scenting prey. Lucifer takes Cain on a journey through time and space, a cosmic Male Display to show Cain that he is nothing and Lucifer is, if not all-powerful, then at least supreme competitor with all-power. Lucifer also shows Cain the underworld, the phantoms of dead races and cultures that came before, all the while humiliating Cain with jabs at his inferiority. Lucifer has access to the whole universe and to all of the past, and yet nothing interests him except Male Envy, winning. He illustrates an important characteristic of Male Envy, namely that it converts everything into itself: everything it sees is assimilated to the obsessions of Male Envy. "Evil minds / Change good to their own nature," as P. Shelley puts it in *Prometheus Unbound* (1.380-81). Milton's Satan is again the model here.

Cain returns to earth, stunned, only to be assailed for consorting with the enemy by his brother, Abel. Abel demands that he participate in a cleansing ritual sacrifice, cutting the throats of lambs in the manner that the God of *Cain* desires. Cain, a farmer, makes a vegetable offering instead. As Abel predicts, God is not pleased with a bloodless offering, and God destroys Cain's gift with a bolt of lightning, while showing favor to Abel's bleeding lamb. Cain is shocked at God's predilection for blood sacrifice, as if God were a god of death to be worshiped by death. In response to Abel's bitter reproaches, Cain impulsively strikes him, and he falls down, dead, much like the repulsive Claggart when Billy Budd strikes him in Melville's story *Billy Budd*. The emphasis on *blood*, treated as magic life-substance, is conspicuous.

The epiphany of death-power is thus the point of the play. For the code of Male Envy, death is the ultimate power, the ultimate reality, and has therefore a deep fascination. The unveiling of death as mystic agency is the final secret, as it were, of Male Envy. The fascination death exerts for Male Envy is not in any sense metaphysical—concerned with an afterlife—rather, it is awe-inspiring and mesmeric. This is not surprising, because death is the ultimate control and a miraculous threat-instrument by which to force subordinates. *Paradise Lost* treats with great care and detail the genesis of death: death is visualized as, literally, a competitor/warrior (he is a figure who appears at the end of Book II of *Paradise Lost*, where, amid much bluster and boasting, he challenges Satan).

One of the characteristic features of Male Envy is its fascination not so much with power as with *immense power*, with impersonal forces that elude comprehension. Such forces can be conceptualized in various forms—for example, as fate or destiny or natural law or even God's will. But the fascination itself is logical enough, because the competitor/controller who can successfully affiliate with greater power *acquires* greater power (or thinks he does). To harness fate or natural law is to become invincible, to be "destined" to greatness, greatness meaning power over others. These mysterious forces are not only impersonal but are typically destructive; they manifest in the form of destruction. They are, in short, the capacity to destroy or kill on a vast scale. Hence the mystic force that attracts the competitor/controller is essentially death; the power to command or control death. What Male Envy loves is not life or the power to create, but the capacity to control life, and that means, in practice, the power to kill it. As the terrorist in Joseph Conrad's novel *The Secret Agent* (1907) modestly explains, "I depend on death, which knows no restraint and cannot be attacked. My superiority is evident."[60]

It is no accident that one of the crucial episodes of *Paradise Lost* is the genesis of Death: when King Death appears at the end of Book II, he is visualized as the incestuous progeny of Satan himself. Allegorically, the Satanic frame of mind is naturally drawn to death and brings death into being: it causes death to happen. Byron's Lucifer shows the same fascination with mystic force, with a power that he has somehow harnessed or represents, and that will make him master of the universe. These motifs will need to be investigated at greater length, disturbing and repellent though they are (see Chapter 4, "Holy Murder").

Cain is a study in the horrors that unfold out of competitive rivalry, not just between brothers but generally, between those who seek power over others, and those whom they must subordinate and use to inflate a sense of identity, between the jealous God of the play and the Lucifer whose burning grudge at his defeated ambition motivates his action. Thus the Lucifer of *Cain* is interested in nothing but the power struggle. Since Male Envy expands to obsess every aspect of existence, a thing interests Lucifer only in so far as it advances or hinders his control. Indeed, things exist for him only in so far as they appear at all on the scale of control. Cain appears to him, because Cain is potentially useful in his struggles. Cain's wife, Adah, scarcely registers on his mind because she is not only useless to him but a distraction factor in his manipulation of Cain.

Lucifer's obsession explains why his intellectual talk is so opaque and frustrating. Its emptiness recalls Dimmesdale's boring obsessions and "guilt," which are in fact the anxieties of male hierarchy—not spirituality. Lucifer and Cain talk at length, with Cain asking questions, but Lucifer has no answers and only responds with more questions, questions that mirror back to him his victim's bewilderment. Lucifer's evasions and verbal aggressions epitomize the kind of arguing that Male Envy engages in. One looks in vain for answers in Lucifer's words—or even simple information. He does not seem to be interested enough to know about anything, since that might distract him for a moment from his vital obsession with control. Male Envy requires constant vigilance, never relaxing, never letting up one's guard. *Cain* is especially clear about the nature of envy as *aggressive*: it is not withdrawn or passive in outlook. By its very nature, it has to have a target and restlessly seeks one if nothing is to hand: it feeds on and hence requires opportunities for hostility. In this respect, Byron's Abel and his Lucifer are very similar.

Byron's Lucifer is anything but a "romantic" figure. He sneers in disgust at sexual love; his attitude toward Cain's wife, Adah, is crudely misogynistic: as a "god," he is proud of being only spirit—flesh, the body, repels him. The fact that Byron could in so many respects replicate the character of Milton's Satan in his own Lucifer, more than a century and a half after *Paradise Lost*, is significant. It indicates how powerfully Milton's creation is a prototype: a preview of the constitution of male identity as warrior-competitor in the context of a nihilistic field of control, where win and lose are the only categories that have meaning, where emotional ties are a dangerous liability and aggression is a norm. "If men need to interpose violence in order to protect themselves from closeness and personal connections, then the threat which they see suggests that men live in a kind of war zone, always on the lookout for a potential enemy" (Formaini 73). Criminologist John Archer sums up: "Those who have power are always having to protect it through violence or threat of violence . . . are always having to protect it or to take pre-emptive action, and they are subject to being usurped by those willing to challenge them."[61] The historical significance of this development—the origin and evolution of Male Envy in the forms traced here— is the topic of Chapter 3, "Object Thinking." One has to be grateful that Male Envy, powerful as it is, is not the only factor governing behavior and thought.

Just as Milton's Satan reveals nothing to Eve in *Paradise Lost*, apart from half-truths and distortions, Byron's Lucifer reveals nothing to Cain, properly speaking. But this "nothing" has a content, nonetheless: fear, obsession, mental division, an incessant itch to damage and hurt others in order to prove that one exists, a compulsive insistence on self-importance (hence generating illusions of control), a need to believe in one's own boasting and to humiliate those who are weaker. It is a chilling prospect altogether and might well incite anybody, like Cain, to kill and die, simply out of panic.[62]

But when one looks at the horrors that history displays, notably the last two centuries, the cruel compulsions of Male Envy are not the anomaly but a ruling principle. What the facts of history suggest is that it is impossible to exaggerate the pain which Male Envy causes. Male Envy could almost be defined as the worship of death. Again, Male Envy takes us into the mystery of evil as few subjects can. Malice is a charcteristic only of human beings, not of animals.

The horror and revulsion of *Cain* disclose an intense yearning to be free of Male Envy, and the difficulty of getting free of it, since attacking it seems only to intensify it. What is "wrong" with Cain in Byron's play is his unwillingness to placate the male hierarchy or participate in its wars. He just wants out. By contrast, total devotion to the male hierarchy is what the religion of his brother Abel amounts to—just as it does for Dimmesdale. For Abel, as for Dimmesdale, the need to placate, manipulate, and identify with greater power is deeply internalized, as is every aspect of Male Envy.

This internalized hate/subservience/fear is personified in Byron's and Milton's Lucifer, a fanatical Manichean, whose vision is endless war, disaster fantasies, terror at losing, no rest ever, obsessiveness: what is, in the phrase of Milton's Eve, "a death to think" (9.830). Male Envy is male alienation, a separation of self from self, and not simply "losing."

Notes

1. René Girard, *A Theatre of Envy: William Shakespeare* (New York: Oxford UP, 1991) 4.

2. "Among the disorders of the soul, envy is the only one no one confesses to," says Plutarch (qu. in Gonzalo Fernàndez de la Mora, *Egalitarian Envy: The Political Foundations of Social Justice*, trans. Antonio T. de Nicolà [New York: Paragon, 1987] 18). "Philosophers have hardly touched it," de la Mora notes (113)—social scientists likewise have left envy virtually *terra incognita*.

3. Joseph Berke, *The Tyranny of Malice* (New York: Simon, 1986) 11.

4. Helmut Schoeck, *Envy: A Theory of Social Behavior* 1966; trans. M. Glenny and B. Ross (New York: Harcourt, 1969); for Berke see n. 3—Berke follows Schoeck closely. Both Schoeck and Berke comment on the fact that there are surprisingly few studies of envy by social scientists—or other analysts.

5. David Hume, *A Treatise of Human Nature*, ed. Ernest C. Mossner (Harmondsworth: Penguin, 1969) 420-429.

6. Max Scheler, *Ressentiment*, trans. William Holdheim, ed. Lewis Coser (New York: Free P, 1961) 53.

7. Tilottama Rajan explains: "The term 'aporia' meaning 'unpassable path,' is best defined by Paul de Man himself as allowing for 'two incompatible, mutually self-destructive points of view'. . . . It is different from 'contradiction,' which implies a logical impasse that can be surmounted through an act of choice, and from 'paradox,' which suggests an apparent contradiction that turns out not to be one from a higher perspective" ("Displacing Post-Structuralism: Romantic Studies after Paul de Man," *Studies in Romanticism* 24.4 [1985]: 453n).

8. Melanie Klein, *Envy and Gratitude and Other Works* (London: Hogarth, 1973) 189, my emphasis.

9. The silence of envy is reinforced by the belief that men should be, in general, silent, like machines. As Jack Balswick puts it, "The traditional definition of manhood includes not only what 'real' men should do, but also what a real man should not do. Inexpressiveness is a male characteristic. . . . men are verbally inexpressive of their feelings because they believe it is the way men should be" (*The Inexpressive Male* [Lexington: Heath, 1988] 1). This is "The first precept of conventional wisdom": "men had to keep certain things to themselves. . . . Men had no persona, they played no role: they were men, and that was the long and the short of it" (B. Mark Schoenberg, *Growing up Male: The Psychology of Masculinity* [Westport: Greenwood, 1993] 1).

10. Thorstein Veblen, *The Theory of the Leisure Class* (New York: NAL, 1953) 40; my emphasis: I refer to *The Theory of the Leisure Class* throughout this study. Cf. Adam Smith in 1776: "The pride of man makes him love to domineer, and nothing mortifies him so much as to be obliged to condescend to persuade his inferiors. Wherever the law allows it, and the nature of the work can afford it, therefore, he will generally prefer the services of slaves to that of freemen" (*The Wealth of Nations* [Glasgow: Oxford UP, 1976] 388, III.ii.10).

11. "Condensation" ("*Verdichtung*") is a key function of the "dream-work" in Freud's *The Interpretation of Dreams*: condensation is the enfolding within one motif of numerous others, on the model of Galton's "composite" photographs. Literary theorists have devoted much attention to Freud's concept of "displacement" (*Verscheibung*), but have shown little interest in condensation, which is a most suggestive concept for what Aristotle might call the *eidos* of literature. On mental images as a mode of thinking, see my *13 Ways of Looking at Images: Studies in the Logic of Visualization* (Los Angeles, 1999).

12. Walter Burkert, *Homo Necans: The Anthropology of Ancient Greek Sacrificial Ritual and Myth*, trans. Peter Bing (Berkeley: U of California P, 1983) 9. This theme is treated in Chapter 4, "Holy Murder."

13. Liam Hudson and Bernadine Jacot, *The Way Men Think: Intellect Intimacy and the Erotic Imagination* (New Haven: Yale UP, 1991) 99.

14. "The man's ego," when threatened, "compensates with inflationary fantasies and inflated personae in its effort to establish itself in the world. These inflations always seem collectively determined, in that they are efforts to conform with that standard, regardless of the actual abilities or personal characteristics of the individual" (James Wyly, *The Phallic Quest: Priapus and Masculine Inflation* [Toronto: Inner City Books, 1989] 105).

15. Steven Cohan, "Masquerading as the American Male in the Fifties: *Picnic*, William Holden and the Spectacle of Masculinity in Hollywood Film" *Camera Obscura* 25/26 (1991): 68. Male Display may or may not include what Cohan calls "a performance of virility" (68).

16. Rory O'Day, "Intimidation Rituals: Reactions to Reform," *Journal of Applied Behavioural Science* 10 (1974): 373-86.

17. Michael A. Messner, "Masculinities and Athletic Careers," *The Social Construction of Gender*, eds. Judith Lorber and Susan A. Farrell (Newbury Park: Sage, 1991) 72-73; my emphasis.

18. See Luise Eichenbaum and Susie Orbach, *Between Women: Love, Envy, and Competition in Women's Friendships* (New York: Viking, 1988).

19. Peter Lehman, "*In the Realm of the Senses*: Desire, Power, and the Representation of the Male Body" (*Genders* 2 [1988], 108). Jeff Hearn notes: "The institutions of patriarchy are means of men's domination of reproductive labour-powers and their products. Men dominate and oppress women and children through these institutions, yet at the same time and by way of them men compete with each other; and in turn oppress each other and are oppressed" (*The Gender of Oppression* [Brighton, England: Wheatsheaf, 1987] 89). "An examination of masculinity, not as a direct oppression of women, but as a category of definition itself is important to any feminist understanding of the operations of patriarchy" (Susan Jeffords, *The Remasculinization of America: Gender and the Vietnam War* [Bloomington: Indiana UP, 1989] 18. "Men's studies" has scarcely begun this examination—the men's movement exemplified by Robert Bly seems largely a new way of inculcating the code of Male Envy.

20. Jeffords 84. As Judith Stiehm puts it in her study of the Air Force Academy: "men do not fight to the finish; they fight to establish hierarchy" (qu. in Jeffords, 61).

21. Jill Radford and Elizabeth A. Stanko, "Violence against Women and Children: The Contradictions of Crime Control under Patriarchy" in *Women, Violence and Male Power: Feminist Activism, Research and Practice*, eds. Marianne Hester, Liz Kelly and Jill Radford (Buckingham, England: Open UP, 1996) 65.

22. Friedrich Nietzsche, *The Birth of Tragedy and The Genealogy of Morals*, trans. Francis Golffing (New York: Doubleday, 1956) 196; my emphasis.

23. See Elliott Leyton, *Hunting Humans: The Rise of the Modern Multiple Murderer* (Toronto: McClelland, 1987). Feminists have scrutinized this subject, e.g., Deborah Cameron and Elizabeth Frazer, *The Lust to Kill: A Feminist Investigation of Sexual Murder* (Cambridge: Blackwell, 1987); Jane Caputi, *The Age of Sex Crime* (Bowling Green: Bowling Green State UP, 1988); Jane Caputi and Diana Russell, "'Femicide': Speaking the Unspeakable" *Ms. The World of Women* 1.2 (1990): 34-37.

24. George L. Mose, "Manliness and the Great War," *Genocide, War, and Human Survival*, eds. Charles Strozier and Michael Flynn (Lanham: UP of America, 1996) 171.

25. Nancy Jay, *Throughout Your Generations Forever: Sacrifice, Religion, and Paternity* (Chicago: U of Chicago P, 1992) offers a particularly lucid critique of Girard's theorem, from a feminist viewpoint.

26. Janice Doane and Devon Hodges discuss "The importance of infantile sexuality, always a troubling feature of Freudian psychoanalysis and perhaps particularly disconcerting in Klein's account of infantile sadism" (*From Klein to Kristeva: Psychoanalytic Feminism and the Search for the "Good Enough" Mother* [Ann Arbor: U of Michigan P, 1992] 20).

27. "The neglect of the ideas of Thorstein Veblen (1857-1929) is a major academic scandal," as his editor, Rick Tilman, argues (*A Veblen Treasury: From Leisure Class to War, Peace, and Capitalism* [Armonk: Sharpe, 1993] ix).

28. In *L'Imaginaire philosophique* (Paris: Grasset, 1980), Michèle Le Doeuff argues that the texts of philosophy conceal and repress the role of mental images in shaping the argument, given philosophy's obsessive privileging of the abstract and conceptual over mental image and sensation: "Aujourd'hui que la pensée en images est une notion qui a conquis droit de cité, la méconnaissance de l'importance des segments imagiers n'est plus possible. Mais il n'est pas simple pour autant d'en faire la théorie. . . . La perspective dans laquelle je me place est tierce, comme on le verra, puisqu'il s'agit de réfléchir sur des lambeaux d'imaginaire à ou, pourtant, sans lui, rien ne se ferait" (11).

29. In *Models of Desire: René Girard and the Psychology of Mimesis*, Paisley Livingston notes the logic of Male Display: "this important desire for social recognition and distinction must express itself in a context where distinction is never fully certain. Insofar as one perceives any sign of real or pretended superiority in the other, this distinction is not believed to be a necessary or lasting mark of hierarchy, but temporary and changeable, a strategic contingency that may be removed with effort or a little luck" (Baltimore: Johns Hopkins UP, 1992) 154-155.

30. The larger context of Lamia is a constellation of character-types that appears at the end of the eighteenth century: (1) a woman struggling for emancipation, flanked by (2) a brutal, power-obsessed male, and by (3) a weak and self-divided male, typically the ineffectual lover of the woman. See Chapter 2 and my "Female Emancipation in Romantic Narrative," *Women's Studies* 18.2-3 (1990): 309-29.

31. Generic coherence and continuity of this type is a fact that literary history has yet to come to terms with. See David Perkins, *Is Literary History Possible?* (Baltimore: Johns Hopkins UP, 1992), especially 121-152. For a fusion of Male-envious themes and New Historicist outlook, see Marlon B. Ross, *The Contours of Masculine Desire: Romanticism and the Rise of Women's Poetry* (Oxford: Oxford UP, 1989), notably in his treatment of Byron, a frequent target of *Schadenfreude*.

32. Edward Alboo, *Who's Afraid of Virginia Woolf?* (New York: Pocket, 1964) 194.

33. *Hawthorne's Short Stories*, ed. Norman Arvin (New York: Knopf, 1946) 206-208.

34. Richard Brenzo, "Beatrice Rappaccini: A Victim of Male Love and Horror," *Nathaniel Hawthorne*, ed. Harold Bloom (New York: Chelsea, 1986) 141-52, 149. Cf. Edward Wagenknecht, *Nathaniel Hawthorne: The Man, His Tales and Romances* (New York: Continuum, 1989) 50-57. As Brenzo argues, the tale "concerns the exploitation of one person by another" (142)—but in this exploitation males use each other, as well as exploiting the female, so as to recall the "désir triangulaire" model in René Girard's *Mensonge Romantique et vérité romanesque* (Paris: Grasset, 1961]), where the reason why A wants B is that C wants B. This early study by Girard is filled with insight; but his elaborate later studies on mimetic desire (envy-as-imitation), sacrifice, violence, and religion seem to assume what I call the code of Male Envy—to assume it rather than explain it, and so belong to the same genre as Freud's *Totem and Taboo*: attempts to reconstruct primitive psychology/anthropology without any archaeological or other empirical evidence. Hence they give the impression of projecting backward on to a mythical prehistory behaviors and attitudes that are actually those of our own historically conditioned culture.

35. *The Scarlet Letter*, ed. John Stephen Martin (Orchard Park: Broadview, 1995).

36. "Le vaniteux ne peut pas tirer ses désirs de son propre fonds; il les emprunte à autrui" (René Girard, *Mensonge Romantique et vérité romanesque* 14-15). "The *vaniteux*—the empty, vain man—is unable to draw his desires from his own depths; he borrows them from others."

37. Sacvan Bercovitch, "The A-Politics of Ambiguity in *The Scarlet Letter*," *New Literary History* 19 (1988): 636. On the masochism of Dimmesdale see Joanne Diehl, "Re-Reading The Letter: Hester, the Fetish, and the (Family) Romance," *New Literary History* 19 (1988): 668.

38. "Desire is always spontaneous" (René Girard, *Mensonge Romantique* 12). An English translation of this important book exists under the title *Deceit, Desire, and the Novel: Self and Other in Literary Structure*, trans. Yvonne Freccero (Baltimore: Johns Hopkins UP, 1965). Girard's further comment makes one think of Hester and Dimmesdale: "un contraste entre l'être spontané qui désire intensément, et le sous-homme qui désire faiblement en copiant les autres" (28): "a contrast between the spontaneous being who desires intensely, and the underling who desires feebly by copying others."

39. Don Sabo, "Pigskin, Patriarchy and Pain: Sex, Violence and Power in Sports," *Rethinking Masculinity*, eds. Michael A. Messner and Donald F. Sabo (Fredan: The Crossing P, 1994): 98.

40. *Great Expectations*, ed. Angus Calder (Harmondsworth: Penguin, 1965) 386.

41. Charles J. Rzepka, *The Self as Mind* (Cambridge: Harvard UP, 1986) 247.

42. Michael Johnson notes: "Patriarchal terrorism, a product of patriarchal traditions of men's right to control 'their' women, is a form of terroristic control of wives by their husbands that involves the systematic use of not only violence, but economic subordination, threats, isolation, and other control tactics" ("Patriarchal Terrorism and Common Couple Violence," *Journal of Marriage and the Family* 57.2 [1995] 284). See Chapter 4, "Holy Murder."

43. Clyde W. Franklin III notes in *The Changing Definition of Masculinity* (New York: Plenum, 1984): "Male youth friendships generally are diffuse and based on competitiveness, aggressiveness, dominance, and the like. . . . instrumental friendships, rather than based on emotional expressiveness. This pattern of friendship-formation for males continues into adolescence and adulthood" (119); "The adult male who is 'appropriately' socialized into masculinity is rendered incapable of forming close ties with other males. . . . how does one reconcile intimate self-disclosing and being emotionally expressive with one's competitors who may attempt to use this in future competitive games?" (120). In Michael E. McGill's blunt words: "Men do not value friendship. Their relationships with other men are superficial, even shallow" (*The McGill Report on Male Intimacy* [New York: Holt, 1985] 184).

44. Michael A. Messner, "Masculinities and Athletic Careers," *The Social Construction of Gender*, eds. Judith Lorber and Susan A. Farrell (Newbury Park: Sage, 1991) 72-73.

45. Heather Formaini, *Men: The Darker Continent* (London: Heinemann 1990) 71

46. William G. Doty, "'Companionship Thick as Trees': Our Myths of Friendship," *Journal of Men's Studies* 1.4 (1993): 363, 364.

47. See Jerry Seinfeld, *Sein Language* (New York: Bantam, 1993) 53. Seinfeld begins his essay "Friends" by assuring readers he is not gay. In the code of male envy, male friendship is always suspect.

48. Sigmund Freud, *New Introductory Lectures on Psycho-Analysis, Standard Edition of the Complete Psychological Works*, trans. James Strachey (London: Hogarth, 1961) 22:125.

49. Ben Greenstein, *The Fragile Male* (London: Boxtree, 1993) 157.

50. Mary Wollstonecraft's great fragment, *The Wrongs of Woman, or Maria*, is a Romantic narrative which illustrates the horror of the female role in the context of male compete/control struggles.

51. Henry C. Holloway and Carol S. Fullerton, "The Psychology of Terror and Its Aftermath," *Individual and Community Responses to Trauma and Disaster*, ed. Robert J. Ursano et al. (Cambridge: Cambridge UP, 1994) 31.

52. Alex J. Tuss, "Divergent and Conflicting Voices: Victorian Images of the Male," *Journal of Men's Studies* 4.1 (1995): 51.

53. In a psychoanalytic study, Pamela Bowker notes: "As in *A Farewell to Arms, For Whom the Bell Tolls* dramatizes the conflict between Hemingway's desire to believe unconditionally in a heroic, masculine ego ideal . . . and his opposing regressive wish to escape from adult responsibility to a fantasy state of primitive fusion with the good mother" (Pamela Bowker, "Negotiating the Heroic Paternal Ideal; Historical Fiction as Transference in Hemingway's *For Whom the Bell Tolls*," *Literature and Psychology* 41.1-2 [1995]: 84). The anxiety of male competition and the yearning for release from its horrors is the point here—not the psychoanalytic diagnosis.

54. Victor J. Seidler, "Rejection, Vulnerability, and Friendship," *Men's Friendships*, ed. Peter M. Nardi (Newbury Park: Sage, 1992) 17. As far as Male Envy is concerned, La Rochefoucauld's maxim on "friendship" has the last word: "What men have termed friendship is only a corporation, a reciprocal arranging of interests and exchange of useful offices; it is finally only a business where self-love always plans on getting something"—"Ce que les hommes ont nommé amitié n'est qu'une société, qu'un ménagement reciproque d'intérêts, et qu'un échange de bons offices; ce n'est enfin qu'un commerce ou l'amour-propre se propose toujours quelque chose à gagner" (François de la Rochefoucauld, *Maximes*, ed. Jacques Truchet [Paris: Garnier Frères, 1967] 26 (Maxime #83). Freud's lieutenant, Ernest Jones, cites a maxim of La Rochefoucauld that is even more famous: "In the troubles of even our best friends, there is something that does not displease us"—"Dans l'adversité de nos meilleurs amis, il y a quelque chose qui ne nous déplaît pas." Jones reflects Freud's fascination with aggression and rivalry in his discussion of this and related expressions in Jones's influential *Hamlet and Oedipus* (New York: Doubleday, 1954) 81-83.

55. Thus Leonard Kriegel: "a homosexual is nothing but a man who has broken under the weight of manhood" (*On Men and Manhood* [New York: Doubleday, 1979] 170)—a defective "male machine." The belief that a gay man is somehow "broken" or defective is deeply ingrained in the code of male envy and in homophobic society in general. As Sedgwick puts it: "Patriarchy structurally requires homophobia" (4). "Little boys learn very early on that they must not simply behave as boys, but, more importantly, they must not behave as girls. . . . 'maleness' = dominance and aggression. . . . Homosexual men are perceived as acting like their status inferiors, and are therefore deemed 'traitors' to men" (Joanne Naiman, "Left Feminism and the Return to Class," *Monthly Review* 48.2 [1996]: 22.)

56. Richard D. Mohr, *A More Perfect Union* (Boston: Beacon, 1994) 66, 62.

57. "It is made clear that homosocial bonds include all forms of masculine interaction, but are not reducible to any one as a stable and transcendent unity" (Richard Easton, 'Canonic Criminalizations: Homosexuality, Art History, Surrealism, and Abjection,' *Differences* 4.5 (1992): 154.

58. Eric Cheyfitz, "Literally White, Figuratively Red," *James Fenimore Cooper: New Critical Essays*, ed. Robert Clark (London: Vision P, 1985): 88. Cf. Richard Slotkin, elaborating what he calls "the hunter myth": "For the American writer, the conflict of cultures meant the replacement or extermination of the Indian. The reconciliation of white and Indian could be seen only as the reconciliation of the hunter and his prey—a flash of sympathy and fellow feeling that caps the climactic moment when the long hunt ends and the kill is achieved" (*Regeneration through Violence: The Mythology of the American Frontier, 1600-1860* [Middletown: Wesleyan UP, 1973] 473). The notion that there could be "regeneration" (note the religious language) through *violence*—inflicting violence—is the kind of absurd thinking that typifies Male Envy. By means of violence, the degraded loser becomes an exalted winner.

59. The image of the wilderness as a graveyard or charnel house is basic to *The Last of the Mohicans*. Cooper's wilderness is anarchic—yet it paradoxically reinscribes the principle of hierarchy as "the social construction of masculinity as transcendence over others" (576). Here "success is achieved through individual competition rather than dyadic or group bonding" (Dorothy Hammond and Alta Jablow, "Gilgamesh and the Sundance Kid: The Myth of Male Friendship," *The Making of Masculinities: The New Men's Studies*, ed. Harry Brod (Boston: Beacon, 1987) 255.

60. Joseph Conrad, *The Secret Agent* (Garden City: Doubleday, 1953) 67.

61. John Archer, "Power and Male Violence," *Male Violence*, ed. John Archer (London and New York: Routledge, 1994) 320.

62. Chapter 4, "Holy Murder," explores this theme (and *Cain*) further.

2

The Tricky Female

*Envy worketh subtilly and in the dark,
and to the prejudice of good things.*
Francis Bacon

One of the recurring themes in the scene of Male Envy is that sex is a reward for winning, for male winning, that is. If you are a winner, you get sex; if you are not a winner, you do not get sex. The corollary is that to have access to sex is a marker of winning. It affirms one's status as competitor/controller. This view of sex amounts to a first principle in Male Envy, and hence one that dictates how Male-envious culture views women. One reason why men in powerful positions engage in extramarital affairs is that this is a means of affirming their winning and power status: it has nothing to do with sex appetite. Thus, in the régime of Male Envy, "love" becomes "strangelove," to use the term of Stanley Kubrick's satiric film: it is love as winning. More exactly, it is love as the *sensation* of winning, so that female roles and female sexuality are seen through the lens of male anxieties about controlling in competition with other males.

Space permits only brief reference to movies here, but one director who is unusually valuable for probing the logic of Male Envy is Stanley Kubrick. In his *Dr. Strangelove* (1964), a general goes insane: he fears his vital male fluids are being subverted by a secret conspiracy. To defeat his anxiety, he orders the launch of a nuclear weapon. The "explanation" he gives to another officer is perfectly unintelligible (bizarre reasoning again). What does seem clear is that he confuses a sexual problem with a feeling of losing. To lose access to sex is to lose, period, not because sex is desirable or emotionally needed, but because sex is the prerogative and signifier of a winner. Hence, facing that nightmare of Male Envy, losing, a dramatic reaffirmation of potency is required. His twisted rationale, where "winning" replaces love, assumes a specific complex of motifs:

- sex as a function of winning in compete/control struggles
- sex understood in terms of abstinence and overindulgence; as the manipulation of a special object or magic fluid, as power condensed in an object to control
- secrecy; self-enclosure; detachment from women
- anxiety (over potency and masculine identity)
- fascination with control over objects in space
- vanity; boasting; attention command
- destructive force
- nuclear weapons (i.e., metaphorically, the symbolic limit of total power)
- misuse of words: opaque, convoluted, or misleading language; deliberate obscurity; use of the big lie; language of intimidation

In *Dr. Strangelove*, a threat to male identity—that is, to placement in Male Envy—is compensated for by a Male Display on literally a global scale, a Display that is a spectacular act of destruction. The officer is clearly missing more than vital male fluids.[1] Curiously, the fantasy of having several women for each man (a standard male fantasy—and a dramatic marker of a male winning over other males) emerges in the midst of what would seem to be the mind-numbing horror of global destruction, as Dr. Strangelove himself explains what life will be like after the bomb is dropped: not so bad, after all—for winners, that is.

Male Envy treats women in a certain way because it sees them in a certain way. Therefore, we have to probe a little deeper into the logic, such as it is, of Male-envious perception before we can trace accurately the roles of women in Male Envy.

The out-of-control general who orders the bomb dropped may be as sane as the Mad Hatter and the March Hare combined, but he goes about his insanity logically enough. His actions require planning, ingenuity, attention to detail. The "method in his madness" is a motif characteristic of envy. Envy is not just an emotion: it is a complicated state of mind in which imagination, reason, emotion —and action—are all coordinated by the will. De la Mora argues that envy originates in "a reasoning process"; hence it is *not* "an elemental instinct, like sensuality or aggression. One does not envy because the genetic code so dictates. Envy is the most intellectual of our emotions; not only because its home and cradle is lacking, but also because, despite its false premise, its origin is in reason."[2] Envy can be impulsive, but its preference is to compare, observe, wait, and plot. It loves to calculate and manipulate. There is an element of deliberateness about envy which is what makes it envy. "Envy is not just an emotion," as Joseph Berke puts it: "It is a profound emotional force that imposes a comprehensive alienation on the whole way that the envious person sees, feels, and acts and on the way that the envied other, the victim, responds."

The nucleus of envy, then, is *perception*: a mode of consciousness that has a particular way of seeing, an understanding that guides the envious will.

> Envy begins in the eye of the beholder, an eye that exaggerates, misrepresents, and selectively chooses things to hate. This eye is especially attracted to prosperity, fertility, vitality, fame, success, pride, power, and any other quality, characteristic, or accomplishment that conveys, or appears to convey, superiority or special advantage.[3]

Notice again the connection with seeing and the eye (also the targeting of fertility). To envy is to see another as a threat, even if he is not: simply by being who he is, the envied man threatens, without his having to do anything. Hence envy is not only a form of perception, but a complicated *distortion* of perception, "the optics of envy," as Helmut Schoeck terms it: "the envious man sees what confirms his envy."[4] The Russian proverb Schoeck quotes, "The envious man sees with his ears as well" (21), emphasizes the fusion of distorted perception with obsession.

Envy sees what is not there, giving it a hallucinatory quality: "Such a perception arises from a deep, gnawing sense of inferiority coupled with an instantaneous and usually unconscious comparison with the envied object. It conveys the essential idea 'Whatever I am, or have, you are much bigger and better'" (Berke 36). The distortions of envy are a standard theme in analysis of the subject: "envy does not provide any valid information about the surrounding environment. On the contrary, it represents the superior person as an enemy and a scandal" (Mora 83). Thus, envy both calculates/controls—and deceives/distorts: "envious perception confirms, and adds to, envy" (Berke 37).

The distortion of envy gives its perceptions a hollowness: what it sees is not merely what it hates, but its own invention, a mirror of its hate. In what it sees, then, there is nothing there, because there is nothing inside the self, a void—an emptying of vital fluids, so to speak. The false perception, an emptiness itself, springs from an emptiness within. Hence the bottom of the compete/control hierarchy is a void, a nothing so terrible that it drives the competitor/warrior to fight to escape it, casting his anxieties on to rivals as a means of escaping it himself. "The truth is that the formal object of envy is not a good; it is, rather, the unaccepted impotence to be able to achieve the superior happiness of others" (Mora 71). The fear of being nothing makes others into nothing.

This feeling of inner emptiness is carried within the competitor, who is constantly aware, consciously or unconsciously, of what losing means, even if he never loses. The bias toward an evacuation of self associated with losing generates a hallucinatory and obsessive quality, a distortion of experience that makes it hard to tell what things are, what they actually are like, independently of the lens of envy. Perception loses its clarity and becomes in itself a means of damaging, reducing, or debasing its object. The result is a sharpening need to have actual *things*, trophies as it were, things one can count and depend upon, and hold up for show: "a tangible, visible result that can be put in evidence and can be measured and compared with products of the same class exhibited by competing aspirants for repute," as Thorstein Veblen says (49). Male Display is not just showing off; it is a vital matter of ego defense—"one must kick ass or be considered a fairy," as William Doty articulates the point.[5] One must make an impact on objects and on people, so as to fill the emptiness within. The evacuated self, or the self threatened with evacuation, needs the outward insignia of display as assurance of identity, an assurance, even, of existence itself.

In Veblen's words:

> The wealth or power must be put in evidence, for esteem is awarded only on evidence. And not only does the evidence of wealth serve to impress one's importance on others and to keep their sense of importance alive and alert, but it is of scarcely less use in *building up and preserving one's self-complacency*. (42; my emphasis)

This pressure gives a certain desperation to the hunger for ego points; nevertheless, this desperation must be concealed from view, because desperation is perceived in the code of Male Envy as an obvious indicator of weakness. Weakness, in turn, or rather the disclosure of weakness to others, makes the competitor/climber vulnerable to attack. If you know your competitor's weakness, you know where to strike. This same pressure to acquire power points, to avoid losing, also has the effect of flattening out personality.[6] In the code of Male Envy, there is no time for personality, as there is no time for genuine emotion.

Winning is the goal of envy, and winning also reaps the gratifying tribute of envy from other men. Likewise, losing is doubly bad, because the loser not only loses, but feeds the ego of the winner, who appropriates and enjoys that envy, even as he looks down upon the loser in this "double movement," as Derrida would say. Given "the nature of ambition," as the philosopher David Hume says, "the great feel a double pleasure in authority from the comparison of their own condition with that of their slaves" (*Treatise* 426). Winning *requires* losing. In Male Envy, the winner derives gratification, not merely from the losing of others, but generally from the *discomfort* of others—irritation, unhappiness, and other insignia and rewards of losing. Taking pleasure in others' misery is basic to Male Envy. By the logic of the compete/control hierarchy, winners shift the horrors and burdens of that hierarchy on to losers, who are by that very shifting degraded and debased. "The traits which characterize the predatory and subsequent stages of culture, and which indicate the types of man best fitted to survive . . . are (in their primary expression) ferocity, self-seeking, clannishness, and disingenuousness—a free resort to force and fraud" (Veblen 153). Veblen echoes Machiavelli. In that masterpiece of the Italian Renaissance, *The Prince* (1513), Machiavelli identifies "force and fraud" (*forza* and *froda*) as the supreme virtues of the ruler and gives them the noble emblems of "lion" and "fox."

In Male Envy, it is not merely that the suffering of others is gratifying. Absence of feeling, especially sympathy for others, has a nobility and virtue: "success on the basis of an impartial self-seeking and absence of scruple" (Veblen 153). The fascination with suffering suggests an inner emptiness in the competitor/controller, a lack of genuine interests—and hence another kind of horror. The hollowness of the competitor/controller manifests as boredom, a lack of engagement with the world, a lack of curiosity, or an inability to make or create anything: a loss of what Veblen termed the vital "instinct of workmanship." Male Envy is incompatible with the spontaneity that characterizes emotion, indeed life and delight in life. Emotion is controlled, but controlling emotion means *repressing* emotion, flattening or eliminating it. Because of its spontaneity, emotion cannot be manipulated: when it is manipulated, it ceases to be actual emotion and becomes its simulacrum. Boredom manifests the inner hollowness of life in the régime of Male Envy, what T. S. Eliot calls "the waste sad time / Stretching before and after." This boredom incites an itch for stimulation, for distraction from the inner emptiness.

Here we arrive at a peculiar and peculiarly disturbing aspect of envy. Paradoxically, it is not caused by someone or something external. It is an inner force looking for a target. It is a void in the self seeking an object to feed on. The envied person thus becomes the arousal or occasion for envy, rather than its cause. It is as if the envied person reminds envy of something it had temporarily forgotten, but once awakened, it becomes fearfully awake and active, like a demon. Here again, the sense is strong that envy is a connection with supernatural and evil powers.

This demonic aspect is presented with penetrating intelligence in C. S. Lewis's *The Screwtape Letters* (1942), which is very much an exposition of Male Envy. In *The Screwtape Letters*, a devil named Screwtape advises his subordinate, Wormwood, on how to snare human victims. Screwtape refers to the victim as the "patient"—a word full of irony; literally, "patient" means "one to whom things are done" (cf. the cognate "passive"), whence it came to mean "one who suffers," i.e., a medical patient. Screwtape explains to Wormwood:

> You will be gradually freed from the tiresome business of providing Pleasures as temptations. . . . You can make him [the "patient"] waste his time not only in conversation he enjoys with people whom he likes, but in conversations with those he cares nothing about on subjects that bore him. You can make him do nothing at all for long periods. You can keep him up late at night, not roistering, but staring at a dead fire in a cold room. All the healthy and outgoing activities which we want him to avoid can be inhibited and *nothing* given in return.[7]

Baudelaire could not have captured the sense of emptiness more exactly than this display of waste. *Screwtape* is not just about Male Envy; it illustrates it. Thus the real struggle in the story is not between a junior devil and his human prey—but between the senior devil himself and his subordinate, and the unsuccessful subordinate ends up losing. His "affectionate uncle," Screwtape, *eats* him.

The need to evade the void, so to speak, to annihilate the feelings of nothingness in the self, incites Male Display. Cars and power objects distract attention, as well as impress it. Objects that materialize identity, so to speak, block out the nothing that threatens the self in compete/control struggles. Thus, it is not so much an object to stabilize the sense of self that is required, as it is the sensation of power over that object. Power and control—"winning"—yield a feeling that is hard to label; it is like pleasure, but "pleasure" is a feeble term for it. The feeling is a kind of intoxication or high that has an intense appeal for many—an addictive appeal. It is not so much a feeling, then, as an overcoming or compensation or substitution for feeling. The standard "object" to provide the needed power boost for identity is a woman, who will serve as a supply base and, if possible, as a marker of status and envy. This appropriation of women as ego points, as objects by which to materialize winning identity in the compete/control hierarchy, is the next area we need to explore. Again, it is not so much an "object" as *control* of the object; control of the woman, that is.

As we shall see, dangers lurk here for the aspiring competitor/controller, grave dangers.

* * *

In the code of Male Envy, a woman who appears to be vulnerable is also a highly erotic object. There is something about the mere fact of vulnerability that makes her attractive, as if weakness were also sexually arousing. The association of weakness with "femininity," that is with being sexually exciting, is a familiar theme and becomes conspicuous in the eighteenth century. Burke's treatise on *The Sublime and Beautiful* (1756) illustrates this association. Burke explicitly projects the "beautiful" as weak—and feminine; the "sublime," meanwhile, is projected as strong—and male. Thus, Burke's argument goes, we are frightened of the "sublime": it is stronger than we are and could destroy us. But we are contemptuous of the "beautiful," which is weaker than we are; the beautiful wishes to please, as if the wish to please were itself an attribute of weakness: in the code of Male Envy, this wish is a need to placate threatening authority, and has nothing to do with pleasure or sharing pleasure.

Vulnerability needs to be carefully formulated here, however, for it does not simply mean being open to attack. It means, more fundamentally, being unattached to a male. Thus the vulnerable woman has no male who "owns" her; or she is away from him, and hence "free"—an openness to be avoided. In this sense, she is like free money: an easy way of transferring power from another male (a male who is weak enough to let her go free), to the male who happens to find her—one thinks of Dimmesdale having sex with the "free" Hester, whose husband is away. A woman who is unowned is vulnerable, and vulnerability makes her easy pickings, so to speak; her powerlessness, in turn, is sexually provocative. One might call this the Andromeda archetype. The fact that she cannot protect herself—or rather, that she is not protected/owned by another male—means that she is "available," in various senses. Here, as so often in Male Envy, sexuality is a function of power relations. I have already noted the emotional sterility and incapacity of Male Envy, which instinctively views sex as the pleasure of control-power. The sexually desirable is that which enhances control, or that which yields feelings of power. A chivalrous knight in Malory or Spenser might protect and honor the vulnerable female, but a likely reaction would be to take advantage of her and *say* that she is being protected and honored; or more economically, simply use and then discard.

The very fact that the vulnerable woman is a target of male control compulsions, however, makes her curiously problematic and tricky. In the code of Male Envy, the main purpose of a woman, apart from her role as status marker (and apart from the important function of confirming a man's male identity by being impregnated by him), is to act as a source of matériel. In sophisticated versions of this relationship, she is like a backer or junior partner to her male, or even a coach to encourage him in his ambitions. That is, she is a resource to draw upon in his competitive struggle with other males, supplying emotional and physical provisions to make him a more effective climber. "The complete loyalty of . . . men to their own freedom and personal goals to the virtual exclusion of significant bonds with other males increases the importance of voluntary support from women at the same time that it prompts them [men] to offer almost nothing in return."[8] If the woman distracts the male, makes demands in her own right, or fails to supply the necessary provisions in the form of emotional cushioning and physical service, she may become a liability, potentially a dangerous liability.

Given the woman's primary role as supply base, the notion of an unowned woman is in evident conflict with the code of Male Envy. Hence such a woman is an anomaly needing to be corrected, possibly even a danger to be eliminated. Her vulnerability—that is, her unowned status—implies that she ought to be destroyed, or taken advantage of, not just to prevent other male-competitors from getting there first, or to drain power points away from a weaker male, but because dangers lurk in this figure. Vulnerability by definition is weakness, but the *appearance* of vulnerability is the appearance of weakness; that is, it is strength. She may look vulnerable but actually be a predator herself. Thus a pose of vulnerability is a standard disguise for strong women seeking to take advantage of males, to attract and even destroy men. In this way, she constitutes a danger of dread emotional intensity, fusing desire with terror, like Keats's "La Belle Dame sans Merci." In this poem, the "belle dame sans merci" specializes in seducing then eviscerating the most powerful males of all—the poem carefully lists "kings," "princes," "warriors" as her victims, her "Male Display."

This brings us then to an important convention of literature, indeed of culture generally: this is a specific type of woman that might be referred to as the "Tricky Female." The characteristic of the Tricky Female is that she attracts, then attacks. She seduces a male—typically by looking vulnerable, and hence erotic. Then, having gained power by means of her sexual attractiveness, she harms him, because she in some way feeds on men. In concentrated, undisplaced expressions, this figure is not human at all, properly speaking, but a witch, vampire, or other supernatural type. In romance—in a form popularized by Mario Praz's book *The Romantic Agony* as the *femme fatale*—she may actually kill, eat, entrap, or magically metamorphose her victim. In works of realism, this figure takes a more displaced form, and instead of eating the man literally, she may use him to get things she needs, hurting—sometimes killing—him in the process.

One of the most fearful examples in drama is the character of Laura, the wife of the male protagonist in Strindberg's play called *The Father*. She effectively guts the "father" of the title; her technique is to insist that he is not the father of their child, as if she did not need him to reproduce herself, therefore nullifying his status marker to the male hierarchy, and hence to himself. As mentioned earlier, a standard marker of male identity in Male Envy is impregnating a woman, as if, without doing so, a man is not "really a man"; that is, not a serious competitor/contender, male identity being constituted as placement in Male Envy.

The Tricky Female is one of the most popular conventions in patriarchal culture: in the person of the disobedient Eve she symbolizes everything that can go wrong. Examples of the Tricky Female range from Delilah in the Bible and Circe in Homer to the greedy murderess of *The Maltese Falcon* (1941), whom Sam Spade (Bogart in the movie version) calls "angel" as he gleefully hands her over to the hangman. Another movie example, and one that created a sensation, is *Fatal Attraction* (1987), where the seductress uses her sexual magnetism to attack the man's middle-class status marker—his family. The Tricky Female embodies primal anxiety, a fear so paralyzing as scarcely to be contemplated by the male hierarchy.[9]

Male Envy is a force field in which plot is enacted, but it is also a subtle presence, with many unspoken principles and silent communications. Again, when they are viewed in terms of Male Envy, canonic texts—often classics of literary tradition—reveal facets that are clearly important but hidden. What is interesting about Male Envy, in fact, is how invisible it is; it disguises itself under varied (if not meritorious) motivations, such as love or greed or ambition —ambition in worthy and unworthy variants—as well as many other feelings and impulses. This is one reason why the figure of the Tricky Female is so useful: nothing brings the dynamics of Male Envy out into the open more than this highly conventionalized, highly familiar figure. Hence I would like to explore one of the most famous examples, Hedda Gabler, in Ibsen's play of that name.

Fiction usually has a single point of view, and so may conceal the tensions of Male Envy, whereas drama has a variety of characters speaking for themselves. Being inherently multiple in perspective, drama can be a powerful instrument for making the inner workings of Male Envy visible. What is fascinating about Hedda Gabler, perhaps the greatest character creation by Ibsen, arguably the major dramatist of the modern period, is that she is not the tricky one, but, like the murderer in a mystery novel, the really dangerous character is the least suspected. *Hedda Gabler* appears to be about a Tricky Female, but in fact is about Male Envy, about female roles in the context of Male Envy.

* * *

Hedda Gabler has a plot as tight as a spring. Like other literary texts in this exploration, it belongs to a complex of *Gedankenexperimente*, imagination experiments, that articulate the code of Male Envy, that treat it not as an abstract system, but as a compound of emotion, character, image, and action from which far more can be learned than from pondering Male Envy in abstract. *Hedda Gabler* is particularly revealing for the present topic.

Somewhat surprisingly, the daughter of the aristocrat General Gabler, Hedda Gabler, has chosen to marry the bumbling academic, Jörgen Tesman, instead of one of her many other admirers. The drama begins as she and her new husband return from their honeymoon. Tesman's motherly maiden Aunt Julle, who with her sister raised Tesman, has rented the expensive house that Hedda demanded; she hopes Hedda is pregnant by Tesman. Hedda humiliates her by pretending that her hat is the servant's hat, showing off what appears to be a haughty, mocking, and amoral, even sadistic temperament. This temperament appears to generate the action and is much in evidence; for example, she disconcerts the pompous Judge Brack by firing her father's pistols at him as he walks on her lawn; she resumes an old interest in an admirer from the past, the writer Ejlert Lövborg, who is brilliant but unstable and a friend and rival of her husband. She humiliates her schoolmate Mrs. Thea Elvsted, who has been anxiously seeking Lövborg, for Thea helped Lövborg overcome his alcoholism as well as his writing block—and she gave up everything, including a respectable marriage, to do so. She is the ideal source of supply for a male competitor/controller. Male Envy evaluates a woman by her ability to supply resources to a man (emotional and material) and by her capacity to mark winning over other men.

As a test of her power over Lövborg, Hedda dares him to take a drink: he takes the drink—and then plunges into a binge in which he loses the manuscript of his new book, which is about the future development of mankind and which everyone regards as a work of genius. Losing his special object is the ultimate horror for Lövborg. Notice the motif of the *special drink*, so often found in the scene of Male Envy: it functions as a power object that precipitates the action. Later, Jörgen Tesman accidentally finds the manuscript by the roadside. Hedda takes it from him and secretly burns it. Her motivation for this shocking destructiveness seems obscure; dramatically, the burning scene is extraordinarily powerful, one of the most memorable moments in drama.

It is also a turning point. Next day, Judge Brack reveals that Lövborg has shot himself with one of Hedda's pistols. Hedda is pleased by Lövborg's unconditioned act, but horrified to learn that he shot himself in the stomach, possibly by accident, and not "beautifully" in the temple. Furthermore, Hedda may have burned Lövborg's precious manuscript—but it has not quite vanished. For Lövborg's mistress Thea has fortuitously kept notes—and Tesman now asks her to help him reconstruct the manuscript. Thea—Mrs. Elvsted—also happens to be Tesman's first love. Tesman invites Judge Brack to occupy Hedda's time while he is working on the project with Thea, so that Hedda will not be "bored," a condition she has bitterly complained of. Brack is delighted with the prospect of having Hedda: what he always wanted, given the boredom he also suffers. The prominence of the motif of boredom, of the threat of emptiness in life, in the configuration of *Hedda Gabler* is no accident. He also has some excellent blackmail material, so as to ensure control over her, for he knows that Lövborg shot himself with Hedda's pistol: she gave it to him. If necessary, Hedda can now be forced to do as he wishes. He has the power-over relationship with her that flatters his vanity and excites a tired sexual palate. Again, the principle is that, for Male Envy, a vulnerable woman is sexually arousing.

The play ends with Hedda shooting herself, beautifully (as she would have it), in the temple, with one of her father's famous pistols, thus achieving the ritual suicide which her male admirer Lövborg failed to do.

In terms of Male Envy, Hedda Gabler represents all kinds of dangers, as her willfulness, lying, concealing, destroying, manipulating, mocking, seducing, and generally pushy ways make plain. She derives pleasure from causing trouble for men, it seems. More subtly, however, Hedda represents a traditional female strategy: since women are not on the compete/control hierarchy, a woman who is ambitious must manipulate males, must use men as proxies to fulfill her need for power and domination. Hedda's energized personality projects her as competitor on the hierarchy in her own right.

The resulting role reversal, with Hedda as competitor/controller, makes the whole code of Male Envy visible and evident in a way that it usually is not. This is one reason why the play has had the notoriety it has had: it brings out in to the open themes and images that are normally repressed. *Hedda Gabler* belongs to a period of feminist agitation and is a kind of experiment in placing a woman directly on the compete/control hierarchy itself and observing the results. By giving a woman the values and attitudes of male competitor/controllers, Ibsen throws into relief the very code of Male Envy that conditions "normal" life for males, and hence also for the régime in which women are contained. Hence it is its open dramatizing of the code of Envy that makes the play notorious, more than the Tricky Female attributes of its protagonist.

This role reversal explains, in part, Hedda's reputation as a monster. Her reputation is as Tricky Female *par excellence*, a manipulator of males who finally gets her comuppance. Hedda has many of the insignia of the Tricky Female, and, as so often happens to such figures, she is also ruthlessly cornered and brought down. A not insignificant portion of commentary on Ibsen's play has been devoted to observing the Tricky Female qualities that Hedda ("she is a monster," says Arthur Ganz[10]) seems to illustrate. Hedda's ancestry in Norse myth has even been traced, so as to demonstrate affinity with an unpleasant folklore figure: "Hedda could be placed directly in the tradition of the demonic *havfru* who lures men to their doom," and even with the figure of a "fairy temptress, the *huldre*," "who is very beautiful, but possesses a repellent physical characteristic that renders her identifiable"—often a cow's tail (one can imagine what the refined Hedda's reaction to the cow's tail would be!).[11]

It is true that Hedda plays the Tricky Female in her manipulation of the hapless Lövborg. But the inner heart of the play has nothing to do with her trickiness, and everything to do with Male Envy, and especially, therefore, the trickiness of her apparently foolish husband. Jörgen Tesman is the person Hedda despises most—and so underestimates the most. Thus he snares and brings down the great general's daughter. This sounds surprising. After all, doesn't everybody agree that Tesman is bumbling, immature, ineffectual, stupid, weak? But then, it is precisely a person who looks bumbling, ineffectual, and so on—and only such a person—who could cause the haughty Hedda to miss her step—and fall.

His fatal attractiveness to her does not lie in his looks (vulnerable or otherwise), but in his *usefulness* to her. There is thus a hidden contest between Hedda and the seemingly ineffectual Tesman: indeed it forms a powerful dramatic tension that builds palpably if subtextually throughout the play.

Hedda is such a magnetic presence in the play that she affects our perception of all the other characters. So strong is her magnetism that we tend to perceive them as she does and therefore ignore elements in their personality that make them more complex than they appear to be. Because of her power, the play is subtly projected from her point of view. Thus the way Hedda sees Tesman is essentially the way the audience see him—and the way the critics have seen him, too. In terms of the logic of action in *Hedda Gabler*, however, Tesman performs a role very different from what his image allows. Hedda views Tesman wholly in terms of someone that she can use: she is not able to see him in terms of his own personality, with its specific traits. In other words, what she sees of him is limited to what is useful to her. He is constituted for her as a useful object: that is why she married him. Anything about him besides that vital fact is superfluous, as far as she is concerned.

Thus she married him partly because he was timely—a handy vehicle to enable her to exit from an awkward social situation, surrounded by rivalrous men who were interested in her when she did not wish to marry—and be subordinated. He is useful, as far as she is concerned, precisely because he can be manipulated and dominated so unresistingly. He offers a safe base from which to establish relations with witty and competitive males at pleasant parties—such that, as one who prefers to flirt, observe and manipulate at a safe distance, she can enjoy herself, without the burdens of commitment or obligation, or, still less, the restrictions created by sexual entanglements. She even views Tesman as a possible medium for her political ambitions. In short he is an all-purpose husband that she can mould to her ends, and she assumes easy control, it seems. He even seems sexually of no account; thus he is, explains one critic, "so entirely a booby, a bookworm, a nincompoop, in everything he does. His ignorance about marital relations, and apparent unawareness that Hedda may be with child after their honeymoon, is heavily handled."[12] If anything, Tesman seems *eager* for Hedda to use him—a kind of masochist that finds the matching sadist for his need for female discipline: Hedda Dominatrix as it were.

But ironically, the brilliant aristocrat Hedda perishes—whereas the boring bookworm Tesman survives and thrives. For someone so stupid, he gets pretty much everything he wants, surprisingly: the right job, the right woman, even the right task: "putting other people's papers in order," he rhapsodizes, "that's just the sort of thing I'm good at" (260). And—before her suicide—he even frees himself of the wife who was an asset to begin with, but who rapidly proves to be a liability. Ibsen's Scandinavian-American contemporary Thorstein Veblen articulates the relevant principle: "Any action on the part of a woman which traverses an injunction of the accepted schedule of proprieties is felt to reflect immediately upon the honor of the man whose woman she is" (but "relatively little discredit attaches to a woman through the evil deeds of the man with whom her life is associated"[13]). Perhaps Tesman is not quite the dummkopf he seems. And if so, then also a more sinister figure.

* * *

Male Envy forms the dramatic matrix of *Hedda Gabler*—the dramatic premise that the plot requires in order for the play to exist at all. Competitive tension lies between Tesman and Lövborg and is noticeable between Lövborg and Judge Brack. Thus Brack is determined to exclude Lövborg from the circle of males that is already beginning to form around Hedda as the play starts. Tesman in at least one important respect is not the booby he would appear to be, and this is in a crucial area: his "love" for Hedda and his reason for marrying her—what the actual basis of his attraction to her was and continues to be. For Tesman, clearly, she was a great catch. The competitive advantage that Hedda represents is practically the first topic in the play. The adoring aunt who brought Tesman up is preoccupied with his winning this advantage, and she is the one character in the play who emphatically does not see him as Hedda or the critics see him. She lovingly reminds Tesman of his win; more precisely, she gloats:

> MISS TESMAN. And to think that you'd be the one to walk off with Hedda Gabler! The lovely Hedda Gabler. Imagine it! So many admirers she always had around her!
> TESMAN. [hums a bit and smirks]. Yes, I dare say there are one or two of my good friends who wouldn't mind being in my shoes. Eh? (171)

Note the sarcastic reference to "friends"—"*good* friends," no less. In Male Envy, males have no friends, only rivals and competitors whose interests may at any time be in conflict, because, really, they already are in conflict. Ibsen emphasizes this later in the play, when the same characters revert to the same topic: Hedda's value as a career weapon in the competitive struggle. As Harold Clurman puts it, "Tesman *preens* himself" on the way his "friends" envy him.[14] Hedda is desirable and much sought after ("So many admirers," rhapsodizes Miss Tesman). We have seen the "many competitors" motif before; it is a standard marker of the presence of Male Envy.

More important: Hedda is another "Rappaccini's daughter," for she is the child of a great man, daughter of the aristocratic General Gabler. Commentators on the play often note that Hedda is very much her father's daughter, but that parentage is more important to the other characters, especially Tesman. Tesman knows his marriage is a great coup. He is very aware that other men want her: he "hums a bit and smirks." He perceives her as a remarkable acquisition, one that has given him the power of Veblen's "invidious comparison." Other men admire his luck—and envy him. Thus her value is constituted as an aristocratic beauty that other males want but cannot have: a high-prestige object, like a Rolls Royce. Veblen's principle applies: "The motive that lies at the root of ownership is emulation" (35). One concludes that Tesman is a climber and competitor—and not a passive object of others' manipulations.

Thus, after Hedda insults his aunt with the "hat trick," Tesman has her *pose* for his aunt, to exhibit his accomplishment in winning her—and therefore his *aunt*'s accomplishment. His aunt, after all, brought him up: "Aunt, take a good look at Hedda before you go! Charming's the word for her, eh?" (178). The aunt responds, "Oh my dear, that's nothing new. Hedda's been lovely all her life." But Tesman persists. "[Following her]. Yes, but have you noticed how well and bonny she looks? I declare she's filled out beautifully on the trip" (178), and he solicits auntie's public assessment of how she has "filled out." Hedda then hotly denies she is pregnant.

But this final proof of Tesman's possession—to be impregnated by him and to incubate his child—is surely the crucial reason why he insists his aunt study her, not just in order that auntie may contemplate her legendary beauty. Here then is the real significance of her pregnancy, and an essential reason why the idea so distresses Hedda Gabler. What pregnancy would show is that Hedda, indisputably, belonged to Tesman. Tesman speaks naively about sexuality, as if he did not know what the difference between boys and girls is. Yet he clearly does not need to speak. In his eyes, he now has her, whatever she, his critics, or anybody else may say.[15] Tesman may be stupid, but to think that he does not understand human sexual biology (after years spent in a university milieu) is even more stupid.

Hedda perceives Tesman as a safe, useful and unresisting instrument that she can manipulate; for Tesman, meanwhile, Hedda Gabler amounts to a significant boost for his career. She is a means to an end for him, as he is for her: here lies the basis of the conflict between them referred to earlier. The idea that Tesman should be a successful competitor against other males seems absurd at first, given his babyish self-presentation. Yet at the same time his competition with Lövborg is essential to the play.[16] In the competition for control, Tesman has done rather well. Ibsen makes Tesman's parental aunt recur to this point early on—she dwells on it and proudly elaborates. "Isn't it the only joy I have in this world, to help you along your road, my darling boy?" she asks, rhetorically:

> MISS TESMAN. And now we're very nearly there, my boy! .... Thanks be to God, you've made good, Jörgen!
> TESMAN. Yes, it's queer, really, the way it all turned out.
> MISS TESMAN. Yes ... and the people who stood in your way ... and wanted to keep you back ... you outran them all. They've fallen by the wayside, Jörgen! And your most dangerous adversary, he fell lower than any of them, he did .... And now he must lie on the bed he's made for himself ... the poor depraved creature.   (174-75)

Thus the meek Miss Tesman crows over Tesman's defeated enemies—Ejlert Lövborg most of all.

The compassionate-sounding afterthought ("poor depraved creature") is for propriety's sake, roughly equivalent to "Give the poor dog a bone!" and in no way expresses true compassion. Miss Tesman "congratulates him with delighted surprise" (Clurman 156)—but clearly much more than congratulation, delight, or surprise are going on here. As his functional parent, *Tante Julle* has in effect created Tesman. She has a stake in everything he does, and his self-image appears to be *her image of him*.[17] In other words, she is entirely enclosed within the code of Male Envy and takes it for granted that her success is the success of the males she sponsors and supplies. Tesman shares her way of thinking so totally that it is instinctive and unconscious. Thus he even quotes her, when at the end, he contemplates his crowning success: editing Lövborg's manuscript (compare her early comment: "Yes, collecting things and sorting them out . . . you've always been good at that" [175]). His winning in male competition is *her* winning, too. For this is a world in which females win by proxy: by manipulating males in the male power struggles that structure societal relations.

That is one reason why Hedda's first action in the play is to humiliate the aunt: there is to be no equivocation over who now controls Tesman. "Few daughters-in-law would be as sharp with a surrogate mother-in-law as Hedda is over Aunt Juliane's hat," and few "would be pleased at receiving an unsolicited visit the morning after returning from a wedding trip and at seeing her domestic authority eroded in the matter of a husband's bedroom slippers" (Ganz 14). The hat and the slippers are tokens in a struggle for control of Tesman—power points. Hedda insists on exclusive proprietorship. Hedda, the wife, controls the domestic center that the slippers represent. Tesman may not be appealing to us— or to Hedda and her select society—but he is vital to her interests. So total is her command that she feels she can transform him and project him on to the political scene: a plan as quixotic as her aristocratic ethos is anachronistic. She appropriates Lövborg's power object, the precious manuscript, and uses it to manipulate Tesman's envy. While she shows little understanding of Tesman, the stereotypic academic, she understands perfectly how female power in her society acts, as a manipulating of male power.

In the dictum of one Duchess of Marlborough: "Women signify nothing unless they are the mistress of a prince or first minister."[18]

Tesman is an *eiron*, one who appears to be less than he really is. With his inane small talk, he looks harmless as a competitor, but already, at the start of the play, he has proven very efficient in the struggle—far more effective, on the evidence, than the brilliant but erratic Lövborg. What is critical is that Tesman's relation to Hedda is constituted as a function of male rivalry. Hedda sees this— but not entirely—she is too blinded by her own wishes, and like the critics, she underestimates the dull Tesman. Judge Brack informs them that with the return of Lövborg, Tesman will not get the professorship he had been promised automatically: there will have to be a competition. Hedda finds Tesman's discomfiture at having to face Lövborg, book in hand, in competition for the professorship entertaining. As an aristocrat, she is above Tesman's arcane interests and petty academic struggles: they do not affect her, she naively tells Brack. Brack meanwhile enjoys playing the role of the interrupter of festivity, the one who breaks up the party so that he can do it his way.

For as the possibility of Tesman's collapse on the success ladder is conjured up by Judge Brack, with the attendant cash shortage, Hedda realizes that Tesman may soon break the contract she had founded her marriage to him on. Tesman was to allow—and enable—her to enjoy a pleasant standard of living: to "entertain." There would be a piano and a nice house and parties with interesting men. The unexpected now seems imminent, as Tesman loses his expectations. Hence she must consolidate control of him; she must do the leading now.

Unless she does so, Hedda's dream of pleasant parties, flirting, and control without commitment may unravel totally. This dream is bigger than the *frisson* of controlling Lövborg, intoxicating as that is. That is why Hedda burns the manuscript. This act is presented as a Medean pagan rite—and it has those overtones, no doubt. But Hedda is practical; she knows that her husband must be secured, must have the professorship. Lövborg must be eliminated from the competition, if she is to have the things she wants.

The need to eliminate Lövborg is paramount. After she burns Lövborg's manuscript ("all of it," she says for emphasis [250]), Hedda makes what amounts to a joke: she did it all, she enthuses, for *him*: "[suppressing an almost imperceptible smile]. I did it for your sake, Jörgen." Like an echo, Tesman gasps back: "For my sake!" By presenting her act under the guise of homage to her husband, she plays on the sensitive spot: envy, what males feel for winning males. "Tesman's naive, admiring envy" of Lövborg, as Stein Olsen calls it (601), may indeed be admiring, but it is hardly "naive." In Male Envy, fear and hatred of others' talents are vital elements of wisdom. Tesman's envy—and fear—of Lövborg are a precondition of the plot: Hedda cleverly manipulates it. How sensitive she is, and how deliberately, almost teasingly, she plays upon it!

HEDDA. You admitted that you envied him for it.
TESMAN. Oh Heavens above, I didn't mean it so literally.
HEDDA. All the same, I couldn't bear the thought that someone else should put you in the shade. (251)

With Tesman rejoicing at her devotion, she adds a bonus for his obedience (and to make plain that he must conceal her role in destroying the manuscript), namely a hint that she is pregnant.

Of course, she is lying when she says she burnt the manuscript for her husband—just as she conceals her revulsion at the idea of pregnancy. Concealment and manipulating are her delight. But her situation is forcing her at this juncture to offer Tesman valued information—concessions, in effect— a thing she would normally never do, given her determination to be always in charge. Ironically, though, she *is* doing it for Tesman; that is, she is doing it for herself via Tesman. She smiles at her own suggestion here, but she may not have the last laugh. The fact that she has to make an offering to Tesman suggests that already she is slipping in the contest for power that joins this man and this wife.

* * *

What makes burning the manuscript so decisive is that, like burning ships and bridges, there is no going back. The *Schadenfreude* which Hedda embodies now modulates into pure hubris: a going-beyond one's place in the scheme of things, followed by a disastrous loss of control. For just as Hedda seems within grasp of extraordinary power over others, a power symbolized by the act of sacrificing, of burning, his "child" as Lövborg calls it (a child that is, to her, illegitimate because its mother is Thea), she slips. As she burns it up, Hedda also refers to the manuscript, with its promise of the future, as Thea's baby: the motif of child sacrifice has immense significance in the scene of Male Envy (see Chapter 4, "Holy Murder"). But Hedda's ecstatic sense of power over others, the intoxicating winning reserved for male competitor/controllers, is really hubris, a dizziness that conceals from her the abyss she is falling into.

As a tragic figure, Hedda Gabler recalls Greek tragedy. She resembles both Medea—and paradoxically, Antigone. Hedda's mythic ancestry as a figure only half-human is in part a metaphor for her aristocratic status (she is a "superior" being). But it also suggests the superhuman: one who has a source of power hidden from ordinary people. As George Bernard Shaw says, "Hedda Gabler has no ethical ideals at all, only romantic ones."[19] Like the heroes of Shakespearean tragedy, she is linked to another kind of reality, a mysterious, even heroic realm. "Ibsen, resolutely refusing to annotate Hedda's mythic yearning, leaves its central mysteries undefined. . . . To burst out of time, to discover a dimension of spiritual intensity no longer discoverable in the obtuse bourgeois parlour, to live *mythically* in a world beyond historical change and death" (Durbach 40). "The sense of transcendent power and beauty that she longs for is inseparable from the fierceness and self-absorption of the Dionysiac frenzy" (Ganz 19).

Hence it is not that "Hedda Gabler is difficult to defend" (Low 43)—Hedda does not need our defending! for she is a kind of superwoman, a female equivalent to Nietzsche's *Übermensch*. One must be clear: Hedda Gabler is no proto/feminist struggling for female emancipation: witness her treatment of Thea (or her view of the "actress" Diana).[20] Rather, her role as "overcomer" makes Hedda one of the few genuinely tragic figures—in Aristotle's classic sense—to be found in modern literature. That is, she is one who arouses the audience's fear (even hostility)—but one who *also* attracts; indeed draws the audience to identify with her. She repels—and fascinates. She cannot be judged simply, as simply good or simply bad: normal categories do not apply, recalling the great figures of tragic drama, from Oedipus to Hamlet. Like them, she evokes intense responses: something about her strikes deep in us.

On one hand, she refuses to be controlled by anyone; she insists on her desires, even if it means humiliating or embarrassing people (witness Auntie Julle and the "hat trick," and upsetting the pompous Judge Brack by firing pistols[21]). There is something appealing here, dramatically and psychologically: perhaps what it speaks to is the rebellious child in us, the part of the self that can be repressed only by killing something vital in our personality. She would rather die than be humiliated, as she demonstrates in the unforgettable final moment of the play. She has a kind of spontaneity that is utterly at odds with the control compulsions of Male Envy, and thus she is too threatening to be allowed to go free. Hedda's rebellious determination to have her way, her defiance of authority —*gammelmandsfornuftigheden* ("the prudence of old men")—is something that Ibsen himself shared.[22] After all, Hedda's predilection for *galskaper* ("bits of mischief") is characteristic of *Ibsen* and his love of stirring up social anxieties and breaking convention. In this respect, Hedda is Ibsen himself.

But on the other hand, Hedda's callous, predatory egoism—her "secret vision of ecstatic violence"—shocks, even terrifies (Ganz 17). Her wish to climb the compete/control hierarchy is in her way as frightening as it is for a ruthless male obsessed with similar compulsions. Ibsen skillfully entwines this shocking strand of her personality with her attractive, even magnetic quality: as John Northam puts it, "the courage, the vision, the poetry are never allowed to cancel out the absurdity, the destructiveness and the triviality."[23] There can be no doubt that, in the century since she first appeared, Hedda Gabler remains one of the supreme character creations of drama.

Hedda is thus a Tricky Female, the character type that the code of Male Envy is very familiar with, but she also illustrates a type that Male Envy has far more difficulty understanding, a type that might be referred to as the desiring female, and a figure that first appears in Romantic narrative. The desiring female is a figure of struggle; she may not be clear what exactly her object is, but she has a boldness and courage that set her apart; she is often associated with sexual love. Whatever she wants, she is inevitably at odds with the compete/control system. Hence she illuminates that system in a useful manner: she attracts two complementary male types that typically accompany her: (1) the ineffectual lover, and (2) the figure of the overbearing, usually older male. The "ineffectual lover" is a male who is defeated in compete/control struggles, self-divided, often preoccupied with the past and with guilt, so that he is unable to act in the present. He is not there when his lover needs him, hence "ineffectual." Whereas the ineffectual lover is a "loser," the overbearing (often older) male is a winner in compete/control struggles, a figure of control and ambition, who utters nihilistic speeches and is associated with rape and violence: the "power male," for short. In *Hedda Gabler,* this configuration appears with Hedda at the center, flanked by the apparently ineffectual Tesman on one side and the overbearing controller Judge Brack on the other; it is characteristic of his type that Brack, who poses as a know-it-all, is determined to force Hedda to be his mistress.

This configuration pits the woman against the culture of Male Envy so as to exert maximum pressure on the woman. We have seen it before. In Keats's *Lamia,* for example, Lamia is the struggling woman; Lycius is an ineffectual lover; and Apollonius is a power male. "Rappaccini's Daughter" and *The Scarlet*

Letter illustrate the same configuration (Beatrice, Giovanni, Rappaccini; Hester, Dimmesdale, Chillingworth).[24] Where Male Envy is a central concern, one can expect to find this trio of character types.

The persistence of this configuration is noticeable in the movies. Alfred Hitchcock's masterpiece, *Psycho*, is an illuminating example. In *Psycho*, the struggling woman, Marian, is flanked, on one side, by the boastful older male, who "flirts" with her in her office by waving money in her face; and on the other side, by her ineffectual lover Sam, who is preoccupied with failure from the past (his divorce), and his inability to make money. The inability to make money is a standard marker of defeat in compete struggles (compare Tesman's painful anxieties on this score). To acquire the money that her lover is unable to provide, Marian steals the older male's cash. In doing so, she over-reaches her role as provider/supporter to a male competitor. She becomes an outlaw in the compete/control system. The ineffectual lover and the power male represent the poles of the compete/control hierarchy: loser and winner.

By taking action as she does, Marian is defying the code of Male Envy itself. No wonder she is killed. Her killer, Norman Bates, fuses in himself the two male character types, the weak and the aggressive. He represents the hidden reality of the compete/control system itself: murderous aggressiveness, deception, insanity, calculating deliberateness, hallucination, control obsessions, voyeurism (control and detachment), convoluted rationalizing, and a terror of inner emptiness. His murder is explained (away) in the famous "producer's scene" at the end as the result of oedipal tensions (an overprotective mother), but the real motivation appears to be the rage of frustrated ambition in male competition for control.

Another example from a classic movie indicates the immense potential this configuration has for plot construction. In Roman Polanski's *Chinatown,* the configuration organizes the plot: at the center is Evelyn Mulwray, struggling to protect her daughter and if possible avenge her husband's murder. The detective she hires, Jake Gittes, becomes her lover, but he proves unequal to her and betrays her, causing her to fall into the hands of her enemy. He is preoccupied, it should be noted, with a past guilt he can only hint at. On the other side is her tycoon father, Noah Cross, who raped her when she was 15 and who remains obsessed with her sexuality: that is, with the violation of innocence. Cross murdered her husband, who was also Cross's former partner and best friend: he candidly admits that this friend also made him his fortune. Cross's attitude toward his "friend" (his "best friend" no less) is typical of Male Envy. In a foolish show of bravado, Gittes confronts Cross with his crime, as if he is going to bring down the mighty Noah Cross all by himself. Cross completely ignores Gittes's threat. Instead he boasts to Gittes of his nihilistic ambition—not satisfied with untold riches, he wants to "own" the future—and he easily defeats Gittes. The result is, again, that Evelyn Mulwray is killed. Gittes, meanwhile, is reduced to emotional life-in-death: the shattered ego that is the reward of losers.

Hedda Gabler treats this configuration with unusual subtlety. Thus, Tesman is a sophisticated illustration of winning strategy in compete/control struggles in the age of the bureaucrat: he has all the marks of the ineffectual lover, but it is a kind of disguise. For unlike Hedda, Tesman knows his own weaknesses in the struggle for control. And his strengths. Thus he knows he cannot compete or win against Lövborg on grounds of originality. When Lövborg reveals that his new book is on "the future course of civilization," Tesman's candor is embarrassing: "Amazing! It just wouldn't enter my head to write about anything like that" (212). Hedda impatiently agrees. After all, the ineffectual "Tesman is an object of ridicule" (Gray 148). Observed more carefully, his behavior is rational: he does not fight where he cannot win. And having nothing to gain (and something to lose) from antagonizing a rival, he does well to congratulate Lövborg: congratulations yield the giver certain advantages. His whole approach to Lövborg shows acute awareness of the nature of his rival and friend (read enemy)—indeed it shows subtlety in handling someone of greater intelligence and ability than Tesman. Moreover, Tesman must cope with the sheer emotional shock of Lövborg's re-emergence, of finding his careful plans shattered by a man who had vanished from the scene long ago, seemingly knocked out of the race, but who has now come back as a potentially unbeatable rival.

What makes Lövborg so dangerous a rival is his unpredictability. Lövborg does not compete in the conventional mode—his power comes from his brilliance and his originality. Lövborg explicitly refuses to compete with Tesman for the professorship, and this refusal, joined with his casual display of the manuscript, constitutes a strong gesture in the code of Male Envy. Announcing that one is not a competitor can be a potent competitive strategy. Instead of lessening the threat, such gestures intensify it, despite Tesman's relief when Lövborg assures him that he has nothing to fear. Tesman's power comes from manipulating the established structure, from climbing in a systematic, bureaucratic manner: on the tortoise principle that safe-and-steady wins the race. Wait for your rival to make a mistake. But of course this is precisely what makes Lövborg so exciting to Hedda: he is bold, uninhibited, daring; a challenge to her powers of manipulation in a way that the insipid Tesman, who acts like that worst of all combinations— the servant who is one of the family—could never be.

That is why, once again, Tesman is exactly suited to bring Hedda down: he is boring, hence written off as of no account. This very fact, however, renders him non-manipulable, ironically. True, he yields to her—when it is in his interest. Hedda thinks she is using Tesman when Tesman is using Hedda. How easily, by contrast, Hedda incites, deceives—and destroys—Lövborg. At first, she lives ecstatically on Lövborg's beautiful death, in true Tricky Female style, deceiving men in order to absorb their life-energy: "Driving him by her will, she would live the act through him, share his defiance, feel his freedom. . . . to realize her longing for a wider psychological liberation" (Ganz 17).

Unfortunately, however, he betrays her commission to die beautifully; his death is not the tribute to her ego that she had longed for. Instead, it was either a shoddy accident, or worse, a tribute to the repulsive Diana, with her lower-class, prostitute's tricks. The idea of being outdone by a female rival is unendurable.

Tesman, meanwhile, lives on, of course. Indeed, what is interesting is the skill with which Tesman follows the code of Male Envy in stripping his fallen rival. For Tesman absorbs Lövborg's greatness, transforming his rival's originality into fuel for his career. Lövborg's manuscript is invaluable material for consolidating that career. Tesman discloses his occult identity as thief. In effect, he takes for himself the benefit from Lövborg's death that Hedda had expected would accrue to her. In doing so, he also acquires the woman who served and saved Lövborg, sacrificing everything for her chosen man, including her respectability as the wife of an important husband: Thea—Mrs. Elvsted—the very woman who "inspired" his fallen rival to create a work of genius!

The absorption of the rival's woman is a standard marker of male winning on the compete/control hierarchy, especially given the quality of woman involved. At first, Tesman outmaneuvered male rivals by getting the aristocrat Hedda Gabler; now he has acquired a better (read *useful*) woman, especially for this stage of his career, the consolidation stage: Mrs. Elvsted. She is a superb resource in terms of compete/control struggles, a source of the highest quality matériel and support for a climber like Tesman. Unlike the leisure-class Hedda, Mrs. Elvsted *works*; she is an ideal wife—and "companion"—for a man like Tesman. Indeed, she was his original love-choice, the woman he really was attracted to, but would not marry because it would have brought no advantage to him or his career (which are really the same thing). Now, he gets her.

Hedda's destruction of the manuscript—metaphorically of Lövborg—would secure Tesman and a solid base for herself, as well as enhance her sense of power. What it really does, however, is to alert Tesman to the crucial fact that she is now a dangerous liability. Her self-determination, her bursts of aggression, her unpredictable impulses, and her insistence on self-expression mean trouble. Any advantage he might gain from her has now been gained. Ironically, her act has also done for Tesman what he could not do for himself—it has removed the threat of Lövborg, permanently. What Hedda did for herself has turned out to be for Tesman, after all—but not as Hedda had mockingly suggested.

This is an important point. It is not that Tesman has a secret master plan whereby he calculatedly manipulates others. That would be more in Judge Brack's line, with his "triangular relationship" and carefully calculated blackmailing schemes. Rather, Tesman shows instinctive skill in turning events to his advantage: in being at the right place at the right time to get what he wants. His "happening" to find the lost manuscript is a metaphor for this instinctive attunement to the needs of competition. There is something about Hedda that is mysterious, even mystic, as if she participates in a kind of reality that is closed to the audience. There is something hidden about Tesman, too—but in an utterly different way. We do not know how much Tesman perceives; nevertheless, the point is that he cannot be as stupid as he is made out to be. This principle applies, for example, to his decision to marry Hedda Gabler in the first place; to his knowledge of the Facts of Life; to his awareness of the importance of Lövborg's manuscript and its secret destruction; to his perception of the interest of both Brack and Lövborg in his wife. As we have seen, Ibsen goes out of his way to show how sensitive Tesman is to the fact other males envy the access to Hedda Gabler that he now enjoys. He knows.

How much he sees is uncertain—he can be played in different ways. Tesman is not on the same level of character creation as Hedda—perhaps Ibsen's greatest dramatic creation—but he is no buffoon. As a dramatic construct, he is artfully made, in the same sort of way that Iago is created in relation to Othello in Shakespeare's play; and, as a man obsessed with his career at all costs, he is evil enough. But it is the evil of Male Envy, the "banality of evil" that Hannah Arendt identified as the form of evil characteristic of our age, bureaucratic and unthinking, yet at the same time cunning, repressive, watchful. Tesman proves able to get what he wants, without the crude blackmail that the sophisticated, clever Judge Brack has to resort to. Nor is he carelessly taken in by the superior Hedda Gabler's machinations, like the ill-fated Lövborg, a man who proves himself to be, in practice, far weaker and more stupid than Tesman is.

Hedda at the end finds she has not only lost the vision of Lövborg's unconditioned act, an act that would for ever function as the ultimate in homage/sacrifice to Hedda herself; she has also fallen under the power of the odious Brack, a sadist who would derive intense thrills from taking control of the proud, ever-so-independent lady. Tesman meanwhile rubs in her defeat with great skill, so as to make the humiliation appear casual and yet actually be total.[25] Tesman knows how to make it hurt. "You go and sit down again, now, with Mr Brack," he says—as if throwing her away. Thus he literally consigns Hedda to Brack—he hands her over to him, knowing how much Brack wants it and how much Hedda does not. Male Envy requires the total humiliation of Hedda Gabler. Only an "absolute" act can redeem her now.

> HEDDA. And is there nothing I can do to help you two [Tesman and Mrs. Elvsted]?
> TESMAN. No, nothing at all. [Turns his head.] We'll just have to rely on you, dear Mr. Brack, to keep Hedda company.
> BRACK. [with a look at Hedda]. It will be a pleasure indeed.
> HEDDA. Thank you. But tonight I'm tired. I'm going to go in and lie down a bit on the sofa.
> TESMAN. Yes, you do that my dear. Eh? (263)

Tesman and Mrs. Elvsted clearly do not let the grass grow under their feet when it comes to reconstructing Lövborg's manuscript. Tesman's climbing the ladder is everything. Shaw mildly observes: "Over the congenial task of collecting and arranging another man's ideas Tesman is perfectly happy, and forgets his beautiful Hedda for the first time" (172). He does not "forget" her: he gets rid of her. Hedda's impassioned burst of piano music, which Tesman finds so intolerable to himself and his new companion, is a dramatic protest: it is hard to imagine Tesman earlier in the play taking so strong a line with the prized wife to whom he had so ostentatiously deferred.

Indeed, Tesman finds the childish piano music so objectionable that, to avoid such interruptions, he proposes to Mrs. Elvsted—his former love—that she move into his aunt's house, which is also Tesman's old home. He is consciously reconstructing his way of living, so as to isolate and exclude Hedda. "Then I'll come up in the evenings. And then we can sit and work there. Eh?"—where Hedda cannot interrupt with unpredictable impulses, her aristocrat whims. (Note the ironic echo here of Lövborg and Hedda sitting confidentially together—a pleasure that was especially keen to Hedda, so keen that she re-enacts it with the album.) As Stein Olsen smugly concludes, "Hedda is, of course, the real parasite in the play" (603). Rather harshly, Tesman punishes Hedda's rebellious noisemaking; and in doing so, the real power figure at last clearly emerges. Hedda must now perform the heroic deed that Lövborg failed to perform for her: she must achieve the unconditioned act she earlier sought only by proxy.

> Mrs. ELVSTED. Yes, perhaps that would be the best . . . .
> HEDDA. [from the inner room]. I can hear what you're saying, Tesman. And how am I supposed to survive the evenings out here?
> TESMAN. [leafing through the papers]. Oh, I expect Mr. Brack will be kind enough to look in now and again.   (264)

Notice Tesman's casual inattentiveness—it is not really casual but studied, and very deft. Tesman has benefited as much as he can from the prized Hedda Gabler. Now she is a liability, hardly an asset, given her aberrations, someone who cannot be trusted where it counts, in the enhancement of Tesman's career. He therefore hands her over to Brack—to "the illicit advances of the ever-willing Judge Brack" (Haugen 88)—"*Hedda Gabler*'s debased satyr" (Fuchs 219).

In every way she is defeated. Tesman looks harmless but has proven deadly. Hedda, having lost Lövborg, has now lost the contemptible husband she had so ostentatiously taken for granted. She has even lost in terms of female competition: her "friend" Thea that she looks down upon has pocketed her husband. Now the loathsome Brack is about to collect *her*.

The great Hedda, however, has one more card to play, and she does.

* * *

The unimaginative Tesman thus demonstrates the combination noted at the outset: distortion fused with calculation, the combination that characterizes Male Envy. His ambition founders on something that Male Envy has great difficulty comprehending: personality. He underestimates Hedda, because he does not see her as she is, but only as a function of the compete/control hierarchy. For the determined competitor/controller, the field of Male Envy is all that is real; hence anything that does not illustrate its obsessions is unreal. Genuine personality is spontaneous and full of surprises, and this is Hedda's outstanding quality: again and again, she surprises. She also shocks.

But that power to shock *ipso facto* serves to emphasize her larger-than-life personality. Tesman, meanwhile, is incapable of surprising; control dislikes surprise, except the calculated surprise used as a weapon against rivals. But to act spontaneously, or on impulse, requires a letting-go which is at odds with the control compulsions of Male Envy. Tesman does nothing that does not advance his own interests, and that means studying every move and avoiding risk, above all avoiding loss of control, including self-control. One cannot control others unless one controls oneself.

The sinister side of this disturbing principle is articulated by Blake in a crucial passage of *The Marriage of Heaven & Hell*: "Those who restrain desire, do so because theirs is weak enough to be restrained; and the restrainer or reason usurps its place & governs the unwilling. And being restrain'd, it by degrees becomes passive, till it is only the shadow of desire." Genuine personality, as a distinctive energy and as opposed to the role-playing of Male Envy, is a function of desire. The erasure of desire in others erases desire in the self, erases the self. Desire as a spontaneous energy thus is the opposite of control, with its compulsions and obsessions.

The implication is that the desiring female is the natural opponent of the code of Male Envy, a metaphor for rejection of the system of Male Envy, the nucleus of the opposition or search for an alternative: a point we will return to.

Hedda's final, explosive action is a parody of the male-competitor, who would die rather than lose on the compete/control hierarchy, whose devotion to control is so great that losing face is far worse than dying. In this peculiar state, while nothing matters, yet total war is required; if one is to lose, then, what the code of Male Envy advises is the destruction of one's enemies and of everything else, in a final sacrifice or Male Display. The figure who embodies this attitude is Hitler in his last days deciding that, if he was going down, then everything, Germany and all, will go down with him. He seems to have been enacting Nietzsche's *Dawn of Day* aphorism: "When some men fail to accomplish what they desire to do they exclaim angrily, 'May the whole world perish!' This repulsive emotion is the pinnacle of envy, whose implication is 'If I cannot have *something*, no one is to have *anything*, no one is to *be* anything'" (see Schoeck's comment 178-179).

Hedda's impulsive decisiveness is literally her death. Her suicide is a blow against her competitor/enemies, a blow that they will never recover from. The disgrace of her suicide will overshadow Tesman, her owner-husband, for the rest of his life. To quote Veblen, once again: "Any action on the part of a woman which traverses an injunction of the accepted schedule of proprieties is felt to reflect immediately upon the honor of the man whose woman she is." Hedda Gabler pays with her life, but she "wins," after all.

* * *

Hedda Gabler is a compendium of female roles in the context of Male Envy. The standard role is represented by Mrs. Elvsted: that of supplier to the male competitor. Tesman's aunt is completely devoted to this function, too, but Mrs. Elvsted also performs the other standard role. Her transfer from the man she supposedly worshiped—Lövborg—to Tesman (after similarly being transferred earlier from her husband, Elvsted, to her lover Lövborg) is typical of the other function of females in the régime of Male Envy, to mark male winning and status in relation to other males. The "actress" Diana, whom we never see, illustrates another female role, that of independent, one who manipulates males in order to survive, and in this respect, she adumbrates Hedda Gabler herself, which is one reason no doubt why Hedda regards her with such contempt. The difference is that Diana has no ambitions, whereas Hedda is all ambition.

Hedda resents exclusion from competition and determines to satisfy her ambition by manipulating a useful male, reversing the normal arrangement, so that Tesman becomes *her* supply base. Unfortunately, in doing so, she collides with the whole ethos of Male Envy, where the exclusion of women is a necessity. At the same time, Hedda's manipulations indicate that women have a potential power within the régime of Male Envy that is far out of proportion with their official subordination within that system. Hence she has the power to mirror the misery and horror of the Male-envious system, to make its pettiness and viciousness appear as what it is, so that while she is a mirror of evil, she is curiously free in the sense that she cannot be pinned down or identified with evil in any simple way. This is a very complex character creation, partly because it twists around the Male-envious system so skillfully and dramatically.

Just as the central place of Male Envy in *Hedda Gabler* is subtle and inconspicuous, the crucial power object in the play is also subtle and inconspicuous, in part because the magnetic Hedda upstages everyone and everything else in the action. That power object is not the manuscript, nor General Gabler's pistols, nor the piano that causes Tesman so much irritation. It is rather something much more vulgar: money: what Tesman may—or may not —be able to supply. In this sense, *Hedda Gabler* is a play about money.

Money crystallizes the magic of commanding—the power to control control, so to speak—more precisely, the capacity to require, if not actually force, someone to do what you want. To adapt Marilyn French's term in *Beyond Power*, money symbolizes a "power-over relationship," and achieving power-over relationships is both a goal of male competition and a means of competition. In a power-over relationship, one does not need to argue or persuade the person in the non-power position: one commands, and the desired action follows. This is the magic of money, which satisfies desire by a mechanism of invisible coercion.

Hedda Gabler belongs to a line of important female figures that emerge in Romantic narrative which I have referred to as "desiring females," noting the way that this character type is usually accompanied by two complementary male types: the ineffectual lover and the power male. Money as materialized or concretized will-power, the will to force others, is associated with these power males, just as failure to make money is associated with the figure of the ineffectual lover. *Hedda Gabler* is an elaborate and in some ways ironic presentation of female roles against the backdrop of a long development of Male Envy. A more condensed treatment of these motifs, in an example from the critical period in which Male Envy emerges, is Keats's *Isabella, or The Pot of Basil*. And money here also has an inconspicuous but critical role.

Keats seems to have had more sensitivity to Male Envy issues than the other Romantic poets. One of his narratives, *Isabella, or The Pot of Basil*, a tale Keats adapted from Boccaccio, is concerned with Male Envy in relation to women. While Isabella herself is completely unlike Hedda Gabler, she follows a curiously similar trajectory to Ibsen's heroine. She also resembles Beatrice in "Rappaccini's Daughter," which is, like *Isabella*, set in Renaissance Italy, the birthplace of modern science and modern capitalism. The plot presents the Tricky Female figure, but as *a function of Male Envy*, so that the scenario of *Hedda Gabler* is an elaboration and variation on the situation described in *Isabella*.

Male acquisitive struggle forms the background against which the plot of *Isabella* unfolds: the ambitions of two merchant-brothers is the necessary prerequisite for the action and a constant point of reference. These brothers have a sister, Isabella, whom they plan to "invest" in a marriage of commercial advantage to them. But Isabella has fallen in love with Lorenzo, one of their warehouse workers. Isabella's love is a serious aberration, from the brothers' point of view, because for them, she is a valuable commodity: in effect, capital. Hence Lorenzo's love is really embezzlement.

In some of Keats's most famous lines, money = materialized will = a webwork of power-over relationships:

> With her two brothers this fair lady dwelt,
> Enriched from ancestral merchandize,
> And for them many a weary hand did swelt
> In torched mines and noisy factories,

And many once proud-quiver'd loins did melt
In blood from stinging whip;—with hollow eyes
Many all day in dazzling river stood,
To take the rich-ored driftings of the flood.

For them the Ceylon diver held his breath,
And went all naked to the hungry shark;
For them his ears gush'd blood; for them in death
The seal on the cold ice with piteous bark
Lay full of darts; for them alone did seethe
A thousand men in troubles wide and dark. (ll. 105-120)

Stylistically, this poignant passage draws in the opposite direction from Male Envy: it is direct, concrete, sensory, and specific—not abstract, general, and distanced. It is also sympathetic—and synthetic—in that it makes connections that link the whole world and the numerous life-forms in that world. Notice the references to blood. Furthermore, Keats goes out of his way to connect human victims—human beings from round the world—with *animal* victims, on the assumption that as Blake puts it, "everything that lives is holy."

The reason why animals are prominent (and so prominently linked with human beings) is that the poem is built around the motif of objects that can be controlled: the reduction of living beings to objects that can be converted into cash. This convertibility, however, requires a power-over relationship: a relationship in which one person controls another and can damage or destroy the other if satisfaction is not given to the person in control. Interestingly, the text makes a significant allusion to child sacrifice (l. 262; the significance of this allusion will be clearer in Chapter 4, "Holy Murder"). For Male Envy, achieving power-over relationships is advantageous in several ways:

(1) The power-over relationship yields what political economist Samir Amin calls "unequal exchange," a system whereby one gives less and gets more, so that one drains wealth out of the weaker to the stronger.

(2) Obligation is not incurred—the person in the power position does not have to take into account the wishes of the person in the non-power position. He owes him nothing.

(3) A power-over relationship converts people into objects, thus enhancing the sense of self and personal power that Male Envy is preoccupied with. One need not waste or lose any time from thinking about oneself and one's desires; one eliminates distractions or obligations posed by other people, since in a sense there are no other people.

(4) A pleasing cruelty is implicit in power-over relationships; by causing the pain of others, one may derive not only power points, but a strangely piquant form of pleasure for those who are so inclined. One imprints one's will in the bodies of lesser beings, and by doing so, one proves that others *are* lesser beings.

(5) Ironically, also, one turns others into nothing, the not-seen. This is also a characteristic of reason in Male Envy: it views what it cannot understand or control as non-existent.[26] Personality and the subjectivity of other people especially need to be ignored if one is to control them with equanimity and efficiency. Cruelty at a distance becomes pleasure close up.

After describing the merchant-brothers, Keats comments on the fact that the miseries they inflict and benefit from are screened from them: "Half-ignorant, they turn'd an easy wheel, / That set sharp racks at work, to pinch and peel" (ll. 119-120). They have succeeded in detaching themselves and their egocentric lives from the horrifying process by which their money is made: a remarkable achievement. The phrase "*Half*-ignorant" is especially interesting, recalling the importance of silence in maintaining the system of Male Envy. In Male Envy, sympathy with others is a dangerous liability, indeed a sign of weakness. It goes without saying that the capacity to understand others as independent human beings, with their own needs and nature, is a distraction, if not an impediment, to winning on the control hierarchy; indeed it is a sin. In the code of Male Envy, ruthlessness is a prized virtue: "Ferocity and cunning," says Veblen,

> are useful to the individual only because there is so large a proportion of the same traits actively present in the human environment to which he is exposed. Any individual who enters the competitive struggle without the due endowment of these traits is at a disadvantage, somewhat as a hornless steer would find himself at a disadvantage in a drove of horned cattle. (174)

The image of the "hornless steer" "in a drove of horned cattle" is a disturbingly apt metaphor for the defective competitor, the ridiculed loser/failure. The castration symbolism here suggests what castration really means in Freud (and in the psychoanalytic revisionists following him): it means defeat in compete/control struggles, and hence collapsed identity, given that male identity is constituted as placement on the control hierarchy.

The plot of *Isabella* could hardly be simpler or more effective in dramatizing the *modus operandi* of Male Envy. Isabella is a desiring female of the type noted earlier. She is surrounded, as to be expected, by the corresponding male figures: an ineffectual lover (Lorenzo) and in this case *two* overbearing males (her brothers: the fact that they are family is not surprising, since rape or incest are often associated with power males in this three-part configuration, as *Chinatown* makes clear). Again, in the event, she dies. Isabella's merchant-brothers casually murder her lover, the lower-class employee of their business operation. This killing is not a matter of emotion for them; it is logical from their point of view. They cannot afford to lose the marriage-investment that their sister represents. It is simply a business necessity: it is not "personal."

As a result, Isabella goes mad, like Ophelia, and dies: one recalls the suicide of Hedda Gabler and the death of Beatrice Rappaccini—in each case, the women show a determination not to be trapped as an object within the competitive struggles of Male Envy, at whatever cost. In a variant of this paradigm Estella in *Great Expectations* is finally stopped by the physical blows of her animal-abusing husband. In Romantic narrative, progressive instincts or feminist sympathies are often featured; they may be defeated, but they must be respected.

After the murder of her lover, Isabella is visited by her lover's ghost, who, in the manner of ghosts of murdered men, begs for some burial rite. Isabella responds by digging up the body and removing the head, which she "plants" in a pot containing the herb basil; hence the title. Subsequently, Isabella lapses into total obsession with the head/pot, in a parody of her brothers' obsession with material objects, that is, with money:

> And she forgot the stars, the moon, and sun,
>   And she forgot the blue above the trees,
> And she forgot the dells where waters run,
>   And she forgot the chilly autumn breeze;
> She had no knowledge when the day was done,
>   And the new morn she saw not.   (ll. 417-22)

The world of sensation disappears. The effect of obsession is to make sensation evaporate. Isabella sees only the object-fetish of her obsession; nothing else exists for her. She is in total control of it, having achieved the power-over relationship with the body/thing, the relationship that reduces people to manipulable objects in the manner so highly approved in Male Envy. Note the fusion of distorted perception and calculating skill; thus Isabella carefully tends the plant—after deliberately exhuming her lover's body, no mean task when one only has, as Isabella only has, a knife to do it with. Like Hedda Gabler, but in a different way, Isabella mirrors the madness of the men who enclose her.

Ironically, of course, her madness means that she is slipping into a kind of freedom, something that the brother-businessmen do not like at all. She is becoming an "unattached" female, like the vulnerable women noted earlier, a woman that is not owned, because perhaps she *can*not be owned. Her bizarre behavior suggests the unpredictable personality of the Tricky Female (cf. in *Lamia*, Apollonius's denunciation of Lamia as a Tricky Female who must be destroyed). For the brothers, Isabella is now becoming worthless as an investment; her mental "freedom" has reduced her cash value to zero. The vigilant brothers respond as one might expect, by trying, even more determinedly, to control. Control—the manipulation of objects—is the magic elixir for all problems in Male Envy. They know that she is obsessed with the pot but do not know what is in it, and they conclude that if the pot is taken away from her, she will return to normal; that is, someone who will do as directed. Isabella's reaction recalls that of Hedda when cornered. She goes mad when her power object, her display piece, is taken from her, and dies. The pot is opened, the brothers' crime is exposed, and they are forced to flee the town. They "lose," after all.

*   *   *

As in *Hedda Gabler* and other examples, the plot of *Isabella* demonstrates in a curious way the futility, irrationality, and destructiveness of social relationships governed by the compete/control hierarchy and its ethos. I have stressed several features in its total field of influence: for example, the impoverishment of feeling, the narrowing of awareness to certain obsessive preoccupations, the cruelty and arrogance. In Male Envy, power is, above all, *differential*, defined not merely in opposition to women, or in order to exploit women; but in relation to other males on a hierarchy that is constantly precipitating out of the competitive struggle for control: control of other people and of objects. The implication is that the oppression of women could not be possible without the prior oppression of men; or, more precisely, the oppression of women is *facilitated* by the oppression of other men. Thus, while the oppression of women appears to be a function of all men and a benefit to all men, the régime of Male Envy immensely complicates this relationship. Male Envy is a process by which women are oppressed by men, because men are oppressed by men. If anything, the result is a doubling of the oppression of women, because male competitor/controllers must make use of women in order to wage their struggle against other male competitor/controllers.

Male Envy articulates power and control struggles—real reality, as it were, "the real world"—but it is also charged with illusions and even hallucinations.[27] One of the most potent of these illusions is the notion that sheer ego—arrogant ambition alone—somehow creates and accomplishes things; that it is a generative source simply by itself without doing anything. This is the view carefully articulated by Satan in *Paradise Lost*. Hence in the logic of Male Envy, in order to understand a man, one must seek out the greedy self-absorption that really animates him, and that is the true motivation for his character and actions. One assumes that everyone is as egocentric and ambitious as oneself. Accordingly, genuine love, spiritual conviction, impartial dedication to a cause or art, the wish to know for its own sake, or other authentic feelings and motivations, or even pleasures, are marginalized, nullified, or ruled out by the intellectual suction of Male Envy and its illusions. Male Envy does not exist in a vacuum; it emerges out of a specific worldview (in Kaja Silverman's terms, "If ideology is central to the maintenance of classic masculinity, the affirmation of classic masculinity is especially central to the maintenance of our governing 'reality'"[28]).

The next step is to probe this worldview and its origin.

Notes

1. "The loss of vital fluids," notes Alan Dundes, "is believed to diminish a finite supply of life energy"—"medical practitioners have sometimes claimed that infertility and erectal impotence were the results of the wastage of sperm through excessive sexual activity in youth" ("Wet and Dry, the Evil Eye: An Essay in Indo-European and Semitic Worldview," *The Evil Eye: A Casebook*, ed. A. Dundes [Madison: U of Wisconsin P 1992] 288). The popular mythology around conserving semen (= masculine identity/ power) is immense.
2. Gonzalo Fernandez de la Mora, *Egalitarian Envy*, trans. Antonio de Nicola (New York: Paragon 1987) 75.
3. Joseph H. Berke, *The Tyranny of Malice* (New York: Simon, 1986) 36.
4. Helmut Schoeck, *Envy: A Theory of Social Behavior*, trans. M. Glenny B. Ross (New York: Harcourt, 1969) 20.
5. William Doty, "'Companionship Thick as Trees'," *Journal of Men's Studies* 1.4 (1993): 365.
6. Alfie Kohn emphasizes this effect: "Depriving adversaries of their personalities, of faces, of their subjectivity, is a strategy we automatically adopt in order to win. . . . the posture is demanded by the very structure of competition" (*No Contest: The Case against Competition* [Boston: Houghton, 1990] 139). Compare Thorstein Veblen, *Imperial Germany and the Industrial Revolution*, 134ff.
7. C. S. Lewis, *The Screwtape Letters* (London: Collins, 1955) 63-64.
8. David Bertelson, *Snowflakes and Snowdrifts: Individualism and Sexuality in America* (Lanham: UP of America, 1986) 76.
9. On the Tricky Female figure see also my "Magic Food, Compulsive Eating, and Power Poetics," *Disorderly Eaters: Texts in Self-Empowerment*, ed. Lilian R. Furst (University Park: Penn State UP, 1994); and "Romantic Desire," *San José Studies* 16:3 (1990): 65-79. Dread of female reproductive power may be at the root of this convention; see Julia Kristeva, *Powers of Horror: An Essay on Abjection*, trans. S. Rondiez (New York: Columbia UP, 1982). The text is Henrik Ibsen, *Four Major Plays*, trans. James McFarlane and Jens Arup (London: Oxford UP, 1981).
10. Arthur Ganz, "Miracle and Vine Leaves: An Ibsen Play Rewrought," *PMLA* 94 (1979): 19.
11. Per Schelde Jacobsen and Barbara Fass Leavy, *Ibsen's Forsaken Merman: Folklore in the Late Plays* (New York: New York UP, 1988) 217, 211, 214. In Elinor Fuchs's Jungian reading, Hedda is a Hecate figure ("Mythic Structure in *Hedda Gabler:* The Mask behind the Face," *Comparative Drama* 19 [1985]: 209-220).
12. Ronald Gray, *Ibsen, a Dissenting View* (Cambridge: Cambridge UP, 1977) 135. Critics love to expatiate on Tesman's absurdity—on what Lisa M. Low calls "Tesmanic mediocrity" (Lisa M. Low, "In Defense of Hedda," *Massachusetts Studies in English* 8.3 [1982]: 47): he is "a somewhat pedantic and self-satisfied young man" (Ganz 9).
13. Thorstein Veblen, *The Theory of the Leisure Class* (New York: NAL, 1953) 230.
14. Harold Clurman, *Ibsen* (London: Macmillan, 1978) 157; my emphasis.
15. Stein Olsen even argues that Tesman represents a high moral ideal—something called "The tesmanesque ethos": "simplicity, naivety, childlikeness, restricted vision, diligence" ("Why Does Hedda Gabler Marry Jörgen Tesman?" *Modern Drama* 28 [1985]:

595), which is what the aristocratic but unfunctional Hedda needs in order to develop as a human being. "Given the value-scheme of the play, Jörgen Tesman is the logical choice for Hedda Gabler" (Olsen 610) because Tesman "offers her what she needs to change her role from aesthetic object to moral agent" (see 605); but she can't let go and, like an addiction, her old values return. This view testifies to Tesman's ability to deceive; Tesman's entire ethic is enclosed in rising in competition for control. The point is not that he plans deliberately what happens—though he is capable of planning: rather, it is his capacity cleverly to take advantage of circumstances as they unfold.

16. In *The Modern Ibsen* (New York, rpt. 1960), Herman Weigand notes Tesman's "instinctive, unavowed wish to deprive his rival of the material evidence of his superiority" (269). In fact, Tesman in the first draft actually suggests hiding the manuscript so as to scare Lövborg. In the familiar Royal Shakespeare film of *Hedda Gabler*, with Glenda Jackson, Tesman wishes to rebuild his "friend's" destroyed manuscript at the end to atone for his wife's act of destroying it. This motivation makes Tesman look good (and his wife look bad)—but it has no textual basis in the play itself.

17. "He addresses Aunt Juliana as *Tante Julle*, a particularly irritating and babylike abbreviation which drives Hedda mad every time he uses it. The last straw is when he asks her to address the old lady by it too" (Michael Meyer, "A Note on the Translation," *The Pillars of Society* [Garden City: Doubleday, 1961] 450). The contrast is Lövborg's sexual language to Hedda, "lust for life" (*livsbegaeret, livskravet*; see Ganz 15; and Errol Durbach's *"Ibsen the Romantic"* [Athens: U of Georgia P, 1982] 41-42).

18. Qu. in Patricia Spacks, *The Female Imagination* (New York, 1975) 317.

19. George Bernard Shaw, *Shaw and Ibsen*, ed. J. L. Wisenthal (Toronto: U of Toronto P, 1979) 169.

20. In a study of Norwegian proverbs in Ibsen, Ansten Anstensen even argues that Hedda "is a thoroughly conventional person whose acts are governed by the dictates of the prevailing social code" (*The Proverb in Ibsen* [New York, 1966], 215)—a half-truth, given Hedda's last act, but a suggestive one.

21. Significantly, the "One doesn't do it" (*"Man bruger ikke det"*) theme first appears —facetiously—in connection with the aunt and the hat, and reappears in Brack's shocked final words. Ganz traces the permutations of the phrase not only in *Hedda Gabler* but in *A Doll's House* (Ganz 11).

22. See Einar Haugen, *Ibsen's Drama* (Minneapolis: U of Minnesota P, 1979) 113.

23. John Northam, *Ibsen: A Critical Study* (Cambridge: Cambridge UP, 1973) 184.

24. Blake's "Visions of the Daughters of Albion" is an early example of this configuration, with the desiring woman, Oothoon, surrounded by the ineffectual Theotormon (the name suggests "God-tormented") and the nihilistic rapist Bromion. Oothoon seems to have been modeled on Mary Wollstonecraft, the great feminist; Wollstonecraft presents the same configuration in her own unfinished novel *The Wrongs of Woman, or Maria*, with the desiring Maria flanked on one side by the pimp-husband Venables and, on the other, the ineffectual Darnford. This configuration of character types expresses the emergence of feminist thought at the end of the eighteenth century.

25. For the nuances of the Norwegian at the end, see James McFarlane, "Meaning and Evidence in Ibsen's Drama," *Contemporary Approaches to Ibsen*, ed. D. Haakonsen (Oslo: Universitetsforlaget, 1966) 43-44.

26. "A fallacy of appeal to ignorance looms . . . if we suppose that because we don't immediately have conclusive proof of something's existence that we can then infer that the thing doesn't exist, and especially when the 'thing' in question is not the kind . . . that readily lend itself to such proof" (Phyllis Rooney, "Rationality and the Politics of Gender Difference," *Metaphilosophy* 26.1-2 [1995]: 29).

27. See Yong Shin Kim, *The Ego Ideal, Ideology and Hallucination* (Lanham: UP of America, 1992); Kim's psychoanalytic approach derives from Freud's *Group Psychology and the Analysis of the Ego*, specifically Freud's fascination with the powerful ego as leader (by corollary, social needs for submission to a powerful ego).

28. Kaja Silverman, *Male Subjectivity at the Margins* (New York: Routledge, 1992) 16.

3

Object Thinking

> *What could stand more in the way of honest inquiry after truth . . . than that conventional metaphysics to which the state has granted a monopoly and whose propositions are hammered into everyone's head in his childhood so earnestly and so deeply and firmly that . . . it retains their impress for ever, so that his capacity for thinking for himself and for making unprejudiced judgements—a capacity which is in any case far from strong—is once and for all paralysed and ruined?*
> (Schopenhauer, "On Religion")

In William Blake's great satire, *The Marriage of Heaven & Hell* (1792), a rebellious devil meets a conservative angel. Each shows to the other what he believes will be the other's "eternal lot"—i.e., heaven and hell. Blake calls the devil a devil, because devils advocate desire, and the traditional attitude of authority is that desire is evil; hence those who believe desire is good are "devils." For the conservative angel, people would be better off without desires and to stick to obeying authority. In the words of Byron, another Romantic rebel: "the angels all are Tories" (*The Vision of Judgment*, 1821).

Blake, like Byron, is an instinctive devil, advocate of desire, and speaks as a "devil": "An Angel came to me and said: 'O pitiable foolish young man! O horrible! O dreadful state! consider the hot burning dungeon thou art preparing for thyself to all eternity'." When the devil challenges the angel to show him this hell, the angel takes him where Hell is traditionally located, under the earth. They descend to a huge cavern; the devil sits "in the twisted root of an oak"— the angel meanwhile is "suspended in a fungus," "head downward into the deep."

> By degrees we beheld the infinite Abyss, fiery as the smoke of a burning city; beneath us, at an immense distance, was the sun, black but shining; round it were fiery tracks on which revolv'd vast spiders, crawling after their prey. . . . we saw

a cataract of blood mixed with fire, and not many stones' throw from us appear'd and sunk again the scaly fold of a monstrous serpent; at last. . . . appear'd a fiery crest above the waves; slowly it reared like a ridge of golden rocks, till we discover'd two globes of crimson fire, from which the sea fled away in clouds of smoke; and now we saw it was the head of Leviathan . . . soon we saw his mouth & red gills hang just above the raging foam, tinging the black deep with beams of blood, advancing toward us with all the fury of a spiritual existence.

A vision of terror has considerable potency in society, and therefore usefulness. This particular visualization—Hell—served as a means of control for centuries, of stimulating obedience not just to the Church, but to the established social structure generally. In precapitalist, feudal culture, to disobey the "lord" of the manor is to disobey the "Lord" of creation. The social hierarchy interlocks with the hierarchy of God. Obedience and disobedience are categories built into the structure of the universe, as is a fixed social hierarchy. According to Dante's Virgil in *The Divine Comedy* (in the Carey translation familiar to writers in the nineteenth century):

Philosophy, to an attentive ear,
Clearly points out, not in one part alone,
How imitative Nature takes her course
From the celestial Mind, and from its art.

Just as nature obeys its overlord, humans should obey theirs.

What corresponds to social terror, in terms of individual psychology, is the *disaster fantasy*: fearful images of what might happen, especially if one pursues desire instead of obeying authority. Disaster fantasies have a controlling, even paralyzing effect on consciousness, and so function as a means to limit the range of possibilities available to an individual. In Freud, the disaster fantasy motif has deep importance; he refers to it as "castration anxiety," as a "castration complex" ("*Kastrationsdrohung*"). The control of awareness by fear is basic to Male Envy.

Blake's angel is so terrified by his vision of Hell that he jumps up and runs away. But then there is a surprise. Once the angel is gone, Hell vanishes, "& then this appearance was no more, but I found myself sitting on a pleasant bank beside a river by moonlight hearing a harper, who sung to the harp; & his theme was: 'The man who never alters his opinion is like standing water, & breeds reptiles of the mind'." Hell, in other words, is the projection of the angel: it is a disaster fantasy, not a reality. And clearly, to deny the validity of the disaster fantasy is to threaten a whole structure of coercion. Inevitably, to reject fear as a valid means of control is to bring oneself into conflict with the code of Male Envy: a point I will return to in the next chapter.

When the devil comes back from "Hell," alive and well and not burnt to a terrified crisp, the angel is astonished. The horror, as he does not realize, is *his* horror, the *angel*'s horror. The devil then reciprocates: he takes the angel to the angel's heaven, located where heaven is traditionally visualized to be, up in the sky. But since heaven for Blake is not a place, this Heaven turns out to be nothingness: the emptiness of space, "if space it may be call'd," as the poet says, wondering how you describe a nothing that is somehow something. The angel's heaven does not exist; it is "nothing," and the place where he thinks it is is just that—emptiness, space, as if nothingness were what was most real. Heaven and Hell are not "in" the physical world; they are not places, but mental spaces. The point that reality is what we experience is the basis of phenomenology (especially that of Merleau-Ponty, who emphasizes the sensory and imagined, as opposed to the abstract). How we see determines what we see.

Fusing perceived and perceiver, Male Envy is communicated and indoctrinated in complex ways that cannot be accounted for in a simple manner. More than words, more than actions or unspoken expectation, is involved in the inculcation of Male Envy. Male Envy is like a magnetic field in which all the individual particles are lined up according to an unconscious pattern, communicating with one another in subtle, often involuntary ways. Blake's primary idea is that perception is creation: that is, creation is an attempt to become conscious of the invisible patterns and lines of force that "magnetize" human consciousness in certain directions, and not in other directions.

In a larger sense, this attempt was characteristic of many of the writers of the Romantic period. What flows from this attempt is that reality is a social construct or, more precisely, that we live in a model of reality rather than reality itself. Therefore, and this is the crucial point, change is possible. The realization that change is possible, because reality is a social construction and not an immutable datum handed down by authority, is powerful—and also threatening. What Blake calls "reptiles of the mind" are still monstrous even if they do not "exist" (i.e., do not occupy space). Like the Dragon in the book of Revelation, which is and is not at the same time, a "reptile of the mind" is worse than a spatial monster. Blake understood that society lives within a model of reality that determines what is done and limits what is thought. Nor is this model of reality an individual creation; it is a social identity—it is participation in a social order. Thus, Blake's angel is part of a complex social system; his devil is a rebel struggling to recreate society and to listen to an inner voice that for Blake guides and reveals, a presence symbolized by the beautiful voice of the harper.

* * *

Society does not live nakedly in nature; it creates a complex picture of reality, and that is what it inhabits: a set of assumptions and expectations that guide action, that shape perception, and that enable it to manipulate nature in various ways. As a cultural envelope, this model of reality intervenes between physical nature and society; between the individual and the social structure which encloses the individual within itself; and between the individual's conscious and unconscious mind. Because we live in a picture of reality, not reality itself, our perceptions and actions are at every point affected by this collectively created, collectively disseminated and shared picture.

This puts the case a little loosely: what a model of reality embodies is a way of thinking about the world that determines social consciousness, and that organizes social labor. It tells you what to do. It embodies what linguist John R. Searle calls *"collective intentionality."* One may not like it—one may rebel—but one is still shaped by it. As soon as one stops resisting its pressure, it springs back unconsciously. This is partly because the model of reality that society projects is not merely a set of abstract proposita: it is rather a complex made up of image, emotion, and narrative. It consists of large governing assumptions that direct awareness along certain axes, just as it directs behavior along certain routines; hence the term "ideology" is far too limited here. In a sense, these assumptions are not ideas at all; they are *images*, paradigms of how things work, and they cannot be simply transposed into abstract ideas. But however one construes them, their effect is powerful because they shape practice and day-to-day consciousness—they are not confined to intellectualizing or to High Theory.

It follows that perhaps the hardest perception an individual can make is to see and understand the model, or cosmology as I prefer to call it, that conditions existence to the point of automatism. This act of consciousness demands detachment, and hence a kind of self-awareness that a cosmology is designed to prevent, for awareness disrupts the social order and the psychological assumptions needed for it to function smoothly. Yet this detachment/awareness seems to be the real locus of creative action. It should be emphasized that a cosmology is not simply an untruth or illusion. On the contrary, it is meant to explain the physical world, and to an important extent it does that: it observes, records, and explains the workings of nature. But it also, in a complex way that is not easy to unravel, rationalizes the existing social order, so that the world becomes a metaphor for that order.

I referred earlier to the figure of Milton's Satan as a paradigm of Male Envy. As an exemplar, Satan makes it evident that the code of Male Envy has a history that needs to be taken into account. We can identify the origins of Male Envy, not in the form of some neolithic dying-god cult, or a tribal contract at the dawn of civilization, such as we find in Freud and René Girard. Nor is Male Envy an eternal fact of reality: it is not just a matter of psychology or (socio)biology ("male sex hormones predispose males to behave aggressively toward other males," etc.[1]). Male Envy as we have observed it is a matter of history. But it is the *history of cosmology*, "cosmology" both in the scientific sense as a model of nature, but also "cosmology" as a paradigm, as a worldview, a mode of perception that organizes social consciousness and social labor.

Thus the image of nature that a cosmology offers is really a metaphor for the social structure that generated that image in the first place. As philosopher of science Jonathan Powers puts it, "A 'worldview' presents both a picture of the physical world and an account of human values in a co-ordinated fashion."[2] As the social structure shifts, cosmology shifts along with it. *Paradise Lost*, with Satan as perhaps its most conspicuous feature, emerges out of a complicated shift in cosmology and signals the hegemony of a new model of reality, roughly corresponding to the shift from feudalism to capitalism. Cosmology-shift is a large and difficult subject; only the determining factors for Male Envy can be dealt with here, and only in terms of the crucial assumptions, abstracting key features in order to make the larger picture clear. The large and fundamental assumptions that we must attend to are, however, what get neglected in favor of details. People see trees easily enough, but they do not see the forest.[3]

Milton is the last major poet to belong to what may be called the Old Cosmology. The most conspicuous feature in this model of reality is a split between two levels of existence: the fallen world and the unfallen world. The unfallen world is the perfect creation that God originally made; it remains now only in the form of the stars and heavens above, and hence is often referred to as the "upper world." The upper world corresponds to the realm of "Being" in Plato and Greek philosophy, as opposed to the realm of "Becoming," the world of time, death, and change that human beings inhabit.[4] In the words of Adam Smith's "History of Ancient Physics," "whatever was below the Moon was abandoned by the gods to the direction of Nature, and Chance, and Necessity."[5]

Christianity assimilated the Being/Becoming split to something that was far more important for it: the split between unfallen and fallen realms. Below the moon ("sublunary"), in the Ptolemaic system that dominated astronomy down to Milton's time,[6] God's originally perfect creation is now "fallen," where human beings are born, live, and die. Human awareness is damaged as a result of the fall, just as the human will is corrupted. The "fallen" world is characterized by mutability and mortality; everything is changing—and everything that is alive is doomed to death. Gertrude instinctively turns to this primary axiom when confronting Hamlet in Shakespeare's play: "Thou know'st 'tis common, all that lives must die, / Passing through nature to eternity." For her society, human death and the mutability of nature are the most obvious of truths. The lower or fallen world is a place of struggle and labor, of sin and pain: it is the result of human disobedience to God, who is visualized as occupying the top of the social and cosmological hierarchy—a "lord" or "king" who is on a cosmic level what a king or lord is on earth.

But in some ways, this is the real point of the Old Cosmology: while it is certainly an attempt to depict the natural world, it is, more profoundly, a projection of the fundamental fact of precapitalist civilization, the split between a hereditary ruling class and the peasantry. The aristocracy correspond to the immutable upper world of authority; the peasants to the lower world, as God has assigned these orders. Some people do no work and are "eternally" fixed; other people labor in the messy, mutable world of the senses. In this manner, the Old Cosmology is a picture of nature that is also a picture of the social system that created the picture. The levels of reality embody what Frank Whigham calls the "founding of an absolute ontological distinction between the ruling class and its subjects."[7] Inevitably, therefore, any interference with this model and its crucial cosmic divide is perceived as an assault on the class structure—as indeed it was when Galileo declared that the upper world was made of the same mutable, physical stuff that the lower world was. What he was implying was that the two basic orders of society were indeed ontologically the same.

In traditional "tributary" culture (Samir Amin's term for feudal or semifeudal societies[8]), Male Envy is limited by a quasi-caste system that assigns to each individual a specific place, the result of birth. One is who one's parents were. If one is a peasant, as almost everybody was in premodern culture, one's child is also a peasant; if one is an aristocrat, one's child is an aristocrat. Changing status —the "social mobility" we take for granted—is scarcely thinkable: "Innovation is bad form" (Veblen 138). As Harvard professor Richard Lewontin explains, "It is hard to realize today the extent to which primary social relations in early feudal European society lay between person and person rather than between persons and things. The relationships . . . entailed mutual obligation."[9] By contrast, the code of Male Envy we have explored here is inextricably identified with a particular model of reality, a model which makes competition a central function and not merely an accidental possibility.

Over a period of centuries, the Old Cosmology disintegrated. More exactly, it was attacked and destroyed, just as feudalism was supplanted by capitalism. The model which replaced the Old Cosmology has characteristics of special importance because they stimulated and even theorized Male Envy. There is a logic to this model, what may be called the Object Cosmology, but it is not a logic of intellect alone, but of image, emotion, and action. "Complexes of metaphors may be constituents of the world," as Carl R. Hausman puts it.[10] The Object model visualizes reality as a collection of discrete material units held together by impersonal laws, laws which act as external forces upon those material units. Reality, in short, is a pile of objects in space. (Wealth, in the same way, is visualized as a vast accumulation of material things—this is the paradigm of wealth that Marx begins *Capital* with.) These objects are by nature quantifiable, so that whatever cannot be quantified is not really real. It is logical that this mode of perception should view reality as consisting of small indivisible objects—"atoms," where "atom" means "not cuttable," objects that are typically visualized like grains of sand, only smaller. The basis of reality is thus matter in the form of an object so basic it cannot be subdivided: hence, psychologically and metaphorically, it is the bedrock truth. What is really real are material objects, irreducibly: this certainty of objects constitutes an absolute or fixed point that at first supplements the existence of God and later replaces Him.[11]

As for society, the Object Cosmology is as atomistic and spatial in its thinking as it is about nature. Thus, society itself is thought of as atomic, a heap of separate individuals, where "individual" means much the same as "atom"—not divided, not divisible. This atomic image, to borrow David Pugh's principle, "must be understood as a psychosexual, cultural phenomenon which found expression in various sectors of the society, including those at odds with each other."[12] Margaret Thatcher said it best: "There is no such thing as society. There are only individual men, women, and families."[13] People-units are much the same: "separateness and uniformity go hand in hand" (Formaini 14). The five properties of matter that Newton identifies in his *Principia Mathematica*—extension, hardness, impenetrability, mobility, inertia—apply equally to the "possessive individual" that emerges along with Object thinking. Just as

reality = an aggregate of material units in space,
so also
society = an aggregate of separate individuals in economic space.

These human atoms, like objects, are scattered separately, deployed according to immutable laws and forces. Such impersonal forces take various forms, depending on context—they may be laws of psychology, for example, or laws of the market (e.g., the "law" of supply and demand, the "iron law of wages" in Ricardian economics). One of the primary metaphors in the early phase of Object thinking is the analogy of gravity and self-interest. Gravity regulates physical bodies, as self-interest regulates human bodies, as well as the commodities that human bodies instinctively trade with one another.

This is naturally, then, almost the first point that Adam Smith makes in *The Wealth of Nations*: human beings have an *instinct*—"a certain propensity in human nature," in Adam Smith's phrase—"the propensity to truck, barter, and exchange one thing for another." This instinct is a defining characteristic of humanity, something that differentiates humans from animals. That is, the market system is inherent in our genes, as one might say now. The isomorphy of gravity in nature and self-interest in society has been integral to the Object Cosmology since at least Malthus. This mirroring of physics in the market system, and vice versa, re-reflects throughout our culture: the "laws" that govern society are continuous with the "laws" of nature. Marx quotes (and ridicules) Edmund Burke's *Thoughts on Scarcity* (1795) to this effect: Burke explains that "the laws of commerce" are the "laws of nature," and the "laws of nature" are, in turn, "the laws of God."[14] Such a God, however, is circular: He is a personification of the laws of nature (and subtextually of commerce) to begin with.[15]

In this model, "Human beings are held to be profoundly separate and isolated from each other," observes Nancy Hartsock:

> Rational economic men are unable to associate with each other directly and instead associate only by means of *things* they pass back and forth between them (i.e., through exchange). A community that bases itself on the self-interested passing back and forth of objects can only be an instrumental community in which exchange and competition lead directly to relations of domination.[16]

This formulation may not be as extreme as it sounds. Historian David Zaret notes, "Puritan theology relied on a very specific model of economic life, one governed by a market rationality. In this model, acquisitive activities are governed by purely contractual patterns of interaction, and they are justified by the doctrine of possessive individualism."[17] The exchange of objects operates like a mechanism. But nature itself and its parts may be visualized as a machine. As Cleanthes in Hume's *Dialogues Concerning Natural Religion* says: "You will find [nature] nothing but one great machine, subdivided into an infinite number of lesser machines, which again admit of subdivisions, to a degree beyond what human senses can trace and explain."[18] Not only is the individual visualized as a machine,[19] but everything that is real tends to be similarly visualized; to see things as mechanism becomes an instinctive way to identify what they are and how they "work," their "mechanism" or "spring."[20]

The machine image applies to people, needless to say, and especially to males. Indeed, identifying the male body with the machine is axiomatic in Object culture. The atomic model of the self is emphasized for males, moreover, by "possessing" a penis—an object that defines or even constitutes who males are; and of course, as Cleland's *Fanny Hill* (1749) shows, an old word for penis is "machine" (cf. "tool"). The logical implication of Object thinking—the Frankenstein implication—is that, as Mark Seltzer says, "*bodies and persons are things that can be made.*"[21] The mechanism paradigm is familiar; the key point is that it allows not only a means of understanding nature, but of facilitating and even requiring the treatment of nature and of other people as objects to manipulate, use, and on occasion destroy. The application to males—"the masculine machine," in David Pugh's phrase (Pugh 38)—is taken for granted and seldom examined. By contrast, the objectifying of the female body has been much discussed—partly because of the anxiety-arousing power of sexual reproduction that, for Object thinking, constitutes women as women.[22]

The Object Cosmology projects reality as objects in space; it follows, therefore, that the primary relation is that of individual and object. Reality is constituted as *subject-space-object*, universally, where the space is a gap or separation (subject-*separation*-object), as well as the "space" in which objects are located. "Natural science conceived of man as a detached spectator of an objective universe. It held the spectator-spectacle polarity to be genuine and fundamental," in Henry Margenau's words.[23] Because the person-thing relationship becomes paradigmatic and unconscious, relationships generally tend to be thought of this way; even other people become external objects that can be, like any other object, measured, controlled, used, manipulated, enjoyed, destroyed —much like ownable things, "property" (literally "what belongs to one"). The aim of life becomes the "pursuit of happiness," as the Declaration of Independence—that most influential of all Enlightenment documents—puts it. But "happiness" is constituted as property, the owning of property being the basis and material means of personal enjoyment: an axiom recognized by the American Constitution in its adaptation of the Independence manifesto. "Happiness" becomes a code word for possession of objects—and success in competition with others: the mystique of property which is so potent an element in Object culture.

The first thing that one owns is oneself—one "owns" (and sells) one's labor: in Victor Seidler's words, "the idea that our relationship to ourselves is essentially possessive, so that we possess this self in the way that we possess any other commodity"; hence "The body is to be used as an instrument to serve our ends, rather than to be listened to."[24] Pondering what was already an unprecedented expansion of wealth, even before the industrial revolution, Adam Smith, a major theorist of what I have been calling the Object Cosmology,[25] sees each individual as by instinct a merchant, someone who buys/sells/consumes. This mode of perceiving is a commonplace nowadays, where people "sell" or "market" themselves, where human interactions are understood on the model of commercial transactions; indeed, where biology is understood in terms of commercial metaphors, with animals "investing" in various reproductive "strategies" to yield maximum returns and cut their losses.

This brings us once again to Milton's Satan. For the poet significantly visualizes the fallen angel and president of demons in terms of a *merchant prince* —a male driven by enterprising ambition. He risks, he makes deals, he ventures into the unknown, he seeks and enslaves others who are useful to him. One of the most memorable similes in *Paradise Lost* visualizes Satan as a merchantman ship sailing the lucrative East India route (1.636-42), one of the prime sources of what Marx refers to as "The So-Called Primitive Accumulation" in *Capital*— that is, the plunder of the non-European world. "The motives which impel Satan," J. M. Evans notes, "replicate, in turn, virtually all the social and political arguments advanced in favor of England's colonial expansion in the late sixteenth and early seventeenth centuries."[26]

Paradise Lost also compares Satan's shield to the moon seen through a telescope. The telescope (and the lens in general) is a paradigm for Object thinking: physicist David Bohm sees it as "indeed one of the key features behind the development of modern scientific thought"[27] (the gun and the clock are other paradigmatic power objects). The telescope was the creation *par excellence* of mercantile commerce: it was not a product of impartial science, seeking to understand nature for its own sake.[28] It was invented in order to signal information from incoming ships, so that the market could be made to yield higher profits at the last minute. The science of the Renaissance is interwoven with mercantile capitalism, because the needs of early capitalism for technology stimulated the growth of science, just as mercantile capitalism did so much to stimulate other developments, from Protestantism to navigation to oil painting to the development of unified nation states. For Milton, poised between the Old Cosmology and the model that replaces it, evil is associated with Object thinking —hence his characterization of Satan, his model of the Satanic.

With the rise of Object thinking, intellectuals begin to conceive God deistically, as a personification of the laws of nature (and of the market). What is really real—what we *know* exists—is material objects in space. Therefore, if God really exists, it follows that we should somehow be able to prove God's existence by studying those objects—that is, by measuring and quantifying them. God can be deduced from what is actually real, objects in space; hence the rise of "natural theology," the belief that the structure of nature reveals the nature of God. Thus God can be proved to exist from the existence of structure in nature: in practice, from the measurability of nature.

The Reverend William Paley produced a number of the most influential statements of this theology (his *Natural Theology*, 1802, retained textbook status throughout the nineteenth century). For Paley, the mechanical view of nature could supplement theology, in a sense supersede theology, because it would be scientific. In Northrop Frye's words:

> Paley's *Evidences of Christianity* used the analogy of a primitive man picking up a watch on a seashore left by some passing mariner. The primitive was supposed to infer that a watch meant a watch-maker, and similarly we should infer that if a complex world exists, somebody must have designed the complications. Samuel Butler pointed out that this assumed primitive would be much more likely to make a god of the watch, as the Lilliputians thought Gulliver did with his watch when he told them that he seldom did anything without consulting it.

In the mischievous spirit of Hume's *Dialogues Concerning Natural Religion*, Frye goes on to note

> The absurdities of the argument from design, such as congratulating the Creator for his ingenuity in dividing the orange into sections for convenience in eating. ... One cannot get very far with speculation on the mental level of a small child who assumes that a cat's tail is a specially designed handle for pulling it around.[29]

The fascination with design/mechanism coincides, paradoxically, with a profound revaluation of chance. Chance becomes positive in Object thinking, far more so than in earlier culture: after all, the merchant/businessman *gambles*. He must be willing to risk—and he must be "rewarded" for risking. Gambling on personal gain is meritorious. The prominence of Chaos in *Paradise Lost* is an index of the increased power of chance in social imagination. Chance begins to be seen as a formative agent, as it becomes in Darwinian evolution, where chance mutations are what drive evolution onward. Chance as a governing principle can, like luck, bring many "chances"—that is, opportunities to take advantage of, without having earned them. These must be seized and used. The combination of chance and personal, private ambition will take the individual competitor to the top of the compete/control hierarchy, in a world where chance interactions are fundamental.

The "Deism" that emerged in the Enlightenment was a progressive social development for many reasons. Most obviously, it made the tolerance of other religions and spiritual perceptions possible, as well as weakening some of the nastier beliefs in traditional Christianity, such as the doctrine that everybody with a different religion is going to hell, or even the doctrine of hell itself, as in Blake's satire. "Intolerance is something that belongs to the religions we have rejected," says Rousseau, perhaps the key Enlightenment thinker.[30] Object thinking itself was a powerful progressive development, in many respects, just as commercial capitalism brought with it numerous benefits, including increased productive power and scientific knowledge, notions of individualism and self-development scarcely available or possible to earlier civilization—democratic ideas generally. These positive aspects of Object thinking are important, but our concern in the present context is with its relation to Male Envy.[31]

One of the effects of deism and natural theology was a change in the conception of God, a shift away from God visualized as a cantankerous feudal-style potentate on a throne in a sky-kingdom, a God who is "punctilious in all questions of precedence and is prone to an assertion of mastery," in Thorstein Veblen's expression (198). This older way of visualizing God was not only Scriptural and traditional: it had, more importantly, a *function* as occupying the top of the pyramid of societal authority. In this way it was an inevitable feature of feudal civilization, a validation device for feudal hierarchy.

By contrast, the new deity—the new way to visualize God—established and validated a field of universal competition/control in nature and society. This God, as creator or personification of impersonal laws, implies equality: the deconstruction of aristocratic privilege. The new deity did not enforce, like God in the past, the privilege of hereditary aristocracy, but of large property-owners generally, regardless of birth. It validated, in short, a belief that independent competitor-owners should be equals before the law, much as objects in space are "equal" before the laws of nature. Hume cynically observes in his *Dialogues Concerning Natural Religion* that theologians have reinvented God: the old vale of tears has suddenly become the best of all possible worlds.

> They know how to change their style with the times. Formerly it was a most popular theological topic to maintain, that human life was vanity and misery, and

to exaggerate all the ills and pains which are incident to men. But of late years, divines, we find, begin to retract this position, and maintain, though still with some hesitation, that there are more goods than evils, more pleasures than pains, even in this life. [Once] it was thought proper to encourage melancholy; as indeed, mankind never have recourse to superior powers so readily as in that disposition. But as men have now learned to form principles, and to draw consequences, it is necessary to change the batteries, and to make use of such arguments as will endure, at least some scrutiny and examination. (213)

It is perhaps not surprising that Hume's *Dialogues* was only published after he was dead. The phrase "superior powers" implies aristocrats. Already in Hume, society is seen as rebuilding religion so as to fit changes in cosmology and in the power relations that project cosmology. This is an important illustration of the logic of imaginable forms. Social imagination creates cosmology, but it does so by breaking apart and transmuting earlier models. Thus, vestiges of the Old Cosmology persist, but are subtly reconstituted and altered, so as to support new social and imaginative needs (monarchy, for instance, is changed into a bourgeois institution).[32]

In *Paradise Lost*, Satan is *constituted* as a competitor. He sees his power as deriving from his private source, his inherently superior identity, which gives him personal control over other living beings and over material objects. On the one hand, he believes in liberty; on the other hand, he believes in hierarchy, a hierarchy of force, which reconciles the two contradictory notions of hierarchy and freedom: everyone is free to dominate everyone else.

This struggle to dominate replaces the old, fixed feudal-based hierarchy. In the new model, the compete/control hierarchy, there are no limits upon ambition, no restrictions by birth or background. It is rather a matter of getting what you can, so that Satan exemplifies the code of Male Envy that we have been tracing, in the very moment of its emergence out of Object thinking, like Sin appearing out of the head of Satan himself. Milton carefully marks Satan as a master of rhetoric, one who uses words to manipulate and control; the language of hate is second nature to him, as is the assumption of perpetual war, perpetual insecurity. He is a believer in chance and luck; his pact with Chaos is indicative. He takes it for granted that lying and deceiving are normal, indeed praiseworthy practice.

In the Satanic cosmology, beings become subordinates, and objects weapons, to signify ambition in a hierarchy of force. Like atoms, the competitive struggle is what is absolutely real, the irreducible residue that is left when everything else is accounted for. As what is really real, it is competition that should occupy one's consciousness constantly. For a male competitor, losing in this struggle is to lose absolutely—to enter "a process of disintegration, dissolution, molecularization—a process that threaten[s] to completely cancel him out as an entity, to attack the controlled coherence of his sense perceptions and explode it into an infinite number of mutually hostile particles."[33]

Such fragmentation, separation, and isolation is implicit in Object thinking already, however. It is also the working assumption of the Satanic order:

> The whole philosophy of Hell rests on recognition of the axiom that one thing is not another thing, and, specially, that one self is not another self. My good is my good and your good is yours. What one gains another loses. Even an inanimate object is what it is by excluding all other objects from the space it occupies; if it expands, it does so by thrusting other objects aside or by absorbing them. A self does the same. With beasts the absorption takes the form of eating; for us, it means the sucking of will and freedom out of a weaker self into a stronger. "To be" *means* "to be in competition."[34]

This is how the devil Screwtape in C. S. Lewis's *The Screwtape Letters* explains reality. Notice the Object thinking here: people are isolated units, exactly as reality is a pile of different objects. Everything is separated from everything else: disconnection is assumed as inherent in the structure of reality. The inference is obvious: existence is struggle-for-existence. "Weaker" and "stronger" are fundamental, irreducible categories of reality. Hence rational behavior requires a predatory impulse, organized (if that is the right word) by means of a control hierarchy that is not fixed but constantly emergent. Thorstein Veblen explains:

> The end sought by accumulation is to rank high in comparison with the rest of the community in point of pecuniary strength. So long as the comparison is distinctly unfavorable to himself, the normal, average individual will live in chronic dissatisfaction with his present lot; and when he has reached what may be called the normal pecuniary standard . . . this chronic dissatisfaction will give place to a restless straining to place a wider and ever-widening pecuniary interval between himself and this average standard. The invidious comparison can never become so favorable to the individual making it that he would not gladly rate himself still higher relatively to his competitors in the struggle for pecuniary reputability. In the nature of the case, the desire for wealth can scarcely be satiated in any individual instance.   (39)

Struggle, unending conflict, dissatisfaction, constantly shifting and disputed ranking, hostility and distrust, inability to relax, and unlimited appetitive ambition: the motifs Veblen identifies here are all enacted by Milton's Satan, and all are constitutive of Male Envy. Milton had already worked all this out in *Paradise Lost*, for his Satan has the sense of an endless nothingness below him threatening to suck him down, with no escape from the primal terror that forms the bottom and fundamental layer of reality:

> Which way I fly is Hell; myself am Hell;
> And in the lowest deep a lower deep
> Still threatening to devour me opens wide,

To which the Hell I suffer seems a Heaven.
(*Paradise Lost* 4.75-78)

Byron detested the compete/control hierarchy; he satirizes it in his apocalyptic poem entitled "Darkness," in a manner that recalls Blake's *Marriage of Heaven & Hell*. "Darkness" presents the universal struggle metaphorically, as a planetary destruction recalling Noah's flood. Only two humans survive. They are male competitor-enemies, and they kill each other by looking in each other's face, shocked to death by "their mutual hideousness." (Notice again the kill-power of the hostile gaze.) In Male Envy, men would die rather than nurture each other. Males are, intrinsically, competitors. As the familiar saying has it, "people are naturally selfish," where "people" means males, given the assumption that women's first loyalty is to supporting the male competitor-controller that they are allied with. This "selfishness"/"self-interest" is not bad; on the contrary, "Greed is Good," in the phrase made famous by the movie *Wall Street*, traditional values notwithstanding.

Another major Object theorist, the Reverend Thomas Malthus, articulates the point clearly: it "is to the established administration of property and to the apparently narrow principle of self-love that we are indebted for all the noblest exertions of human genius, all the finer and more delicate emotions of the soul, for everything, indeed, that distinguishes the civilized from the savage state."[35] Self-interest is not only the gravitational instinct inherent in human atoms; it is the golden secret, the ultimate good, and creator of good in the world. Malthus, whose *Essay on Population* is as much about theology as it is about demography, also redefines original sin in a form that makes sense to Object thinking—that is, in a manner that Object thinking can use for its own purposes: "The original sin of man is the torpor and corruption of the chaotic matter in which he may be said to be born" (118). Original sin is not disobedience to a divine being, but the natural laziness of the working class. It follows that whatever interferes with self-interest must be suspect. The Object Cosmology translates problems of power relations into relations between objects. Not surprisingly: Object thinking sees people as essentially objects (compare Marx's concept of commodity fetishism, whereby commodities just appear, as if by magic, instead of being the product of coordinated human work). Thus, the Object Cosmology is a validation device, designed to rationalize what L. J. Jordanova calls "A form of social relations which treated persons as objects."[36] It assumes that exploitation is the working of the laws of nature.

Theoretically, competition rewards merit; merit is typically valorized as "efficiency" or "frugality" or some other term by which superiority is brokered—rationalized and sanitized. In practice, however, competition means identifying others' weaknesses and taking advantage of them, so that the weaknesses and defects of others are primary elements of the system. Skill at cheating—to get the better of others in exchange-acts—is highly prized. To make one winner requires many losers; that is why ruthlessness is virtue. "Freedom from scruple, from sympathy, honesty and regard for life, may, within fairly wide limits, be said to further the success of the individual in the pecuniary culture" (Veblen 151). The Object Cosmology implies satisfaction at others' troubles; winning at their expense; getting what one wants, whatever others get. If it did not do so, the system would not survive; civilization, according to Malthus, would collapse, since everything of value is the result of self-interest. "The canons of pecuniary decency are reducible for the present purposes to the principles of waste, futility, and ferocity" (Veblen 228): that is, Male Display.

To live—survival—becomes inseparable from using others, in this zero-sum game. To be weak is miserable, where "miserable" does not denote unhappy—it denotes, rather, degraded—exploded on the scale of male competition, to have one's identity eviscerated. We saw what this means, concretely, in the case of Lycius in Keats's *Lamia* and of Chillingworth in *The Scarlet Letter*, a fearful shriveling of identity that is worse than death, indeed may result in death. It is better to die than suffer such defeat; defeat means self-implosion of identity as a kind of object lesson to others. One does not wish to be someone else's trophy, a locus for others to gloat.

Male Envy is thus the corollary of "possessive individualism," to use the term coined by political historian C. B. Macpherson: the governing ideology that emerges together with the Object Cosmology. It requires contempt of weakness (in oneself and in others), where "weakness" means not so much inability as mutual dependency, co-operation, and deviation from competitive values. Inevitably, it also demands the disruption of cooperative/equalizing arrangements, and so makes constant vigilance of aggressiveness necessary. One must guard the competitive field, keeping women and weaker males, as well as other races and nations, at the bottom of the compete/control hierarchy, or off it altogether.

This vigilance is internalized, so that it monitors consciousness in the manner of an unforgiving Freudian superego. One cannot police others without policing oneself. Such "censorship" is the hidden underpinning of society's obsession with individual success. It is thus no accident that Freud derived his concept of mental "censorship" in *The Interpretation of Dreams* from the political censorship of the Austro-Hungarian empire with which he was familiar: socio-political and personal control/repression interpenetrate.[37] Hartsock's dictum again comes to mind, "power appears as domination not only of others but of parts of oneself" (203), a point Klaus Theweleit elaborates in *Male Fantasies*.

* * *

As Object thinking intensifies, certain characteristic markers indicate its presence, especially the following assumptions:

- Reality is a pile of objects in space. That is, reality is *subject-space-object*.
- Hence the primary relationship is that of person-thing (with countless variants, e.g., society-nature, self-other, subject-object). Hence one relates to objects by controlling, measuring, using, wasting—manipulating from inside objects outside at a distance, in accord with the subject-space-object paradigm.
- Knowledge is a distillation or abstraction of material objects in space. Likewise, language is understood to be a mapping of objects, in which words are like labels corresponding to objects. Ideas and words that do not conform to this paradigm are suspect and are likely trivial or meaningless.
- People are driven by interest, that is self-interest, so that self-satisfaction is the aim of existence, expressed in the form of controlling other people and consuming objects.
- Religion becomes increasingly a matter of personal, private opinion, like other "free" "choices" in the "marketplace" of ideas.
- Since reality is objects in space, the actual basis or pediment of reality is space itself, and space is nothingness (compare the motif of emptiness in Male Envy).
- The model for reality, the way to understand it, is mechanism.

It should be emphasized, again, that the Object Cosmology had many progressive consequences, but the concern here is with the way its assumptions drive Male Envy, its destructive shadow. It should also be clear that "Object thinking" is a way of experiencing and perceiving: it is not the same as materialism in the philosophical or technical sense of materialism. It is a paradigm or mode of living in the world and not just a theory or philosophical position.

Male Envy is inevitable in Object thinking in the sense that it is *historically conditioned* and emerges as the Object Cosmology emerges. Milton's Satan is a herald of this mode of consciousness, but its real hegemony does not come until the period of the Industrial Revolution (after 1780), which is also the period in which the civilization we know today originates. The Industrial Revolution corresponds closely with the Romantic period; that is one reason why I have drawn upon Romantic narrative for examples. "In 1600, atomism was a 'radical' philosophy, destructive of the still prevailing scholastic world-picture. By 1700, atomism as a mechanical philosophy was, in England, the conservative view," notes Robert Kargon.[38] Other strains of thinking coexist with it, needless to say, but by about 1800, Object thinking dominated England and America and economically powerful areas of Europe, whence it spread throughout the world. Its roots and intellectual ancestry go back to ancient Greece, at least, but without capitalism—especially in its industrial phase—the Object Cosmology would have remained a latent, oppositional model of reality, just as science as we know it would have remained embryonic and undeveloped.

Once again, a cosmology in the sense of the term used here is a model of nature; but it is, much more, a picture or even mirror of the society that creates it, and that uses it as an essential means to rationalize its social structure—the class division and social roles imposed on its members. Hence it is not something speculative, primarily; it is something *practical*, something that defines for its members what they should do, and what they should not do; what is desirable, and what is not desirable. More subtly, it defines what is possible, and what is not possible; what is thinkable, and what is not thinkable.

It follows that "meaning" really comes down to conformity or resonance with the established cosmology. The more powerful that resonance, the "truer" the meaning, the more persuasive it is.

In other words, a cosmology establishes limits: it imposes a necessary frame of consciousness upon its members, and while different people may, individually, have different modes of thinking/seeing, they can no more choose their cosmology than they can choose their parents. Cosmology is always changing, of course; and one may not agree with the dominant model, or one may specialize in some variant on it, but to live in society requires thorough familiarity with its basic image-assumptions. A cosmology in this sense is a part of what people are and is as socially necessary as a common language is. Indeed, properly speaking, a cosmology *is* a language. Just as a language is infinite in complexity and in its effect on people, so is a cosmology; hence certain features that may seem simple or obvious require repeated attention, because complicated and unexpected consequences flow from them.

* * *

The actual working of Male Envy as a function of Object thinking must be understood concretely, not merely theoretically. A central text of Romanticism, Coleridge's *Rime of the Ancient Mariner*, is especially illuminating here. The poem is one of the most familiar in the language, but it looks different when explored from the point of view of Male Envy. With that purpose in mind, it has to be approached not as a "text," but as an imagination experiment, in the same manner as *Lamia* and other literary works in this study. I treat it in terms of thinking-in-images rather than as (failed or confused) abstract reasoning.

The Ancient Mariner has been subjected to decades of intensive academic processing, but its point as an illustration of the logic of Male Envy has seldom been attended to. Nevertheless, *The Ancient Mariner* is a lucid account, in the language of metaphor and image, of the inter-relations between Male Envy and Object thinking. More precisely, this narrative is a complex reaction *against* the

Object Cosmology, a probing of its horrors. It also poses an alternative model of reality in opposition to Object thinking, a shift which requires our most careful attention.

The Rime of the Ancient Mariner uses archaic language and is presented in the form of a ballad, an oral form with a history probably as old as human language itself; Romanticism supposedly celebrates subjectivity, but this poem has, like the ballad, the impersonality and plainness of the voice of authority. Moreover, the poem's archaism is a screen, in the manner of Freud's "screen memories": what *The Ancient Mariner* presents, in the language of metaphor and image, concerns Coleridge's own civilization, the culture of England in the rising surge of industrialization. Hence, the poem has a deeply contemporary resonance, as Jerome J. McGann and other critics have noted.[39]

In *The Rime of the Ancient Mariner*, a ship departs on a voyage into the Atlantic, but no hint is given of what the purpose of this voyage is. A terrible storm drives the ship off course, forcing it south into the Antarctic. We can be confident that this is not a trip for the sake of voyaging, nor a voyage of exploration, except by accident; it must be a commercial venture. A commercial venture heading south into the Atlantic Ocean in the late eighteenth century suggests a slaving expedition: the slave trade accelerated in the last half of the eighteenth century, peaking in the 1780s, providing a crucial source of the "so-called primitive accumulation," the unprecedentedly vast investment pool required by the "take-off" stage of the Industrial Revolution, with its heavy capital demands. Economic historian Roderick McDonald notes, for example, that "In both value and volume, the slave trade to Jamaica reached its peak between 1783 and 1808."[10] The figure of the Storm as a pursuing spirit (ll. 41-62) is an appropriate metaphor, driving the ship off its commercial course into the place of lost direction: the place where even the ocean freezes, and the ice becomes a monstrous predator ("It cracked and growled, and roared and howled" [l. 61]). Spiritually, all this is correct, suggesting a protective and protesting energy that rejects the cruel use of people as object-machines.

When the ship is lost in the Antarctic, the region of terrifying isolation and death, then, unexpectedly and mysteriously, the saintly Albatross appears. The crew greet this miraculous bird like "a Christian soul." Its advent signals salvation, for the ice suddenly opens up, and the ship is able to escape. In undisplaced terms, the Albatross is not simply a bird, but a spiritual being who makes the ice open and sets the ship free. If we see it in more displaced terms, as simply a bird, the Albatross saves the crew psychologically, showing by its very presence that there is life and hope even in the midst of death. In any case, Coleridge's bird is charged with profound significance, a fact perhaps most evident from the proverbial status that the Albatross has acquired in subsequent culture. The resonance of this image is not a matter of mere "figures" and verbal "tropes" or rhetorical "devices," but of the human imagination as it tries to comprehend reality in terms of meaning and non-meaning.

This is why what follows is so horrifying: the Mariner, without warning, kills the Albatross. This killing—one instinctively calls it murder—is performed with a "cross-bow." Apart from the pun on "cross," indicating that the killing of the Albatross is a ritual execution of the same type as the crucifixion of Christ, the cross-bow is a screen image for what is more likely a gun, just as the expedition itself belongs to the eighteenth century and not to some archaic period of ballad-making such as in "The Ballad of Sir Patrick Spence" (a favorite of Coleridge's), or similar relics of archaic time. I have already cited the gun as a power object: it is, more precisely, an emblem of Object thinking. Like the telescope, the gun possesses *power over distance*, in a worldview where space is what is ultimately real—is that which constitutes material objects as material objects. No space: no objects. And no objects: no reality.

But whether it is a gun or a cross-bow that the Mariner uses to kill with, the way it is used is very revealing. In fact, a number of elements in the murder of the Albatross are conspicuous—and puzzling. The obvious puzzle is why the Mariner does it. No explanation is given. The killing is presented brusquely and unexpectedly. He simply does it. We are told that the bird follows the ship and perches at night. Then, with a look of agony, the Mariner telling the story just says: "With my cross-bow / I shot the Albatross" (ll. 81-82). Extraordinary emphasis is given to this action: "Albatross," capitalized, is the final, climactic word of Part I. The action simply breaks at this point, in what is really an aporia. The story picks up again, in Part II, after a gap.

Gripped by a disaster fantasy, the superstitious crew at first angrily denounce the Mariner. Still, they are safe, the breeze blows, everything seems fine, nothing bad happens. So the crew change their mind and commend him for killing the bird. The "gloss" that Coleridge wrote and placed in the margin of the poem notes that "when the fog cleared off," the crew "justify" the killing of the Albatross, "and thus make themselves accomplices in the crime." But what the crew does not ask, and what the gloss does not explain, is the obvious question: Why does the Mariner kill the Albatross?

Inexperienced readers often regard the killing of the Albatross as a kind of scientific experiment. The crew are, in the manner of sailors, superstitious. The Mariner kills the bird to deconstruct superstition, to show there is nothing to fear; they should not believe in omens or spirits. This explanation resembles the pre-feminist reading of *Frankenstein*, that Victor Frankenstein is essentially good—a purist scientist totally dedicated to his experiment, an impartial and objective seeker of facts, who made a tragic mistake or "went too far." This is in fact Victor's view of himself; thus, his midnight raiding of graveyards and frequenting of slaughterhouses for body parts and his torturing of animals are simply scientific dedication. Likewise, the Mariner ignores human feelings of affection (if not obligation), because he is such a pure, honest seeker of truth, one who wishes to enlighten his fellow men—much as Victor claims his purpose was to bring intellectual light and freedom into a world of darkness. These views illustrate the values of Object thinking and merely compound the original question of why the Mariner does his violent deed. After all, the world of *The Ancient Mariner* is full of alien beings and mysterious forces, and not to believe in omens and spirits in such a world is to be out of touch with reality.[41]

There may not be an answer to the question, why does the Mariner kill the bird? a question which obviously has many layers and no single solution. But the sheer act, in itself, is revealing enough. The details are significant: (1) the killing of the Albatross was not an accident. The act required the utmost skill and a certain amount, at least, of planning. The Mariner did not, for example, lean by chance on the weapon, which then went off accidentally. On the contrary, he had to gain access to the weapon, which then had to be loaded (presumably also checked over and cleaned), aimed, and fired with care and precise timing. This is an act of calculation, planning, attention, careful observation. He would have to measure the height and position of the bird before firing; otherwise he would miss it. He fires only once—indeed, if more than one shot was needed, he likely would not have succeeded. The Mariner seems to be a good shot.

(2) The *deliberateness* of the Mariner's act is conspicuous, perhaps its most outstanding quality, especially when one recalls that the Mariner must have done it quickly. It was a *surprise*. If the other sailors had seen him, or seen him in time, they would have interfered; they did not do so, because the Mariner acted swiftly, decisively, ruthlessly, and secretly, like the general with his nuclear attack in *Dr. Strangelove*. This is not an act that can be undone or taken back.

(3) The Mariner is a man in control of his emotions: if he felt anything for the bird—or if he respected the crew's emotional attachment to the bird—he would have had difficulty shooting it, indeed would fail. One thinks of Robinson Crusoe on his island, unable to kill the first of the goats he raised: it had become a companion with whom he had emotional ties—more honestly, he loved the animal. Any feeling for the bird on the Mariner's part, or any feeling of respect for his fellow crew-members, would impede successful attack on it. The act is therefore most cruel and ungrateful, apart from being calculated and deliberate.

Another interesting feature of this killing is (4) the reaction of the crew. The crew loved the bird, even if the Mariner did not. They react strongly to his crime, first condemning it, then condoning it. The change in attitude is conspicuous, but in some ways this weathervane behavior is not the point. What matters is that the Mariner knows that the crew will react strongly—the poem goes out of its way to emphasize the love of the sailors for the bird and the eagerness with which they welcome it "in God's name," treating it "as a Christian soul," and feeding and watching it, as it, apparently, watches over them, and as, meanwhile, a mysterious spirit is said to "love" the bird from deep under the sea, and watches over it, as the Albatross watched over the crew.

What does this add up to, then? In a word: attention; command of attention. Commanding the attention of others, as noted earlier, is a vital element in the code of Male Envy. By killing the Albatross, the Mariner steals the attention of every single person on the ship: he seizes center stage. No one can ignore him now. He achieves instant notoriety. The absorption of attention, the focusing of the male gaze on the self, is a great desideratum of Male Envy, and the Mariner gets it in abundance. The assumption is clear: violence is the basic form of attention-getting, just as it is a basic form of entertainment.

The importance of this craving to control attention is evident at another bizarre moment of the story. When a mysterious ship appears in the distance, the Mariner thinks their problem—*his* problem—is solved:

> With throats unslaked, with black lips baked,
> We could nor laugh nor wail;
> Through utter drought all dumb we stood!
> I bit my arm, I sucked the blood,
> And cried, A sail! a sail!
>
> With throats unslaked, with black lips baked,
> Agape they heard me call:
> Gramercy! they for joy did grin,
> And all at once their breath drew in,
> As they were drinking all.
>
> See see! (I cried) she tacks no more
> Hither to work us weal;
> Without a breeze, without a tide,
> She steadies with upright keel   (ll. 157-170)

Again, what is striking here, when viewed in terms of Male Envy, is the way the Mariner seizes the attention of others by a grotesque and outlandish act—that of biting himself and drinking his own blood. He could have alerted his comrades to the approach of the ship (which we discover brings death for the crew) in some other, less extravagant way. Ships have bells, after all. The suggestion that the crew are able to speak without drinking their own blood—they're not that dry!—hangs over the passage. The phrase "Gramercy! they for joy did grin" sounds as if they *cry out* "Gramercy!" Hence the Mariner's act must be seen as what it is: violent attention-getting. Note also that this attention command *is* violent, in the sense of inflicting pain, whether on others, or on himself, as if the fundamental way to gain attention in Male Envy were by inflicting pain. The appearance of the motif of the special fluid (blood) is noteworthy here, too.

The killing of the Albatross is thus an act characterized by:

- mechanism; mechanical force and violence

- deliberation, not accident; planning and foresight; careful timing
- calculating reason: measurement (height and motion must be taken)
- skill in the use of weapons: prominence of the motif of the weapon
- hostility to his fellows, who would have stopped him if they could: not much "male bonding" here!
- power over an object at a distance: the epitome of control
- hence an act of isolation, self-identification, and separation from others, who are, in turn, demonstrated to be inferior to him
- neutralized feelings (no affection, no obligation, no sympathy)
- hence an act of objectification
- hence, too, a defiance of spiritual values; assertion of raw force as the principle governing reality

Above all, the killing of the Albatross is a potent bid for attention; a seizure of the gaze of others. In Male Envy, the male gaze is not bad—as it is in feminist analysis of the treatment of women; it is rather a *source of identity*, a way to prove importance in the eyes of others, which is what Male Envy is all about.

Indeed, as an object of attention, the Mariner substitutes himself for the Albatross. He has not only supplanted the Albatross as an object of attention, but he has seized the attention that the Albatross had gained for himself, and redoubled that attention by killing the bird. Killing the Albatross is a quite creditable Male Display. After all, the killing of animals is traditional as a means of creating tableaux of power, as a glance at the iconography of royalty, from the most ancient times onward, makes clear. Killing animals is a standard means of gaining attention from the powerful, from the gods, especially, and therefore also a means of demonstrating power to others. This may be one reason why it has been so popular with males; it is a strong power boost in the code of Male Envy.

In the background of this tableau is the principle of sacrifice: instead of sacrificing animals to a god, one sacrifices animals (preferably in large numbers) *to oneself*, as a means of generating feelings of inflated importance and personal power. Also, as a sacrifice, the Albatross is the only available victim—apart from fellow crew members. The feeling that it is a ritual killing hangs over this scene. Subtextually, it also suggests an offering to a god of rage, an offering given in order to secure exit from the horror at the bottom of the world—and also necessarily an act of worship. It suggests obeisance to the power—the *numen*—of ruthless, violent control. One kills as an act of worshiping kill-power.

In terms of Male Envy, killing the Albatross can only be viewed as a high accomplishment, worthy of praise. Hence the Mariner's omission. One does not say why one kills the animal: that would violate the sanctity of the blood-sacrifice involved, and the god it honors. In the code of Male Envy, silence is the speech of power.

In Veblen's analysis, hunting is a mode of conspicuous consumption: "It is, indeed, the most noticeable effect of the sportsman's activity to keep nature in a state of chronic desolation by killing off all living things whose destruction he can compass" (171).[42] There is only one animal in the Antarctic available to kill, and the Mariner finds it and kills it. He has in effect killed nature, or symbolically demonstrated mastery to the whole of nature. In Veblen, sports such as "hunting . . . afford an exercise for dexterity and for the emulative ferocity and astuteness characteristic of predatory life" (173), where "predatory life" is Veblen's expression for competitive market culture. It is a means of training the skills and exhibiting the values of that culture. The Mariner shows "emulative ferocity" in his seizure of attention and "astuteness" in the skill of his killing, his manipulation of death.

We are now in a position to offer an answer to the question, why the Mariner kills the Albatross. In terms of the code of Male Envy, the question needs to be rephrased: why *not* kill the Albatross? It is obviously a rational, desirable thing to do. *Of course* a man would want to cruelly kill the animal that had done so much for him and for his group of fellows. Evidently, therefore, killing the Albatross does more than gain attention: it demonstrates the personal power of the Mariner. It shows that he is not dependent. In the code of Male Envy, nothing is worse than weakness, and weakness is by definition a state of dependency: precisely the state that the Albatross symbolizes to someone of the Mariner's mentality. For in the icy desert of hope in which horrible death is imminent, he and the crew are utterly dependent on the bird, who came to them at their time of greatest need.

By killing the Albatross, the Mariner erases the humiliation of dependency. He shows that he is dependent on nobody—almost, like Satan's explanation of his origin in *Paradise Lost*, self-generated. He needs nobody and nothing, because he is strong.

* * *

Another aspect of the murder of the Albatross has to be noted, therefore: the Mariner's achievement of a power-over relationship with the bird. He kills it, and by killing it he shows not only that he can do what he likes to the bird, but that the bird's life is owing to him and at his pleasure. He annexes the bird's identity to himself; this annexation later is acted out in ironic form when the bird's carcass is hung round his neck. Once again, achieving power-over relationships is a primary goal of Male Envy and in itself a means to other goals. A power-over relationship enables one to dispense with obligations to inferior beings (humiliating obligations clearly), allowing one to enjoy egocentric gratification, with less inhibition. The avoidance of obligation is a recurring motif in Male Envy and discloses the revulsion that commitment to inferiors inspires in the dedicated competitor. To be obliged to inferior beings, whether people (women, children, weaker males) or animals, is simply to become inferior oneself, to drop on the compete/control hierarchy, a fate to be avoided at all costs, since it entails a threat to one's very identity as constituted by that hierarchy.

The Rime of the Ancient Mariner presents the mystery of evil with unmatched force and precision. Indeed, it is one of the few works of highbrow literature that has had a hold on the imagination of subsequent culture generally, and for good reason, since it spells out fundamental anxieties and obsessions of the model of reality that has dominated society since Coleridge's time.

But the precision with which it translates the axioms of Object thinking into images and acts needs to be grasped with equal precision. Object thinking takes it for granted that reality consists of a pile of objects in space. These objects can be controlled, because they are deployed according to predictable laws. Since reality is visualized in this way, so are people: as objects deployed according to fixed laws. People are more complicated objects than most objects, to be sure, but they are objects nonetheless. Hence they are subject to control, too, if one has the knowledge—and daring—to seize that control.

Therefore, this model of reality inevitably privileges certain ways of relating to experience: in its view, for example, knowledge is essentially the measurement of objects (and the collation of measurements); it valorizes calculation and power over objects at a distance. This power to control and move objects at a distance, as Keats notes in *Isabella*, is what merchants possess, recalling the mystic power of gravity, which also controls objects at a distance (as if merchant power were equally a part of the constitution of nature). The killing of the Albatross in *The Ancient Mariner* illustrates key attitudes of the Object Cosmology generally: it enacts Object thinking. If reality is a pile of objects in space, it is rational to try to control/accumulate those objects; in fact, one *must* do so in order to survive. This process of control/accumulation requires parallel attitudes toward human beings and life forms generally. Measuring, controlling, and owning in turn feed back into the axiom that reality, as objects in space, is to be used and discarded.

The belief that everything can be explained by the configuration of objects was a major advance. For instance, the idea that natural disasters are the result of divine anger weakens dramatically with the rise of Object thinking: such horrors are the result of the movement of objects in space—not of God's desire to punish human disobedience. The unprecedented expansion of productive power was a related advance: this is the true starting point of Adam Smith's *Wealth of Nations*. Smith attributes this expansion of wealth to "the division of labor," but the division of labor is only a partial explanation; indeed, the division of labor is a screen for the real reason, which is that society can now produce, with the same quantity of labor, far more than ever before—thanks to the refinement of *capitalist* social relations. In other words, it is the market system and its values that have generated the expanding current of wealth, and not the division of labor in or by itself.

In fact, Object thinking stimulates the great dream of civilization, the dream of the end of poverty and the possibility of abundance for all. William Godwin's *Political Justice* (1793) insists on the things that truly do matter: decent food, clothing, and shelter for everybody; the capacity to travel, to learn, to communicate; and the right to realize one's potential as creator or worker. Such authentic goals are a permanent legacy of the Enlightenment. But the benefits of the Object Cosmology were accompanied by evils, evils that were both new in kind and essentially identical with the horrors of Male Envy. Thus, in Object thinking, the logical goal of human existence is to accumulate objects, as a means of achieving happiness in this life (not in some afterlife). But this goal brings with it two disturbing byproducts. One is a conviction that taking advantage of others is not only necessary but a positive good; so that exploitation is rationalized and valued in ways that would have been impossible before. The second is alienation as the feeling of meaninglessness.

These require closer examination, identifying the consequences of Object thinking as the basis of Male Envy:

(1) Exploitation. If other people are essentially objects in space, then it is right and reasonable to use them and to discard them when they are no longer useful. In fact, people *must* be exploited—exploited in the technical sense that people receive less than the value of what they produce. And what would be the point of hiring someone unless the wages paid to that person were less than the value of what the person produced? Without exploitation, there is no accumulation of capital—and hence no civilization. The capacity to cheat and betray becomes essential when it is essential to take advantage of others' weaknesses. This process need not be as nasty as it sounds, for the boundary line between getting a good deal and cheating or lying is very difficult to ascertain with moral exactitude. Isn't the definition of a good business deal buying cheap and selling dear? How does one determine when this is cheating someone? One praises such practice, not condemns it. Taking advantage of others acquires the character of a positive good in Object thinking, even if it is seldom stated openly. Silence is golden, after all.

In truth, there is a serious difficulty for ethics under the hegemony of the Object Cosmology. If reality is a pile of objects in space, then what sense does it make to speak of "good" and "evil"? Logically, these can only be subjective notions—something inside the head, not something "objective"—i.e., not something real. Therefore the tendency is to translate "good" and "evil" into some form of natural law. Thus, "good" means following the laws of nature, and evil breaking them—or rather, trying to break them, for by definition a law of nature cannot be broken. That is why it is a "law," an invariable principle, as opposed to a deliberate, willed command. This is the basis of Malthus's arguments about property and population in his *Essay on Population*. Any attempt to reconstruct property or power relations in a more equitable way is in fact a violation of the laws of nature, laws that are ordained by the Almighty.[43]

The absurdity of such arguments as identifying property with divinity has not diminished their effectiveness. As Joyce Appleby puts it, in a classic study: "No more powerful notion came out of the seventeenth century than that of a natural order of economic relations impervious to social engineering and political interference."[44] The seventeenth century is a bit early for such thinking, which becomes hegemonic later: "The nineteenth century was virtually unanimous in seeing the human as an aggressive animal," notes Peter Gay.[45] Once this way of thinking is established, it intensifies and ramifies in all directions, especially because of Darwin. Darwinian evolution offered a protected space in which to articulate social principles that would normally have to be accepted in silence and not openly proclaimed. Nonetheless, for Object thinkers, inequality is sacred, and the freedom to exploit others is equivalent in sanctity to one of Christ's Beatitudes. Nothing must be allowed to interfere. This in turn is expressed in the compete/control hierarchy itself, which is a monument to inequality.

(2) Alienation. The term "alienation" has a venerable history in nineteenth-century thought, in Hegel and in Marx. But, of course, the concept of alienation goes much further back, originating in the Christian belief in the Fall of humankind.[46] In traditional Christian and feudal civilization (the Old Cosmology), human beings are fallen. Alienated from God by sin, the troubles they endure in this world are morally intelligible, because they are the result of human disobedience to divine authority, and God's anger as a response to that disobedience is just and reasonable. At the same time, a final reconciliation is imminent, either with the second coming of Christ, or with death, judgment, and an afterlife, hopefully in Heaven, as Blake's angel assumes. There is a reward for all the suffering—for those who obey, that is.

In the Object Cosmology, however, while it is an advantage to get rid of the notion that the evils that plague human beings—famine, earthquakes, disease, etc.—are punishments inflicted by an angry God, nevertheless, the old God took at least an interest in human beings. He was not merely a mechanical force or a personification of impersonal laws—something one can hardly imagine praying to. As the Object Cosmology evolves, by contrast, God becomes increasingly problematic, if not actually unnecessary. At first, as noted earlier, intellectuals tend to reconstruct God in deistic terms, as an engineer or "providence" that oversees the machine of nature and keeps it wound up and running. God becomes, in short, a kind of businessman with an investment in nature and therefore is obliged to maintain nature in good running order. Ultimately, this attitude becomes a deification or worship of the market system.

Christianity itself, meanwhile, tends to glue the old God, the warrior-judge-king, on to the Object Cosmology, where He does not really fit, but where He supplies certain necessary functions—the functions of looking after His believers when they are dead and punishing their enemies. The notion that the Bible can be read "literally" is in fact an Object notion. It assumes that reality is actually a pile of objects in space, and words are a mapping of those objects—and the Bible is no exception.[47] Its words correspond to actual movements of physical objects in space; this correspondence is what makes it "true," not its origin in a higher being. What such literalism really does, clearly, is to deify Object thinking. It does not concern faith, but is the worship of a certain way of thinking about words, and hence about reality, and has nothing to do with God.

Indeed, the inner logic of the Object model would seem to be atheistic. Philosopher of science E. J. Dijksterhuis notes:

> No more glaring contrast between an idea and its elaboration is conceivable than the antithesis between Newton's conviction that the order of the planetary system constitutes an irrefutable proof of the existence of an intelligent First Cause and the reply which Laplace, the author of *Mécanique Céleste*, is reported to have made to Napoléon when the latter asked him why he had not mentioned the Creator anywhere in his work: *Sire, j'ai pu me passer de cette hypothèse.*[48]

"Sire, I have been able to do without that hypothesis." God is not necessary to the machine of nature, any more than a king is necessary to oversee the market, which runs quite well on its own—again, like nature. Logically, for Object thinking, death is extinction, like a candle going out.[49] The Object Cosmology is not only atheistic, but essentially amoral. Given these implications, it becomes ever more urgent to let self-interest have free rein in the pursuit of happiness now. Get it while you can.

Panic thus underlies Object thinking. It is a reasonable panic. For if reality consists of objects in space, it follows that what is really real is not so much objects, as space itself. Space is a very difficult concept for philosophy to make sense of, because the notion of space as a measurable entity, when there are no limits, no containing walls, no reference points, is intellectually impossible to encompass.[50] But in the practical world of imaginative sense, space is visualized as emptiness, like air: it is an opening to be filled. If there were no space, there would be no objects; no reality. Hence the primal, ultimate reality is that which makes objects possible—space: but space is fundamentally nothingness. Object thinking thus treats space as the ultimate and absolute and, to that extent, deifies it. One notices this tendency as early as Newton, where space is visualized as the "sensorium" of deity, in effect the mind of God.

It is interesting that Milton's Satan is already very familiar with this logic and argues to his subordinate devils that "Space may create new worlds." That is, reality mysteriously comes out of the nothingness of space and may return to it, as if space were a new god. The primacy of space in Object thinking is one reason I began this chapter with Blake's *Marriage of Heaven & Hell*. The angel's heaven turns out to be empty space: his heaven is "nothing." What he really believes in, therefore, is thus space; that is, nothingness. And if you believe in nothing, then you are authorized to do anything.

Moreover, if what is most real is nothing, the feeling of alienation is built into the very construction of reality. It is not surprising, as a consequence, that imagery of the void, of the abyss, of emptiness, and of related gaps and spaces,[51] becomes prominent in Romantic and post-Romantic literature, as an emblem of "inner" emptiness, of alienation in its most terrifying form. One seeks the ultimate—and finds a nothingness there. An emblem for this alienation is the Marabar cave in E. M. Forster's *A Passage to India*, in which the character Mrs. Moore has a shocking encounter with nothingness that leaves her nauseated, psychically crushed. Angst, as the fear of nothing, has a peculiar intensity because of the way Object thinking permeates our culture. It coheres with the metaphysics of the Object Cosmology. As a feeling that responds to the metaphysical nothingness that is the ultimately real, it implies that it is better not to feel at all; better ignore the nothingness and simply numb oneself to its horror, like a machine, by means of routine or drugs. Or the most potent anodyne of all: the drug of controlling and numbing others.

Thus, alienation becomes the feeling that one is a machine oneself, just as becoming a machine is, ironically, a solution to alienation. One no longer feels it. But either way, machines do not matter. Hence it is all right to use and exploit people-machines, including oneself, so that alienation supports exploitation, just as exploitation sponsors alienation.

Machines do not have feelings, needless to say. Or rather, feelings may well exist, but they are regarded as of no consequence. They are a kind of distortion of the reasoning-calculating power, which, as we have seen, is the valid approach to take toward reality, given that reality is a pile of objects in space. One can see here how Object thinking underlies the code of Male Envy, where emotion is simply weakness. Emotion is a dangerous opening to one's enemies, something to hide, silence, or eliminate. Males are told not to feel pain; they must "take it like a man," but to take it like a man in practice means making someone *else* "take it like a man." The paradigm of the body as machine thus applies to men with double force. The intensive association of guns with the male body, and cars with the male body, is familiar enough. A man is a mechanism, requiring various kinds of fuel, of course ("calories")—but not requiring emotion, any more than a tank or a forklift require emotion. The exception is anger, which is the acceptable male emotion in the code of Male Envy. Anger, however, is really a weapon in itself and so does not count. The fact that this metaphoric equation (male = machine) is utterly absurd has not, once again, diminished its effectiveness. That is because it resonates so closely with the dominant cosmology, as well as facilitating the working of Male Envy. If one is a weapon oneself—if one is constituted as a weapon, as a force-inflictor—one is more likely to "succeed." It is an advantage to be a machine without feelings.

Alienation is the feeling that one is ultimately nothing, and that life is meaningless. It is itself a feeling, but it is a peculiar one, because it does not have the sharp edges or clarity that emotions such as grief, joy, or fear have: it is a compound of "despair, meaninglessness, absurdity, anomie," as Laurel Holliday puts it.[52] In fact, alienation is more like the erasure or repression of feeling, and in this respect it is merely consistent thinking. Machines do not feel, therefore I do not feel: logic run amok. One should recall the feeling of "losing" in connection with the compete/control hierarchy. Alienation may be understood variously, but it is in substance *the same as losing*, the experience of being defeated in control struggles, including the dread of being defeated. For as already noted, one of the ways that the alienation of the Object Cosmology can be repressed and silenced is by "winning" on the compete/control hierarchy, a process exactly designed to divert feelings of meaninglessness, burying them deeper within the self.

To put this more precisely, alienation opens up another aspect of the winning/losing axis. If reality is a meaningless concatenation of particles, and people are equally a meaningless concatenation of human particles, and the self is a random event; then it is only reasonable that one would be inundated by painful feelings of alienation. To silence these feelings, one rises on the compete/control hierarchy, a total package of distraction from the anxieties of alienation, but yielding "a restless proclivity for interaction that will be competitive and conflict-oriented in style."[53] A prominent element here is satisfaction derived from the envy of others and, where possible, the losing or suffering of others. This suffering has the added advantage, apart from being diverting and pleasing to observe, of magically transferring pain away from the self on to the sufferer-losers. It is a kind of anodyne, and like anodynes in general, it is addictive.

One of the typifying features of Male Envy is that it is not only malicious, but obsessive. Ironically, obsession is by definition a loss of control: one cannot choose whether to be obsessed or not; if one could choose, one would not be obsessed. As a logical result, obsession merely reinforces feelings of alienation and loss of control: the very feelings it is determined to wipe out.

* * *

The Rime of the Ancient Mariner is concerned deeply with the assumptions of Object thinking. The crucial event, the Mariner's killing of the Albatross, in particular displays its logic. In Object terms, the killing is rational and logical, even if there is no practical utility to be gained. What is even more interesting is the way Coleridge unfolds the consequences of this action; that is to say, the consequences of Object thinking itself, with its Male-envious afflatus.

After the Mariner kills the bird, everything looks fine. Denounced by the crew at first, he is then hailed and commended, so that he gets the benefits of both negative and positive attention, as well as the excitement of triumph, of saying to the crew, in effect, I told you so. I am a winner.

But it all begins to fall apart when the ship is becalmed. They are suspended in a limbo, a twilight zone of lifelessness and unreality:

> Down dropt the breeze, the sails dropt down,
> 'Twas sad as sad could be;
> And we did speak only to break
> The silence of the sea!
>
> All in a hot and copper sky,
> The bloody Sun, at noon,
> Right up above the mast did stand,
> No bigger than the Moon.
>
> Day after day, day after day,
> We stuck, nor breath nor motion;
> As idle as a painted ship
> Upon a painted ocean. (ll.107-118)

The eerie feeling of descending into a world of two dimensions could hardly be expressed more powerfully: this is the real unreal. The physical evaporates into a hallucination, as the sensory dissolves into an alien and hostile pressure.

Then the Mariner sees the spectral ship approach, and bites himself. He wants, it seems, to be credited a second time with bringing good fortune—first when he killed the Albatross, the desired wind sprang up; now, he has sighted a ship on the horizon that will rescue them. Little does he know that the ship is a metaphor approaching, not a ship at all; and that that metaphor is "Life-in-Death" (= Alienation) for him, and "Death" (that is, release) for the crew. The ship that appears contains two figures, a female being named "Life-in-Death" and a spectre identified as "Death," and they are casting dice to decide which one will "win" the Mariner and his fellows. *Chance* is the arbitrator-master. At its fundamental level, reality is chance mutation, a clash of conflicting forces.

In the event, chance consigns the Mariner to "Life-in-Death." The decisive part place of chance in *The Ancient Mariner* recalls the conspicuous role of Chaos in *Paradise Lost* and of chance in Satan's thinking. "Life-in-Death" resembles another personification, the allegorical character named "Sin" in Milton's *Paradise Lost*, whom Satan finds beautiful and monstrous; she is accompanied by a shadowy warrior named "Death." The crew in Coleridge's poem die, finding the release that the Mariner cannot find. The Mariner is now the prey of an alien female power. In terms of Male Envy, he is utterly collapsed, nullified. He is alone on the ocean, surrounded by monsters and hallucinations, unable to relax or rest, without water to drink in the extreme heat. Above all he is vulnerable: totally exposed to whatever forces may pass by; he

Object Thinking

has no protection, no control over his situation. From being in the power position, he is now a passive object even to himself. He is isolated and does not know where he is; all he knows is that he is surrounded by the dead, while he is still alive. In fact, given the terror of vulnerability and the horror of physical contact with the dead, he wishes to die—but cannot. Desire and control dwindle to utter frustration. This is what the oxymoron Life-in-Death means: total alienation. We have seen the same sort of state before, when Pip is eviscerated by the return of Magwitch; when Chillingworth is evacuated by Dimmesdale; when Apollonius annihilates Lycius.

The Ancient Mariner sums up this state of dread with peculiar completeness and intensity, as follows:

- isolation, aloneness; no communication—no one to communicate with
- inability to pray; evacuation of spiritual identity, including pity
- exhaustion and physical discomfort, even mental dissociation; confused thinking
- reality is random; random interaction is fundamental
- no rest; sleep deprivation
- extreme thirst, extreme heat
- inability to die or let go; to be emotionally dead while still alive
- obsession: nothing changes or moves
- disappearance of time
- total vulnerability; no protection; exposure to random or unknown forces, forces that can neither be predicted nor controlled
- frustration
- hallucinations and monstrous perceptions, disaster fantasies

Also: Coleridge emphasizes the evil-eye gaze, the torment of being stared at by those who are hostile but more powerful, so that his prize of being the object of other men's envious attention now turns inside out, into its terrible opposite:

> I closed my lids, and kept them close,
> And the balls like pulses beat;
> For the sky and the sea, and the sea and the sky
> Lay like a load on my weary eye,
> And the dead were at my feet.

The Mariner may close his eyes, but he cannot shut out the horror:

> The cold sweat melted from their limbs,
> Nor rot nor reek did they:
> The look with which they looked on me
> Had never passed away.

> An orphan's curse would drag to hell
> A spirit from on high;
> But oh! more horrible than that
> Is the curse in a dead man's eye!
> Seven days, seven nights, I saw that curse,
> And yet I could not die.   (ll. 248-262)

Coleridge's gloss to the poem adds: "the curse liveth for him *in the eye of the dead men*," of whom there are not a few: "four times fifty." The passage is blackly ironic, as far as Male Envy is concerned. The Mariner now possesses that great desideratum, the gaze of his fellows—and he wishes he didn't.

And yet, in this appalling solipsism, the Mariner is curiously compulsive:

> Alone, alone, all, all alone
> Alone on a wide wide sea!
> And never a saint took pity on
> My soul in agony.
>
> The many men, so beautiful!
> And they all dead die lie:
> And a thousand thousand slimy things
> Lived on; and so did I.
>
> I looked upon the rotting sea,
> And drew my eyes away;
> I looked upon the rotting deck,
> And there the dead men lay.
>
> I looked to heaven, and tried to pray;
> But or ever a prayer had gushed,
> A wicked whisper came, and made
> My heart as dry as dust.   (ll. 232-247)

What is the whisper? This question is nowhere answered, and in this respect resembles the prior, determining question of why the Mariner kills the bird. First mentioning, then silencing, the "wicked whisper" draws attention to it: what for? The saint in heaven no more pities the Mariner than the Mariner pitied the Albatross. Male Envy is tenacious to the point of compulsion, and a logical inference about the "wicked whisper" is that what it says is: "I'm glad I did it!" No remorse, no pity; but a compulsive holding on and refusal to change, like Pharaoh in the Exodus narrative, whose hardened heart led him to grip his power position unrelentingly, in spite of being opposed by the creator of the universe. In other contexts, this persistence might be a virtue; here it is the pride that would rather die than accept dependency, whether dependency on nature, on lesser beings, on others, on one's own vulnerable emotional life, or on God or some spiritual identity. In Male Envy, the ego is self-begotten, alone, absolute, and can do what it likes.

This self-absoluteness is profoundly characteristic of Male-envious yearning. Hence it underwrites what is the standard fantasy of science fiction: the fantasy of attaining total world domination. Normally, it is the villain who wants this domination, but the fantasy is projected on to the villain as if to exculpate the protagonist (and others) from the same fantasy. This scenario turns up in science fiction with what would be irritating frequency, if it were not the expression of something so central to Object thinking; in other words, it repeats and re-enacts a central fantasy–in effect a fetish—of the dominant cultural mode of perception itself. When a fantasy is so fundamental, repetition appears to be highly original and new, rather than what it is: the hypnotic display of a primary datum of social consciousness. Its primacy in Object culture is indicated by how early it appears; it is already the basis of Percy Shelley's *Prometheus Unbound*, in the form of Jupiter, who seeks total mastery of the cosmos; and it is "always already" present in what is usually called the first science fiction novel, Mary Shelley's *Frankenstein* (not to mention Satan in *Paradise Lost*). It achieves apotheosis in Orwell's *1984* (1948), where the goal of the ruling class is not simply obedience by its subordinates, but their total, "voluntary" devotion, which is what it calls "love." "Love" in Male Envy is, after all, simply control power.

The Rime of the Ancient Mariner traces the logic, or rather the horror, of Male Envy and the framework of assumptions that supports it, Object thinking:

- measuring, calculating (requiring separation, detachment)
- controlling; using
- owning; claiming exclusive access/mastery
- competing
- destroying (control-use-discard)
- power at a distance
- person-thing relations; power-over relationships

In *The Ancient Mariner*, the action takes us from this complex, condensed in the murder of the Albatross, into the total alienation illustrated by the Mariner's horrors, or what Coleridge refers to as "Life-in-Death." This sequence is causal: one leads to the other. Exploitation unfolds as alienation. Male Envy, which is the ongoing exercise of the values of control, is thus permeated by horror: what Marlow in Conrad's *Heart of Darkness* (1899) finds at the supporting bottom level of European "civilization": an utter nightmare too appalling to be seen directly for more than a moment, before it must be screened off—and silenced.

* * *

The Rime of the Ancient Mariner illustrates the code of Male Envy as it emerges out of the Object Cosmology. But *The Ancient Mariner* is comprehensive in another way. For it also poses an alternative model to Object thinking. This alternative model of reality can be found throughout Romantic writing and is in fact implicit in the genre of Romantic narrative itself. Some account of this alternative model, or "Transform" thinking as it may be called, is necessary, before descending in the next chapter into the hell of Male Envy, where violence becomes a noble and even holy imperative, and the very basis of morality. Violence is the corollary of male fascination with anger—the sacredness of male rage.

The Ancient Mariner has a clearly marked turning point, the blessing of the water-snakes:

> Beyond the shadow of the ship,
> I watched the water-snakes:
> They moved in tracks of shining white,
> And when they reared, the elfish light
> Fell off in hoary flakes.
>
> Within the shadow of the ship
> I watched their rich attire:
> Blue, glossy green, and velvet black,
> They coiled and swam; and every track
> Was a flash of golden fire.
>
> O happy living things! no tongue
> Their beauty might declare:
> A spring of love gushed from my heart,
> And I blessed them unaware:
> Sure my kind saint took pity on me,
> And I blessed them unaware.
>
> The self-same moment I could pray;
> And from my neck so free
> The Albatross fell off, and sank
> Like lead into the sea.   (ll. 272-291)

The gloss to the last stanza reads: "The spell begins to break."

What happens in this passage is the opposite and the counterpart of the killing of the Albatross. It is a not-doing, rather than a doing: the deconstruction of the killing. Indeed it is the deconstruction of action in general conceived as controlling, for it is an act that is not an act. The Mariner blesses the water-snakes *without thinking about it*; it is involuntary, not deliberate; it is an act of sensation and spontaneous expression, and not of calculation and reason. It originates with the mere experience of *seeing*, nothing more (as if looking were simple!). The mere sensory opening unfolds into a dramatic feast of the senses, and of imagination:

- light ("tracks of shining white")
- mesmerizing motion ("They coiled and swam; and every track / Was a flash of golden fire")
- color ("shining white," "Blue, glossy green," "velvet black, "flash of golden fire")
- tactile sensation ("hoary flakes," "rich *attire*")

When the Mariner spontaneously watches the water-snakes, it is a looking which unites. It does not separate, as in the subject-space-object paradigm with its control-over-distance compulsion. This in turn decodes the preoccupation with the eye in Male Envy, where gaze is a means of establishing and commanding distance, a signifier of power-over.

This feast of the senses is precisely what Isabella in Keats is excluded from. In heightened sensation, the ego-centered consciousness is suspended or surrounded and transformed by sheer sensory power. But this sensation is not merely a physical event; it has the effect of expanding consciousness. The vivid heightening of experience modulates into a burst of inner energy: "A spring of love gushed from my heart." Emotional life revives after the desiccating egoism that has preceded—emotional sensation which connects the Mariner with that most alien of creatures, the sea-snake. But it also connects the conscious mind with unconscious feeling. Finally, it connects his ego-self with a spiritual identity, so that suddenly he is able to bless—and to be blessed—and to pray: "Sure my kind saint took pity on me, / And I blessed them unaware. / The self-same moment I could pray." It is a complex moment of re-connection, in which the human, the natural, and the divine are linked together.

It is also a moment of release: the guilt and the horror of the past slips free—the body of the martyred Albatross falls from his neck and is absorbed by the sea. In the lines that follow, the Mariner praises the power of sleep. That is, his ego is able to let go, and he is able to rest, after a long period of exhausting self-assertion and obsessiveness. The motif of *release*, of letting go of the control compulsion that makes life hell, is prominent: release unfolds as refreshment and rest. He sleeps (and dreams); dew falls (an image of grace); it rains; his whole being drinks in the refreshing liquid:

I moved, and could not feel my limbs:
I was so light—almost
I thought that I had died in sleep,
And was a blessed ghost.   (ll. 305-308)

Metaphorically the Mariner has indeed died and been resurrected ("ghost" here means "spirit," not night-terror). The motif of the divine suddenly becomes prominent, but here it is the divine visualized in *female* terms: "To Mary Queen the praise be given!"

Nature, once stuck in an hallucinatory two-dimensional unreality, abruptly comes to life, too—"soon I heard a roaring wind":

> The upper air burst into life!
> And a hundred fire-flags sheen
> To and fro they were hurried about!
> And to and fro, and in and out,
> The wan stars danced between.   (ll. 309, 313-317)

Nature is celebrating.

This phase of *The Ancient Mariner* displays certain key motifs:

- a moment of receptivity that interrupts obsession
- heightened sensation: color, motion, texture: seing more, and more deeply
- absorption of ego-consciousness into intense sensation
- spontaneous utterance; recovery of power of speech; communication power
- recovery of emotional life; return of the power to love
- re-connection: the human with the natural; the self with the self—with the unconscious mind and with emotion; the human with the divine
- release; letting go of the past and of obsession
- peace, refreshment, sleep, dream, renewal; waking, resurrection
- water symbolism (imagery of life, grace, rebirth)
- animals (snake, albatross—later, singing birds)
- recovery of energy in nature; celebration
- valuing of the unconscious

The contrast with the horrors of vulnerability/obsession in the earlier phase of the plot could hardly be more dramatic.

The Mariner undergoes other ordeals, but a decisive change has occurred. The poem ends as the Mariner returns home, and the narrative rejoins its frame —the Mariner telling his story to a guest at a wedding. As people pour out of the church, the Mariner speaks of his love of prayer:

> To walk together to the kirk,
> And all together pray,
> While each to his great Father bends,

Old men, and babes, and loving friends
And youths and maidens gay!

Farewell, farewell! but this I tell
To thee, thou Wedding-Guest!
He prayeth well, who loveth well
Both man and bird and beast.

He prayeth best, who loveth best
All things both great and small;
For the dear God who loveth us,
He made and loveth all.   (ll. 605-617)

The Mariner mysteriously disappears, and the Wedding Guest is left with the shock of his tale.

Usually, the content of the final lines is regarded as trivial—as hopelessly unequal to the various miseries and struggles that have preceded, as though nothing could match the painful disasters that dominate the narrative (especially ideas that look so simple). Critics scorn these stanzas, as if the open expression of spiritual convictions, in simple and direct language, were *ipso facto* inferior. But these lines are ironic in the reverse sense; that is, they look simple, even simplistic, but actually convey profound significance that resonates and deepens when studied with attention. In part, this is because of the emphasis on images in the poem, the posing and contemplating of mental images, which have their own kind of logic, the logic of imaginable forms. This logic, as the French feminist philosopher Michèle Le Doeuff argues (and also Freud in *The Interpretation of Dreams*), cannot be simply reduced to abstract ideas or transposed to propositions which can then be proved or disproved. Like a cosmology, images are both hypothetical and practical, rather than simple assertions: a guide to reality rather than a representation of reality.

The Ancient Mariner closes with a subtle reconstitution of religion. Prayer and love are identified with each other—to love is to pray: this is hardly orthodox Christianity, by any means. And this love extends to all beings, whereas in traditional Christianity love is love of God and of one's neighbor—the difference is significant. The emphasis, furthermore, is *communal*: spirituality unites people with one another, just as it unites the human and the natural—and the divine with the human. It is not an individualizing or ego-oriented function. Finally, the simplicity of the language suggests an appeal to another level of identity than that of the analytic-evaluative or self-conscious ego. The concluding lines thus repeat the blessing which is the turning point of the action.

The religion of the concluding passage is expressed in the language of traditional Christianity, but the actual content and substance is not orthodox.[54] Thus, the human, the natural, and the divine are fused—whereas traditional Christianity is built on separation. In traditional Christianity, God is emphatically *not* His creation: this separation is the starting point of orthodox theology. Human beings are not God (except once, in Jesus), they are separate from Him and need to be redeemed by Him. Nature, in turn, is specifically subordinated to the use of human beings and has no spiritual value in traditional theology. The subtly different spirituality of the concluding lines of *The Ancient Mariner* is consistent with the way that the divine is visualized in the poem, usually in female terms rather than in male, as in the reference to "Mary." Animals—the Albatross and the snakes—are unusually prominent, perhaps more prominent than in any fiction before Coleridge. The use of the snake is itself striking, given its negative associations in Christianity, in the crucial Garden of Eden story especially (it might be added that sea snakes are among the most poisonous creatures on earth). The theology, if that is the right word, of *The Ancient Mariner*, is that sin originates in human separation from the divine/human/natural identity. Indeed, that is what sin is: not so much an act or set of acts, as a state of mind which generates destructive actions. "Sin," in short, becomes the destructiveness of Object thinking.

This in turn draws attention to another peculiar feature of Coleridge's narrative. When the Mariner "blesses" the water-snakes, the action is not an action of the same type as his killing of the Albatross—it is a receiving—an "act" of receptivity, and hence implies a redefinition of action. Meaningful action is not the exercise of control over a separate object, in the Male-envious context of competing with others, but is rather a receptivity that unfolds into action from a deeper level of the self than the conscious will or acquisitive ego. It is not a matter of control but of the release of control.

Furthermore, the Mariner is alone when he sees and blesses the transcendent beauty of the world, and participates in that beauty as a spiritual event; nevertheless, his aloneness is not the solitariness of egocentric control compulsions. On the contrary, his experience of the blessing is incomplete until he communicates his tale to others, so that he has become a kind of evangelist:

> I pass, like night, from land to land;
> I have strange power of speech;
> That moment that his face I see,
> I know the man that must hear me:
> To him my tale I teach.   (ll. 586-590)

The Mariner resembles a reformed alcoholic or drug addict: one who struggled out of a horrendous enslavement to false thinking and destructive practice. The Mariner's telling of the tale—his spreading of the message—is not a matter of personal individual will, but rather a synchronizing of his will with another kind of rhythm, over which he cannot exercise conscious control:

> Since then, at an uncertain hour,

> That agony returns:
> And till my ghastly tale is told,
> This heart within me burns.   (ll. 582-585)

The rupture with the continuum of the human/natural/divine is a permanent scar; the Mariner always will understand what alienation means—not as an abstract idea, but as lived experience.

* * *

The code of Male Envy is rooted in Object thinking; hence the exploration of this large and complex subject in this chapter. One simply cannot understand the logic of Male Envy without grasping its rootedness in the Object model of reality. *The Rime of the Ancient Mariner* illustrates the experimentation with an alternative worldview which is characteristic of the Romantic writers. Thus, once Object thinking becomes established and the code of Male Envy is increasingly understood as its unavoidable, rational, and indeed necessary consequence, a reaction begins. Writers formulate a critique of Object thinking and an alternative to it. This reaction is largely unconscious, even instinctive; it is not a matter of deliberate calculation, and includes some rather uninhibited speculation.

When Romantic literature is approached as a complex of imagination experiments, it acquires an interest that it lacks when taken as a collection of historical artifacts only, or as a concatenation of texts to be deconstructed in the familiar manner of post-structuralist mechanisms. In particular, these imagination experiments are attempts to reformulate the model of reality that society lives within. I referred to this reformulated model as "Transform" thinking (see Chapter 6). "Transform" thinking is not complete by any means; it remains experimental and speculative, with nothing like the force or social power behind it that the Object Cosmology possesses. Nevertheless, social models of reality evolve over time, as, for example, Object thinking itself grew out of and supplanted the earlier model of reality. Transform thinking has been evolving in various forms since the Romantic period, and continues to evolve, gaining rather than losing in persuasiveness.

For the writers who engage in it, much of this experimentation is clearly unconscious. The subject is a vast one, but the main points, those that affect the code of Male Envy, can be noted in abbreviated form and must be considered, however briefly, if the full meaning of Male Envy is to be grasped. For the basis of resistance to Male Envy seems to be this alternative model of reality.

Object thinking separates everything from everything else. *"Tout autre est tout autre,"* as Derrida puts it.[55] For Transform thinking, by contrast, reality is a whole: it is a totality in which everything must be regarded as linked together. This interconnectedness is fundamental. The human, the natural, and the divine (however the divine is understood) are thus seen as interpenetrating aspects of a single identity, and not visualized atomistically. In Hegel's dictum in *The Phenomenology of Mind*, "The truth is the whole."[56] This way of thinking, while it can be traced in a number of earlier writers, has been much stimulated in recent times by the evolution of physics, as physics has grown past its Newtonian/mechanical phase. It is not that Object thinking is "wrong," but rather that it is incomplete and is not absolute. As Robert Nadeau puts it:

> We are accustomed in everyday experience to conceiving of ourselves and external objects as utterly separate and discrete. The view of the actual physical character of physical reality in quantum physics suggests, however, that this is a macro-level illusion. From the perspective of quantum physics, all seemingly separate and discrete collections of matter, including ourselves, are inextricably interconnected.[57]

What affects one thing affects everything else. Nothing is really separate. Hence the attempt to separate stimulates the control compulsions that typify Male Envy —and alienation and exploitation. One cannot act upon things at a distance, without consequences flowing back; the object is not isolated from the subject. Things that appear separated in space are actually linked in complex and subtle ways. If you poison the river, the river will poison you. Since everything is connected, what one does to others is something one is actually doing to oneself. Hence, in this mode of perception, if a man treats others as objects to exploit, he is treating himself in the same way, or inviting negative consequences that he did not intend and that he cannot control. One of the most difficult perceptions of Transform thinking to conceptualize is that subject and object are phases of the same thing, not utterly separate entities sealed off from each other. Object thinking inculcates separation as an absolute datum, a datum that conditions every aspect of consciousness, and any attempt to revise it has to reckon with its pervasive presence, Blake's famous "cloven fiction."

In the Transform model, everything is a part of a larger whole; and the larger whole is present in each of the parts. This is the second characteristic of Transform thinking. The relation between part and whole replaces, in importance and function, the relation between subject and object, person/thing, that epitomizes Object thinking. The awareness of this part-whole identity is the point of Blake's famous lines from his "Auguries of Innocence":

> To see a World in a Grain of Sand
> And a Heaven in a Wild Flower,
> Hold Infinity in the palm of your hand
> And Eternity in an hour.

This quatrain articulates a moment of heightened sensation and expanded awareness, of a type we have already seen in the Mariner's blessing of the water-snakes. Male Envy, with its obsessions and preoccupations, has no room for such perceptions; it cannot relax long enough or deeply enough—it cannot attain what Wordsworth called "wise passiveness"—simply because of its obsessive character and its need for control. The contrast between alienated consciousness, which sees only separation, on one hand, and heightened sensation and expanded awareness, which sees interconnection and identity, on the other, is common in both Transform thinking and the Romantic writers we have been drawing on. Reality is not a pile of objects in space, but an interpenetrating complex, a field or web of identity. Subject cannot be separated from object, and vice versa; indeed subject and object are fused so as to make the distinction between them of limited value. How you see, again, determines what you see.

A final characteristic of Transform thinking is a shift from space to time. Thus reality is not simply a thing in space; it is a power-in-time. More accurately, it is a transformation-in-time. To quote Hegel's *Phenomenology* again, "Appearance is the process of arising into being and passing away again, a process that itself does not arise and does not pass away, but is *per se*, and constitutes reality and the life-movement of truth" (Hegel 105). Everything is becoming something else all of the time. It is not simply sitting there, an unchanging or fixed quantum pushed around by forces external to it. This intuition is essentially the basis of contemporary physics: that reality is a complex of energies, not a pile of inert "things." The objects that comrprise reality, furthermore, are replacing themselves constantly. To that extent, everything is alive, or as if alive. Inevitably, therefore, life itself becomes a model or metaphor for understanding reality, in contrast to the mechanism that typifies Object thinking. The organic paradigm that the Romantics experimented with has been much pooh-poohed by literary theory (dismissed as "Romantic ideology," for example), but it is far too important to be reduced to facile deconstruction or waved away as ideological mystification.

The parallel with modern physics is an indicator of the rise of an alternative way of thinking about reality—alternative, that is, to the Object model that has dominated social consciousness since the hegemony of capitalism. Another parallel that should be noted is Marx's model of wealth, a model he presents immediately at the opening of *Capital*. Wealth, he suggests, is not a pile of objects in space, even though it appears in that form. It is rather the power to make those objects, the coordinated social labor of a very great many people. In other words, wealth *looks like* a pile of things; but the reality is the hidden activity that created those things. Here illusion and reality reverse themselves. The illusion is the objects in space; the reality is the invisible labor-in-time (*"Arbeitszeit"*) that generated the objects. Marx uses a most suggestive expression for these objects; he calls them "labor crystals" (*"krystalliserte Arbeit"*). The phrase is very much in the spirit of Transform thinking. One may adapt Marx's phrase, and say that objects appear to be objects, but are really "time-crystals"—

congealed time, congealed energy, and not really object-things in space.

In Transform thinking, the control compulsions we have been observing become nonsensical instead of rational, like trying to push a river back up the hill: everything is transforming-in-time, nothing can be really controlled, certainly not totally, without, of course, doing damage to oneself and others. One thinks here of Isabella and her basil pot—or of her brothers and their attitude toward their sister. Just as Object thinking tends to see everything as a mechanism, Transform thinking tends to see everything as alive, as transformation-in-time, with its own logic of metamorphosis. Isabella's basil plant goes on transforming itself in time, whereas she enters the void of alienation caused by the control compulsions she is immersed in. There must be a better way.

Notes

1. Drury Sherned, "The Bonds of Men: Problems and Possibilities in Close Male Relationships," *The Making of Masculinities: The New Men's Studies*, ed. Harry Brod (Boston: Beacon, 1987), 227. For a critique of sociobiology in the area of sex roles and male aggression, see Sandra Lipsitz Bem, *The Lenses of Gender: Transforming the Debate on Sexual Inequality* (New Haven: Yale UP, 1993), especially "Biological Essentialism," 6-38; and also Joseph A. Kuypers, *Man's Will to Hurt: Investigating the Causes, Supports and Varieties of His Violence* (Halifax: Fernwood, 1992), passim: Kuypers's study deserves to be much more widely known.

2. Jonathan Powers, *Philosophy and the New Physics* (London: Methuen, 1982) 170. Please note: I am not arguing that cosmology is mere ideology or an arbitrary fiction.

3. See John Neubauer, "Models for the History of Science and of Literature," *Bucknell Review* 27.2 (1983): 17-37.

4. The political implications of this split are laid out with unusual clarity by Alban D. Winspear, *The Genesis of Plato's Thought* (New York: Russell, rev. ed., 1957), a study in the cultural-materialist or New Historicist vein.

5. Adam Smith, *Essays on Philosophical Subjects*, ed. W. P. D. Wightman and J. C. Bryse (Oxford: Oxford UP, 1980) 115.

6. The most lucid guide to the Old Cosmology remains C. S. Lewis's *The Discarded Image* (Cambridge: Cambridge UP, 1961); of special value is the final chapter on "models."

7. Frank Whigham, *Ambition and Privilege: The Social Tropes of Elizabethan Courtesy Theory* (Los Angeles: U of California P, 1984) 63.

8. Samir Amin, *Class and Nation, Historically and in the Current Crisis*, trans. Susan Kaplow (New York: Monthly Review, 1980).

9. R. C. Lewontin, Steven Rose, and Leon Karin, *Not in Our Genes: Biology, Ideology, and Human Nature* (New York: Pantheon, 1984) 37. "Feudal society was quite unsuited to a growing mercantile, manufacturing, and eventually capitalist system. First, social and economic life had to become disarticulated so that each individual could play many different roles. . . . Second, individuals had to become 'free' . . . Ties to specific

places or persons had to be eliminated, freeing workers to leave land and lord in order to become manufacturing laborers. . . . landowners had to be free to alienate the land. [Third,] presumptive equality for the growing bourgeoisie. Entrepreneurs needed to acquire and dispose of both real and personal property, which required a legal system that would guarantee them redress against nobles, and, above all, access to political power" (39-40).

10. Carl R. Hausman, *Metaphor and Art: Interactions and Reference in the Verbal and Nonverbal Arts* (Cambridge: Cambridge UP, 1989) 205. Foucault is much interested in cosmology-shift, but for this study, which works with the logic of imaginable forms, his emphasis on abstraction depletes his usefulness: he showed no interest in writing a history of the imagination. See Mark Johnson, *The Body in the Mind: The Bodily Basis of Meaning, Imagination, and Reason* (Chicago: U of Chicago P, 1987, especially ch. 1. I use the term "Object Cosmology" in a number of essays; e.g., "Gertrude's Poison Cup," *LIT: Literature, Interpretation, Theory* 8 (1997): 1-23; "Stevens' Sound Cosmology," *The Wallace Stevens Journal* 18.1 (1994): 63-80; "Sex and Spirit in Wollstonecraft and Malthus," *The Journal of the History of Ideas* 51 (1990): 401-23; "Female Emancipation in Romantic Narrative," *Women's Studies* 18.2-3 (1990): 309-29; "Indeterminacy in Byron," *English Studies in Canada* 16.1 (1990): 35-53; "The New Cosmology in Romantic Poetry," *The Wordsworth Circle* 22 (1989): 123-31.

11. Object thinking is not to be confused with "object relations" psychology—though Object thinking, in my sense, pervades the psychology of Melanie Klein, a leading member of this school. (John Bowlby and D. W. Winnicott, other "object relations" psychologists, are somewhat different.)

12. David G. Pugh, *Sons of Liberty: The Masculine Mind in Nineteenth-Century America* (Westwood: Greenwood P, 1983) 28.

13. Margaret Thatcher, *Monthly Review* 40.4 (September 1988) 46.

14. Marx quotes Burke in a footnote to *Capital*, vol 1; see Ben Fowkes, trans. (Harmondsworth: Penguin, 1976) 926. It goes without saying that modern physics—relativity, quantum mechanics, etc.—represents a model very unlike Newtonian physics, and the "fit" with the market system lapses. See my "The New Cosmology in Romantic Poetry," n. 10 above.

15. "God is depicted both as a person and not as a person. He is both identified and not identified with gravity. He is a platonic architect, a geometer, a biologist, a mathematician" (Robert H. Hurlbutt, *Hume, Newton, and the Design Argument* [Lincoln: U of Nebraska P, 1965] 87-88).

16. Nancy Hartsock, *Money, Sex, and Power: Toward a Feminist Historical Materialism* (Boston: Northeastern UP, 1983) 50. Cf. Samir Amin, "Historical and Ethical Materialism," *Monthly Review* 45.2 (1993): 44-56, especially 46.

17. David Zaret, *The Heavenly Contract: Ideology and Organization in Pre-Revolutionary Puritanism* (Chicago: U of Chicago P, 1985) 201.

18. David Hume, *Dialogues Concerning Natural Religion*, ed. Norman Smith (New York: Bobbs, 1947) 143. Cf. Carolyn Merchant: "As the unifying model for science and society, the machine has permeated and reconstructed human consciousness so totally that today we scarcely question its validity. Nature, society, and the human body are composed to interchangeable atomized parts that can be repaired or replaced from outside. . . . The mechanical view of nature now taught in most Western schools is accepted

without question as our everyday, common sense reality" (*The Death of Nature: Women, Ecology, and the Scientific Revolution* [San Francisco: Harper, 1980] 193).

19. See John Neubauer, "The Freedom of the Machine," *Eighteenth-Century Studies* 15 (1981-82): 275-90, especially 281.

20. In his classic book, *The Mysterious Universe* (Harmondsworth: Penguin, 1931), Sir James Jeans makes a definitive comment on the mechanical cosmology; notice Jeans's striking *battlefield* metaphor: space is isomorphic with the Male-envious field of universal conflict. Jeans quotes Newton as saying "'would that the rest of the phenomena of nature could be deduced by a like kind of reasoning from mechanical principles.' Out of this resulted a movement to interpret the whole material universe as a machine, a movement which steadily gained force until its culmination in the latter half of the nineteenth century. It was then that Helmholts declared that 'the final aim of all natural science is to resolve itself into mechanics,' and Lord Kelvin confessed that he could understand nothing of which he could not make a mechanical model. He, like many of the great scientists of the nineteenth century, stood high in the engineering profession; many others could have done so had they tried. It was the age of the engineer-scientist, whose primary ambition was to make mechanical models of the whole of nature. Waterston, Maxwell and others had explained the properties of gas as machine-like properties with great success; the machine consisted of a vast multitude of tiny round, smooth spheres, harder than the hardest steel, flying about like a hail of bullets on a battlefield" (27-28). Reality is a *zone of conflict*: it is the arena of Male Envy.

21. Mark Seltzer, *Bodies and Machines* (New York: Routledge, 1992) 152; italics in the original.

22. It is no accident that the Object Cosmology has aroused intensive feminist scrutiny: it is associated with both the start of modern feminism—and with a qualitatively new phase of the oppression of women (in "Female Emancipation in Romantic Narrative" [n. 10], I argue that early feminism is related to experimentation with an alternative cosmology, a model close to the "Transform" thinking that the Romantic poets experimented with).

23. Henry Margenau, *Physics and Philosophy* (Derdrecht: Reidel, 1978) 262. The detached or impartial spectator is a figure essential to Object thinking (and morals, as in Smith's *Theory of Moral Sentiments*)—despite the many philosophical problems involved in the notion of a detached subject; see John W. Yolton, *Perceptual Acquaintance from Descartes to Reid* (Minneapolis: U of Minnesota P, 1984) especially 204-223.

24. Victor J. Seidler, *Rediscovering Masculinity: Reason, Language, and Sexuality* (London and New York: Routledge, 1989) 26, 65.

25. See Stewart Justman, *The Autonomous Male of Adam Smith* (Norman: U of Oklahoma P, 1993) for further analysis of Smith and Object thinking.

26. J. Martin Evans, "Milton's Imperial Epic," *Of Poetry and Politics: New Essays on Milton and His World*, ed. Paul Stanwood (Binghamton: Medieval and Renaissance Texts and Studies, 1995) 233. "Satan rehearses virtually all the major roles in the repertoire of English colonial discourse. By turns buccaneer, pilgrim, and empire-builder, he embodies not only the destructive potential of imperial conquest but its glamour and energy" (234).

27. David Bohm, *Wholeness and the Implicate Order* (London: Ark, 1980) 144. Bohm emphasizes the lens as a paradigm: "the photographic lens is an instrument that has given us a very direct kind of sense perception of the meaning of the mechanistic order, for by

bringing about an approximate correspondence between points on the object and points on the photographic image, it very strongly calls attention to the separate elements into which the object can be analysed. By making possible the point-to-point imaging and recording of things that are too small to be seen with the naked eye, too big, too fast, too slow, etc., it leads us to believe that eventually everything can be *perceived* in this way. From this grows the idea that there is nothing that cannot also be *conceived* as constituted of such localized elements. Thus, the mechanistic approach was greatly encouraged by the development of the photographic lens" (*Wholeness*, 176-77; emphasis in the original).

28. What philosopher of science David Faust calls "the dependence of prescriptions for science on assumptions about the world" has been intensely controversial (David Faust, *The Limits of Scientific Reasoning* (Minneapolis: U of Minnesota P, 1984) 138.

29. Northrop Frye, *Creation and Recreation* (Toronto: U of Toronto P, 1980) 42.

30. Jean-Jacques Rousseau, *The Social Contract* (1762), trans. M. Cranston (Harmondsworth: Penguin, 1968) 186. On the impact of deism see Andre Tadie, "Lord Herbert of Cherbury's Idea of Ultimate Reality and Meaning and a Note on the Popularization of Deism," *Ultimate Reality and Meaning: Interdisciplinary Studies in the Philosophy of Understanding* 18 (1995): 264-274.

31. For example feminist and philosopher of science Sandra Harding notes that "objectivity" is not just a delusion: "The notion of objectivity has valuable political and intellectual histories" and remains "useful" ("Whose Science," *Centennial Review* 36.3 [1992]: 461). Cf. Lois McNay, *Foucault and Feminism: Power, Gender and the Self* (Cambridge: Polity P, 1992) 192; and Karen Green, *The Woman of Reason: Feminism, Humanism and Political Thought* (Cambridge: Polity P, 1995).

32. Compare Marx's analysis of the leaders of the French Revolution: its leaders "performed the task of their time in Roman costume and with Roman phrases, the task of unchaining and setting up modern bourgeois society. The first ones knocked the feudal basis to pieces and mowed off the feudal heads which had grown on it . . . a century earlier, Cromwell and the English people had borrowed speech, passions and illusions from the Old Testament for their bourgeois revolution. When the real aim had been achieved, when the bourgeois transformation of English society had been accomplished, Locke supplanted Habakkuk" (*Eighteenth Brumaire of Louis Napoleon* [Moscow: Progress, 1935] 11).

33. Klaus Theweleit, *Male Fantasies, Vol. 1: Women, Floods, Bodies, History* (Minneapolis: U of Minnesota P, 1987) 123. The notion that the self is really a concatenation of isolated atom-states is deeply ingrained in Object thinking; already Hume in 1739 in *A Treatise of Human Nature* vividly expresses it: we "are nothing but a bundle or collection of different perceptions, which succeed each other with an inconceivable rapidity, and are in a perpetual flux and movement. . . . The mind is a kind of theatre, where several perceptions successively make their appearance; pass, re-pass, glide away, and mingle in an infinite variety of postures and situations. There is properly no *simplicity in it at one time, nor identity in different*" (ed. Ernest C. Mossner [Harmondsworth: Penguin, 1969] 300-301). The uncanny anticipation of poststructuralism, where identity is really an assembly of "subject positions" or "constructions" (not to mention the notion of "difference" here) is noteworthy. Object thinking—the images that organize consciousness—is still very much hegemonic today, as it was in Hume's time.

34. C. S. Lewis, *The Screwtape Letters* ([1942] London: Collins, 1955) 92.

35. Thomas Malthus, *Essay on Population*, ed. Philip Appleman (New York: Norton, 1977) 98.

36. L. J. Jordanova, Intro. to *Languages of Nature: Critical Essays on Science and Literature*, ed. L. J. Jordanova (London: Associated UP, 1986) 112.

37. By contrast with the Object Cosmology, "True vision cannot be achieved by looking *at* the world, as if from a distance, or by thinking about the world as a collection of *objects-in-general*"—this "feminist perspective" is one that assumes a wholly different cosmology (Linda Holler, "Thinking with the Weight of the Earth: Feminist Contributions to an Epistemology of Concreteness," *Hypatia* 5.1 [1990] 7).

38. Robert Hugh Kargon, *Atomism in England from Hariot to Newton* (Oxford: Oxford UP, 1966) 133.

39. Jerome McGann relates the poem to "a field of discourse saturated with political connotations and addressing itself to issues raised in the work of Godwin and Paine: the incompatibility of reason and humanity with a society based on domination and fear" ("The Meaning of *The Ancient Mariner*," *Critical Inquiry* 8 [1981]: 3). Cf. David Punter, "Social Relations of Gothic Fiction," *Romanticism and Ideology*, ed. David Aers et al. (London: Routledge, 1981) 103-117.

40. Roderick McDonald, "Measuring the British Slave Trade to Jamaica 1789-1808," *Economic History Review* 33 (1980): 253.

41. The epigraph to the *Rime of the Ancient Mariner* is a long quotation from Burnet in Latin, which begins *Facile credo, plures esse Naturas invisibiles quam visibles in rerum universitate*—"I easily believe that there are more beings that cannot be seen in the universe than can be seen."

42. Cf. Veblen's comment on sport in *Imperial Germany and the Industrial Revolution* (New Brunswick, NJ: Transaction P, 1990): "a *tour de force* of inanity. . . . The deadening of the sense of proportion implicit in addiction to this round of infantile make-believe is not to be achieved in one generation" (142).

43. Richard C. Lewontin notes that "Sociobiology is the latest and most mystified attempt to convince people that human life is pretty much what it has to be and perhaps what it ought to be" (*Biology as Ideology: The Doctrine of DNA* [Toronto: Anansi, 1991] 63). What-is becomes what-has-to-be.

44. Joyce O. Appleby, *Economic Thought and Ideology in Seventeenth-Century England* (Princeton: Princeton UP, 1978) 242.

45. Peter Gay, *The Cultivation of Hatred* (New York: Norton, 1993) 529.

46. For background on the inter-relations of Hegel, Marx, and early Christianity, see Nathan Rotenstreich, *Alienation: The Concept and Its Reception* (Leiden, The Netherlands: Brill, 1989).

47. For this point, let us cite a psychologist, Raymond Gibbs, instead of a philosopher or literary theorist: "the view that reality is made up, objectively, of determinate entities with properties and relations holding among these entities at each instant. This view of reality leads to a related view that meaning is also an objectively determined entity. For example, semantics is taken as consisting in the relationship between symbols and the objectivist world, independent of the minds of any beings" ("Metaphor, Mental Imagery, and Dreams," *Journal of Mental Imagery* 16.1-2 [1992]: 104).

48. E. J. Dijksterhuis, *The Mechanization of the World Picture*, trans. C. Dikshoorn (Princeton: Princeton UP, 1986) 441.

49. Hence the process of "Discovering that Nature does not evidence a perfect and harmonious machine and that it cannot comfort a soul longing for immortality," as Christopher Johnson puts it, becomes a *rite de passage* for thinking people (Christopher D. Johnson, "A Spiritual Pilgrimage through a Deistic Universe," *Early American Literature* 27.2 [1992]: 117).

50. See Henri Bergson's meditation on this point in *Time and Free Will*, trans. F. L. Pogson (London: Allen, 1910) 90-104.

51. Cf. "aporia." In *Aporias* (trans. Thomas Dutoit [Stanford: Stanford UP, 1993]), Derrida lists a series of terms equivalent to aporia that designate his preoccupation: "marks of undecidability—and the interminable list of all the so-called undecidable quasi-concepts that are so many aporetic places or dislocations; the *doublebind*" (15). Aporia as gap, or space, adumbrates the ultimate aporia, death: "with the motif of the nonentity, or of nothingness, the motif of death is never very far away" (13). Chapter 5, below, probes the significance of this link, aporia as death.

52. Laurel Holliday, *The Violent Sex: Male Psychology and the Evolution of Consciousness* (Berkeley: Bluestocking Books, 1978) 172.

53. Carl A. Bersani et al., "Personality Traits of Convicted Male Batterers," *Journal of Family Violence* 7.2 (1992): 132.

54. The Mariner "has had some vital experience, the implications of which he can neither understand nor communicate in any other than the terms of conventional piety" (Sara Dyck, "Perspective in 'The Rime of the Ancient Mariner'," *SEL* 13 [1973] 603).

55. Derrida, *Aporias*, 22: "Everything other is everything other." Derrida's emphasis on this principle shows that his writing is subtextually structured by Object thinking, despite the fascination with elusive and undecidable "particles": these derive their identity from the image of reality as *an infinite array of separated objects in space*, somewhat like shadows from physical bodies.

56. G. W. F. Hegel, *The Phenomenology of Mind*, trans. J. B. Baillie (New York: Harper, 1967) 81.

57. Robert L. Nadeau, *Mind, Machines, and Human Consciousness* (Chicago: Contemporary Books, 1991) 212. Cf. Percy Shelley's remarkable fragment "On Life," where the self is interwoven with other selves rather than separated: "The existence of distinct individual minds [is] a delusion. The words *I, you, they*, are not signs of any actual difference subsisting between the assemblage of thoughts thus indicated, but are merely marks employed to denote the different modifications of the one mind."

4
Holy Murder

Thou shalt not kill.
God

In Stanley Kubrick's movie *The Shining* (1980), based on the novel by Stephen King, the lead male, Jack Torrance, attempts to murder his wife and child, after he has a powerful hallucination which is not quite a hallucination. Torrance is the winter caretaker of a mountain hotel which is closed for the off season; he is all alone with his wife and son. To his surprise, Jack finds that the bar of the hotel is not shut down for the winter after all. For an alcoholic like Jack, this is a joyous discovery: as far as he knows, there is nobody else in the hotel, which is completely isolated by snow and storm. He saunters into the bar and orders a drink. The bartender explains it's on the house, but regrettably, before he can enjoy his elixir, a waiter bumps into him and spills a drink on his clothes.

As a director, Kubrick is fascinated by scenes of drinking and eating—scenes charged with complex power associations. In fact, eating and drinking are central to the semiosis of power. This particular scene is one of Kubrick's most memorable examples.[1] The waiter is super-attentive and apologetic, and takes "Mr. Torrance" into the washroom to wipe off the spilled drink, which is sure to leave a stain if not attended to promptly. Once they are alone together, however, the waiter discloses that he is a messenger from the "management" of the hotel (he does not add that the "management" are what appear to be evil spirits). His message is that Jack's young son is disobedient; that the child has telepathic powers, which he is using to receive warnings of danger and to communicate with "a nigger cook." This is the hotel's chef, who is wintering in Florida, and who is also telepathic—and increasingly anxious about the boy (the casual racism is typical of the premium Male Envy puts on expressing contempt for others; sneering is an art-form). Here then is the message from the hotel "management": the boy must be "corrected," as the waiter phrases it. The waiter reveals that he also had had at one time to "correct" his children (and subsequently his interfering wife). He did the "correction" by axe-murdering them. He knows how to do it, and he knows how important it is to do it.

The euphemistic and misleading language is conspicuous, especially the verb that the waiter uses. He is to "correct," not kill, still less "murder." Jack's child (and necessarily the mother) must be "corrected." They are "wrong"; they deviate from an established norm, and the solution to this deviation, the correction, is to kill, possibly chop them up, as the waiter did with his family.

What was their crime? The family threatened the rules. In Male Envy, this means that they threatened the compete/control hierarchy, and the standard way in which a wife and child do that is by asserting ties of domestic obligation. That is, they hold that the man's identity is with them (he is obliged to them—and not just they to him); his identity is not constituted by his placement in the competitive struggle with other males. More precisely, they pose a conflicting obligation on the man, as if their needs meant something: a dangerous notion. "Correction" by murder is a kind of Male Display in itself, an intimidation ritual that goes beyond intimidation. Jack takes his duty—"contract" is his word—very seriously. Killing children is a very serious duty, after all—and he almost succeeds. He succeeds in killing the African American cook, who endures severe dangers to reach the hotel, so fearful is he of what is taking place there.[2]

The hallucinatory appearance of what seem to be evil spirits in the hotel recalls the "voices" that deranged murderers claim to hear, instructing them to kill people. The sense that murder is a *transcendent duty*, a categorical imperative, brings us to the theme of the sanctity of violence that is the most horrifying element in the code of Male Envy, and in many ways the most important and therefore the most silenced. The fact that killing becomes a transcendent duty enables the murderer to face its unpleasant aspects (blood, mess, smells, disagreeable emotions and noises, undignified struggles) with equanimity, even pleasure.

The figure of the multiple murderer as a deranged male who kills for no sane reason, often preying on women, amounts to a cultural paradigm that haunts and also fascinates society. This figure has a numinous horror: his crime, often involving mutilation or rape, obliterates justice and nullifies faith, and so marks a kind of absolute. Even if dreadful things are done to him, his victims—including relatives and friends of the dead—cannot have their loss restored or their traumas effaced. As a crime for which, emphatically, no restitution is possible, such murder makes a quasi-metaphysical statement: No rule but the power of the powerful.

In Robert Browning's dramatic monologue "Porphyria's Lover" (1836), the "lover" kills a woman who loves him—he strangles her with her hair—and then the "lover" concludes cheerily, all's well with the world: "God has not said a word." God doesn't mind, it would seem, such crimes.

* * *

In a study of the rhetoric of multiple murderers, sociologist Elliott Leyton rejects the common view that they are too crazy for rational comprehension. "Their rebellion is a protest against their perceived exclusion from society," but —and this is a crucial point—their rebellion is not "an attempt to alter [society] as befits a revolutionary." On the contrary, Leyton argues, these men are conservative. They are not crazy, nor are they oppressed rebels driven to fight against authority, however irrationally. They are not radicals seeking political justice: "they pose no threat to the established order—neither in their ideology nor in their acts."[3] "On the surface of things they appear to be doing it for the thrill of sexual excitement or the intoxication of conquest, but the truth is they do it to relieve a burning grudge engendered by their *failed ambition*" (Leyton 298; my emphasis). In this view, their crime is not an assault on the compete/control hierarchy itself, a protest against its evils, but against their exclusion or defeat on it; they wish not to overturn it but to express their rage at feelings of nullification on it. Murder soothes the offended ego. *Male* ego, that is.

In short, the multiple murderer is a phenomenon of power relations—not simply relations of oppression, but of *ambition and competition*—of climbing on the compete/control hierarchy. In this respect, therefore, as a function of the compete/control hierarchy, the figure represents an element of the social order itself, not something outside it: "it is worth remembering that the original 'Ripper'," notes Rosalind Miles, "was never caught. So-called psychopaths are usually found to be functioning fully in society. . . . For madmen, in fact, psychopaths are remarkably sane."[4]

Leyton argues that the murderer chooses as victims not just anybody, but vulnerable members of the social class that he perceives as a threat to him—the stratum of society that either excludes him or that threatens to exclude him. He is well described by the former magistrate and crime novelist P. D. James, as a man who, having suffered feelings of inferiority and of being despised throughout his life, now will never need to have such painful feelings again.[5] Hence what psychologist Alfred Adler calls "the tortured feeling of inferiority" is crucial.[6] The multiple killer exorcizes anxieties of frustrated ambition and fears of loss of control, by means of spectacular acts of brutality. Thus he individualizes what happens on a social scale when a threatened ruling class instinctively turns to horrifying crimes to intimidate the opposition—one thinks of the *matanza* in El Salvador, an Intimidation Ritual on a scale hardly imaginable, until one recalls the horrors of Nazism and of Stalin.

Women are a key target of the multiple murderer, on the Veblen principle that possessing women is a means of Male Display on the compete/control hierarchy. The murderer seizes power by seizing women, thus using women as a means of war, not just against women, but against other *males*. Feminist analysis has studied this figure as in effect the gestapo of patriarchy. But this is too simple. Women are the means of reproduction: by killing them, he attacks the future of the excluding social stratum, their existence-power, as it were. Hence the assault on women is also a way of waging war against power-holders, the male structure that threatens him socially and torments him psychologically.

In waging what amounts to class war, the killer typically uses rhetoric that has a moralistic, crusading intensity, in the manner of the quasi-religious ranting of Hitler's *Mein Kampf*: a Nazi obsession with imagined wrongs. "It is in the act of representing his act that the killer lays claim to his position in our culture," note Deborah Cameron and Elizabeth Fraser,[7] as if murder were an ideological statement. Murder thus is sanctified as holy duty, as it is for the "soldiermale" of Klaus Theweleit's disturbing *Male Fantasies*. Such murder expresses ownership, ownership being understood not merely as the right to sell property, but as something mystical, something going beyond the right to dispose of it as one likes. Above all, what this mystic jurisdiction includes is the right to *destroy* it. For, in the logic of control, how can one truly own something, unless one can also destroy it? Destruction is the ultimate form of possession: paradoxically, the ultimate proof of possession. To destroy means more than to create.

By this logic, destroying becomes a perverted form of conspicuous consumption that proves a man is strong. The unpleasant corollary is that one can prove his right to what one destroys by doing just that—by destroying it. Hence to destroy becomes the clearest index of the exclusivity of title that constitutes ownership. It becomes, moreover, a way of *claiming* ownership rights, and so powers, and with them the attendant ego-gratification and ego-inflation which is compulsive in Male Envy.

This control-compulsion manifests painful feelings of weakness, where "Power," again in Nancy Hartsock's words, "appears as domination not only of others but of parts of oneself."[8] By murdering those who symbolize his exclusion, the murderer enjoys empowerment and is exalted as by an addictive "high." He rises above the enemy/excluding social stratum by appropriating and disposing of its members, in such a way as to proclaim indisputable power. The detective novelist and former magistrate P. D. James captures the self-inflation of the murderer, the feeling of being a god who can take life and (bizarrely) give life (James 406). In this kind of murder, the ruthless destruction of life is thus equated with creating life. This paradigm informs *Frankenstein* (1818, 1831) and has been much commented upon in connection with nuclear weapons, as if the vision of utter destruction—the flash of the fireball and the mushroom cloud—were understood to be the power of creation, or perhaps, more exactly, a seizure of that power.

The notion that destroying is somehow creating, while bizarre and chilling, is the kind of paradoxical reasoning that Male Envy seems instinctively to favor. I have already noted the predilection of Male Envy for convolution of language and opacity of thought. Holy murder is not a matter of intellectualizing or abstraction, but of emotion and aggression; hence it is necessary to bring out this emotion and clarify it. Its rhetoric, like the thinking processes of Male Envy, is convoluted and opaque, and its pretensions must be exposed if its nature is to be understood. One must make the absurdity and the horror of its practice plain.

As my reference to *Frankenstein* implies, this type of multiple murderer enters literature in the Romantic period. The timing is no accident. Leyton may not have the answer to why multiple murderers murder (various theories have been put forward: sociologists have a sociological theory; psychologists have psychological theories; historians have historical theories—none seems to respect the others). But Leyton's analysis is peculiarly resonant for probing the emergence of this figure in Romantic narrative.

The late eighteenth century was a period of crisis in many spheres, especially in England, as commercial/manufacturing power transformed the social structure.[9] A crucial if underestimated facet of this transformation has to do with religion. "Above all," notes G. S. Rousseau, "the Enlightenment did actually generate, almost for the first time in Western culture, a thoroughgoing materialist strand, which was generally . . . associated with a strident religious freethinking verging on atheism: true materialism would expose theistic idealism as false consciousness."[10] Critics and historians tend to step around the fact that the Romantic period has to be regarded as a period of religious shock; and that in this shock, genuinely spiritual and not merely ideological concerns were at stake. Whatever else Romanticism was, it was a struggle (1) to purge traditional religion of its errors, (2) to find an alternative to Object thinking, and (3) to reconstitute spirituality in new terms, even for those who maintained traditional Christian doctrines, like Coleridge or Wordsworth.

This religious crisis informs the type of murder which crystallizes the most fearful aspects of the code of Male Envy, where control and ego-enhancement find their ultimate expression. In Male Envy, the suffering of others is a means of self-inflation or gratification and also, according to the Doctrine of Good Suffering, the means of solving problems; so that, in this logic, killing is especially efficacious. It is indeed a transcendent duty, hence "holy." Holy murder is embodied in a specific, recurring plot that now needs to be explored.

In this plot, God commands a male to kill as an essential moral duty; in variant form, God orders a male to witness, approve, or will the death of others —or abandon others to death. In short, this is murder that God Himself validates, thus making plain the holiness of murder. Typically the killer hears schizophrenic "voices": God or some superhuman being commands him to kill as a way of punishing those who have threatened true Authority. Holy murder is thus visualized by the killer as a vital cleansing; it asserts true authority, removes/ corrects deviant or offending humans, and installs correct power relations. It is a "correction." Paradoxically, while humans are infinitely weaker than God, literally infinitely weaker, yet God is somehow threatened by those same beings, by their thoughts and actions. Furthermore, despite His unimaginably vast power to destroy, He must employ some humans to kill, to "correct," others, and sometimes to prove their piety by doing so. He needs, in effect, subordinates to carry out his wishes, subordinates who are utterly at his disposal and command.

The context of holy murder in Romantic narrative is a set of anxiety-arousing progressive ideas that are in conflict with the code of Male Envy:

- interrogation of authority; interrogation of fear as means of control
- non-Christian or deistic belief
- female emancipation; respect for children
- domestic obligation (e.g., men are obliged to their wife and children)
- democratic vistas of equality: ideas of Godwinian "political justice"[11]

Holy murder fuses two areas of especially intense social anxiety: (1) male/female relations (and male/child relations in the background); and (2) society's image of God, its way of visualizing the divine. Romantic narrative supplies a number of "imagination experiments" that illustrate the inner workings of holy murder— notably Charles Brockden Brown's *Wieland* (traditionally regarded as the first American novel), James Hogg's *Confessions of a Justified Sinner*, and Byron's *Heaven and Earth*. These "imagination experiments" ponder (1) the reconstitution of religious motifs in the régime of Male Envy; (2) power as kill-power; (3) the ethos of control-without-commitment; (4) the meaning of spirituality in the context of Male Envy. The fact that *Wieland* is such a primary text in American literature should be kept in mind, for it suggests the centrality of the holy murder plot in American literature. It is, so to speak, the first thing that comes to mind.

Holy murder is a factor in Byron's *Cain* and Mary Shelley's *Frankenstein* (also her husband's poetry, especially *Prometheus Unbound* and *The Cenci*), and Blake was influenced by this paradigm, too; holy murder and its God recur in his prophecies. Even in Wordsworth and Coleridge, there are important traces of these motifs. In the culture of Male Envy it has continuing popularity; for instance, one finds it used even in Dashiell Hammett's *The Dain Curse* (1929). It is true, of course, that killing or suicide commanded by God through an "inspired" prophet/leader is a recurring motif in American cultural history: a sort of culturally recognized event, like hara-kiri in Japan.

A late example in literature, almost a parody, appears in *Huckleberry Finn* and is in effect its opening and constitutive scene: Pap tries to murder his son, after kidnapping and imprisoning him. Pap plunges into terrifying drunken hallucinations in which he sees his son as the "Angel of Death," so that Pap is *defending himself* by attacking his son, who would seem to be utterly at the stronger man's mercy. Huck escapes, in a complicated substitution of an animal victim (the narrative stresses the animal's blood). Attack on the weaker male is rationalized as defense of the stronger. This inversion is bizarre but not unfamiliar to the logic of Male Envy; indeed it almost defines Male Envy, where damaging those who are weaker is a sacred obligation. The motif of the drink is again conspicuous. Note the way that, in *Huckleberry Finn*, Pap's "religious" hallucination of "the Angel of Death" (executioner of the Egyptian first-born in Exodus), with its mystic overtones, displaces what is actually a *property* motive: the father wants to steal his son's cash. In other words, madness and alcohol notwithstanding, there is a "rational" motive, requiring calculation and observation (the capabilities required by the Mariner to kill the Albatross). These motifs recur in the scene of Holy Murder. What appears to be madness is actually under the control of a rational motivation, if a cruel and amoral one. Compare Raskolnikov's killing in Dostoevsky's *Crime and Punishment*: bizarre intellectualizing displaces a property motive; the killer is obsessed by loser/inferiority feelings which killing is designed to placate and ease.

To kill someone as a show of obeying God assumes a particular way of visualizing the divine: a certain model or image of God. Holy murder is conceived as the ultimate expression of obedience in C. B. Brown's *Wieland*, for example; Wieland sees it as a humble, defensive act whose intent is to affirm true religion. In practice, "true" religion functions as a specific set of power relations in society, by which some people obey other people. Since the God who presides over these power relations does not do His killing for Himself (except via plagues, famines and other rather blunt instruments), the effect is to authorize those who *can* kill—or who can command to kill. Here again a metaphysical statement emerges; by killing, the holy murderer asserts a particular image of God. In this model, God is visualized as absolute master who cannot be disobeyed without disastrous results: a warrior-king whose word is law. Having created all things, He has the power—and the right—to destroy all things, as He demonstrated in, for example, Noah's Flood. And destruction *is* coming: an apocalyptic *culbute* is to be the fate of the earth, with a subsequent death/damnation of a huge proportion of humanity—almost all, according to some authorities (144,000 saved, in the book of Revelation—male celibates, it seems).

Liberal-minded Christians tend to forget how savage the model of God is that long dominated society. It is one thing to read Noah's Flood as Blakean allegory of losing higher consciousness: it is another to take it "literally" as an historical event in which millions of people perished at a stroke, not to mention virtually every animal, plant, and even insect. Yet Christianity took the latter view for granted as historical and moral truth. In this model of divinity, God displays rage and jealousy, and by so doing endorses such outpourings of hostile energy; He resorts to violence as a matter of course. "Moses said unto them Now therefore kill every male among the little ones, and kill every woman that hath known man by lying with him" (Numbers 31:17).[12] One thinks of Tom Paine writing disgustedly in 1794 in *The Age of Reason* of the murderous aspect of the Bible: "People in general do not know what wickedness there is in this pretended word of God" (92). Thorstein Veblen, as usual, sums up:

> It is only on second thought, if at all, that the devout fancy of modern worshippers revolts at the imputation of ferocious and vengeful emotions and actions to the object of their adoration. It is a matter of common observation that sanguinary epithets applied to the divinity have a high aesthetic and honorific value in the popular apprehension. (199)

Kill-power is sacred.

To kill on God's command is to share His power and entails more than simple obedience: it transmits some of the total destructive power that makes this God—this *model* of God—so awesome. In the language of the psychoanalyst: "the partially inverted man feel[s] incomplete and inferior without a hero, a leader, or a God . . . In His strength he regains his own strength."[13] Hence killing becomes a dramatic form of self-enhancement. In this model, power is constituted as coercion, and coercion, in its essential, primary form, is kill-power. The only way to make someone really obey you, in the final analysis, is to have the power and the willingness to kill. It follows that what makes God God is not His power to create, but His force to control.

Moreover, this model of God also implies a certain model of good and evil, a rather crude model to be sure, but not the less effective. According to this model, good = obeying authority—preferably unquestioningly. The better one is, the more perfectly one obeys. Parents assume this model of good when they tell their children "be good"—and actually mean "do what you're told": goodness = compliance. By the same token, then, evil = disobeying authority. Failure to obey —failure to be "good"—warrants harsh punishment. Hence the *basis* of good in this model is the power to require obedience—ultimately, on pain of death, or even damnation. Also, then, the more dramatic the act of obedience—say, killing wife or child on command—the more impressive one's goodness must be.

These ideas pervade *Wieland*. Wieland, earnestly seeking to prove his piety, hears a "voice" that commands him to kill his family; as in Numbers 31, God insists. His sister, the narrator of the novel, escapes; but, she says,

> His wife and children were destroyed; they had expired in agony and fear; yet was it indisputably certain that their murderer was a criminal? He was acquitted at the tribunal of his own conscience; his behaviour at his trial and since was . . . uniform; not for a moment did he lay aside the majesty of virtue; he repelled all invectives by appealing to the deity, and to the tenor of his past life; surely there was truth in this appeal: none but a command from heaven could have

swayed his will; and nothing but unerring proof of divine approbation could sustain his mind in its present elevation.[14]

How can one expect mercy from a God who views mercy as a sign of weakness —as reluctance to obey?—as evidence, in short, of flagrant *dis*obedience. After all, reluctance to obey is itself disobedience. In his own mind, Wieland is a man of exceptional goodness and divinely favored.

Indeed, he has accomplished miracles.

* * *

Holy murder shows the way older modes of perceiving are adapted, absorbed, and used for new purposes and in a different social context. Holy murder begins as divinely sanctioned killing—then modulates into a conviction that murder is holy, that kill-power is the highest good (an irrational belief we have already seen in "Rappaccini's Daughter": Rappaccini makes his daughter poisonous and regards this as the ultimate gift). What Male Envy does, then, is to transform holy murder from an act sanctioned by an external being called God, into a régime where "God" is conflated with the killer, who thereby becomes a kind of human god, wielding ultimate power and expressing righteous anger, like the deranged general of *Dr. Strangelove*. On a lesser scale, the self-righteous Jack Torrance of *The Shining* angrily insists on his duty to his "contract," but not to the life of his only son.

To understand this transformation, we must observe holy murder in its initial form, in the Bible's concern with it. Holy murder is in fact one of the first things that the Bible displays, in one of the most discussed passages in Scripture: God orders Abraham (via an angel) to sacrifice his son Isaac as a first-born offering. The test and measure of Abraham's "goodness"—that is, his willingness to obey —is his capacity to kill a close family member.[15] One can imagine what would have happened if Abraham had refused to obey (to say nothing if Isaac resisted). Remember Abraham's sister-in-law, Lot's wife. She was one of the chosen, too, and not one of the alien tribes or religions, whose treatment is plain enough, and what happened to her was instant death and metamorphosis into an object to commemorate God's anger and total control-power. (She was turned into a pillar of salt, for those who need to be reminded.)

By agreeing ritually to kill his son, Abraham proves that he deserves God's favor, and thus God rewards him: He lets Isaac live. Since Abraham was *willing* to kill his only son, he doesn't have to. Positively interpreted, this story is a moving renunciation of human sacrifice—hence a historic turning point in moral evolution; Christians also read the story typologically, as prophesying Christ's self-sacrifice; or it may be read as in Kierkegaard's *Fear and Trembling*, as a prophetic test of faith.[16] But as World War I poet Wilfred Owen saw, another reading seems more obvious. God is to humans as absolute master, to be obeyed even if obeying means killing those to whom one has deep human obligations or emotional ties. In paintings of the sacrifice of Isaac, there is a surprising degree of consistency: Abraham "submits to the divine command as a matter of course, the same way his son submits to him. He must—and wants to—prove that his obedience is stronger than what he calls his love for his child."[17] How else, really, can one show one's first priority than by offering—by killing—what has second priority? Holy murder is heroic: a test of devotion like the self-sacrifice of the *kamikaze* pilot dying for his emperor-god.

When Abraham displays such heroic willingness to sacrifice, God is ecstatic: "By myself have I sworn, saith the Lord, for because thou hast done this thing, and hast not withheld thy son, thine only son: That in blessing I will bless thee, and in multiplying I will multiply thy seed as the stars of the heaven and as the sand which is upon the sea shore" (Gen. 2:16-17). The conspicuous repetition and hyperbole suggest delirium—and a bizarre equation of kill-power with life-power. For Abraham's *willingness to kill* is what generates the immense—indeed unimaginable—progeny that God promises his loyal servant. Willingness to kill the son is what makes the son—and therefore the father—so fertile.

Therefore, too, on one level the tale of Abraham and Isaac proscribes human sacrifice. But on another level, it enshrines it as the ultimate act of faith: and so the ultimate act of submission to—and thus union with—God. And this is exactly Wieland's view of his murders: they are the ultimate good deed. Hence the religious intoxication (the "high") he enjoys: "nothing but unerring proof of divine approbation could sustain his mind in its present *elevation*,"[18] as his sister puts it.

Holy killing is crucial to the Old Testament; its origin appears to be *akeda*: "the Ancient Near Eastern practice of sacrificing the first-born offspring," in theologian John Yoder's words.[19] The subtext of sanctifying murder in the Abraham/Isaac story coheres with the Bible's obsession with blood sacrifice generally.[20] "The meaning of the 'holy war' tradition has been for centuries a focus of moralistic debate and embarrassment"—"the prima facie contradiction between the killing of Amalekite and Canaanite peoples on the one hand, and on the other the peace and justice visions not only of the New Testament but even of the Hebrew prophets" (Yoder 346). Divinely ordained massacre is basic to the Bible—the paradigmatic example is the Angel of Death's slaughter of first-born Egyptians, as if an offering to Israel's God: indisputable demonstration of Jehovah's authority. One cannot argue with this display—one can only obey. Even Pharaoh, the most powerful human of them all, indeed a human god, is forced to yield. Samson shows renewed devotion to God by killing God's enemies *en masse*. Saul's troubles result from hesitations about mass murder.

While fundamental to the Old Testament, blood-sacrifice is also basic to the

New Testament, where Christ is sacrificial victim, dying to spare others from God's all-consuming rage. The need to be "washed in the blood" of Jesus, the Lamb of God—that is, a sacrifice to God, a bleeding child-animal with its throat slit—has been crucial. "Christianity has always insisted on hanging redemption on a cross."[21] This theme and its disturbing, not to say revolting, imagery has been sacred in Christianity, with its grisly crucifixes.[22] It also appealed to the evangelical Protestantism of the Romantic period, as E. P. Thompson shows in his analysis of hymns in *The Making of the English Working Class*. Thus, when Jesus insists "I have set my heart on mercy, not on sacrifice," he rejects a point vital to theology: the need for blood sacrifice—Jesus's blood specifically—to atone for the human sin of disobeying the Father God, a God defined by a willingness to kill, indeed torture forever, those who do not obey. "For sacrifice is not always optional; the gods demand it."[23] Once again, this God's murderous proclivity is not confined to the Old Testament: when Ananias and Sapphira do not give all their property to the Christian brotherhood, God strikes them dead for being reluctant to "share" (Acts 5:1-11: this is the type of God that modern "cults" would love to have working for them). Those who cannot be controlled voluntarily may have to be killed.

* * *

There is a prototype in the Bible itself for the sacrifice of Isaac, and that is the story of Cain and Abel. This story is the archetypal narrative of male conflict, and hence an implicit reference for all aspects of the code of Male Envy. The two narratives share important motifs in common:

- male family members with a significant difference in age
- divine commands, divine intervention; angelic visitation: the presence of superhuman beings
- questions of responsibility and obligation
- blood sacrifice; contested offerings
- ritual

In fact, the Cain and Abel story sounds very like the story of Abraham and Isaac gone wrong. For the younger, innocent male family member (brother, in this case, not son) actually *is* slaughtered, in connection with a sacrificial blood ritual meant to placate a death-controlling God. Hyam Maccoby notes: "in the original version of the Cain story, Cain was not a murderer at all. He was the performer of a human sacrifice, and in the very earliest form of the story . . . it was a meritorious act, just as the sacrifice of Isaac by Abraham would have been, if God had allowed it" (11).

Out of this complex of motifs Byron created his drama *Cain*, one of the most fascinating texts of English Romanticism. *Cain* is a Romantic reading of the Bible story, but it goes beyond that, beyond questioning traditional Christianity: its true focus is the Object values that have in practice replaced Christianity, as the prominence of Satan, the paradigmatic competitor/controller, indicates. Adding Satan is Byron's most significant revision to the original story: there is no Satan in the account in Genesis. His appearance in the play suggests that Satan has "won"—that is to say, metaphorically, the compete/control model of reality has won. It has become the dominant mode of understanding. The earlier model, with its fixed hierarchy, has been supplanted by a field of universal competition for control. Market culture has replaced feudal culture.

For our purposes, *Cain* sets out the matrix of holy murder, with a directness characteristic of Byron, as follows:

- uninhibited interrogation of religious and social assumptions
- a threat to established power and power relations
- a God visualized as authoritarian patriarch (where authority means absolute control)
- good conceived as obeying—or placating—authority
- hence evil correspondingly understood as disobedience
- Male Display: competing tableaux of offerings—competition for divine approbation (and hence a win-lose dialectic)
- judgment: public evaluation of personal worth: identity as placement in a hierarchy
- authority/subordinate relations, e.g., creator over creature, father over child, age over youth, man over woman, humans over animals; and above all: winner over loser
- blood sacrifice: a fascination with blood, with manipulating and controlling a numinous life-substance or body-power: the bodily *material* of life
- ritual as hypnotic focus of social attention; the enactment of male attention-command

More closely observed, this matrix is simply the code of Male Envy itself, in rudimentary or germinal form. It follows that confronting holy murder is to confront the code of Male Envy as it comes into maturity, in its most uninhibited form, and this is precisely what Byron's drama does: it confronts Male Envy.

Byron carefully avoids idealizing Cain, who is presented as no worse than the average man.[24] What is different is that he questions and thinks. He cannot see why things are the way they are, why all humanity is punished for what his parents did, why the punishment was so severe—death, drudgery, pain, exile: being deceived and eating a fruit do not seem such dreadful crimes. Adam and

Eve, his parents, are not saints—but neither are they monsters. Whatever they did cannot be as bad as the suffering imposed on all humanity. Yet Cain's family fully acquiesce in their punishment.

Cain frantically seeks a moral reason for God's authority, whereas the real basis for that authority is superior control-power. Eve and Adam, like Milton's Belial in *Paradise Lost* Book II, are thus terrified of arousing God's anger and will do anything to placate Him. As Veblen notes, "Propitiation was the end, and this end was sought, in great part, by acquiring facility in subservience" (236). They wish that Cain would shut up; knowledge, as they learned to their cost, matters nothing. Abel, Cain's brother, goes further. Abel is presented as a religious bigot of the most unattractive type; he is not merely obsessed with his beliefs, but with policing others, on the assumption that "belief" is really social conformity, and difference is a threat to his own power. Blake's line from *The Marriage of Heaven & Hell* again comes to mind: "Those who restrain desire, do so because theirs is weak enough to be restrained." Abel specializes in coercing others to participate in the throat-slitting rituals that he and his God prefer. Abel's first principle is that, as he puts it, he loves God more than he loves life: almost a definition of the fanatic. It could be Wieland's motto.

By contrast, Cain is paralyzed by questions. Like many intellectuals, he does not understand that power relations determine his place, not ideas. Hence, when Lucifer appears, he thinks he can get answers, given God's refusal to speak. But Lucifer won't answer Cain's questions: he clearly has no answers, except competitive war. He talks a lot, but his words are no more enlightening than God's silence. Lucifer despises Cain, as he despises all inferior—that is, all weaker—beings. Unlike Cain, he is "practical." He has a war to win, a war in which Cain may be useful. Lucifer demoralizes Cain to the point where he calls himself "nothing" and, in this stunned state, kills God's chief worshiper, Abel: a win for Lucifer—in his books a not insignificant win. As noted in Chapter 1, God dramatically rejects Cain's vegetable offering—not enough blood. Abel then denounces Cain. Cain strikes Abel—Abel falls dead: chalk one up for Lucifer. Intellectual questions are a red herring in the code of Male Envy, where control is everything, because it yields everything else as spoils. Intellectualizing is the afflatus of power and has no independent content or authority of its own. In the régime of Male Envy, "knowledge" = power over others.

The motif that precipitates the crisis of *Cain* is sacrifice, the killing of an animal. Cain thus refuses to do what the Ancient Mariner is eager to do and needs no motivation to do. It is at first surprising how frequently animals turn up in the scene of Male Envy. But, of course, abusing, brutalizing, and killing animals is standard training for Male Envy, on the principle that Male Envy is the eating of weaker beings, the absorbing of their identity. Animals are very close to children in the language of images (as children are to women): they are beings less powerful, more vulnerable, than adult males and are thus the perfect object of male rage and its need for ego-inflation. The capacity to use others is what the divine is in the eyes of Male Envy. The emphasis on the *animal*, at the center of Byron's play, crystallizes the theme of power relations, of male competitive struggles for control, that makes this play so profound and complex.

Cain immediately repents his impulsive attack on his brother. He begs to die for Abel and even asks to take his place, so as to atone for his crime. The sense that Cain is suicidal is strong. The closing scene, when "The Angel of the Lord" enters, is the crucial one:

> ANGEL. Where is thy brother Abel?
> CAIN. Am I then
>   My brother's keeper?
> ANGEL. Cain! what hast thou done?
>   The voice of thy slain brother's blood cries out,
>   Even from the ground, unto the Lord!—Now art thou
>   Cursed from *the earth, which opened late her mouth,*
>   *To drink thy brother's blood from thy rash hand.*
>   Henceforth, when thou shalt till the ground, it shall not
>   Yield thee her strength; a fugitive shalt thou
>   Be from this day, and vagabond on earth! (my emphasis)

The critical point is the blood involved; as soon as the Angel thinks about blood, rhetoric begins to bloom. First, the Angel's language projects Earth as a *female* being. She "opened" "her mouth," so as "To *drink*" Abel's "blood"—blood shed by Cain's "rash hand." The wasted blood has a "voice," which "cries out," as if blood talked (cf. Genesis 4:10-11), as if Abel were essentially blood. For the Angel—for God, too, presumably—blood definitely "talks." After all, the Angel's Master, God, in a stunning display of anger, has just rejected Cain's vegetarian offering in favor of Abel's sanguine one.

The Angel clearly has blood-sacrifice on the brain: he visualizes Cain's murder of Abel not as murder but as sacrifice—*but to the wrong god*. In biblical tradition "The blood of human beings and animals was sacred, reserved for God only" (Williams 34). Abel's blood has been wasted—poured out "rashly" for the delectation of an alternative deity: Earth. Cain is a farmer, like the homonymous Canaanites; it would be natural (as for so many agriculturalists) to worship mother earth, the female deity posited by the Angel's rhetoric. The subtext of rebellion, of defying authority—of "worshiping false gods"—is unmistakable. If Cain had immediately declared Abel a special sacrifice, perhaps the murder would have been gratefully accepted by God as holy. Abel is a martyr now, anyway: he is already a sacrifice to God, in effect if not intent. And Abel dies happy: he attains a satisfying martyrdom that is honored here and hereafter; God, who can bring Abel back to life if He wishes, does not wish.

At any rate, the Angel (and God) do not think it necessary to investigate exactly what took place. On the evidence, Cain's crime is not that of murder, but of *threatening established power*. Cain's questions; his willingness to talk to The Enemy; his inability to accept the mysteries that Abel worships; and his reluctance to join in official ritual (couldn't he just do it and keep his thoughts to himself?) pose a threat that must be neutralized. The rest of the angelic dialogue confirms this. When the Angel makes Cain an exile, Cain's wife, Adah, boldly objects: "This punishment is more than he can bear"—

> ADAH. 'Twill come to pass, that whoso findeth him
>   Shall slay him.
> CAIN. Would they could! but who are they
>   Shall slay me? Where are these on the lone earth
>   As yet unpeopled?
> ANGEL. Thou hast slain thy brother,
>   And who shall warrant thee against thy son?
> ADAH. Angel of Light! be merciful, nor say
>   That this poor aching breast now nourishes
>   A murderer in my boy, and of his father.
> ANGEL. Then he would but be what his father is.
>   Did not the milk of Eve give nutriment
>   To him thou now seest so besmeared with blood?
>   The fratricide might well engender parricides.—
>   But it shall not be so—the Lord thy God
>   And mine commandeth me to set his seal
>   On Cain, so that he may go forth in safety.
>   Who slayeth Cain, a sevenfold vengeance shall
>   Be taken on his head. Come hither!

The Angel's language is very revealing. His final words open with a dry sarcasm ("Then he would but be what his father is"). His rhetorical question denigrates Eve—though she is as fanatically obedient as Abel, her favorite, is. Clearly, to the Angel, no degree of obedience is really sufficient.

But then something seems to cross the Angel's mind—something that seems to pop out before he realizes what he is saying; namely, that the only man available to kill Cain would have to be his child. That would be parricide: the ultimate crime: a very disturbing idea. Indeed, an idea so disturbing that it causes him to break off—in mid-sentence, as if in a gasp of aporia. "The fratricide might well engender parricides.— / *But it shall not be so*—the Lord thy God / And mine commandeth me . . . " He changes the subject at once; that is, he shifts to what is for him the real point: God's command-power. The real problem with Cain is that if one can kill a brother, one can kill a father; and the killing of fathers—something not even to be thought of (hence the verbal stop-sign "But it shall not be so")—implies an assault upon the whole authoritarian principle by which this particular God rules. Metaphorically, killing a father = disobeying the father God—holy murder, but of a different sort.

Here emerges a key feature of the dialogue: the devaluing of human life as essentially sacrificial material. The Angel sees Abel in terms of a sheep—the sacrificial animal *par excellence*:

> CAIN. What
> Wouldst thou with me?
> ANGEL. To mark upon thy brow
> Exemption from such deeds as thou hast done.
> CAIN. No, let me die!
> ANGEL. It must not be. [The Angel sets the mark on Cain's brow.]
> CAIN. It burns
> My brow, but nought to that which is within it!
> Is there more? let me meet it as I may.
> ANGEL. Stern hast thou been and stubborn from the womb,
> As the ground thou must henceforth till; but he
> Thou slew'st was gentle *as the flocks* he tended.

The last line is a blatant lie: Abel is not "gentle"—he is a tough bully. God was enraged with Cain, meanwhile, and even thunderbolted Cain's bloodless offering: a stunning display, by which God (1) prefers Abel's sacrifice of throat-cut lambs, and (2) attacks Cain. It is obvious what Abel would have done if he thought that God wanted Cain dead: he would kill Cain without a qualm.

Yet the Angel's saintly version of Abel is not actual lying: on the contrary, it is merely carelessness—it doesn't matter, really, what Abel was like. What does matter is that he was absolutely obedient; hence he was outstanding as a subordinate, whatever his individual traits were (if he had any). In Veblen's language, Abel embodies "the archaic habitual sense of personal status—the relation of mastery and subservience" (215). With an irony familiar to the age of Derrida and Foucault, renouncing holy murder simultaneously exalts and enshrines it. Cain, true to his stoic personality, continues to be torn by anguishing thoughts and doubts.

> CAIN. After the fall too soon was I begotten;
> Ere yet my mother's mind subsided from
> The Serpent, and my sire still mourned for Eden.
> That which I am, I am; I did not seek
> For life, nor did I make myself; but could I
> With my own death redeem him from the dust—
> And why not so? let him return to day,
> And I lie ghastly! so shall be restored
> By God the life to him he loved, and taken
> From me a being I ne'er loved to bear.
> ANGEL. Who shall heal murder? what is done, is done;
> Go forth! fulfill thy days! and be thy deeds

Unlike the last!

How casually the Angel dismisses Cain's offer! It is nothing—and nothing can be done about the death. Cain, the stoic, contemplates the nature of existence, but the practical angel, by contrast, is in a hurry. He cuts off the discussion with a familiar non-argument: "what is done, is done." He is a busy bureaucrat, an angelic dean with an administration to run and no time for mere mortals. Cain's offer is evidently not anything he needs to consult higher management about. Cain emphatically is a subordinate, by definition a person one need not—indeed *must* not—treat with respect or at all as an equal. The Angel does not deign to respond to Cain's offer: a sacrifice of self that no just being could wave off with such careless indifference.

In *Heaven and Earth*, Byron's dramatization of Noah's flood, the Archangel Raphael exhibits the same attitude. To this archangel, the destruction of life on earth is of less moment than having two low-ranking angels go AWOL from his command. In Cain's case, once God has let him live, thoroughly traumatized, God will torture him, properly according to orthodoxy, in hell for ever. Or Cain as vaporish ghost will vanish into Lucifer's hades—booty in the cosmic war—implying that God and Lucifer are not so much different as competitors in a single system, not opposites: the system of Male Envy, holy murder.[25]

The point of *Cain* is that "God" in Byron's play is a metaphor for the anxiety of maintaining control: an anxiety generated by the fact that hierarchy is no longer an established and stable one, but a constantly threatened arrangement—that is, it is not so much a hierarchy as a field of competition/control out of which hierarchy as an unstable struggle is constantly emergent.

* * *

Cain is much more complex than a critique of traditional Christianity (Byron always identified himself as a Christian, though he was clearly not an orthodox Christian[26]). God in this poem is an absence, on the one hand; but on the other, He is a model of the winner in control struggles: inscrutable, distant, controlling, capable of spectacular displays of power over others, preoccupied with death, blood, and public rituals involving sacrifice focused on acknowledging and celebrating His power as opposed to the power of any imaginable alternative.

Byron uses the motif of sibling rivalry to probe the logic of male/male competition, with its control compulsions and atrocities, in a field of alienation. *God disappears as a spiritual being and reappears as a paradigm of the victor in control struggles*: someone seeking absolute power over others and over the objects that signify his supremacy. A winner of this type may or may not be able to create things, but he can certainly destroy them. A figure, in short, of pure terror; a holy murderer and a god to whom the holy murderer sacrifices, together in one person. The holy murderer conflates his god with himself. By the same logic, Byron's Lucifer demands that Cain worship him. (Cain refuses.)

The image of an absolutist God cohered with aristocratic/feudal culture, where it had an important function, as a validation device for hereditary autocracy (not just the absolute monarchy associated with mercantilism). But a society in which feudal autocracy and absolute monarchy are obsolete implies, necessarily, a new kind of deity, a deity to cohere with society organized on free commercial lines. As we saw in the last chapter, instead of the old absolutist king-judge, an impersonal, providential, and deistic God that personifies both the laws of nature and of commerce is required, an "Invisible Hand" to personify the order of commodities—and atoms—alike. One of the conspicuous features of the Object Cosmology is its fusion of classical ("Newtonian") physics with capitalist social relations, each being a metaphoric mirror to the other.

Since Object thinking visualizes reality as a pile of objects in space, it privileges—indeed fetishizes—the idea that everything is a separate unit independent from other units, and hence automatic laws—gravity in physics, supply and demand in society—control these units.[27] With the hegemony of the Object Cosmology, human relations are seen increasingly as commercial transactions, matters of personal liberty and private will—all of which had hitherto, under feudalism, been suspect, like the lending of money at interest. Thus the appearance of holy murder in literature coincides with epochal social changes: the image of God, the method of determining legitimate authority, the power relations in society, the role of women, the constitution of domestic intimacy and dependency: all these areas face crisis—and all are connected in the plot of holy murder.

It requires genuine strength, psychologically, to abandon belief in God as the patriarchal despot of tradition. In effect this is to reject the disaster fantasy which cannot be rejected without profound mental struggle. It is not a simple matter of choosing something different in the supermarket of ideas. Inevitably, it means confronting deep fears about the primal facts of existence, including the oedipal anxieties that Freud found to determine the male psyche, anxieties that seem, more correctly, to be the tensions of Judaeo-Christian patriarchy itself: that is, Freud's Oedipus complex is really the compete/control hierarchy itself, but projected as Greek myth. To attain more liberal religious perceptions means, in effect, defying the old God. And, as we have seen, that God notices threats.

The reaction of advanced thinkers was to revisualize God, usually in deistic form. Such a deistic God, precisely, is endorsed by the authors of *Wieland* and *Confessions of a Justified Sinner*, indeed assumed by them: a "god of nature" that is essentially the god Paine passionately advocates in *The Age of Reason*. This deity must be visualized as a providential mechanic, overseer (or even capitalist manager), or simply as a personification of nature's laws, its automatic consistency and predictability. At first, the new image of God is socially progressive. An impersonal deity before whom all are equal weakens aristocratic privilege, as all material units are equally subject to gravity—this God does not sit on top of a social pyramid that subjects commoners to their noble "betters."

Hence the revision of God validates belief in equality, with the aim of deleting hereditary privilege from the structure of creation. Hence, too, there is a loosening of power relations, as the rhetoric of equality inspires oppressed people of all kinds and stations. The beginnings of feminism and the anti-slavery movement are indices of this loosening of power relations, as is the "rights of man" vision so notable in Paine, Godwin, Wollstonecraft, the "Jacobin" and early feminist novelists, as well as the Romantic poets, and later in radical American writers such as Thoreau (and even Emerson). A God who must have blood, even metaphorically, is increasingly viewed as illusory superstition. In Blake, this image of God is not a mere illusion, but is really what the devil is, for it functions in the mind as a demonic voice—very like the nihilistic Lucifer of *Cain*: a voice that urges (self-)destruction and recalls closely the hostile voices that schizophrenics suffer from.[28] The identification of a certain model of God with the devil is the basis of James Hogg's superb Scottish fantasy *Confessions of a Justified Sinner*.

The struggle to create a new way of perceiving God, of redefining the divine, is filled with difficulty. The Romantics begin by absorbing the deist model of God, and then go beyond it, to an intuition of the divine as a power present in all beings—not as a control-force that is independent of reality, of reality visualized, that is, as a pile of objects in space. Transform thinking, as I called it, generates this kind of speculation, and in a sense must generate speculations of this kind, simply because of its perception of reality as a complex of interrelated forces in time, rather than as objects-to-control in space.

The rhetoric of liberty and equality that accompanied Object thinking had a practical purpose, like the similar rhetoric of liberty and equality that Satan uses in *Paradise Lost*: the practical purpose of destroying aristocratic privilege, and, at the same time, promoting the power of the merchant class. The goal was a "society which demanded formal equality but required substantive inequality of rights," in C. B. Macpherson's words[29]; "The phrase 'the people'," as economic historian Rajani Kanth observes, "was a synonym for the middle classes and those few among the labouring masses who could demonstrate loyalty to 'middle-class' society, a loyalty indexed, initially, by property ownership."[30] At first, the new way of visualizing God validates equality and emancipation, because it undermines aristocratic privilege. But, as commercial relations come to dominate society, the enemy ceases to be the old aristocratic order, with its various impediments to the market system. The threat becomes the unpropertied and subordinated classes of society, hence "the rising need of the bourgeoisie to defend instead of attack the social order" as Ernest Mandel puts it.[31]

This explains why deistic reconstructions of God are progressive to begin with but disclose a reactionary aspect as time passes, as God declines into a personification of natural law. Nature, as part of the same process, ceases to be a benign mechanism, the handiwork of an intelligent cosmic craftsman, and becomes instead the display of cunning and ferocity, as in that insightful poem of Blake's called "The Tyger" (1794). Natural "law" becomes simply survival of the fittest for destruction: no rule but the rule of the powerful. Here again, the physical subsumes the metaphysical into itself. As "God" comes to personify the forces of nature, the category of God disappears, and nature takes its place—that is, nature in the sense of an amoral conflict, where cruelty and aggression are normative. Naturally, the old God could to a certain extent be adapted to the new régime and made to justify and personify the eternal lawfulness of the new system, including its negative effects, its waste, alienation, and exploitation.

Thus, once its power over society is secure, the commercial class shifts from attacking the established arrangement of society to advocating that arrangement. After the revolution, attacking the system becomes a crime again. As Roy Porter notes, "the once populist Whigs, having come to power with the Hanoverian succession, began to transform certain oligarchical tendencies into a full-blown system of government."[32] Hogg's *Confessions of a Justified Sinner* is set in the revolutionary phase of expanding market culture in the seventeenth century; and, in *Sinner*, holy murder dismantles aristocratic privilege: the "illegitimate" second son murders his legitimate older brother, heir to property and status. *Wieland* is set later, and in a reactionary phase of market relations, and holy murder is used to conserve authority, as a defense against equalizing impulses in society generally.[33] Safeguarding established property relations was, of course, a major preoccupation of the founding fathers of the American confederation.

* * *

In Hogg's *Confessions of a Justified Sinner*, a young man named Robert Wringhim realizes he is "saved," in the manner of evangelical Protestants. As soon as he realizes he is one of the predestined elect, however, he meets the devil, who looks just like him. Perhaps that is why he does not recognize him as a devil: this devil presents himself as very pious, as a warrior for God. The two then proceed to holy-murder people. Robert's key target in this campaign is his older brother—heir to their father's estate. Thus Robert takes literally the words of his pastor and the "cursing psalm" (#109). The pastor proclaims,

> "Lord, I give him into Thy hand, as a captain putteth a sword into the hand of his sovereign, wherewith to lay waste his enemies. May he be a two-edged weapon in Thy hand, and a spear coming out of Thy mouth, to destroy, and overcome, and pass over; and may the enemies of Thy church fall down before him." (122)

Robert naturally concludes from this prayerful exhortation that there isn't much point in trying to convert people already predestined to hell. A higher calling beckons: "How much more wise would it be," he thinks, "to begin and cut sinners off with the sword! for till that is effected, the saints can never inherit the earth in peace. Should I be honoured as an instrument to begin this . . . purification, I should rejoice in it."[34] As in Byron or Blake, this "God" is really the same as the old devil. A God of predestination is a devil of predestination. More exactly, a God who accepts holy murder is just that: a god of murder.

For the Justified Sinner, earth belongs to the elect—namely, Robert and his co-religionists. As Leyton's model implies, a power/property relation informs the Sinner's motive, as it does Pap's grotesque brutality toward his son in *Huckleberry Finn*. Like the Israelites entering the promised land, the "Sinner" must clear away false possessors, so that the true possessors may inherit: usurpers must be destroyed, in this case an older brother "predestined" by primogeniture to inherit their father's property. The market assumption that open competition is the real basis of social relations is implicit in Robert's attack on a brother. The devil calls Wringhim to kill this brother: he embodies the old Tory aristocracy, whereas Robert represents the interloping ultraprotestants determined to wrest control for their class. Ironically, the brother he kills is in every respect decent, kind, generous, tolerant, and humane—unlike Robert. But then, that is what envy is all about: destroying the goodness of others.

In this manner, however, crime becomes holy; a murderer is transmogrified into God's "instrument" in a "purification." The commencement of Robert's campaign is marked by a horrific vision: he sees a gigantic face in the grey fog, staring balefully: the evil eye could hardly be more graphically inserted into the symbolism of the narrative, pouring forth hatred. Distorted perception again signals the alienated identity implicit in Male Envy. Compare the similar figure of the huge face looming over the grey ash heaps in *The Great Gatsby*—again, the evil eye incarnate—in a novel that is much preoccupied with Male Envy.[35]

The last in the series of Robert's crimes is suicide. Wieland also commits suicide. It is often the case that the multiple murderer consummates murder with suicide. Suicide puts him beyond judgment, like a demonic god.[36] He cannot be punished, however ghastly his crimes, for he has overcome the limitations that restrict lesser—less powerful—beings, such as mere humans: he is a kind of *Übermensch* for which Nimrod or Macbeth are prototypes, and Dracula, with what seems to be a fantasy of world domination, an avatar. Hitler's suicide, coinciding with his attempt to stage national suicide, an extraordinary Male Display, is a chilling historical application of the paradigm. The disaster fantasy is enacted in holy murder, much as the crazed general of *Dr. Strangelove* launches nuclear annihilation to reassure himself of his potency—then commits suicide.

"Confessions of a Justified Sinner" is a pun: "Justified" does not mean merely one who sins with reason, with justification. It is a technical term ("justified by faith"), meaning in effect predestined to salvation—hence one whose sins do not count. Indeed, the sinner of the title holds "all the righteousness of man as filthy rags"; he believes "that the more heavily loaden with transgressions, the more welcome was the believer at the throne of grace" (114). The worse one is, the better one is. The effect of the Sinner's "justification" is to cut off any inlet of self-questioning or self-awareness[37]: to doubt or question, after all, is to disobey, as Cain discovers in Byron. The whole notion of "justified sin" in Hogg's novel is insightful and original, for it suggests that what was regarded in the past as wrong is now in practice correct and good. In a sense, there is no such thing as "sin" anymore. There are winners who can do what they like, and, really, there is nobody else, since others do not count.

The Sinner is in the power position—or believes he is, and can exercise its authority, as if he has absorbed God's will/power into his own. One should compare the attitude of someone who is the *victim* of the Sinner's attitude; in Brockden Brown's novel, Clara Wieland gives an eloquent account of what it is like to be the target of holy murder. For she confronts this kind of insane reasoning—as its target:

> I was hunted to death, not by one whom my misconduct had exasperated, who was conscious of illicit motives, and who sought his end by circumvention and surprize; but by one who deemed himself commissioned for this act by heaven; who regarded this career of horrors as the last refinement of virtue; whose implacability was proportioned to the reverence and love which he felt for me, and who was inaccessible to the fear of punishment and ignominy! (213)

Wieland is perfectly at ease after murdering his family. In fact, he is confident of greatness. Likewise in Hogg's tale, for those predestined to election, crimes actually enhance/glorify God. (It is interesting that it is the "election" speech that Dimmesdale in Hawthorne's *The Scarlet Letter* chooses as the occasion for his public confession, then dies triumphant.)

Such legalistic reasoning is associated with holy murder, as it is the mark of Male Envy generally, "the knowledge of the unknowable," in Veblen's sardonic phrase: "By those whose habits of thought are not shaped by contact with modern industry, the knowledge of the unknowable is still felt to be the ultimate if not the only true knowledge" (237). Thus any "sinful doubtings" which the "justified" hero of *Confessions* may suffer, "always" come down to "one point: I doubted if the elect were infallible, and if the Scripture promises to them were binding in all situations and relations" (157). For the holy murderer, the worst sin is to doubt the commands he has received—i.e., the worst sin is to disobey the authority that is making him, in effect, a god. But the anxiety that he might be wrong is a gnawing feeling of loss of control that will not go away—that is, unless it is killed away. Noah in Byron's *Heaven and Earth* is thus enraged by his son's blasphemy that the people being killed are as good as Noah is. The holy murderer's reasoning is a fog of rationalization and Pharisaic legalism, which is so absurd that it readily dissolves into frustrated rage.

Hogg treats his subject accordingly, fusing horror with a wild jocularity; *Wieland* is far more serious in tone, even claustrophobic. The prior action that sets up *Wieland* is the mysterious death of Wieland's father. A devout protestant with a guilty conscience, the father was a man of intense religious conviction—too intense, Brown implies. The most remarkable thing about him is his death. He dies uncannily, vanishing in a flash of light—spontaneous combustion? This horror occurs while he is praying alone in a chapel built on a cliff. Perhaps God struck him down (or the devil! again, it is hard to tell God apart from the devil): the use of fire from heaven is suggestive, with its sacrificial or punishing overtones. As if to exorcize the horror of this death, his children convert their pious father's chapel into a gazebo. Here they enjoy enlightenment conversation, books of advanced ideas, pagan classics, and the playing of secular music—the "pursuit of happiness" being, for a deistic religion, pious, not to say an "inalienable right," as the Declaration of Independence proclaims it.[38]

To convert a shrine of conservative religion into, in effect, a temple of delight—the site of deistic liberalism—is, precisely, to raise Cain. An angry God of judgment and obedience, the God of Jonathan Edwards and of the Great Awakening roughly contemporary with the action of *Wieland*, is dropped in favor of natural theology, a liberal conviction open to godless, humanistic ideas, such as the emancipation of women. The son, the Wieland of the title, has inherited the father's serious personality—but not, it seems, his father's religious obsession. He is presented as a colorless man: the introverted, quiet type that no one ever imagines could be a killer. Against this background, the son starts to hear voices commanding him to murder sister, wife, children, and friend, as a special act of worship: proof of his piety and the means to attain true contact with God, after impious doubts and confusion.[39] Killing is an *ultimate* act, a definitive, incontrovertible act: as Byron's Angel in *Cain* carefully notes, killing cannot be undone. It is a gesture of control designed to demarcate authority.

Clearly, the angry God of conservative religion does not like the new democratizing beliefs: He is determined to regain authority by means blunt enough to preclude any argument. In this respect He recalls the murderous Duke in Browning's "My Last Duchess" (1842) who does not "stoop" to argue with subordinates, still less females, least of all a wife.

* * *

The power relations of holy murder inform a novel that derives from *Wieland*, but one that is richer and culturally more important: *Frankenstein*. Mary

Shelley read Brown extensively, in part because Brown was a disciple of her feminist mother, Mary Wollstonecraft. Indeed, Mary Shelley read *Wieland* just before writing *Frankenstein*. And *Frankenstein* has a "holy murder" plot.

Victor ("Winner") Frankenstein presents himself as paragon of enlightenment rectitude, morality, and scientific commitment. In phony-sounding language, he paints rosy scenes of an ideal childhood: all sweetness and light at its liberal bourgeois best. As in *Wieland*, religion is presented as a matter of aesthetic appreciation of nature: there is not a hint of any God of rage in Victor's account of his upbringing—only a peculiar fascination with the destructive power of nature.[40] Victor describes his upbringing as perfect; in the same phony manner he explains in his self-justifying speech at the end of his life that he created a man out of dead body parts that he took from graves and from slaughtered animals as essentially an accident. He did it, he says, "in a fit of enthusiastic madness," as though years of calculation, study, and effort were a momentary and unaccountable impulse. Victor has a habit of referring causes to "accidents," assuming the Object view of chance interactions as the formative agency of reality. Thus, Victor presents his discovery of the "secret" of life as an accident —he happened to find something that had eluded his professors at the university all these years, as he carefully notes. The motif of (academic) rivalry is lightly touched but definitely present (cf. Tesman "happening" to find his rival's MS).

The way Victor presents his discovery is itself interesting, for it indicates how completely he thinks in Object terms. Life is visualized as a "thing"—an additive, that one finds and *adds to* a dead body—something external that can be manipulated, as if it could be bottled and stored. Life is not inherent in the living being; it is instead like an object one can do things with. "To understand life one must first have recourse to death," Victor explains,[41] with the kind of logical illogic that is typical of him and Male Envy generally. For Victor, death has priority over life, because life is contained by death, and death is the ultimate in control. Victor's brooding self-absorption and intellectualizing anticipates Dimmesdale in *The Scarlet Letter*; both men abandon the woman they ostensibly are in love with. In the code of Male Envy, love is really nothing.

Moreover, once he stumbles on his momentous find, Victor keeps it secret to himself: he tells no one but continues to work on it in hiding, alone, in typically Male-envious manner, like Dr. Rappaccini. Victor is extraordinarily secretive, and in general conceals, lies, misrepresents, and evades. He demands distance: no one is to make claims on him. The fantasy model here is the old God: to be an absolute being, independent, capable of creating (therefore owning) people, who thereby owe total obedience while he has no obligations to them. Indeed, because total obedience is required, inferior beings must be willing to die and kill for him. As in *Wieland*, the eponymous hero's intimate connections are all killed: brother, servant, friend, bride, and (as a result) father.

Then, at the end, Victor mysteriously gets religion. He tells Walton, the explorer who rescues him from the polar ice (a *Mariner* motif), that Heaven has ordered him, arming him with spirits of vengeance, to kill his creature/son. He closes the serial of murders by converting back to a religion of holy murder. Victor's Geneva is one of the great cities of the Enlightenment, home of the liberal Rousseau and site of a French-style revolution. Geneva is also one of the great cities of Christianity: the home of Calvin, whose doctrine of predestination informs *Confessions of a Justified Sinner*. This complex—a liberalism that thinly overlies the fanatical/murderous—recurs in holy murder. It implies that power, when threatened, may revert to an earlier and harsher religion in self-defense. Thus Brown's America was the site of murderous puritanism (and of continuing religious mania)—then of advanced liberalism; likewise Scotland is the scene of John Knox as well as home to the seminal Scottish Enlightenment.

The scenario of *Frankenstein* is that of holy murder, as follows:

(1) liberal upbringing (no religion, except appreciation of nature, and it seems, a deistic God)
(2) vision of destructive power, implying the primacy in the universe of the power to destroy
(3) lying rhetoric, (self-)deceiving rationalization; language of convolution
(4) murder of family
(5) a suicidal, God-commanded duty to kill: conversion *back* to an earlier phase of belief, one that accepts, indeed venerates, holy murder.

Critics note that Victor represents the bourgeoisie, and his wretched monster the ugly revolutionary proletariat newly created in the traumatic changes of the period.[42] Once the commercial/manufacturing class of society has eliminated the old landholding aristocracy as its primary obstacle, their interests merge, and the real enemy becomes the unpropertied mass of wage-labor. Hence authority in general needs to be defended rather than questioned. The issue is not just the triumph of the new propertied class in society; rather, like *Wieland*, *Frankenstein* represents a war against emancipation in general and, in this respect, tallies closely with Malthus's *Essay on Population* (1798). Malthus is obsessed with curtailing the reproductive power of the nascent industrial working class. Similarly, Victor Frankenstein is panicky about the reproductive capacity of the Wretch, his monstrous creation. Malthus also carefully theorizes a god who sanctions death on a mass scale (punishment for the much-to-be-regretted "reckless breeding" of the unpropertied, as Joseph Banks delicately phrases it[43]).

Women are the typical target of the multiple murderer. Victor makes a point of deliberately ripping up the unfinished bride of his Wretch in front of the monster, thus inflicting maximum anguish on his "son" and displaying his life/death power: his power to refuse life to an individual—and even to a species. This is how deity responds to offending subordinates. The Wretch reciprocates by killing Victor's bride, Elizabeth, after vowing to be there on Victor's wedding night. Victor disingenuously declares this threat to be directed against *himself* (not his bride), and hence had no responsibility to guard, or even warn, his bride. But then, Victor saw no need to tell her what he was doing in his years away from her, when he was busy in grave, charnel, and slaughterhouse—or that the monstrous being he created virtually vowed to kill her: facts his bride might possibly wish to hear of. He exposes her to danger, before consummating the marriage: she dies a virgin. To a man of power, the restricting obligations of intimate connection are unthinkable and must be "corrected."

Victor has an explanation for why he abandons his creature: "it" was ugly. It was not beautiful like his "dream." He may be a body-snatcher, but he is a sensitive body-snatcher; he frequents slaughterhouses, but he is squeamish; he tortures living animals, but he is a refined dissector of carcasses. The counter-implication seems more likely, that he enjoys these activities and that he uses them as, in effect, training for ambitious plans of another kind. Thus, his explanation of why he rejects his creature masks something utterly different from distaste at its/his ugliness, or even from the sudden realization that he may not be able to control his creature completely. It suggests primal fear, perhaps fear of the old God, for Victor wished to displace/replace Him.

This fear—Freud would call it "castration anxiety"—turns to the Doctrine of Good Suffering for relief: it transforms fear into the suffering of others as a means of placating or releasing the fear. Victor thus atones for threatening God's authority by inflicting maximum suffering on his "child": he abandons the son to fend for himself (as God abandoned the "ugly" Adam, His creature). The "son" must be sacrificed; it is symbolically significant that the first person to die is a little boy—Victor's younger brother, an Abel figure (not an Abel figure like Byron's, but the traditional image of Abel as innocent and childlike). To kill what one creates—compare "first-born son"—is to win favor in the eye of absolute power, hence validating the self, in the manner characteristic of Male Envy. Victor wishes to complete the abandonment of the son, at the end of the novel, by killing him. The deaths that result from his sadistic experiment could have been predicted—and therefore could have been prevented. The implication is that Victor wanted murder. On the evidence, he wanted Elizabeth dead; after all, Elizabeth posed obligations as wife. The Wretch makes clear, in his last words, that if Victor had let Elizabeth alone, instead of marrying her, he would have left her alone. Victor's sudden decision to marry her was the signal to the Wretch to attack, and guaranteed her death, especially since Victor makes a point of leaving his bride alone on their wedding night.

But in Male Envy, the power to create/procreate is identified with the power to destroy/kill. Killing *is* creating.

As in *Wieland*, a religion of blood, of inviolable control, lurks behind liberalized enlightenment values. It seems culturally impossible to pass from one to the other without overcoming a murderous guilt at defying authority. In Freud's anthropological fantasia *Totem and Taboo*, the killing of a primal father causes generations of oedipal guilt in male descendants: one way to make sense of Freud's late Victorian myth is to see this primal male not as neolithic god-king, but as the traditional image of God, as visualized *qua* authoritarian, absolute monarch. This image first underwent a major crisis in believability in the Romantic period, the death of God being a subsequent obsession of nineteenth-century culture, and a determining influence on Freud, as *The Future of an Illusion* makes plain.[44]

Interestingly, what motivates Wieland is a *yearning to believe*, a need to prove absolutely the existence of an absolute God. He wants God to "speak" to him. But this obsession with certainty is not really a spiritual quest at all; it is essentially bad faith. Rather, it is a sensation of weakness yearning for power, for control: to be free of any claims made on him by family obligation. The target of this control-compulsion is those who embody emotional ties; such ties are not consistent with the control/contract relations by which authority now treats subordinates. Wieland is especially obsessed with the need to kill his sister, Clara. Not surprisingly: Clara is, as far as any woman can be in his world, an emancipated female, with significant property of her own, well-educated and "unattached": she is a woman slipping dangerously free of simple domination. Clara is a "esiring female," of the type noted earlier, flanked by her ineffectual lover (Pleyel) and a fanatical power male (her brother). From the point of view of Male Envy, she is a potential Tricky Female. It is significant that she is also the narrator of the story:[45] *Wieland* has a feminist subtext. Brown's first work was a tract in the Wollstonecraft/Godwin vein, a mode that had a deep influence on Mary Shelley (and on her circle—including Byron).

Thus, killing Clara Wieland (sister, not brother) makes up for her threat to the male God and the control system He projects. Besides: women, children, and "friends" *must* learn their place.

* * *

Similar needs drive Victor Frankenstein: he is fascinated by destructive power. Victor has a secular epiphany—his burning bush—when lightning annihilates a huge tree (cf. the fiery fate of the elder Wieland). He seeks, above all, total power over others: the power of life *and* death. He fantasizes a race that would receive him as god. The unspoken fantasy that drives Victor seems to be a vision of immense destructive force, a force that would give anyone who could wield it unlimited control.

Hence what must have occurred to Victor is an army of creatures that would be totally dedicated to him. With the power to create people, one could manufacture and re-manufacture an army that in the era of Napoléon could make one the master of nations; and Napoléon's history-shattering example is very much to the point. Fighting battles in which tens of thousands of soldiers were slaughtered, he climbed from Corsican nothingness to control of Europe. I have already cited the fantasy of world domination which is so central to science fiction. What you create, you own and may use as desired—possibly even to control/destroy others, just as the traditional God uses subordinates to perform killings that He desires. In acting out his fantasy of control, Victor risks the lives of some and causes the death of others. His plan fails. But when the explorer Walton rescues him from the polar ice, Victor tries to palm off on Walton the "duty" (Victor's word) of holy murder. Thus Walton (and the crew) are to risk their lives in order to fulfill his own murderous egoism and kill his creature for him, whatever the risks to themselves. Victor is not an appealing character.

But the utter egocentricity that Victor enacts, the determination to be a winner, has great resonance in Male Envy. Here one may compare him with Robert Wringhim in *Sinner*: Wringhim is especially distressed by the idea that he might possibly not be infallible after all. He has the control-compulsion typical of the holy murderer, the need to be absolutely right, to convert the attention of others into fuel for his ego. Again, eliminating family ties = devotion to God: i.e., devotion to power/control. In *Wieland*, the killer demonstrates the ethos of *control-without-commitment* that constitutes market culture, where "The hierarchy of social position is replaced by a hierarchy of personal force," as Julie Ellison expresses it.[46] His victims are those who are a threat to control-without-commitment; notably, intimate family members whose claim on him cannot be dissolved—except by divine decree.

Victor likewise has a commitment to his creature, a responsibility he even goes so far as to acknowledge at one point—before promptly disclaiming it: the whole novel documents his rejection of obligation. Victor, via the Wretch, wages war on intimate connection: on those who threaten to make claims on him. His friend Clerval saved him from illness, and Clerval is murdered. Clerval had no right to check what his secretive friend was up to. It is not proper for Victor to be indebted to anyone. The denial of intimacy and of the obligations of intimacy; the denial of awareness and subjective reality in others, as though they were objects to control, or as if they must be reduced to such objects; and an insistence on control over others are crucial elements in the logic of holy murder.

The anxiety over dependency which Victor displays epitomizes Male Envy: as Stevie Smith puts it, "Because of its denial of fear, vulnerability and dependency, stressed masculinity promotes exaggerated levels of fear; indeed, much of male anger may be understood as masked fear."[47] This fear recalls the hollowness or spiritual desiccation at the heart of Male Envy, the incapacity for sincere or authentic feeling—a condition that Victor consistently displays. In *Separation Anxiety and the Dread of Abandonment in Adult Males*, Gwendolyn

Stevens and Sheldon Gardner argue that "Men are socially conditioned simultaneously to deny their innate attachment needs and to assert their domination over the women to whom they are intimately related. . . . The competent man needs help from no one. The successful man dominates. The powerful man is a loner." Victor Frankenstein must be viewed, then, not as a freak, but as an exemplar of the values of the code of Male Envy, what Stevens and Sheldon refer to as "the masculine dream," which neutralizes the "separation anxiety" that is chronic in males.[48] The horror of dependency, I suggested, is a major factor in the Mariner's murder of the Albatross.

I mentioned earlier the recurring fascination in Male Envy with vast impersonal forces, which the competitor/controller in fantasy identifies with—destiny, nature, fate, etc.—generating the sensation of being selected for greatness. Hitler is a clear enough illustration from history. What this power comes down to recurrently is the power to kill on a wide scale, from Dr. Rappaccini's poison experiments to Frankenstein's capacity to construct living beings to the science fiction fantasies of world domination, and even the ultimate power of nuclear weapons to wipe out life on earth (as in *Dr. Strangelove*). The sense of secret affinity or even outward affiliation with such powers amounts to a kind of religion of Male Envy for the competitor/controller.

But in the early phase of the Object Cosmology, the decisive model for total control is the traditional God. This being is absolute in control of life—*and* death: one who can decree others' death, because He controls everything. Given this logic, gaining the power to kill makes one a kind of human god. Kill-power and divinity are parallel, once again; indeed, metaphor-synonyms. This nasty equation informs *Frankenstein*, as it informs Byron's *Heaven and Earth*, which supplies our final insights into holy murder. What Object thinking introduces, then, is the fantasy of in effect *displacing or becoming the old God*.

Heaven and Earth, with its angels, demons, Noah and sons, and doomed mortals, has a bold, original, cinematic quality. As in *Cain*, God is conspicuously absent in *Heaven*. When the play opens, the ark is ready; the waters impend. But something is wrong: Noah's son Japhet does not show the zeal appropriate to a patriarch's son. Instead, he is seen brooding over his girlfriend, Anah, who doesn't love him anymore, and who, more to the point, belongs to a race God is about to correct by drowning. In his grief, Japhet hears incongruous sounds of celebration coming from a cave, where, it turns out, a party of devils celebrating the death of life on earth is in progress. Ironically, God and His enemies both desire holocaust: again, God and devil are not so much different as competitors in a universal field of conflict. Both are satisfied to kill those who are weaker. How God can be hurt (or helped) by beings so inferior—still less, benefit from killing them *en masse*—is one of those obvious questions no one seems to ask.

The finale is a nightmare: people, facing sudden genocide, struggle to save themselves and their children. Facing this horror, doomed mortals express love, dignity, faith, even vision. Noah, by contrast, is a bigoted Abel who presides over a blood-sacrifice far more impressive than slaughtered lambs. He looks after himself and his followers without a qualm about the catastrophe swallowing everybody else, including his son's beloved. His mission is to witness holy murder, to approve it unswervingly, to show how thoroughly one can will the destruction of others as the highest good. Not surprisingly, Noah "in the original stories was a practitioner of human sacrifice" (Maccoby 45-46).

Heaven would be utter horror but for some typically Byronic twists that recall the black humor of Hogg's *Confessions of a Justified Sinner*. Thus, Anah gave up the ineffectual Japhet not because Japhet's father, Noah, rejects her as racially inferior and doomed by God—but because, like her sister Aholibamah, she has found a more energetic lover: a disaffected angel who has deserted from the heavenly marine corps. When Noah seeks out the delinquent Japhet (he should be on board now), the father finds the son, to his horror, in the company of disobedient angels and doomed women. What outrages Noah is the, in effect, cross-racial sex—love between human females and angels: exactly the sort of disgusting thing that has forced God to wipe everybody out. The solution to sin is to eradicate sinners; God has to destroy the city, as it were, to save it.

Noah is fulminating against the angels for deserting, and for their godless love, when the archangel Raphael arrives in search of the delinquent seraphs. What worries Raphael—it worries him greatly—is how it will look on his CV to have lost two angels under his command. He appeals to their "better" nature, their class solidarity in effect; "Together," he says,

> Let us still walk the stars. True, Earth must die!
> Her race, returned into her womb, must wither,
> And much which she inherits: but oh! why
> Cannot this Earth be made, or be destroyed,
> Without involving ever some vast void
> In the immortal ranks?

"Earth must die" (and "her race"), but why let that spoil things for us? in the angel's mind, humans are pieces of dirt—literally. Their death cannot matter.

The climax of *Heaven* is Aholibamah's speech attacking Japhet, Noah, and the religion that liquidates others to display control-power. Aholibamah is the woman who eludes the compete/control compulsion of the male hierarchy. Unlike Justine and Elizabeth in *Frankenstein* or Wieland's wife, she refuses to be holymurdered. She is a reinvigorated Clara Wieland; the Wretch's bride who never got to choose for herself: the victim who refuses to be a victim. This figure emerges in the very face of destruction and implies an alternative to the horrors of Male Envy. She, Anah, and their angel-lovers then fly away in search of a better world.[49] We never learn whether they make it to another world or are shot down by God. This exit into the unknown is a metaphor for seeking a new way of organizing reality.

The logic of imaginable forms is metamorphic. Thus, society does not simply discard old forms, it reconstitutes them, just as the hereditary feudal ruling stratum was subsumed within the new merchant/manufacturing social class. Holy murder begins as the expression of an absolutist religion, of a God who is visualized as king, with life and death power over His subordinates, above and outside the world of ordinary human work. Once Object thinking is established, the old God becomes a kind of model or paradigm for the successful competitor/controller—someone who is absolute and self-subsisting, separate from an inferior world that He dominates, whose wishes are enacted on command. In Object thinking, the subject-space-object paradigm is universal and correlates with a major value, namely control without commitment, which the successful competitor/controller must have if he is to succeed. Unswerving dedication to self-interest is transmogrified into a sacred necessity. If this requires that others die, then death becomes a necessity, even a holy duty. Not only are property motives thereby moralized, but frustration, painful sensations of weakness, and delight in the misery of others are satisfied, as in effect the rewards of success, the privilege of winning.

* * *

Originally, the term "victim" referred to a living being devoted for sacrifice to a god. The need to "sacrifice"—to make holy by killing—has deep psychosocial roots. God insists that harming people solves problems; indeed, the assumption that one can alleviate anxiety by inflicting pain is common enough. It follows from this—the Doctrine of Good Suffering—that *killing* must be especially efficacious: to make the problem "go away"—to achieve "final solution." When Salmon Rushdie writes certain words, makes certain marks on a piece of paper, the damage to God can only be remedied by killing him.[50] Killing pleases—and placates—authority. The assumption here is consistent with the irrational thinking of Male Envy: this is the assumption that destroying what is valuable is good, and one should desire it, as if the best must also be the worst, and therefore something that should be destroyed.

In the sacrifice of Isaac, Isaac is not only Abraham's child: he is *weaker* than Abraham: the sacrifice enacts a power relation. The preferred victim is one who cannot resist and is, metaphorically speaking, an emblem or metaphor of vulnerability. Thus, holy murder has a logic: the logic of total commitment to authority—authority constituted as coercion. Given this model of authority, God is above all He who has maximum power of coercion at his disposal. In the morality of authority-as-coercion, good and evil are simply submission and rebellion. Hence "morality" becomes, in this way of perceiving, not an abstract intellectual matter, but a concrete, psychological, even alogical mode of experience, one in which primal fears have more weight than principles or systems. And primitive pleasures, too: the pleasures of seeing pain in others, of damaging them, of violence as a means of relieving tension and resolving social complexities, simply by liquidating them. In her studies of child abuse, Alice Miller comes to the same conclusion reached by Anna Freud in *The Ego and the Mechanisms of Defense*: by making others into victims, the murderer stops feeling like a victim himself. Thus he transmutes himself into a winner: into a "victor," like Frankenstein.[51] One achieves the power over others which defines both God and, at the same time, superior social status.

The key target is *weakness*; one attacks those who are vulnerable, and hence one is somehow externalizing weakness and vulnerability in oneself. But the logic of holy murder goes deeper. It is not only what is weak in oneself that must be destroyed, but something else that cannot be controlled, namely that which is creative in the self. By piously damaging the best in oneself, that which poses a threat to authority (typically the genuine creative impulse in the self), one reassures authority that one is "good," safe, obedient. In Freudian metaphor, one castrates oneself in order to demonstrate to authority that one is harmless and not a threat. Destroying one's creative power (in sexual terms, reproductive power) translates metaphorically as killing one's progeny or dependents, so as to recall, on one hand, Freud's oedipal conflict, and on the other, Victor's assault on female sexual power itself.

Hence the voice of protest within the self must also be silenced; one must be made unaware of it. Victor tells his tale with a practical aim, to manipulate Walton into doing his dirty work for him. But the need to reconstruct motivation and feelings is involved, too, a censoring/self-justifying process that silences inner protests, by establishing a public version of events. Walton takes notes of Victor's narrative, which Victor carefully edits for "accuracy"—he is a good editor, it seems. Thus Victor is also motivated by his need to be a winner in the end, after all, and casts himself in the role of blighted genius, memorialized/honored by the naive Walton, who will make of Victor's story a Male Display of glory and fame that will put him at the top of the compete/control hierarchy. Who could do so much—or suffer so much—as the great Victor?

The holy murderer is a spiritual suicide; what he is really trying to kill when he murders is a sense of threatened identity, a sensation too painful to endure. To kill this feeling, he kills those who can be made to represent it—exactly as God condemns to death the human race for disobeying Him, implying that, by doing so, God reassures Himself of His own existence, His own identity as master of all things, despite annoying resistance and opposition from inferiors. In the context of a society that makes a fetish of power over others,[52] in which "to be weak," as Milton's devil says, "is miserable," the holy murder's killings are sacrifices to the demonic voice that proclaims he is inferior. The holy murderer, like the soldiermale of Klaus Theweleit, is at war with himself[53]. This control-compulsion manifests painful feelings of weakness, where "Power"— Nancy Hartsock's dictum again—"appears as domination not only of others but of parts of oneself" (203). As Rosalind Miles says,

> Only through the blood, pain and suffering of those weaker than themselves can they achieve those idealised masculine norms of strength and dominance which they are lacking in every other respect. Aggression, criminality, by creating a pitiful weakness and vulnerability in its victim, allows the young aggressor to transcend his own. The assumption of power, however brief, over others offers him a kind of heroism, a starring role, a naive dream of self-realization through the truth of pure behaviour untrammelled by conscience, reason, or even hesitation.   (218-219)

Notes

1. Cf. the motif of magic fluids in the scene of Male Envy. On power and food, see my "Gertrude's Poison Cup," *LIT: Literature, Interpretation, Theory* 8 (1997): 1-23; "The Scene of Eating," *Recherches Sémiotiques* 14.1-2 (1994): 285-382; "Magic Food," *Disorderly Eaters*, eds. Lilian Furst and Peter Graham (University Park: Penn State UP: 1992): 43-60; "Eat—Or Be Eaten: An Interdisciplinary Metaphor," *Mosaic* 24.3-4 (1991): 191-210; and "Food and Power," *Mosaic* 20.3 (1987): 37-55.

2. In Stephen King's novel, the cook survives and is not axe-murdered by the young boy's father.

3. Elliott Leyton, *Hunting Humans: The Rise of the Modern Multiple Murderer* (Toronto: McClelland, 1987) 27. Cf. Jane Caputi, *The Age of Sex Crime* (Bowling Green: Bowling Green State UP, 1988) 116; and her "Sexual Politics of Murder," *Gender and Society* 3 (1989): 437-56. The "holy murderer" discussed here is related to the perpetrator of child abuse and rape, but (as Leyton argues) there are differences; cf. Carl A. Bersani et al., "Personality Traits of Convicted Male Batterers," *Journal of Family Violence* 7.2 (1992): 123-4.

4. Rosalind Miles, *The Rites of Man . . . the Making of the Male* (London: Grafton, 1991) 212.

5. See P. D. James, *A Taste for Death* (New York: Penguin, 1988) 367.

6. Alfred Adler, *Understanding Human Nature*, trans. Walter B. Wolfa (New York: Greenberg, 1946) 75. For Adler's treatment of envy, see 223-28. Adler formulated the famous "Napoleon Complex."

7. Deborah Cameron and Elizabeth Frazer, *The Lust to Kill: A Feminist Investigation of Sexual Murder* (Cambridge: Cambridge UP, 1987) 139. Carl R. Lovitt comments on the rhetoric of "murder as a heroic act" (30) in "The Rhetoric of Murderers' Confessional Narratives: The Model of Pierre Rivière's Memoir," *Journal of Narrative Technique* 22.1 (1992): 23-34. Motivated by "Rivière's fantasies of restoring male dominance in society," "he projects himself into a narrative that will immortalize him as a martyr": "an

instrument of divine justice, he is repositioned as a hero" (31, 32).

8. Nancy C. M. Hartsock *Money, Sex, and Power: Toward a Feminist Historical Materialism* (Boston: Northeastern UP, 1983) 203. For a sociobiological account, see Adrian Forsyth, "The Biology of Murder," *Equinox* 5.5 (1986): 80-93.

9. As Joel Black puts it, "Cultural historians agree about dating the modern phenomenon of crime from the late eighteenth century and finding its first literary appearance during the romantic era" (*The Aesthetics of Murder: A Study in Romantic Literature and Contemporary Culture* [Baltimore: Johns Hopkins UP, 1991] 30). In *The Frenzy of Renown*, Leo Braudy identifies a similar shift in the concept of fame—in fact, the *creation* of the notion of fame in its current sense. "Fame was beginning to be a matter of talent, learning, and personal virtue rather than of birth and inherited rank": that is, a matter of competition/control rather than of a pre-fixed hierarchy (*Frenzy* [New York: Oxford UP, 1986] 586).

10. G. S. Rousseau, Intro. to *The Languages of Psyche: Mind and Body in Enlightenment Thought*, ed. G. S. Rousseau (Berkeley: U of California P, 1990) 31-32. Significantly, though, "Outright atheism had been a rare phenomenon in the eighteenth century" (J. C. D. Clark, *English Society 1688-1832: Ideology, Social Structure and Political Practice during the Ancien Régime* [Cambridge: Cambridge UP, 1985] 330).

11. Cf. the historical case analyzed by Foucault and his followers in *I, Pierre Rivière*, where an unruly woman is an offense against God; the need to assert authority motivates the murderer. For the context of social cruelty in the Romantic period see James Twitchell's discussion of "The imaging of violence in early modern popular culture" (*Preposterous Violence: Fables of Aggression in Modern Culture* [New York: Oxford UP, 1989] 48-103. "According to the London Bills of Mortality, from the middle of the seventeenth to the middle of the nineteenth century the execution rate was higher than the homicide rate," notes Jean-Claude Chesnais, who concludes that "Capital punishment, in fact, assumed a religious significance. Much more, its very essence was religious" ("The History of Violence: Homicide and Suicide through the Ages," *International Social Science Journal* 132 [1992]: 230, 231).

12. In Tom Paine's *The Age of Reason*, written in the 1790s (the most important English critique of Christianity), this scene is used to show Moses to be in effect a sociopath: "the character of Moses, as stated in the Bible, is the most horrid that can be imagined"—"What is it the Bible teaches us?—rapine, cruelty, and murder" ([Baltimore: Ottenheimer, n.d.] 89, 177).

13. R. Money-Kyrle, *The Meaning of Sacrifice* (London: Hogarth, 1920) 68.

14. Charles Brockden Brown, *Wieland, or The Transformation and Memoirs of Carwin the Biloquist*, ed. Fred Pattee (New York, 1926) 204-05.

15. See Northrop Frye, *The Great Code: The Bible and Literature* (Toronto: Harcourt, 1982) 183-86, for the power relations here, especially the motif of sacrificing the firstborn; also Hyam Maccoby, *The Sacred Executioner: Human Sacrifice and the Legacy of Guilt* (London: Thames, 1982). (René Girard begins *Violence and the Sacred* [trans. Patrick Gregory (Baltimore: Johns Hopkins UP, 1977)] by treating the Cain/Abel story; for Girard, unlike Byron, the prohibition of murder in favor of animal slaughter enables the establishment of human social order. For Girard's theorem, see Chapter 5, "The Academy of Envy.") C. M. Wieland's *Der Gepryfte Abraham* (1754) influenced Brown (see Alan Axelrod, *Charles Brockden Brown: An American Tale* [Austin: U of Texas P,

1983] 61-63)—much as Gessner's *Death of Abel* influenced Byron.

16. A subtext of Kierkegaard's *Fear and Trembling* is that the willingness to sacrifice Abraham symbolizes a response of faith to the alienation of capitalist social relations. Hence he begins, "Not just in commerce but in the world of ideas too our age is putting on a veritable clearance sale" (*Fear and Trembling: Dialectical Lyric by Johannes de Silentio*, trans. A. Hannay [Harmondsworth: Penguin, 1985] 41)—the erosion of legitimate authority by capitalist social relations can be eased by a willingness to kill what is most dear to one.

17. Alice Miller, *The Untouched Key: Tracing Childhood Trauma in Creativity and Destructiveness*, trans. H. and H. Hannum (New York: Doubleday, 1990) 140. Her analysis of the "poisonous pedagogy" enshrined during the Romantic period is valuable context for this study (see her *For Your Own Good* [New York: Farrar, 1983]).

18. "The culture of murder as transcendence" is related to "the theme of the Faust or superman who transcends conventional morality, who kills in the cause of his freedom and power" (Cameron and Fraser, 140). The "high" or "transcendence" associated with killing someone—making someone into an object over which one has total control, is a preoccupation of Joel Black's *Aesthetics of Murder*. This "high" is related to a mystique of "evil" that fascinates many shallow persons, "a mysterious, inescapable wickedness which cannot be understood by society at large" (Cameron and Fraser, 136). I have already cited the fascination with death as mystic agency in the régime of Male Envy.

19. John H. Yoder, "'To Your Tents, O Israel': The Legacy of Israel's Experience with Holy War," *Studies in Religion* 18 (1989) 346. *Akeda* is a complicated and controversial subject, as is interpretation of scripture generally. I want to my emphasize that my intent here is to look at scripture *from the point of view of Male Envy*, to see how it reads and absorbs the Bible, and not to provide definitive interpretation of scripture.

20. On the important "redeemer of blood" motif in Biblical law, see philosopher Marvin Henberg, *Retribution: Evil for Evil in Ethics, Law, and Literature* (Philadelphia: Temple UP, 1990) 68-74. For exegesis of the claim of God to firstborn sons in the Bible, see James G. Williams, *The Bible, Violence, and the Sacred: Liberation from the Myth of Sanctioned Violence* (New York: Harper, 1991) 117-121.

21. James Wetzel, "Can Theodicy Be Avoided? The Claim of Unredeemed Evil," *Religious Studies* 25 (1989) 13. Feminism raises similar problems for theology: "We can either accept the patriarchal biblical text as sacred and content ourselves with exposing its patriarchy . . . or we can expose its patriarchy and reject it as sacred and authoritative" (Paula Milne, "The Patriarchal Stamp of Scripture: The Implications of Structuralist Analyses for Feminist Hermeneutics," *Journal of Feminist Studies in Religion* 5.1 [1989] 34); feminists early on realized that the notion of a "male" God creates virtually insoluble problems for theology; see Naomi Goldenberg, *Changing of the Gods: Feminism and the End of Traditional Religion* (Boston: Beacon, 1979).

22. "Lovely was the death of Him / Whose life was Love," as mild-mannered Coleridge puts it in "Religious Musings" (1794; ll. 28-29); i.e., the crucifixion was not simply an act of "love" but something *beautiful* ("lovely") to behold. On the basis of Proverbs in the Bible, traditional Christians likewise see the necessity of beating their children as a means of love—a notion most upsetting to Aunt Polly in *Tom Sawyer*, who ruefully acknowledges the necessity to hit Tom.

23. Henri Hubert and Marcel Mauss, *Sacrifice: Its Nature and Function*, trans. W. Hall (Chicago: U of Chicago P, 1964) 100.

24. The consensus from S. C. Chew on is that Cain is basically good (*The Dramas of Lord Byron* [1915; rpt. New York: Russell, 1964]).

25. Byron's religion remains controversial, having attracted attention from the start, at least as early as Kennedy's *Conversations with Lord Byron on Religion* (1825). Byron's play was pivotal in the evolving of Cain as a literary-cultural figure; see Ricardo Quinones, *The Changes of Cain: Violence and the Lost Brother* (Princeton: Princeton UP, 1991), especially 87-108—Cain is significant because it shows "a diminution in the role of the parental figure but also . . . a weakening in the very structure of authority itself. . . . the vindication of Abel and the authority of the father are correlative" (96).

26. A surprising amount has been written about Byron's religion. See David E. Goldweber, "Byron, Catholicism, and *Don Juan* XVII," *Renascence* 49.3 (1997): 175-189.

27. The separable unit as paradigm underpins the notion of objectivity; see Lorraine Daston and Peter Galison, "The Image of Objectivity," *Representations* 40 [1992]: 81-128: "The machine also provided a new model for the scale and perfection to which standardization might strive. Echoes of the popular fascination with the ubiquity and standardized identity of manufactured goods crop up elsewhere in the scientific literature. . . . James Clerk Maxwell, following John Herschel, used them as a metaphor for atoms too similar to be distinguished" (119). Note the nexus here: atom::commodity::abstract unit of scientific measurement.

28. For the psychology of these hate-filled or self-righteous "voices," see Robert W. Firestone, *Voice Therapy: A Psychotherapeutic Approach to Self-Destructive Behavior* (New York: Human Sciences P, 1988).

29. C. B. Macpherson, *The Political Theory of Possessive Individualism* (London: Oxford UP, 1962) 247.

30. Rajani Kanth, *Political Economy and Laissez-Faire: Economics and Ideology in the Ricardian Era* (Totowa: Barnes, 1986) 139.

31. Qu. in Black, 42. Cf. Caputi: "the Witch craze [was] an ideological response to a deep need for redefinition of moral boundaries in a medieval social order that was being shaken to its roots by profound social changes" (Caputi 103). Social anxiety is eased by ritual killing, the Doctrine of Good Suffering applied at its most extreme.

32. Roy Porter, *English Society in the Eighteenth Century* (London: Penguin, rev. ed., 1990) 108.

33. Historian David W. Kling notes: "Throughout the 1790s the decline of Christianity and a fear for the survival of the nation were universal themes among the clergy" in the United States, though "Prior to 1798 [the year *Wieland* was published], most clergy welcomed the French Revolution" with its "happy triumph of republican ideals and the defeat of Catholicism" ("For Males Only: The Image of the Infidel and the Construction of Gender in the Second Great Awakening in New England," *Journal of Men's Studies* 3.4 [1995] 337, 339).

34. James Hogg, *The Private Memoirs and Confessions of a Justified Sinner*, ed. John Carey (Oxford: Oxford UP, 1970) 234; cf. similar language used in the satirical prayer of "Holy Willie" by that great Byronic rebel Robert Burns. The cursing psalm is the basis of a famous ghost story by M. R. James, "The Uncommon Prayer-Book."

35. Cf. also the mocking face of "Plotinus Plinlimmon" staring out of the window at the protagonist in Melville's *Pierre, or The Ambiguities*, which is, like *Gatsby*, full of Male-envious themes. A related example is the looming face of Big Brother in George Orwell's *1984*, whose eyes appear to follow one wherever one goes. The motif of the staring face of hatred is surprisingly common and surprisingly potent. All indicate the power of the evil eye in literature and culture.

36. On the fusion of murder and suicide, see Black, 210-17. A similar configuration appears in E. T. A. Hoffman's "The Sandman," a story that fascinated Freud. Freud analyzes it, inevitably, in terms of castration and oedipal anxieties in his famous essay on "The Uncanny." For Freud, circumcision is a displacement of castration rather than, as anthropologists now believe, a displacement of human sacrifice.

37. For theological background, see John Bligh, "The Doctrinal Premises of Hogg's *Confessions of a Justified Sinner*," *Studies in Scottish Literature* 19 (1984): 148-64. The religious establishments in Gothic fiction often practice a cult of holy murder, worshiping the power to coerce/control, to mutilate, frustrate, kill. Burying Agnes alive in *The Monk*, for example, is a holy murder. Even in conservatives like Radcliffe and Scott, religion has such overtones (especially Radcliffe's *The Italian* and Scott's *Ivanhoe*). Poe, inheriting these motifs, deleted the religion from his murderers—religion becomes superstition, an object of ridicule and manipulation, as in Poe's *Narrative of Arthur Gordon Pym*.

38. In this transformation of Christianity, the fallen world—the vale of tears—changes into the place to pursue happiness. This is a key point in Hume's satiric *Dialogues Concerning Natural Religion*.

39. Jay Fliegelman's analysis of pre-revolutionary writing on both sides of the Atlantic emphasizes the shift in the parent-child metaphor. "An older patriarchal family authority was giving way to a new parental ideal characterized by a more affectionate and equalitarian relationship with children" (*Prodigals and Pilgrims: The American Revolution against Patriarchal Authority 1750-1810* [New York: Cambridge UP, 1982] 11). This "paralleled an evergrowing sense of incompatibility of the Old Testament with its insistence on man as God's obedient servant and the New Testament with its insistence on man as God's loving son" (170; see "Assault on Jehovah" 156-63—which cites Byron's German source, Gesner). "The great challenge of eighteenth-century politics, familial and national, was to make authority and liberty compatible, to find a surer ground for obligation and obedience than 'the fear of the rod'" (14).

40. On Victor's early lack of religion see my "Frankenstein's God: Religion and Oppression in the Gothic" *Literature of the Oppressed* 2 (1989): 5-10; Robert Ryan, "Mary Shelley's Christian Monster," *Wordsworth Circle* 19 (1988): 150-55 (especially 151). "The evacuation of spiritual presence from the world of the novel," as Paul Sherman says, is conspicuous ("'Frankenstein': Creation as Catastrophe," *Mary Shelley*, ed. Harold Bloom [New York: Chelsea, 1985] 137-67). See John Dussinger's subtle analysis of family politics, "Kinship and Guilt in Mary Shelley's *Frankenstein*," *Studies in the Novel* 8 (1976): 38-55; and further on this aspect, James Davis, "*Frankenstein* and the Subversion of the Masculine Voice," *Women's Studies* 21.3 (1992): 307-22; and Joseph W. Lew, "The Deceptive Other: Mary Shelley's Critique of Orientalism in *Frankenstein*," *Studies in Romanticism* 30 (1991): 255-83.

41. On this point see my "Romantic Secrets," *San José Studies* 17.3 (1991): 41-58 and compare Barbara Duden's study of body-perception, of the body as a living entity, as opposed to the body as a quantified object (*Disembodying Women: Perspectives on Pregnancy and the Unborn*, trans. Lee Hoinacki [Cambridge: Harvard UP, 1993]).

42. Apart from Jerome J. McGann, Carlo Moretti and David Punter have both written eloquently on this point. See also Anne K. Mellor, *Mary Shelley: Her Life, Her Fiction, Her Monsters* (New York: Routledge, 1988).

43. Joseph A. Banks, *Victorian Values: Secularism and the Size of Families* (London: Routledge, 1981) 19.

44. See Hans Küng, *Freud and the Problem of God* (New Haven: Yale UP, rev. ed., 1990), especially 39-40.

45. "The single most important advantage possessed by male heads of household in early modern England [was] their virtually absolute right to demand obedience from their subordinate and the corollary right to discipline their subordinates" (Margaret Hunt, "Wife Beating, Domesticity and Women's Independence in Eighteenth-Century London," *Gender and History* 4.1 [1992]: 18).

46. Julie Ellison, "The Gender of Transparency: Masculinity and the Conduct of Life," *American Literary History* 4 (1992): 594.

47. Stevie Smith, "Men: Fear and Power," *Men's Studies Review* 8.4 (1991) 20-27, 24.

48. Gwendolyn Stevens and Sheldon Gardner, *Separation Anxiety . . . in Adult Males* (Westport: Greenwood, 1994) 1, 2. Hence, they argue, "the social forces affecting gender distinctions create males who are uniquely unprepared to deal with separation and cannot accept their dependency needs" (62).

49. Critics are gradually discovering a feminist strand in Byron (e.g., Marina Vitale, "The Domesticated Heroine in Byron's *Corsair* and William Hone's Prose Adaptation," *Literature and History* 10.1 [1984]: 72-94); Caroline Franklin, *Byron's Heroines* (Oxford: Oxford UP, 1993); cf. my "God, Noah, Lord Byron—and Timothy Findley," *Ariel* 23.2 (1992): 87-108. The epigraph to Byron's play, *Manfred*: "There are more things in heaven and earth, Horatio, / Than are dreamt of in your philosophy" likely suggested the title *Heaven and Earth*—where reality has far more possibilities than tradition allows.

50. "When Khomeini gave the order to have Salman Rushdie murdered, he was turning the whole of the Koran into Satanic verses," as Northrop Frye noted in *The Double Vision: Language and Meaning in Religion* (Toronto: U of Toronto P, 1991) 15; his discussion repays study (40-58).

51. "Identification with the aggressor" is a key procedure of self-defense in psychoanalysis; see *The Ego and the Mechanisms of Defense*, trans. Cecil Baines, rev. ed. (London: Hogarth, 1966), 109-21 (Anna Freud cites her father as the original theorist here). This strategy seems simple but is actually very complex, with far-reaching implications; see Marilyn French, *Beyond Power*, and Alice Miller, *For Your Own Good*.

52. Cf. criminologist Gerhard Falk: "the need for power and control is taught from early youth on and reinforced constantly by word and deed. . . . the belief that people must have power and must have control over others, at least some of the time, at least on occasion" (*Murder: An Analysis of its Forms, Conditions, and Causes* [Jefferson: McFarland, 1990] 91); see his meditation on alienation and objectification, 189-95.

53. In many ways the holy murderer sums up the code of Male Envy, and Victor Frankenstein, in turn, crystallizes the figure of the holy murderer. Victor's predilection for convoluted rhetoric and confused reasoning—we never do get an intelligible explanation of why Victor rejects his creature (at the very moment when he has succeeded in creating him)—are combined with a continuing hunger for fame and power over others. Apart from Victor's constant lying, one notices the *doppelganger* symbolism of his creature/son. Victor's need to kill his creature/son and to destroy his reproductive power are essentially a war upon *his own* creative and reproductive power. For Victor, creating and destroying, are, precisely, under the régime of Male Envy, the same.

5

The Academy of Envy

*Science is a form of competitive and aggressive activity, a **contest of man against man** that provides knowledge as a side product. That side product is its only advantage over football.*
                                         Richard Lewontin (my emphasis)

"What do you think of his new book?"
"That guy?! — Oh! Well, he's humping for a full professorship."
                                         Overheard at a conference

The purpose of this chapter is to explore the effects of Male Envy on ideas. It is tempting and even logical to begin such an exploration with anecdotal evidence, with academic horror stories. My concern here, though, is not with individual careers but with the effects of Male Envy on ideas and currents of thought. The academy has always been associated with Male Envy. Academic rivalry is the axis of Hawthorne's "Rappaccini's Daughter"; it is conspicuous in *Hedda Gabler*, where it provides both the motivation and also the framework of the plot. Hawthorne's tale appeared in 1844, but its university scene is set centuries earlier, in Renaissance Italy: yet the academy is already a byword for the obsessions of Male Envy—for, in Veblen's phrase, "invidious distinction." The academy is, as Derrida would say, "toujours déjà," "always already," the site of malice, rivalry, and disturbing ambitions, which can be either vicious or absurd, or both. The intensity of the conflict, according to former Harvard professor Henry Kissinger, is owing to the smallness of the prizes.

The concern of this chapter is not the truth-content or validity of ideas, but how they illustrate and contribute to Male Envy considered as an intellectual force. So far I have focused on literature to identify the code of Male Envy, its logic as a constellation of character-types, practices, ideas. The usefulness of literature as a complex of "imagination experiments" indicates one of the subsidiary themes of the present study, that literature itself has a social function. In part, this social function is to confront Male Envy. Several qualities of literature make this possible.

First, literature is a distancing device. It gives perspective and so clarifies and focuses, and given the detachment of distance, things become visible that function invisibly, simply because they are taken for granted. What is staring us in the face is the hardest thing to see. Furthermore, literary texts are imagination experiments. They are *posed* events; they have a hypothetical (rather than a direct) relation to actual struggles and conditions. The potential application to actual social struggles, consciousness, and conditions is therefore not limited; the relation between literature and life is not confined to a one-to-one reflection or correspondence with social circumstances. Literature illuminates without forcing.

Second, the phase of literature I have concentrated on—Romantic narrative—coincides with the triumph of Object thinking, which is the ground of Male Envy. Object thinking has conditioned all intellectual activity from its appearance to the present time, and Romantic narrative furnishes insights into it that remain penetrating and useful. Romantic narrative does not so much reflect Object thinking as probe its effects and question its validity.

Third, literature furnishes not just historical/ideological or intellectual materials, but a complex of emotion and image, and thereby allows us to observe the code of Male Envy in a way that abstract reason alone cannot. Literature has the advantage of being holistic, not fragmenting; by its nature, it connects and synthesizes, and Male Envy is too complicated to be approached except through synthetic, holistic perception. And this is precisely what literature offers: vision.

Having observed the workings of Male Envy in the context of literature, it is easier to trace its effects on the academy and on ideas and intellectual life generally. These effects are tacitly denied entry to consideration, even though they are pervasive and familiar. The academy is well-known for malice and sneering, for its obsessive snobbery, and for the envious hostility of its members to originality or brilliance in others. Hence, the familiar pattern of simultaneous awareness/unawareness that we noted earlier in the scene of Male Envy is particularly conspicuous here.

Prestige is a fetish in the academy; one thinks of academic journals that publish only from a select list of schools, the name of an institution being more important than the content of what is said. Likewise, the valuing of the "margin" as opposed to the "center" is now in fashion, but this fashion has not affected the actual working of the academy, which is committed to Veblen's "invidious distinctions." An invidious distinction is an identification, but at the same time it is "invidious," as if identity were constituted as the putting-down of others, which, of course, in Male Envy, identity very precisely is. The snobbery of the academy, deep and obsessive as it is, has a meaning in the sense that it articulates the contempt of the top of the social hierarchy toward those who are below it. The sanctity of differential valuation in the academy is thus the sanctity of inequality itself. Hence one must investigate the subject not from the viewpoint of conservative critics seeking to justify inequality or reject innovation, but by means of the theoretical model developed earlier in this study.

The damaging effects that flow from the reign of Envy in the academy are a matter of some urgency, but my concern here is with the prior matter of Male Envy as a force in the domain of ideas itself: to see how Male Envy as a code or logic has determined the construction of key concepts. And, given the commitment of the present study to literature—to literature as a complex of *Gedankenexperimente*—some consideration of the presence of Male-envious motifs in literary theory is essential. Literary theory is curiously transparent in its conveyance of Male-envious themes and is therefore useful in illustrating what Male Envy does to ideas generally.

There are certain cues that mark the presence of Male Envy. These are assumptions and motifs that, like the proverbial litmus test, show the presence of Male Envy, often in unexpected places. These cues include, for example,

- the assumption that the intellectual world is *constituted* as a field of competitive struggle
- the concomitant assumption that the function of ideas is to demolish or expose other ideas, and replace them with one's own; hence the irrefutable argument—the knockout punch—is the goal of intellectual activity
- the belief that everything is determined by ideology or reducible to ideology (a conviction often stated with fervor); the win-lose logic of competitive struggle is what ideas "really" are
- a belief that if one cannot control the field of intellectual struggle, then one must hold as much of the attention of others as possible
- the motif of a conglomeration of separate items or objects—the motif of one thing after another, but without connection or ordering
- the use of intellectual claims to broker "invidious distinctions," in Veblen's phrase, where arguments presented as impartial are actually weapons to attack others and enhance ego[1]
- a fascination with convoluted or opaque language
- reliance on irrational arguments or contradictory arguments (for example, to assert one thing proves that the opposite is true; or an insistence that hurting people actually helps people).

Old ideas do not simply fade away: they struggle, die, are transmuted and reconstituted in various forms over time. This transmutation is especially true in the case of "ideas" taken in a broader sense as "paradigms" (Kuhn's sense), as ways of thinking, or as images in the sense of a mode of perceiving. "Object thinking," as I have termed it, is one of these modes of perceiving. Object thinking provides the essential base for Male Envy, its theory, so to speak, by visualizing reality as an immense collocation of separate objects in space; hence society is likewise visualized as an aggregate of separate individual persons. But, as is plain from a great range of disciplines, from physics to ecology, this way of perceiving shows clear signs of having reached its limits and entering obsolescence; it makes less and less sense of how things actually work.

Nevertheless, when a mode of perceiving becomes obsolete, it often intensifies rather than merely disintegrating. The doctrine of the Divine Right of Kings became a political force in England at the very time royal power was weakening. When a way of thinking is threatened, it often responds by becoming atavistic, by retreating into stronger and stronger versions of its base assumptions, like a defeated tyrant retreating into a fortified bunker. Object thinking seems to be following the same pattern, intensifying and hardening, in a determination to keep control whatever the consequences, and in spite of the fact that it makes increasingly less sense. The code of Male Envy, threatened by a variety of forces in society, has responded by tightening its core beliefs, so that there is plenty of evidence to indicate that, rather than disappearing, Male Envy is becoming more and more dominant.

I have found it useful, in pondering this difficult subject, to reflect upon the example of two prototypical intellectuals, whose names have come up throughout this study: Malthus and Freud. Few intellectuals have had greater influence on society than they have had. More to the point, few have had more success in the competitive struggle of ideas. Hence they are fascinating because their work rationalizes and codifies important elements of Male Envy as a cultural force, but also because, as competitors themselves, their careers exemplify success in Male Envy itself. They demonstrate Male Envy even as they rationalize/expound it.

But this is a curiously common feature: the *form* of Male-envious relations becomes the *content* of theory, the content of what is taken for knowledge.

* * *

The Reverend Thomas Malthus published his *Essay on Population* in 1798. It would be hard to find many intellectuals who have had more influence in the last two centuries than Malthus. His discovery that people reproduce faster than the food supply had a major effect on Darwin (see Chapter 3 of *The Origin of Species*[2]). And, through Darwin, Malthus is the grandfather of sociobiology. Furthermore, Malthus's idea is close to the center of neoclassical economics, the economics taught at university and that organizes the official way of seeing the economy—the production and distribution of goods. One cannot overestimate the influence of *An Essay on Population*.

An Essay on Population is regarded as launching the science of demography, but it was not conceived as demography; on the contrary, it was conceived as a political argument. As A. M. C. Waterman has insisted, the *Essay on Population* is first and foremost a polemic against radical social ideas.[3] Viewed from a literary perspective, *Population* belongs to the Romantic period and is related to the emergence of the form of Romantic narrative. *The Rime of the Ancient Mariner* and Charles Brockden Brown's *Wieland* also appeared in 1798, and both relate to the same concerns that *Population* does. Moreover, *Population* was a response to the radical intellectual (and Gothic novelist) William Godwin, specifically to Godwin's *Political Justice* (1793). In *Political Justice*, Godwin argues that humanity is capable of unlimited improvement: a capacity he refers to as "perfectibility." Godwin believed that, through improved education and expanding self-awareness, society would gradually attain greater co-operation and equality, creating a society without power-over relationships and therefore, from our point of view, a society where the code of Male Envy was obsolete. Godwin speculated that, thanks to improvements in health and scientific knowledge, human life expectancy would lengthen in ways hardly imaginable in the 1790s. What Godwin means by "justice" is essentially social relationship without invidious distinctions, without competitive aggression.

Malthus despised Godwin. The intent of his *Essay on Population* was to prove, definitively, that Godwin's hopes for political reform and better social conditions were impossible, in fact ludicrous, contemptible. Malthus demonstrated that no significant improvement in the life of the mass of the population was possible, apart from minor adjustments. The most that could be hoped for, he argued, for the vast majority, is the condition of the American colonists *before* that regrettable revolution of theirs:

> Were I to live a thousand years, and the laws of nature to remain the same, I should little fear, or rather little hope, a contradiction from experience in asserting that no possible sacrifices or exertions of the rich, in a country which had been long inhabited, could for any time place the lower classes of the community in a situation equal, with regard to circumstances, to the situation of the common people about thirty years ago in the northern States of America. (95)

The period Malthus refers to is the 1760s, while the colonies were still under the British crown, and it is certainly not Canada ("northern") he is referring to.

In the wake of American and French disorder, *Population* is firstly a polemic against revolution. It differs in this from Edmund Burke's earlier polemic, *Reflections on the Revolution in France* (1790), in an important respect. Burke attaches his critique of revolution and democracy to a conservative, traditional view of society as a hierarchical unit sanctioned by God. Burke believed that sudden, willed attempts to reconstruct society *a priori*, according to abstract principles, were doomed. Society was a natural growth that evolved slowly; hence it was disastrous to try to remake society by destroying the pre-existing social growth and replacing it with a system based on invented political projects.

Malthus takes a different tack. Unlike Burke, he shows no interest in conservative beliefs or organic visions of society, in his task of refuting Godwin and demolishing democratic arguments for reconstructing institutions—especially property relations. "His unrelenting defence of the landlord class," as Alexander Field puts it, "still causes one to wince today."[4] Malthus's aim was to rationalize the social order, an aim that had nothing to do with demography; on the contrary, demography was a novel and original tool. Nullifying Godwin is the point. Malthus shows great skill in attacking and destroying competing ideas: he is a prototype of the intellectual, so common in our own time, who is devoted to defending and rationalizing the principle of inequality, inequality being the *sine qua non* of Male Envy, as well as the basis of existing property relations. In Malthus, the existing distribution of wealth (a tiny minority with vast property vs. a vast populace with tiny property) was the "natural" arrangement. Without this inequality, without some unproductive consumers to absorb the surplus generated by the whole, civilization would fall to pieces.[5] His aim from the outset was to produce the irrefutable argument: the irrefutable argument would put him in the forefront of the intellectual life of society. This requires *winning* ideas, rather than just, moral, logical, scientific, or humane ideas *per se*.

On the one hand, intellectual activity is to expand knowledge; on the other hand, it is to reinforce the power relations in society, to "win."

What Malthus did was to provide scientific proof that altering social relations was not simply wrong or immoral, but a violation of the laws of nature: "it has been clearly proved" that "independent of any political or social institutions whatever, the greater part of mankind, from the fixed and unalterable laws of nature, must ever be subject to the evil temptations arising from want, besides other passions" (*Population* 92). Nature's laws create poverty, and therefore poverty is ineradicable. Malthus built his polemic into the structure of the universe—into a cosmology, in short—the Object Cosmology. This could only be possible if Malthus was articulating a core paradigm of Object thinking. His persuasiveness was owing to his crystallizing of a crucial paradigm of the worldview of his own time and of the ruling social order which that worldview rationalized. Malthus accomplished this with brilliance and originality. What he did was to appropriate the deistic, democratic language of the free-thinking intellectuals of his time—and turn it against them.

Object thinking had many advantages over the preceding model of reality; for example, it stimulated democratic impulses. The image of reality as a pile of separate measurable objects has its counterpart in a society visualized as an aggregate of separate individual persons. Tearing down aristocratic privilege in favor of merchant (later manufacturing/industrial) power generated the rhetoric of equality. This equality was, of course, never intended to go beyond large property-owners—it was not meant for wage-labor (or women or slaves). Nonetheless, the rhetoric of equality had the effect of inspiring all elements of society to seek political and economic justice. The underpinning of this rhetoric of equality was the liberal theology of deism, which detached God from the old hierarchical structure, with its pre-fixed landowners and peasants, and redefined God as a skilled providence that maintains the equalizing mechanism of nature: "the order of nature and reason," in Adam Smith's characteristic expression.[6]

Thus, in its early phase, Object thinking was much preoccupied with reconstructing God; with revisualizing Him in a new form. As we saw in the last chapter, the traditional image of God sees Him as an all-powerful potentate in a heavenly kingdom: King of Kings and irresistible Judge and Master of all creation. Such a God cohered closely with feudal and aristocratic civilization, but made increasingly less sense in a society built around capitalism and market relations, governed by laws of exchange, of supply/demand, where it is "wrong" for an aristocratic few to have special privilege—special legal status, for example (not to mention exemption from taxes). What is required is a deity to reflect the market system and treat property equally.

Inevitably, this way of visualizing God comes to think of "the deity" as a personification of the laws of nature—and subtextually of the laws of the market. Such a God is impersonal and detached, views individuals equally, and regulates the workings of nature, according to reason in the form of uniform laws that cannot be arbitrarily broken or interfered with—a god, as Newton put it, "very well skilled in mechanics,"[7] and by implication skilled in the laws of commerce.

These laws of nature, being isomorphic with the laws of the market system, are summed up in the dictum of Edmund Burke cited earlier: "the laws of commerce" are the "laws of nature," and the "laws of nature" are, in turn, "the laws of God."[8] The facts of society and the facts of nature operate on the same plane. Daniel L. LeMahieu encapsulates this interpenetration of market ideology and divine will thus: "Man suffered; some starved, but overall there was an economy of evil as just and compensatory as the Law of supply and demand."[9] Godwin, who shifted from Protestantism to atheism, himself articulates the underlying reason for this isomorphy between nature and commerce: there is a "principle in the nature of human society by means of which everything seems to tend to its level, and to proceed in the most auspicious way, when least interfered with by the mode of regulation."[10]

In this model, impersonal laws apply uniformly to all, and no superior beings may intervene arbitrarily (whether artistocrats or divinities). With its paradigm of equal objects equally subject to the same laws of nature, Object thinking thus attacked aristocratic privilege and the various remnants of the feudal and mercantilist systems that sustained aristocratic privilege; and it advanced the power of commercial property in society. In undermining superstition and despotism, Object thinking was socially progressive. But as commercial power becomes demonstrably more in control of the state, Object thinking switches from attack to defense: "society . . . demanded formal equality but required substantive inequality of rights," to quote C. B. Macpherson once again.[11] "Imbedded in the liberal ideal of equal opportunity is a strong belief that inequality is part of the natural order," as Michael A. Messner expresses it.[12] Malthus is at the cusp of this transition, and his originality lies, in particular, in the way he seizes the ideas and the language of critical intellectuals like Godwin and Thomas Paine and uses it against them, to attack democratic and equalizing aims. This appropriation of Object thinking for conservative purposes marks a cultural innovation of real importance.

Malthus's argument is well-known, and can be summarized (as he himself does) in a few words: population increases faster than the food supply. Hence there will always be more people than there is food; hence much of the population will always be poor, if not destitute, because people will reproduce up to the limits of the food supply and beyond it; hence inequality is the basis of social existence; hence real social change is impossible. Like the motions of physical bodies in Newton, sex and food are governed by a fixed, mathematical formula: population increases in geometric proportion (1, 2, 4, 16), whereas food supply increases in arithmetic proportion (1, 2, 3, 4). The excess population are ineluctably doomed: there is simply nothing for them. Therefore, inequality and the struggle to survive are not only built into the nature of things, but they should be: what-is is what-ought-to-be. The attempt to alter property or political institutions will simply exacerbate the population/food conflict, will result in more people and not more food. Improvement will not take place, but civilization will be threatened. Not surprisingly, Malthus insists on "the strict and necessary connection of the interests of the landlords and of the State," as he himself phrases it, years after *Population*, in his *Principles of Political Economy*.[13]

For a modern reader, what is peculiar about the *Essay on Population* is its obsession with theology. *Population* is preoccupied with God and God's role in the world. A thoroughgoing deist, Malthus takes it for granted that God is a personification of the laws of nature. Scripture is all right in its way—but it can hardly match nature as a guide to the divine nature. To know what God is like, we must, he says, cast "our eyes to the book of nature, where *alone* we can read God *as he is*."[14] Physical nature—objects in space—is the only certain revelation. Thus, if nature ordains frustration and conflict, with privilege for some at the expense of others, this is not simply natural law; it is also the decree of a perfect God, so that both sources of authority are covered. Any attempt to circumvent the law (say by contraception, which Malthus totally rejected) not only defies nature, but the Almighty whose law is embodied in nature—in objects in space. Significant social change is not only impossible but immoral; more importantly, it is impossible whatever the morality. In the manner typical of Object thinking, the physical conflates the metaphysical.

Why, then, has a perfect God created a system that dooms humanity to misery? Malthus's answer is illuminating for the code of Male Envy and dramatizes certain assumptions:

(1) Malthus's identification of nature with God's nature essentially deifies nature in the sense of material objects in space: whatever is, is right. There is no distinction between the way things are and the way they should be. Hence human desire is fundamentally illusory.

(2) Deprivation—evil generally—derives from human desire: the desire for sexual gratification creates babies nature cannot support. The desire for social improvement is blocked by human desire itself. The solution is for desire to neutralize itself (restraint, the "moral check"): what Freud was to call "sublimation." People have to stop wanting: the way to desire is to stop desiring.

(3) Good is reconstituted as personal self-gratification: those who own property are sanctioned by nature, and thus by God, to use it as they please. Marriage, like all personal relationships, has to be understood via the paradigm of commercial exchange, which is in turn thought of as the reordering or exchange of material objects in space. "Marriage was not automatic, it was a choice, the outcome of cost-benefit calculations for both men and women," as Alan MacFarlane insists.[15] Thus, self-interest—"self-love," in Malthus's term— is the *primum mobile* of society. It is the source of everything good.

Indeed (4) Malthus identifies self-interest with Newtonian physics: "self-love" is "the moving principle of society" (note the physics metaphor).[16] We return to a point noted earlier: it "is to the established administration of property and to the apparently narrow principle of self-love that we are indebted for all the noblest exertions of human genius, all the finer and more delicate emotions of the soul, for everything, indeed, that distinguishes the civilized from the savage state" (*Population* 98). The hyperbole is striking: everything good, every advance of civilization, derives from self-interest—from what hitherto was said, in traditional Christianity, to be the greed or pride that was the root of evil.

Hence (5) Malthus must jettison traditional Christianity *in toto*, especially the old doctrine of original sin and the notion that we live in a fallen world damaged by human sin. On the contrary, if nature is God revealed, then nature, with all its deprivation, frustration, and cruelty, is God's specific design. Malthus thus redefines original sin, as we have seen: "The original sin of man is the torpor and corruption of the chaotic matter in which he may be said to be born" (118).[17] From this, Malthus goes on to argue that reality is designed to compel people, by means of the threat of destitution, to transform from matter to spirit; from uncontrolled urges (for sex and food), to abstinence and labor.

What Malthus does, then, is to replace the traditional split between the upper, unfallen world and the lower, fallen world, with a new, Cartesian split: between matter, which is visualized as chaotic, and spirit or mind, which is lawful and orderly, and is in effect a sublimation of matter. This is very different from the old split, which articulated the contrast between aristocracy (unfallen world) and peasantry (fallen world). Similarly, Malthus's new split articulated the contrast between property owners ("spirit") and wage-labor ("matter"). In Peter Bowler's words, Malthus "worked with a simple view of society as divided into two classes: a small group controlling enough wealth to escape the general misery and the great mass of the laboring poor."[18] Wealth, by contrast, comes from wealthy people, from the mystique of ownership itself. This mystique is symbolized by the fertility of the soil and has nothing to do with the actual labor required to generate that wealth. Control has precedence over creation.

This is Malthus's answer to the question why God created such a dreadful world, with its conflict between sex instinct and food supply. God wants people to become all spirit, and the best way to do this is to force people to deny their appetite and work harder. Presumably this metamorphosis is what property-owners have already achieved. Thus, the exercise of sexual appetite is to be a function of property ownership: legitimate for those with property, illegitimate for those without. The sexual function—and this is a feature of Male Envy that we have seen many times—becomes a mark of power in the control struggle. Winners get sex; losers must do without. Winners reproduce; losers perish.

What one notices in Malthus is the reductive impulse, to explain all human phenomena as deriving from a simple formula: the incompatibility of production and reproduction. In this respect, Malthus saw himself as the Newton of moral philosophy: someone who had uncovered the basic moving principle of all social phenomena, a moving principle that was simple, elegant, and easily articulated as a mathematical law, with its arithmetic/geometric ratio. Malthus's achievement was to lay bare a law which governed all things—all social phenomena—much as physical nature could be reduced to certain, simple, irreducible mathematical formulas, controlling basic building blocks of matter. Having found this momentous truth of nature (compare Victor Frankenstein happening upon the "secret" of life), Malthus annexed to himself the theory that no one could disprove: the ultimate success for intellectual competitors.

The dependence of culture on agriculture was hardly a new idea and is plain enough in Adam Smith, Sir James Steurat, the physiocrats, and many other economists before Malthus. Nothing could be more self-evident. Malthus's concern was not with the fact that people need to eat, and therefore food supply limits population; he was concerned with proving that social conditions could not be bettered: with, that is, an ideological proposition, not a scientific one. Malthus was articulating key elements in Object thinking; it was his skill and his timing in doing so that made him important. He managed to capture central elements in the perception of reality that the Object Cosmology projects, and it was this articulation of cosmological motifs that comprises his real achievement.

What, then, are these central elements? (1) Human beings are essentially

Newtonian inert matter: they must be forced. The notion that people must be compelled to act is an index of the struggle of an industrializing society to break in a restive, unruly labor force socialized in the less rigorous rhythms of agriculture, but now required to run the machines at the lowest possible wage. It coheres, too, with a view of human beings as person-objects driven by external forces, as on the paradigm of the stimulus-response mechanism (a paradigm which is a development of Object thinking as applied to human beings).

(2) Human desire, the wish for sex, is so strong and so irrational, that unchecked it would destroy the world. This is true in at least two senses: in that the sex drive would create more offspring than society could support; and in that sex desire, generating irresponsibly, also generates a wish to change social institutions and redistribute property. The implicit metaphor is typical: changing social relations is equated with destroying the world. Subtextually, Malthus supplies and rationalizes a key point for Male Envy: there must be many losers if there are to be any winners. Hence the vision of frustrated masses has in fact a definite appeal and is desirable for its results as well as for its esthetic value.

(3) Human sexual desire, with its political/economic subtext (the sexual desire of the unpropertied is a metaphor for their political desire), is so dangerous that it can only be kept in check by harsh measures: as an extreme social danger, almost any measure is justified against it. "Given the natural tendency of population to increase faster than capital" in Malthus's analysis, "the only hope for real relief of poverty was a drastic reduction in the numbers of the poor" (Kanth 52). In plain terms, the reason why there is poverty is that there are poor people; if poor people would stop existing, there would be no poverty. The genocidal ethos implicit here recalls the logic of holy murder explored in the last chapter (I will return to Malthus's fascination with mass death later).

(4) Socio-political thinking is projected as natural law. The physical is identified with the metaphysical. That is, the aggressiveness and even violence represented by self-interest is rationalized as the working of spirit, as the will of God and of nature. The need to clip equalizing ideals is packaged as the "law" of population, which rules out social reform as impossible. Political and social imperatives are encoded within the structure of nature.

(5) As the physical becomes metaphysical, the substratum of reality is disclosed as conflict; its primal nature is aggression. Hence the imperative to win is categorical, so to speak, and winning means controlling rather than creating.

In Malthus, the paradigm of wealth is food—an *object collected from nature*; it is not something created by human action (a point that Godwin seized on in his reply to Malthus). Inequality is sanctified as an ultimate value. His achievement is a remarkable one, not as science, but as ideology.

* * *

The canonization of Malthus's "theorem" of Population in the nineteenth century was controversial but also inevitable. Darwin extracted from it the axiom that life is constituted as a struggle to survive, in which the weak—those without food or that cannot reproduce aggressively enough—perish. Hence the fundamental datum is the necessity of aggression, which, like other necessities, metamorphoses into a virtue. At least, this is the cultural paradigm: the Darwin that society re-created in its own image. Here we reach the axiom of the code of Male Envy: reality is force—that is, aggression. Reality is a field of hostility in which individual competitors struggle to control. What is real is the ability to dominate: a value articulated by Milton's Satan that weakness is criminal: "To be weak is miserable / Doing or suffering." Hence weakness *ought* to be exploited and punished, without hesitation, as a duty, indeed the most important duty. Cruelty, aggression, winning, and the Doctrine of Good Suffering are ultimate ethical truths, to be justified and sanctified as high morality.

Thus Malthus provided, more directly, another essential element in the code of Male Envy: the Doctrine of Good Suffering, whereby hurting people solves problems. In Malthus, God designs nature such that human beings' sexual desire is so great that it causes them to reproduce beyond the means to sustain offspring (apart from wealthy property owners). The purpose of this arrangement is to convert matter into spirit, by forcing people to control their sex desires, under threat of famine, war, and other apocalyptic horrors, horrors which are the result of their natural inclination for sex—and also ironically its punishment and solution. Ultimately, Malthus coheres with the hostility to sex which according to Foucault is central to the history of sexuality.[19]

The reward of workers not reproducing is, paradoxically, survival and the maintenance of existing social relations, where the index of spiritual development is property. If frustration improves people, the greater the difficulty, the greater the improvement. The worse things are, the better they are, and the more God likes it. More exactly, frustration is good for those without property; those with property may indulge *ad libitum* (the notion that the rich should own sex or should have exclusive access to sex as a kind of luxury commodity haunts Male Envy and is clearly marked in Malthus). To interfere—by means of legislation, property redistribution, charity, or support to the unpropertied—violates the very constitution of God and nature (and not merely existing property relations). Few rationalizations for the Doctrine of Good Suffering could be more ingenious. Destitution is good, because it encourages people to stop being destitute. Interfering with this only creates more destitution; indeed, the attempt to interfere with destitution is regularly regarded as the cause of destitution.

This rationalization inaugurated important values: namely, that power and wealth are meritorious; that weakness is criminal; that weakness should be taken advantage of; that ruthlessness and power-over relationships are inevitable, and hence desirable; that vast inequalities are good in themselves, as ordained by

God/nature, but also beneficial for society as a whole. What is conspicuous about Malthus is his *skill in adapting reasoning to rationalizing*. In a manner that is typical of Male Envy, theology, the relation between the divine and the human, becomes a rationalization of cruelty and power-over relationships, by which some people use and hurt other people: a remarkable achievement and accomplished without recourse to Scripture. The underlying implication for religion is a god that is a god of force: a god worshiped by winning, dominating, controlling, and above all, despising weakness: a god of holy murder. Again, 1798 is not only the year of *An Essay on Population* but of Brockden Brown's *Wieland*.

Ironically, another legacy of Malthus is the scientification of Male Envy. His use of mathematics, his giving of a "law" to humanity and (via Darwin and sociobiology) to the whole of animated nature; and the installation of scarcity as the basis of academic economics are significant indices of his influence—more precisely, his consistency with the emerging values of Object thinking. Malthus's recourse to a mathematical formula was a brilliant validation device. In Louis Dumont's words: "There is so little ground for assuming a geometrical progression on the one hand, an arithmetical one on the other, that one may well ask whether this genial trick is not at bottom a mathematical expression of nature's superior creative power as against man's."[20] Or as Frederick Rosen puts it, "The principles were stated in a manner which made them incapable of clear proof or refutation, once the initial assumptions were granted."[21]

Not only did Malthus supply Male Envy with important theoretical elements, but he also applied its principles. For Malthus was an intellectual "winner," and his *Essay* made him famous. He saw himself as having accomplished for social phenomena what Newton had accomplished for physics, laid down the basic laws of motion. Thus Malthus became a "genius," someone whose ideas are so major that they change reality—a man who climbed to the top of the compete/control hierarchy to dominate the intellectual world. There is a kind of academic subgenre of making obeisance to Malthus which recalls the tribute paid to figures like Newton or Darwin or Freud.[22] Malthus illustrates success in the code of Male Envy itself. He defeated the ideas of Godwin and other intellectuals; he gained fame (and infamy), attracting enormous attention to himself; he became valued among the wealthy and powerful; he was hated by intellectuals, rivals who could not defeat him; and his idea was not just an idea—it gained practical application in one of the most influential pieces of nineteenth-century legislation, the Poor Law of 1834. The 1834 Poor Law set the tone and ethos of what Proudhon was to call "the philosophy of poverty," in which blaming the victim was an essential value, and the Doctrine of Good Suffering was its practice.[23]

* * *

In curious ways, Malthus anticipates Freud. His fundamental idea is the conflict of sexual desire ("population") and social control ("restraint"); and he declared that this conflict was not merely unfortunate or dreadful, but designed by God for the good of humanity. Specifically, the purpose of this conflict was the transformation of matter to spirit—that is, sexual desire into property. Freud's essential paradigm is closely related, indicating the way that Malthus's ideas are implicit within Object thinking itself; hence they keep reappearing in different form over time, displaying the inner image-assumptions of the Object Cosmology, in a sort of ritual repetition.

In Freud, the self is divided in three parts: (1) the superego, a social construct; (2) heaving sexual and aggressive energies ("libido" in the unconscious "id"); and (3) a self-conscious ego perched anxiously in between id and superego. The superego is the internalized system of social control which the ego absorbs as part of education; that is, socialization, because the "natural" form of the self is one of instinctive sexual violence and aggression. In Freud, the substratum of reality is, once again, violent disorder. Without the superego, imposed by society to force restraint on the id, society would explode into chaotic violence and sexual rapacity. More precisely, it would revert to the originary chaotic violence. In Malthus, the individual restrains his sexual urges, if he wishes to avoid famine and plague and war; and by this restraint, he metamorphoses from shapeless violent matter into the order of the spirit; that is to say, property ownership. Spirit replaces matter, in Malthus, just as ego replaces libido/id in Freud: the "sublimation" which was the goal and the essential basis of civilization for Freud. Social restraint, imposed upon the individual's id by way of the ego, prevents sexual violence and anarchic aggression, and enables the individual, and hence society itself, to survive.

The distrust of human desire, with its sexual base, is common to both Malthus and Freud. Freud's dictum is definitive: "What is characteristic of illusions is that they are derived from human wishes." Freud identifies illusion with desire—in more virulent form, with delusions, which are clearly "in contradiction with reality. . . . Thus we call a belief an illusion when a wish-fulfilment is a prominent factor in its motivation . . . the illusion itself sets no store by verification."[24] This theme is a master motif in post-structuralist theory, notably that of Paul de Man, where desire and self-deception can hardly be separated from each other. (It is interesting that in Lacan, who is much preoccupied with desire, desire functions in practice as something little different from frustration or even the opposite of what is normally called desire: in this respect, Lacan makes explicit what in Freud is implicit: desire is deception.)

Freud's *self-perception* also recalls Malthus; that is, he saw his ideas as epoch-making intellectual breakthroughs, comparable to those of Newton, the archetype of genius. And again like Malthus, few intellectuals can claim to have had the influence that Freud has had. Freud was attacked, as Malthus was; but here, too, such attack is an index of success in competitive struggle. Freud thus illustrates the code of Male Envy in terms of his career as a competitor, and his techniques of struggle are themselves worthy of note. As R. C. Tallis observes, "Freud's theories, notoriously, have an inbuilt survival kit: disagreement with them is regarded as a symptom of the very resistance they themselves predict, and therefore counts as confirmatory evidence. Psychoanalysis thus enjoys an extraordinary ability to shake off decisive criticism."[25] Note the parallel with literary theory: the strategy of treating disagreement as confirmation. In terms of academic competitive struggle, psychoanalysis has been a model for how to succeed and is influential in this respect—as a paradigm for successful competition in the kind of struggle that uses ideas (far more influential than is justified by its success as a therapeutic technique).[26]

Freud emerges as a figure of competition and control as much as of medicine or psychology. It is interesting that, despite renewed criticism (from many directions), Freud's potency as an influence remains surprisingly unimpaired among literary critics/theorists. Freud has enormous appeal for intellectuals. His system is all-embracing, all-explanatory, as well as neat, elegant, and presented as impartial/scientific—it also defies criticism with conspicuous success: it adapts and survives, as the popularity of Lacan indicates (Lacan being, like René Girard, a complicated revision of Freud). For literary theory, the obvious example of the influence of Freud is Harold Bloom. Bloom's theory of "the anxiety of influence" is explicitly integrated with the influence of Freud. As David Perkins encapsulates it, "For Bloom, the principle of literary change lies in the oedipal struggle of poets with predecessors as fathers. A poet creates a poem by misunderstanding the poem of a predecessor."[27] Bloom's fascination with Freud has numerous implications, but for our purposes Bloom's value lies in the way he brings out into the open the fact that Freud is the expositor of envy rather than of sex, so that sex in practice is a metaphor in Freud for envy.

As a result, Freud's preoccupation with Male-envious themes has meant that assumptions about sexuality often turn out to be the penetrations of envy, covert or metaphoric treatments of envy. There are important consequences, because for critics, Freud is still, by far, *the* theorist of mind, and hence discussions of sexuality and other matters are often covert discussions of envy. The center of Freud's thought is the Oedipus Complex—Freud explicitly viewed it as the *pons asinorum* of psychoanalysis; acceptance of it divides adherents from non-adherents. When examined from the point of view of Male Envy, the Oedipus complex acquires a rather different emphasis from that accorded it by Freudians or by popular culture. Its real focus is not sex, at all: it is not incest, with all the fascination and *frisson* that incest holds for popular culture. Nor is it relations generally between son and mother. What counts is male-male relations; and on this axis, the female figure evaporates.

Hence one must pass—as Freud himself did—from the Oedipus complex, with its female entanglement, to the real issue: namely, male hostility toward other males. For the weaker male, this "hostility" manifests as castration anxiety ("*Kastrationsdrohung*"), which is in every way more important—is explicitly stronger—than the Oedipus complex. It must be stronger, because it is that which overcomes or suspends the Oedipus Complex. The fear of being castrated is more than a "fear"—"fear" is a feeble word for this primal terror, something which can really never be verbalized or made fully conscious, because it is so basic, so determining and firmly lodged in the hidden layers of the male psyche. Again, the primary level of reality is a field of universal aggression, as in Hobbes's "state of nature." Thus when one deletes the appearance of civilization, its veneer, so to speak, what one finds is untamed aggressiveness, a predatory impulse entirely free from morals or values apart from self-aggrandizement.

For Freud, the boy ceases to desire his mother because he fears castration by a stronger male (his father). It is ironic that castration anxiety "resolves" the Oedipus complex, for this castration anxiety is the fear and hate of males for other males: it does not resolve but fetishizes it; and, in power terms, it has clear priority. The Oedipus complex thus reduces to male hostility: to the compete/control hierarchy itself, whereby males defend their place by attacking younger—or less powerful—male-competitors. The woman once again is not a sexual being but a medium of male war necessary to measure who wins, who loses. In the contest of older male (father) against younger (son), the older one wins; victory, as usual with Male Envy, is marked by possession of the female. Once again, Male Envy implies that, in structure, the locus of oppression is male-over-male, which sponsors, intensifies, and necessitates male oppression of females.

It is significant that Freud shows almost no interest in how the Oedipus Complex looks from the point of view of the father: how a father reacts, or should be expected to react, or should react, to the Oedipus complex. One looks in vain in *The Collected Psychological Works* of Freud for significant discussion of a father's feelings toward his son. Apart from brief references, there is no treatment of the subject in Freud. It is assumed that the father is threatening and hostile to the son and cannot be otherwise, even if he wanted to be.

The myth of Oedipus corresponds in certain respects to the Biblical story of Cain and Abel. The actual narrative sequence has a number of subtle features in the context of Male Envy. In the myth, Oedipus smashes the old male and seizes the female. Therefore, the murder of King Laius, Oedipus's father, though presented as accidental, is no accident: it is simply normal war between a strong male displaying control and a young male determined to win and not submit to another male. The appropriation of the older man's woman by the young man hence signals disintegration in control terms. Laius is not merely dead—his power is annihilated. He is collapsed on the compete/control hierarchy, like old Chillingworth in *The Scarlet Letter*. The fact that the loser happens to be the *father* signifies that the ambition of the young male does not recognize the limits of established authority in traditional Greek culture. And here lies the crime: the crime is that of endangering male established hierarchy itself—the ultimate crime in classical and Christian civilization alike. By violating established power relations, Oedipus metaphorically attacks the cosmic order itself. Hence it is logical that plague and natural disaster follow in the wake of his blinding daring.

For Male Envy, the sex taboo is peripheral, of minor importance compared to male aggression. That is, the incest taboo holds, but primarily as a way to demarcate power relations and not as something important in its own right. Freud himself is completely clear on this point. In *Totem and Taboo*, he remarks that "the forbidden contact [incest] has evidently not only sexual significance but rather the *more general one of attack, of acquisition and of personal assertion*."[28] In short, "The tip of the Oedipal triangle, which Freud called 'mother,' is a phantom," as Klaus Theweleit puts it in *Male Fantasies* (Theweleit 368). But the Oedipal rebellion must be defeated if male hierarchy (and hence civilization) is to survive; there has to be a way of accommodating the terrible tensions generated by the control hierarchy, without destroying the stability of the compete/control hierarchy itself, and Freud has a solution, namely the triumph of castration anxiety. The advantage of incest in the Oedipus Complex is that it pulls attention away from male hatred, which is the real theme (what attracts more attention than unorthodox sex?). Male hatred, in turn, is something that must be shown—and like so many sacred truths, not shown—at the same time.

Thus, Freud grasps the male resolution of the Oedipus complex *not* as simple maturation, as gradual recognition of one's male adult role in the hierarchy, but as *psychic rape*: "In boys . . . the complex is not simply repressed, it is literally smashed to pieces by the shock of threatened castration" forming "the nucleus of the superego."[29] Note the extraordinary drama here, the emphasis on "shock" and "smash." The language is hyperbolic, as if we are approaching the inner temple of the theory: no ordinary language will do. The Oedipus complex is not simply ended, dropped, dissolved, resolved, transcended, grown out of, or even broken: it is "literally smashed to pieces by the shock": *"Beim Knaben . . . wird der Komplex nicht einfach verdrangt, er zerschellt formlich unter dem Schock der Kastrationsdrohung."*

What Freud does, therefore, is to withdraw the myth from its original context in a fixed-hierarchical society, where Oedipus's crime is not so much incest as *hubris*—a tragic hubris of the Antigone or Prometheus type. That is, by going beyond the limits permitted to mortals, Oedipus threatens a structure of authority that is divinely ordained, and therefore inviolable, and he is punished for his sacrilegious boldness. Freud then replaces the Oedipus myth in the context of Male Envy in its capitalist setting. Freud's obsession with the Oedipus complex thus inscribes a prior obsession—a prior obsession with power relations.

Freud's theory of sexuality is phallocentric in that the penis is visualized as a thing that the male possesses, rather than as a member intrinsic to the male body. It becomes an appendage that appears to be—the word "*penis*" says it all—a "tail." It is visualized as an object only tenuously possessed.[30] Thus, penis "ownership" is a metaphor for property-ownership. Because of this metaphor, to be male is to be, by definition, the owner of property; that is to say, one who controls, since property = control-power and the mystique of control-power. Property/penis ownership is inseparable from Male Envy: "The motive that lies at the root of ownership is emulation . . . The possession of wealth confers honor; it is an invidious distinction" (Veblen 35). Put in class terms, capital = penis; property-owner = male. The relation of males to females is thus like a capital relation: possessors of capital vs. those not. Castration anxiety—so obsessive in Freud—is not just a matter of private psychology, therefore. It is a *property* anxiety. It is a metaphor for loss of property—for proletarianization: the ultimate terror for those of social power, and charged with a numinous horror.

Metaphorically, this loss is equivalent to conversion into a woman, i.e., into the propertyless—the un-penised. The rise of the Object Cosmology coincided with systematic curtailment of female property rights (Blackstone's 1758 *Commentaries* on the law make this clear). To be male is to be—as it were by definition—an owner.[31] It is to possess a power object, sexuality being understood as the private manipulation of that object in various private sites, as on the model of purchase and exchange acts. Ownership of the penis (as with property) is exclusive. The absurdity of all this is cleared up somewhat when one realizes that under the régime of Male Envy, female identity becomes a metaphor for being a loser-male, a man who has been defeated in compete/control struggles and cast off: that which a man must not be, not because it is not a man (and not because it is a woman), but because it is a loser-man.

In this way, the penis becomes a portentous Lacanian "phallus": a mystic, fetishized power object that condenses the Oedipus complex as the locus of unending struggle by males against males: "The phallus is the cryptic thing symbolized in numerous figures, images, and objects," in the words of Jean-Joseph Goux.[32] As so often in Object thinking, the physical ironically becomes metaphysical. No one knows how the actual penis relates to the "phallus" in Lacan's complicated theorizing. The "phallus" is a crux in Lacan's thought that is insoluble and inevitable, given the explicit hostility to anything metaphysical that is a standard marker of Object thinking[33]: it is physical but it is treated metaphysically. In this way of comprehending sexuality—as exclusive male ownership of a particular detachable object-unit—woman must be seen as penis-absence, as not-owning the unique object whose ownership defines males: to be constituted in effect as propertylessness. This adds another dimension to the anxiety of losing, of collapse on the control hierarchy, whose horror we have traced in a number of examples—Lycius demolished by Apollonius, Giovanni by Baglioni, Pip by Magwitch, etc. "Castration anxiety" is *loser* anxiety and has little or nothing to do with genital organs.

Since, for Freud, to lack a penis is the *sine qua non* of femaleness, envy is inescapably built into female identity—a notion that feminists have perhaps dealt with sufficiently. For Male Envy, by contrast, penis envy is not the reaction of female to male, but is rather the reaction of *male* to male. As Joseph Berke puts it, "Penis envy is the vengeful union of kindred impulses—spiteful hostility and begrudging deprivation. It may or may not coincide with the wish to be male."[34] In part, penis envy is simply anxiety about penis size. Size anxiety is endemic among males in our culture. It would be interesting to know whether size anxiety is as intense in all societies. Indeed, the exact effect of anxieties about size is unknown but is surely immense, given that it is so common among men. Size anxiety is inevitable in Male-envious culture, where comparing, competing, measurement, display, and quantification are obsessive. This preoccupation is not merely an anxiety, in fact, but a kind of doctrine.

What this "penis envy" signifies, then, is the cultural hatred of males for males. This hatred includes the subtly different hatred that males reserve for "weaker" males. It also refers to the anxiety of losing power/property—a function of the compete/control hierarchy. "Penis envy" is thus (1) a synedoche for Object thinking generally, where reality is measurable and quantifiable; (2) fear of "being small" (= inadequate or inferior); (3) the impotence (a matter of size/shape) that smallness metaphorically implies; and (4) envy of males who are "bigger and better," as they say: "well hung." As a consequence, male identity is visualized as external to itself (alienated almost in Marx's sense of self-separated)—a thing one can "measure." But this typifies Object thinking: the self is visualized as an object which one owns, rather than the being one participates in, the point of access to and connection with reality, not a self-enclosed opacity. The logic of Object thinking is to see male identity as measurable by external objects; by, in short, ownership, as a thing outside the self. Hence, in turn, the vital function of Male Display, which acts as a guarantee of identity. Unless the man can erect Male Displays, he cannot rise on the compete/control hierarchy.

Penis envy and castration anxiety refer to the primary layer of male identity in Freud (subtextually in Male Envy itself). The fear of castration "solves" the dilemmas of the Oedipus complex; but really, something else is going on here. Castration anxiety is an intense fear, a feeling of vulnerability associated with the most fragile, least armored/protected, and most sensitive area of the male body. What this anxiety marks is not merely vulnerability, then, but a need to *hide or conceal vulnerability*. The terror of exposure is the driving force, the "stick," behind the compete/control hierarchy. The need to rise on that hierarchy is not a mere compulsion to control objects and to compete, but a dread of vulnerability and dependency, which is almost too intense to be allowed into consciousness. Hence the code of Male Envy functions as a distraction, as displacement behavior. But, of course, the more one tries to distract or obliterate such feelings of vulnerability and fear, the more intense they become on an unconscious level.

Freud takes up the theme of primal anxiety in *Totem and Taboo*, which amounts to a late-Victorian fantasy in the same general area as Rider Haggard's *She* (one of Freud's favorite books) or Conrad's *Heart of Darkness*, with Sir James Frazer's killing-the-king rituals not too far in the background. As René Girard notes restrainedly, "Personne n'a jamais pris *Totem et Taboo* au sérieux."[35] Philosophy, history, and anthropology may ridicule *Totem and Taboo* —it "would not be accepted by current methods of social anthropology," observe Michael Arbib and Mary Hesse with polite understatement.[36] But as Freud, of all people, knew, fantasy has truths of its own. And *Taboo* unveils key assumptions. Primarily, *Totem and Taboo* is an allegory of the displacing of traditional religion and its God, ultimately of religion itself: a process already visibly underway in Malthus's *Essay on Population*, where God is tacitly reduced to the laws of nature, that is the movement of objects in space. Like Freud's neolithic male horde killing their alpha male, science has murdered this external God-patriarch: "élimination radicale" in Girard's term (114), annihilating Him in the mind of scientific, enlightened people.

Again, the curious persistence of the religious theme in connection with Male Envy is noticeable, and another parallel with Malthus. Freud's crusade against religion was integral to his project; it was not a mere byproduct or a late Enlightenment attempt to free humanity from oppressive superstition. Given its pivotal role in Freud's corpus, one understands why *The Future of an Illusion* is so powerful that it has become a classic. The male compete/control hierarchy is thus reconstituted: the metaphysical top position, formerly occupied by a male God, is deleted (as metaphysics in general is deleted in modern thought), thereby freeing individuals to maneuver on the control scale as their power allows. This is a very important aspect of the plot of *Totem and Taboo*. The deletion of the king-male-God in one way ends the control hierarchy, but in another way it also reconstitutes it—and in a more uncompromising, ruthless manner. It collapses the hierarchy as a pre-fixed structure and installs it as a universal competition. Ironically, furthermore, *Taboo* diagnoses the very guilt that traditional religion has used as its preferred instrument to control people. It is really the inherited guilt of killing God. Now one may go as far as one can in the competitive marketplace that constitutes human existence. Given this universal competition, penis envy is inevitable: intrinsic to the contest of male competitors.

The fact that Freud holds such fascination for literary critics/theorists is full of significance, for he is the exemplar of competition. One may contrast, in this respect, Freud's neglected contemporary, the great American sociologist Thorstein Veblen, from whom literary criticism has perhaps more to learn than from Freud and his penis anxieties and castration obsessions (not to mention Lacan's revision of Freud into an ever more elaborate web of phallus, father, language, mind, none of which has empirical evidence as a base to build on). Curiously, Veblen was hardly a winner in personal competitive struggle in the academic world, as his career at Stanford makes all too plain, whereas Freud (like Malthus) was spectacularly successful, attracting attention from all sides, acquiring the reputation of a kind of saint of scientific rectitude and dispassionate commitment, and shaping popular consciousness to an unprecedented degree.[37]

Veblen's *Theory of the Leisure Class*, fertile in so many respects, remains neglected, especially by literary critics. This may be because its peculiar baroque style is scarcely tolerable for 10 pages, let alone 300, whereas Freud was a superb stylist and had gifted translators. Yet Veblen's style is functional, too, as a distraction device: it diverts anxiety awakened by his attack on societal values, the area of Male Envy, which is essentially his topic, being (once again) virtually taboo. Veblen deploys his attack from the stance of a detached observer—a kind of Gibbon who contemplates all of Roman madness but does not gag. In Veblen, "all that considerable body of morals that clusters about the concept of an inviolable ownership is itself a psychological precipitate of the traditional meritoriousness of wealth" (89). Owning becomes a fetish: desired not for material advantage, but for its own sake in a Baudrillard-style precession of simulacra. (Baudrillard's complicated exegesis of signs and "simulation" has a logical ancestor in Veblen.[38]) This in turn assumes the cultural primacy of envy: "a life of self-seeking, force, fraud, and mastery" (Veblen 234). In traditional morality, envy is understood as being in opposition to self-interest—Samuel Johnson's *Rambler* essay #183 is a marvelous exposition of this traditional view —but in Veblen, one feeds the other. Envy and self-interest (in the sense of aggressive greed) are interconnected forces in a single system, a system responsible for untold cruelty, suffering, and horror.

The curious emptiness of Male Envy is a recurring theme in Veblen. This emptiness usually appears by way of contrasting what he calls "the instinct of workmanship" (the delight and power to create things of value), on one hand, vs. "invidious distinction" (the manipulation of appearances through display or control of things of value), on the other. Veblen's insistence that "workmanship" —creative action or the wish to make and to perfect—is an instinct needs to be observed carefully. For it is radically different from Freud's drives and instincts, with their aggressive base, or from Adam Smith's instinct to trade and barter things (not make things—there is no instinct to create in Adam Smith, and work is regarded as drudgery, as something to avoid). Indeed, Veblen's belief that people have a need and an innate power to create is at odds with Object thinking generally and is practically meaningless in terms of the code of Male Envy.

Whereas in Malthus wealth is something controlled, in Veblen it is something created, and the controlling function (the unproductive consumption by the propertied classes advocated by Malthus) is a perversion or aberration. Without the creating work, the controlling function is literally nothing, and has literally nothing—except control.

* * *

In the academy, the need to be in the limelight—or rather, to control the limelight—is silent and unremitting pressure, like hunger in Malthus. The ethos of the academy is pervaded by Male Envy, an ethos perhaps plainer in the case of literary studies than in most disciplines, perhaps because the content of literary studies has become so contested and uncertain. What proportion of literary criticism/theory is really the product of compete/control struggles, an expression of the *form* of competition? How many changes of theoretical direction are simply the result of the needs of competition? In the régime of Male Envy, the desire to illuminate literature/culture for its own sake is considered too naive for serious consideration. Perhaps it is not an accident that so many mystery novels are set in English departments, where there seems to be plenty of motivation in the form of hate, resentment, envy, grudges, and malice generally.

The effort to win attention for its own sake—not as a contribution to the study of literature or culture—is a basic motivation. This motivation generates the book-a-year syndrome, the compulsion to publish incessantly. One result is that new areas are constantly sought, since publication is easier where there are no "precursors," as Harold Bloom would say, to compete with; the power relations within the academy bring areas into being at least partly because of the competitive form that constitutes academic identity. Male Envy constantly seeks for new fields in which to display control. This compulsion applies not only to junior academics struggling to survive on the compete/control hierarchy, but also to established critics and theorists. For without incessant publication, loss of influence threatens. Aside from the book-a-year syndrome, another result of the operation of Male Envy is the need to be encyclopedic: to comment on everything. Hence, anybody who treats any subject must of necessity cite the encyclopedic critic. Such impulses are noticeable in many critics—J. Hillis Miller and Harold Bloom come to mind. Even Derrida, that most influential of theorists, not only publishes constantly, but publishes on every possible subject. The will to be encyclopedic dovetails with the need to produce the irrefutable argument: to see words as units in competitive struggle, to nullify others and displace them.

The best-known expositor of envy as the basis for literature itself, not just criticism, is Harold Bloom, in particular his *Anxiety of Influence*. The Anxiety of Influence constitutes poets as competitors with poets—and critics as competitors with poets (needless to say, the competition of critic with critic is a given, in this model). Thus Harold Bloom himself, in prophetic mode:

> Every poem is a misinterpretation of a parent poem. A poem is not an overcoming of anxiety, but is that anxiety. Poets' misinterpretations or poems are more drastic than critics' misinterpretations or criticism, but this is only a difference in degree and not at all in kind. There are no interpretations but only misinterpretations, and so all criticism is prose poetry.[39]

In short, "A poem is a poet's melancholy at his lack of priority" (Bloom 96). Bloom's melancholy vision of "influence," as a competition-pathology charged with envy-anxiety, correlates closely with the meaninglessness—"alienation"—of the Object Cosmology. A paradigm that functions similarly in practice is articulated by Stanley Fish: critics antagonistically struggle to impose their interpretation so as "to enhance the importance of [their] activities,"[40] like so many roosters strutting in the barnyard.

The assumption again recalls the emptiness of power points: the poet achieves poetry not by writing, but by dislodging someone else. The need to defeat others, and acquire envy, is more important than the desire to create something, according to Bloom's model: a model that grotesquely overestimates the inner strength of envy, which is scarcely able to create anything, however skilled it may be at using, manipulating, damaging, or concealing the creations of other people. It is as if paying attention to the work of the poet is somehow taking attention away from oneself, hence damaging that self or reinforcing its sensation of inferiority. The goal of seizing and holding the attention of others has a compulsive quality, as noted earlier. This compulsiveness suggests an inner emptiness needing to be hid: in this case, the fear of having nothing genuine to contribute. "A poem is a poet's melancholy at his lack of priority": "priority" is not merely *coming before*, but *being more important than*. Thus, a poem is the despair that others might have more importance than oneself. The concomitant notion that criticism is just a feebler kind of poetry is really an unconscious joke, given the unreadability, predictability, and dullness of so much criticism/theory.

The need to hold attention rather than create or add knowledge implies a disturbing subtext in Bloom's central conception of "misprision" ("misreading"). In misprision, one fails to understand another writer; one substitutes one's own meaning for the author's; misprision is also an unavoidable failure to understand, say an unfamiliar word (as in verbal "false friends") or a cultural practice that is new. Looked at from the perspective of Male Envy, however, misprision has a very different and far more sinister meaning. For it implies the need to *destroy the work of other writers*—to "misread" not in the sense of "misconstrue," but in the sense of obliterate or break up, like an Egyptian pharaoh defacing the inscriptions of a "precursor" potentate from temples and monuments.

Hence misprision is not simply creative or inevitable misreading, but rather a program of sabotage, by which a precursor is "castrated," so as to make room for oneself; that is, to allow one to announce or demonstrate one's superiority. Even if it is unconscious, then, misprision is a way to enhance one's ego at the expense of earlier and other writers. One recalls here the curious principle in Male Envy that destroying is the same as creating; that the power to destroy has priority over the power to create. Destruction is a means of commandeering attention and demonstrating power, and a basic form of Male Display, a decisive test of whether one truly controls something. To destroy someone else is the classic means of self-inflation. This kind of "misprision" leaves an inevitable trace in deconstruction as a theoretical enterprise, a "trace" that is seldom acknowledged. That is, the wish to damage or destroy literary texts and traditions is unavoidably a part of the deconstructive project, which is not just a demonstration of features that were previously invisible. This is merely standard procedure in Male Envy: the way to establish oneself and one's importance is by eviscerating the identity of others.

Nevertheless, since poetry is inherently social in nature—a writer could never write without having read other writers—the competitive model is profoundly contradictory. Literature is a social creation; or rather, it transcends the split between individual and society. Literature is communication, for example (however much it fails to communicate), and communication, as the word implies, is interdependent with community. The language that one writes with is a social energy in which the writer is immersed, and the plots, characters, ideas, and images that a writer uses are taken unavoidably, not so much from personal experience, as from other and earlier writers. I say "taken" here, but I do not mean "stolen": the absorbing and revising of earlier stories is in itself the way by which literature grows and replicates itself, just as children "take" the genetic materials of their parents.

Still, it must be affirmed that Bloom's anxiety of influence is a powerful theory. But that power is not because it is correct, but because *it echoes the hegemonic ethos of Male Envy*, and so acquires a plausibility far out of proportion to its truth content; this plausibility is really isomorphy with the assumptions of the dominant cosmology. The obvious antecedent for Bloom's dismal vision of universal competition was W. J. Bate, who made the anxieties of Male Envy a paradigm of cultural entropy. Thus he closes *The Burden of the Past and the English Poet* with a portentous evocation of the traditional canon:

> The arts mirror the greatest single cultural problem we face . . . that is, how to use a heritage, when we know and admire so much about it, how to grow by means of it, how to acquire our own "identities," how to be ourselves. . . . In the experience of the eighteenth century we have exemplified—if we choose to look at it with a "greeting of the spirit"—what the old epigram said of Plato . . . in whatever direction you happened to be going, you meet him on his way back.[41]

Bate's axiom that the past threatens identity is the key to Bloom's notion of "influence" and "anxiety." The problem with all this is that Bate forgets that knowing the past enables us to know ourselves, rather than threatening our identity. Unless, of course, our identity is *already* threatened, as indeed, in the régime of Male Envy, it is.

It is significant that *The Burden of the Past* focuses on the eighteenth century, the period of the rise of Object thinking, with its inherently competitive mode of perceiving/understanding. The individual does not simply exist: the individual is a competitor in a field of control. Writers, by the same token, must be, irretrievably, competitive producers whose work succeeds only in so far as others' fails. Control is everything.

By contrast, literary tradition is strangely unaware of this way of thinking. For example, the medieval conception of authorship is quite different; it assumes that the writer is an adapter, who receives, changes, and transmits the inherited literary tradition. In other words, literature uses writers, rather than the reverse. This is perfectly apparent in folktale and oral literature, where stories circulate, growing, fragmenting, adding, subtracting, passing from language to language, and from one geographical location to another, picking up and discarding local cultural motifs as they transform. In this line of thought, we find a tradition of poets *recreating* poets, so that earlier writers live on within new generations, again recalling genes replicated through family trees. Spenser speaks of Chaucer in this manner: Chaucer lives on in Spenser. Writers are famously quarrelsome, notoriously with predecessors, but even the revolutionary original, Milton, the strongest of Bloomian "strong" poets, recreates the tradition he has inherited, with its Classical and Biblical basis—he does not destroy or supplant it. There isn't a line of *Paradise Lost* that is without a Biblical or Classical allusion: the poem *is* the Bible and the classics, recreated. Once more, the change in attitude comes with writers whose consciousness is trained by Object thinking, in the eighteenth century.

Even there, however, writers see themselves only gradually as originals, in the sense of producers who "own" their product but write, in practice, as recreators. Thus, we find the important tradition of translation and "imitation" in Dryden, Pope, Johnson, and the rest (including female authors)—that is, a history of remaking and communicating the inherited tradition, and this includes quarrelling with that tradition. In the Romantic poets, this process becomes, not the recreating of a bunch of *things*—a collection of previous texts by dead writers—but the transmission of a power or energy-in-time. Thus, in the Romantics, both tendencies are noticeable: the tendency to see writing in terms of the competitive marketplace, with its Male-envious implications, and the tendency to see writers as recreating/transmitting a tradition. Blake visualizes Milton entering his body in his brief epic *Milton*, and his own poetry as a purging/recreating of the earlier poet's. Percy Shelley's *Defence of Poetry* elaborates a theory that writers are all co-operating thoughts of a single mind—producing "episodes of that cyclic poem written by Time upon the memories of men": an astonishing intuition.

But what Shelley and Blake really indicate is a third model: neither the traditional notion of poets as receiving/transmuting/handing on a tradition, nor of writers as competitors in a field where the purpose is to hold the attention of those who matter, like businessmen competing for market control. This third model is typical of what I termed Transform thinking. The commercial model, which underwrites Bloom's theory, replicates the more prestigious "hard sciences," as in the aphorism of biologist Richard Lewontin in my epigraph: "Science is a form of competitive and aggressive activity, a *contest of man against man* that provides knowledge as a side product. That side product is its only advantage over football."[42] That is, Bloom's theory adapts the unrelenting competition of businessmen, of scientists and technologies, and transposes it into literature. In the hard sciences, Male Envy operates with large stakes, not only grants, prestigious teaching and research positions, labs, and internationally recognized prizes to use as power points but lucrative contracts with large corporations and influential sectors of government: something approaching real power and not merely the simulacrum of power that academics typically seek.

In literary studies, the goal of Male Envy is to seize and hold the attention of professors and students. This compulsion generates what I termed the book-a-year syndrome. Without incessant publishing, there will be a lapse of awareness: people will forget one exists, where existence is constituted in the Male-envious manner, as holding-the-attention-of-others. One will be overtaken and left behind by a new fashion. The image of Dante's demonic pursuit in Canto 16 of the *Inferno* comes to mind: the denizens of this particular circle of Hell endlessly chase a banner; although they can never catch up, if they stop for a second, they turn instantly to dust: "Fear in a handful of dust," as T. S. Eliot says in *The Waste Land*—"dust" being an old metaphor for nothingness and emptiness. Dante's "banner" motif reappears in Part I of *Gulliver's Travels*, with the politicians doing showy tricks in public and receiving prestigious bits of colored thread. Bloomian and deconstructive literary history "replace[s] notions of tradition and revolution with the notion of repetition as displacement or decentering"[43]: whether this model accurately describes literary history or not, what it certainly does describe, in projected form, is the competitive struggle of theorists, displaced on to literary history. Again, the form of competitive struggle is transmuted, as by some Hegelian *Aufhebung*, into the content of theory.

Bloom himself seems gripped by the book-a-year syndrome, producing or editing books on a vast array of subjects; but, as noted before, many familiar critics, such as J. Hillis Miller, and important theorists such as Derrida himself seem to suffer from the influence of this particular anxiety. In *Aporias*, Derrida begins by listing a number of conceptions that he has introduced in his many books, all with their special vocabulary, which he notes all mean effectively the same thing. He all but states thereby that the quantity of writing he has produced does not match, so to speak, its real content. The book-a-year syndrome is accompanied by two related symptoms: apart from the encyclopedic need to comment on as many subjects as possible, there is the *incessant shifting* of point of view, so as to keep up with trends, hoping to turn them in one's own direction. If one goes back over criticism written earlier, it is sobering to see how much of it is simply a function of the fashion popular at the time, and hence almost contentless: a clear warning that much of what is now being produced is equally a function of fashion, a repetition of certain motifs that have obsessive interest for a time, rather than new insights or even genuine content.

* * *

One theorist who did not suffer from the book-a-year syndrome was Paul de Man. For its huge influence, his body of writing was relatively small—a few thin volumes of essays (not counting his "wartime journalism"[44]). However, de Man extends our analysis of the code of Male Envy in important ways. First of all, de Man was a conscious stylist. Few critics could match his cultivated manner, his subtle terminology, and his sheer verbal performance, with its polish, its artful balance of clause and phrase. What his style projects is Olympian authority and detachment—superiority to the fray of critical competition. He is the aristocrat of critics, the personification of refinement. The style partly accounts for the curious veneration accorded to de Man as a kind of saint, which has often been noted, as if he were the very embodiment of scholarly rectitude, of devotion to impartial scrutiny, whatever disturbing conclusions that scrutiny might reveal.

The stylishness of his rhetoric makes it difficult to know exactly what his meaning is. When, however, one separates the ideas from their rhetorical setting, the ideas tend to reduce in size. De Man's main idea is easy enough to identify, simply because he reverts to it so often, and in so many forms, and that is the illusoriness of figures of speech. For de Man, as for most critics throughout history, figures of speech epitomize literature—especially metaphor, the trope or figure of speech that identifies one thing with another, as when Hamlet speaks of death as "the undiscover'd country from whose bourn / No traveller returns." For de Man, as for other Object thinkers, figures of speech are extremely problematic—in a sense, they are tricks: verbal claims that cannot be made good. Death is obviously not a country, discovered or otherwise; travelers do not visit it, whether they return or not. What Hamlet says when he uses words in this fashion does not correspond to reality—that is, to the conglomeration of objects which constitutes reality. His trope is ultimately meaningless, just as the nothing which is death is meaningless and renders meaningless.

De Man frequently recurs to the aporetic unintelligibility of tropes, to "figural evasion," as he stylishly calls it.[45] Exposing their identity as a bogus claim is a primary strategy. In de Man's own words, "Metaphor is error because it believes or feigns to believe in its own referential meaning."[46] One wonders: who is doing the believing here? Metaphors do not "believe" anything. Metaphor is not a matter of belief. Nor is metaphor a truth claim. Whatever one thinks of this "error," de Man's technique of denying metaphor, in the sense of vitiating it as a mode that communicates, has another kind of force altogether.

Deconstructing metaphor is not simply a technique of analysis but a weapon for intellectual conflict, where it has the effect of ending further discussion. That is, his intellectual argument may be an argument; what it certainly is is a technique of competition/control.

In de Man's model, a trope is like an NSF check—there is "nothing" to back it up; it has no material basis, no correspondent reality. The deconstruction of tropes is basic to de Man's theory, but this deconstruction is not simply negation: it is at the same time the careful advocacy of a particular *worldview*. Namely, reality is a collocation of objects in space, and there is nothing else. Indeed, this is literally true in Object thinking—there are objects and there is nothing, and the nothing is what the objects exist in. To call it "nihilism" here would be too crude; it has values, but they are the tacit values associated with Male Envy.

De Man articulates this worldview with special incisiveness in his influential essay on the radical visionary, Percy Shelley, whose death by drowning fascinated de Man. He entitled the essay "Shelley Disfigured." Shelley's body was so badly decomposed that he could be identified only by the contents of his pockets. Such is the fate of the radical visionary, who thought his words made a difference—an error, as de Man demonstrates in "disfiguring" Shelley. The title of this essay is a ghoulish pun. Thus, de Man combines (1) the deconstruction of Shelley's figures of speech ("dis-figured"); (2) the decomposition of the body of the man named Shelley; and (3), the mutilation (castration?) of Shelley's writing. The sly interposition of mutilating Shelley's writing with deconstructing his figures is noteworthy. The task of destroying a hated author is skillfully and impudently screened by an appearance of impartial investigation.

The climax of de Man's essay is a widely quoted sentence. Notice its conspicuous hyperbole: "Nothing, whether deed, word, thought, or text, ever happens in relation, positive or negative, to anything that precedes, follows, or exists elsewhere, but only as a random event whose power, like the power of death, is due to the randomness of its occurrence."[47] Shelley *disproved*, not just disfigured. This famous sentence is intended to be quotable and is rhetorically crafted for that purpose. It is also a metaphysical assertion, indeed a metaphysical assertion of remarkable certainty, coming from a school of thought for which metaphysics is self-delusion generated by the manipulation of words,[48] a school of thought which in fact despises metaphysics.

The notion that "nothing happens in relation to anything else" is profoundly at odds with Shelley's thought (whether Shelley's thought is right or wrong): no poet asserted more determinedly that everything is connected to everything else. Hence one wonders why de Man insists on it in connection with a poet whose work he is ostensibly explaining. But this is really the point. The idea that "Nothing" "happens" "in relation" "to anything" else, except "as a random event," is the essence of Object thinking.

One is struck by the rhetorical fireworks—the anaphora, the hyperbole—in de Man's statement. This is language used to impress, even overpower, rather than communicate: there is a loss of control, as if the vision held something mesmerizing that the author could not resist. The vision of utter destruction fascinates; its rhetorical impact can hardly be matched. One senses a certain heightening here: no ordinary language will do when approaching the inner heart, the determining impulse, of one's vision.

And with this, we return to Malthus, whose visions of death on a mass scale are the prototype: there is a rhetorical history behind de Man's fascination with the power of death. In Malthus, for example, here is what happens when there are too many people, not enough food:

> Famine seems to be the last, the most dreadful resource of nature. The power of population is so superior to the power in the earth to produce subsistence for man, that premature death must in some shape or other visit the human race. The vices of mankind are active and able ministers of depopulation. They are the precursors in the great army of destruction, and often finish the dreadful work themselves. But should they fail in this war of extermination, sickly seasons, epidemics, pestilence, and plague, advance in terrific array and sweep off their thousands and ten thousands. Should success be still incomplete, gigantic inevitable famine stalks in the rear, and with one mighty blow, levels the population with the food of the world.

Malthus makes no attempt to conceal the mounting excitement that this vision—this disaster fantasy—arouses. The rhetoric here is the rhetoric of Edmund Burke's "sublime"—a vision of terror and vastness, of irresistible force. In Burke, of course, the sublime is sublime from the point of view of the privileged spectator, who is exempted and can watch, untouched and safe.[49]

A fascination with the power of death, almost as fetish, is implicit in Object thinking, as we have seen. René Girard's theory of the origin of civilization makes this fascination explicit as, almost exactly, a sort of deification: "we view culture as originating in a mystified deferral of violence, in sacrifice, whereby human violence is rerouted via the sacred, which is a safe place for us both to abhor and adore it," in Andrew J. McKenna's paraphrase of Girard.[50] Violence —destructive force—and the sacred become equivalent terms. The subtext in the *Essay on Population* is the same as that of de Man: a subtext of fascination with the power of death—"the terror of encrypted death," as de Man phrases it in his essay on Hans Robert Jauss.[51] The stylistic virtuosity in such expressions as "the terror of encrypted death" is typical of de Man when he writes about death, what he calls elsewhere "the most extreme of alienations," the style here showing a noticeable relish, as it always does when death is his topic. The fascinated veneration of death as mystic agency is, of course, characteristic of Male Envy.

The need to gain/keep control typifies the Object thinking that is de Man's underlying point; more precisely, the point that is assumed in his work and that makes his judgments correct, even inevitable. Thus his essays have a logic, a technique not only of deconstructing tropes, but of deconstructing rival critics, so as to make plain de Man's own superiority. The rhetorical *topos* of modesty is the starting point: typically de Man praises other critics, sometimes fulsomely. Then, however, he goes on to explain that his subject is regrettably defective, indeed seriously if not fatally flawed, and will not do.[52] (Thus, de Man follows a standard Male-envious pattern: sabotage others and replace them with oneself— i.e., shift attention from them to you, like the Mariner with the Albatross.) The typical reason why the critic/writer is found unsatisfactory, furthermore, is that the writer he is scrutinizing actually has confidence in his/her metaphors and does not seem to realize that metaphor is really deception.

The prime example is Shelley, and the choice of Shelley is no accident. For Shelley was the most radical of English poets, the follower of Godwin and Wollstonecraft, the visionary who believed in social transformation and equality, and in the immortality of the soul; who believed that death was not ultimate–a blasphemy in Male Envy. Moreover, Shelley actually believed that his words had meaning and existential force: a nonsensical notion, because words belong in a special verbal realm that is not objects-in-space, but an illusionary subjective site that is unreal (it has no spatial location). A writer such as Shelley must be "disfigured," as a duty if not a pleasure.

The split between verbal and spatial domains is the basis of de Man's concept of "allegory"; it is an application of assumptions in the model of reality that de Man takes for granted as simply reality.[53] Hence it is not merely tropes that are unreal, finally, but words and verbal constructs themselves: their authority is an illusion, given that the ultimate authority is extinction, whether extinction in the form of death, or in the form of the nothingness in which objects exist. The supremacy of this nothingness partly explains why the imagery of the "gap" (and its many variants—absence, aporia, emptying, etc.) has had such resonance in contemporary literary theory. The gap is more "real," so to speak, than the text that surrounds it, just as the nothingness in which material objects exist and that makes them possible must be more real than the objects located in it. In other words, the motif of the gap articulates the subject-space-object paradigm of Object thinking.

De Man used another technique, especially in his essay "The Resistance to Theory," that deserves note. The term "resistance" resonates with its technical Freudian meaning of denying the truth. In "Resistance," de Man argues that those who resist theory are just producing more theory, hence confirming theory.[54] This is a variant on the technique R. C. Tallis identifies in Freud: a technique that is essentially begging the question. The arguer assumes the truth of what the arguer is supposedly trying to prove. Begging the question is a potent *topos* in the rhetoric of competition—and a potent temptation, for it appears to guarantee winning. The use of reason as a means of rationalization—the treatment of reason as one more weapon in a struggle for control—is typical of the code of Male Envy. Just as repressing something reinforces it, those who disagree are proving the very thing they disagree with, simply by disagreeing. Derrida, a more formidable figure than de Man, works with this technique extensively. The argument that texts, against their will as it were, say implicitly the opposite of what they say explicitly, is a related paradigm. A similar argument—it is really a rhetorical *topos* again—is to dismiss negative reaction or disagreement as (unintelligent) misunderstanding. Therefore, disagreement deserves no respect; and it may be treated Male-enviously, with contempt. The form of competition becomes the content of theory (just as the physical absorbs the metaphysical into itself, even as the metaphysical is being theoretically repudiated).[55]

The impact of "pen envy," in Geoffrey Hartman's phrase, has been immense, on both the form and the content of literary study, especially in the high prestige area of theory. Most theorists do not deal with the subject of "pen envy" openly or allow it to appear that control in the marketplace of ideas is a vital concern: the need to absorb as much attention of others as possible (or more precisely, the attention of those who count, notably prestige institutions). Harold Bloom is valuable here because of his candor about the compulsions of Male Envy. In the form of his theory of "influence," Bloom canonizes Male Envy—indeed, deifies it—as a force in literary criticism. He also gives his preoccupation a Nietzschean "genealogy" in the preoccupation of Freud. The "anxiety of influence" is really a synonym or circumlocution for "envy." Again, the form of Male Envy replaces the content of knowledge. But this in turn is isomorphic with the Object assumptions of society at large, the Object assumptions of *Male-envious* society.

* * *

From many angles, Male Envy has an impact on knowledge. It affects what lines of thought get pursued and what do not. Feminists have probed the ways in which science has been constituted by gender imperatives, and historians have paid attention to the formation of disciplines in the academy. But Male Envy as a force field in the academy remains obscure. What is the significance of knowledge, when it is valued not for itself, but as a competitive token, a means of competing with others in a control hierarchy? Or when its function is to rationalize power relations? If the purpose of research and publication is to acquire advantage over others, to rise on the compete/control hierarchy in order to stay on it at all—and not to add to the understanding of reality—what is the effect on consciousness and on knowledge? and therefore on human power to act and create intelligently? What is the effect of Male Envy on the academy as the place where learning goes forward—on students, on the process of learning?

At the center of these difficult questions is a distinction between intellectual production in order to enlighten and intellectual production as a token in the competitive struggle of Male Envy—as an ego point. This distinction actually corresponds to one of the fundamental paradigms of our culture as a whole. Ego points must be quantifiable and visible, in accord with Object preoccupations with measurement and control. In some respects, this paradigm is at its clearest in professional sports, where winning is more important than playing; more exactly, the *frisson* or thrill of winning and dominating over others is a large factor in the popularity of competitive sports (and this is apart from the fact that a team can win, not because it is athletically better, but for other reasons—weather, financing, personal factors, specifics of the physical environment, etc.). Another familiar example is valuing paintings not for artistic reasons, but for the amount they fetch in the market: their value is not art but what Veblen calls "the traditional meritoriousness of wealth." In the academy itself, two areas are especially revealing in this context: economics (neoclassical economics, that is: what is taught in the academy); and the immense development known as post-structuralism that has grown up around the linguistic formulations of Saussure.

Neoclassical economics descends from "classical economics." As a cultural development, classical economics corresponds closely to the period of Romantic narrative that has furnished most of the examples we have been pondering in this study. Its main figures are Adam Smith (*The Wealth of Nations*, 1776), Malthus (*Essay on Population*, 1798), and especially David Ricardo (*Principles of Political Economy and Taxation*, 1819). Classical economics is built upon the labor theory of value, unlike its neoclassical descendant: according to the labor theory of value, all wealth comes from human work. If labor is the origin of wealth, "Labour, therefore, is the real measure of the exchangeable value of all commodities," as Adam Smith puts it: "Labour alone, therefore, never varying in its own value, is alone the ultimate and real standard by which the value of all commodities can at all times and places be estimated and compared. It is the real price; money is their nominal price only."[56] The labor theory of value coheres in classical economics with another fundamental assumption. This is the distinction between "use value" and "exchange value": what a thing is worth subjectively, as an object of consumption ("use"), and what a thing will fetch as a commodity on the open market (where "commodity" means an object produced for sale, not immediate use by its producer). Use value is universal and ancient; exchange value is a function of the market.

As Adam Smith explains, exchange value is quantitative. A certain quantity of labor is required to produce a commodity, which can, furthermore, be exchanged for a certain quantity of money. By contrast, use value is qualitative and cannot be quantified, certainly not in the same way as exchange value. In classical economics, it is assumed that a commodity has to have use value in order to have exchange value—no one will buy something that has no use. If it has no use, it is simply wasted labor. The distinction between use value and exchange value is a necessary corollary of the labor theory of value, which is the assumption that all economic goods are the result of human beings working, and the labor theory of value, once again, is basic to classical economics, especially Ricardo's.[57] Hence the distinction between the two kinds of value—value in exchange and value in use—was abandoned when the labor theory of value was abandoned, and for the same reasons, by the "neoclassical" economics which supplanted the earlier variety in the later nineteenth century, and which is now standard in the academy.

Neoclassical economics collapses the two kinds of value. For it, "use value" can be quantified, in the sense that a thing is worth whatever someone is willing to pay for it; and this willingness to pay is in practice a measure of use value. That is, because willingness to pay manifests as a quantity of money, it effectively makes the use-value concept of classical economics unnecessary. This price, in turn, is the basis of the key doctrine in neoclassical economics: the doctrine of "marginal utility," which is that value is determined by the amount purchasers are willing to pay at the break-even point for the seller.

Usefulness becomes curiously dematerialized in this conception. The use value of money is its power to generate more money—not things, as it were, not useful or desired products. One invests in whatever will yield the highest return, so that investment money is inherently speculative. In contemporary society, the emphasis on speculation is enormous, especially in international finance.

> Every day about U.S. $1 trillion worth of currencies change hands on world markets. The vast majority of these transactions don't involve the trade of goods and merchandise but are purely speculative. . . . When Keynes first warned [in 1936] against the danger of finance dominating the real economy, financial exchanges were about twice as large as merchandise trade. Today financial transactions are seventy-two times greater than trade.[58]

Usefulness (the point of Veblen's "instinct of workmanship") could hardly be further away from the speculative transactions that govern the global economy. Financial transactions control investment in the production of actual goods and services, whereas in the past it was the other way around: the needs of production determined investment flows. Likewise, the needs of investment for production are increasingly subordinated to the needs of *marketing*: "In 1992 U.S. business spent an estimated $1 trillion dollars (one in every six dollars of GDP) on marketing, simply convincing people to consume more and more goods."[59] In currency speculation, even tiny shifts in exchange rates can yield substantial profits, if the amount speculated is large enough. This vast capital pool is not "used" for anything, but acts like a token in a Derridean chain of endless deferral—an electronic "trace" hurried from one bank's computer to another. It is also liable to turn into nothing, as happens when the market drops. Physical things may not disappear, but money in the form of speculative representations certainly can. The profound irrationality of this arrangement is mirrored in the idolatry of inequality. As Daniel Singer observes: "We're living in a world in which the wealth of its 447 dollar billionaires exceeded in 1996 the income of half of the world's population."[60]

In classical economics, use value is direct, exchange value is indirect; use value is the thing itself—exchange value is a "representation" that is involved in an endless chain of representations, separated from any specific commodity. In curious ways, the distinction between the two kinds of value parallels Saussure's distinction between "signified" and "signifier." The latter is a sign that stands for the former. Saussure regarded this signifier-signified relationship as arbitrary: the signifier bears no necessary connection with what it represents (the signified), any more than the word "star" is stuck on to the little light that twinkles in the sky. Post-structuralism separates the signifier (word) from the signified (thing); it renders the distinction obsolete, much as exchange value is separated from use value in neoclassical economics, floating free into an arbitrary economic space, governed by speculation and chaotic metonymic exchanges. Baudrillard's theorem of the "precession of simulacra" and Derrida's notion of endless deferral are parallel, where appearances disclose only further appearances, not realities; and signifiers unfold into more signifiers, never a signified.

But this kind of paradigm is implicit, ironically, in Object thinking itself; or rather, in the Object model of language. For Object thinking naively regards words as correlating with material objects in space, like labels (word corresponds to thing); that is why words mean something—they are metonyms and "stand for" real things, for actual reality—that is, objects in space.[61] The eminent critic J. Hillis Miller explicates: "Naming or speaking in fact depends on seeing, since literal language, the base and origin of all metaphorical transfer, is defined as the match of the word with the perception of the thing. We see the sun and we call it 'sun'."[62]

However, poetry, he explains, defies every "possible physical fact," for it

> includes anomalous, unlawful, and alogical features [i.e., figures of speech; hence] it is in fact a series of impossible metaphors. 'Impossible' is here meant as a *discrepancy between the language and any possible physical fact*. Rather than being grounded in nature, in things as they are, in perception leading to knowledge leading to naming and then to that interchange among such firmly grounded names called *metaphor*, such alogical language indicates the unsettling freedom of language from perception and its ability to pour into the mold of its syntactical and grammatical patterns forms of locution which, in relation to the empirical world, are, strictly speaking, nonsense. (156; my emphasis)

Miller emphasizes the same hostility to figurative language and inability to accept it that we saw in Paul de Man. In this way of thinking, as soon as words are separated from their legitimate mapping function, they become problematic—

not merely undecidable, but effectively meaningless, not just in the primary sense of lacking denotative content, but in the more sinister sense of being without point or value. For de Man, as for Miller, however, this is characteristic of literature; under this régime, literature can scarcely be said to mean anything, except in the sense of disclosing its own meaninglessness (the process that de Man termed "blindness" and "insight"). In Derrida, the proliferation of signifiers without signifieds is functionally all that there is, since we can only discuss things by means of more words—texts discussed by texts; it is thus texts that are real, therefore, whatever else is. The contempt for literature that saturates this kind of thinking is not a matter of individual critics making up theories: it is a disclosure of Object thinking generally toward literature, as something useless and unreal, instead of a significant social resource.

The notion that words correlate with objects in space, that that is how words are meaningful, is such an oversimplification that it is of no value; but the deconstruction of this notion in Derrida actually reinscribes it, because it assumes that it was there to begin with. That is, by arguing that signifiers are part of an endless chain of signifiers, with no signifieds—no things—no "presence"—to back them up, one is arguing against an idea that was not true to begin with; one is assuming something to be there that is not there, and never was there. Words are infinitely more complicated than labels for objects. The result is not to end the assumption that words map objects, but to keep rebuilding it. Truly to refute it requires *the posing of an alternative model*, which is not possible within the ironic terms of reference that enclose deconstructive theory.

The alternative that has emerged to deconstruction and post-structuralism is New Historicism, the belief that literature is a subset of history, that it can be reduced to a historical artifact on the same plane as scrimshaws and cookbooks. But in the crucial area, the New Historicism has not been an advance on deconstruction. For by treating all texts as equal, and as equally ideological, the New Historicism does not offer a model of literary works and metaphoric language. On the contrary, it abandons the category of literature altogether—a category that will not simply go away merely because history has no understanding of literature. This difficulty in formulating a theory of literary/metaphoric language reveals, in turn, an even greater difficulty: the problem of getting past Object thinking and the Male-envious relations that it sustains, and that replicate and police its authority in the academy.

In the meantime, the quest for the perfect argument, what will permanently collapse others, is built into the Male-envious structure of the academy.

* * *

In Male Envy, competitors accumulate power points as the means of rising on the control hierarchy. Power points take many forms and need not have content independent of their "exchange value," their capacity to impress others, in the manner of "empty signifiers." Thus, one does not need to "do" anything to rise on the compete hierarchy, in the sense of finding, creating, or constructing things, or exercising "the instinct of workmanship." What one does have to do is control others, to manipulate consciousness. The mystique of control is thus possible only with the collusion of people at large, even though it is appropriated by the individual successful competitor, who acts as though power came from himself, instead of being the donation of those who create it. The feeling that sheer ego creates or is inherently meritorious typifies this mystique. In the irrational world of Male Envy, the empty power points that the successful competitor accumulates enable him to control the lives of others. These power points are meaningful, not because they are meaningful, but because the social order accepts them as such. The appearance is individual ego-power, displayed by the successful competitor. The reality, the substance, is complex social communication and cooperation that has been pressed into the service of the controller/competitor. It is therefore inseparable from self-delusion.

The vast quantities of currency that shift around the globe via computers may be "nothing" in the sense of having no concrete content or substance, yet their movements control the lives of millions. Signifiers may be empty, but they are resonant with meaning and emotion that communicate, because human beings are connected by more than words and texts. Control is real, even if the power points that signify it are not. Control manifests as the power to command the attention of others, a command necessary to reassure one of one's own identity or even existence. Thus, power points are inherently "empty," because they are pure coercion, the means of social control.

We return here to the beer commercial cited at the outset of this exploration: the young man values the two beautiful women not so much because of their beauty (their use value, as it were), as because his companions—his "friends"—envy him for having them ("exchange value," as it were). In the code of Male Envy, the accumulation of power points is all-important, and these power points, to put it in post-structuralist terms, appear to be empty signifiers. They have power only in the eyes of those who endow them with power. But that is the point.[63] Power in Male Envy is the manipulation of other people's power; it is a social datum, interpersonal, intersubjective—it cannot be understood by means of Object thinking. Power, control, self-control, perception are facets of a complex social organism: a field of control in which individuals are inextricably linked, whether or not they understand or are conscious of that linking.

Male Envy has the effect of distorting what is important. Power points are themselves distortions. What is valued in Male Envy are not things in themselves, or their capacity to feed, warm, comfort, or enlighten, but their symbolic function as means of intimidation and control. The fact that power points dominate social consciousness and social action, devaluing the things that people actually need and genuinely desire, mirrors the curious inversion of power within society itself:

> John Jay, the President of the Continental Congress and the first Chief Justice of the U.S. Supreme Court, held that "the people who own the country ought to govern it." The political system as well as the social system was designed to serve the needs of the propertied classes; others might benefit incidentally, as conditions allowed. And so affairs have proceeded since.[64]

In other words, the distortions of value embodied in power points mirror the distortions of power within the social system as a whole, whereby what is genuinely desirable and possible is devalued in favor of the insignia of domination—a process Veblen articulated with unusual subtlety.

Male Envy is constituted by Object thinking—but it cannot be understood by means of Object thinking. It requires a different model of perception to comprehend it, a model that has different principles from Object thinking.

Notes

1. See Liam Hudson and Bernadine Jacot, *The Way Men Think* (New Haven: Yale UP, 1991) 99ff.

2. Alfred Russell Wallace also drew his idea from Malthus. See Peter Vorzimmer, "Darwin, Malthus, and the Theory of Natural Selection," *Journal of the History of Ideas* 30 (1969): 524-42.

3. See A. M. C. Waterman, *Revolution, Economics, and Religion: Christian Political Economy, 1789-1833* (Cambridge: Cambridge UP, 1991).

4. "Malthus's Methodological and Macroeconomic Thought," *History of European Ideas* 4 [1983] 135-49.

5. John Maynard Keynes admired Malthus precisely because of Malthus's emphasis on the tendency of capitalism toward underconsumption (hence stagnation).

6. *The Wealth of Nations*, 145. In Smith, an intensely empirical, pragmatic and anti-metaphysical thinker, a gravity-like impulse constantly equilibrates the conglomeration of separate objects that constitute social and physical reality. For example, "The natural price, therefore, is, as it were, the central price, to which the prices of all commodities are continually gravitating. Different accidents may sometimes keep them suspended a good deal above it, and sometimes force them down even somewhat below it. But whatever may be the obstacles which hinder them from settling in this center of repose and continuance, they are constantly tending towards it" (*Wealth of Nations*, 75; cf. n.7 below). Smith's sentence is almost a purely metaphysical statement without any content.

7. Qu. in Alexandre Koyré, *From the Closed World to the Infinite Universe* (Baltimore: Johns Hopkins UP, 1957) 186.

8. Burke, *The Collected Works of Edmund Burke* (London, 1825) 5:151. Marx quotes Burke in a footnote to Capital, vol. 1 (trans. Ben Fowkes [Harmondsworth: Penguin, 1976]) 926.

9. Daniel L. LeMahieu, "Malthus and the Theology of Scarcity," *Journal of the History of Ideas* 40 (1979): 468.

10. *Political Justice*, ed. Isaac Kramnick (Harmondsworth: Penguin, 1965) 765. Cf. Adam Smith, n. 5 above, and his comment at the end of Book 4 of *The Wealth of Nations*: "All systems either of preference or of restraint, therefore, being thus completely taken away, the obvious and simple system of natural liberty establishes itself of its own accord. Every man, as long as he does not violate the laws of justice, is left perfectly free to pursue his own interest his own way, and to bring both his industry and capital into competition with those of any other man, or order of men. The sovereign is completely discharged from a duty, in the attempting to perform which he must always be exposed to innumerable delusions, and for the proper performance of which no human wisdom or knowledge could ever be sufficient; the duty of superintending the industry of private people, and of directing it toward the employments most suitable to the interest of the society. According to the system of natural liberty, the sovereign has only three duties to attend to [defense, judiciary, and essential public works]" (*The Wealth of Nations*, 687).

11. C. B. Macpherson, *The Political Theory of Possessive Individualism* (London: Oxford UP, 1962) 247. To quote Rajani Kanth again: "The phrase 'the people' . . . was a synonym for the middle classes and those few among the laboring masses who could demonstrate loyalty to 'middle-class' society, a loyalty indexed, initially, by property ownership" (*Political Economy and Laissez-Faire: Economics and Ideoogy in the Ricardian Era* [Totowa: Barnes, 1986] 139.

12. Michael A. Messner, "Sports and Male Domination: The Female Athlete as Contested Ideological Terrain," *Women, Sport, and Culture*, eds. Susan Birrell and Cheryl L. Cole (Champaign: Human Kinetics P, 1994): 76.

13. Thomas R. Malthus, *Principles of Political Economy*, 2d ed. 1836 (rpt. New York: Kelley, 1968) 194.

14. Thomas Robert Malthus, *An Essay on Population*, ed. Philip Appleman (New York: Norton, 1977; my emphasis) 201. *Population* went through numerous editions and revisions, as Malthus responded to criticism and accumulated statistics; this passage is from the 1803 edition.

15. Alan MacFarlane, *Marriage and Love in England: Modes of Reproduction 1300-1840* (Oxford: Blackwell, 1984) 20. Note the commercial metaphor.

16. Smith thinks in similar Newtonian terms (see n.3 above), as does Marx, who uses the same metaphor in his attempt to lay bare "the laws of motion" of capitalism. The identification of self-interest with gravity is a standard paradigm in Object thinking.

17. D. L. LeMahieu notes that "Malthus constructed a theodicy without ever mentioning Jesus, perhaps because Christ saved men from sin, not laziness." Malthus's "theology" has attracted a good deal of attention from scholars; it was certainly conspicuous enough in his own time, for he was asked to delete most of it and obligingly did so. See R. Remond, "Malthus and Religion," *Malthus Past and Present*, ed. J. Dupâquier (London: Academic, 1983); F. Rausky, "Malthusianism and the Secularization of Jewish Thought," *Malthus Past and Present* 183-93; M. Harvey-Phillips, "Malthus' Theodicy: Intellectual Background of His Contribution to Political Economy," *History of*

Political Economy 16 (1984): 591-608; and A. M. C. Waterman, "Malthus as Theologian," *Malthus Past and Present*, 195-201; and my own "The Eleventh Commandment: Sex and Spirit in Wollstonecraft and Malthus," *Journal of the History of Ideas* 51 (1990): 401-23.

18. Peter Bowler, "Malthus, Darwin, and the Concept of Struggle," *Journal of the History of Ideas* 37 (1976): 631-50. Malthus's concept of struggle was actually different from Darwin's: in Darwin, animals compete with one another; in Malthus, humans struggle against nature.

19. This is a key theme of volume 2 of Foucault's *History of Sexuality*. Malthus has an important place in the history of sexuality, a place that has been curiously neglected in view of his influence. "Population" after all is a codeword for "sex": the result is a metonym for the cause.

20. Louis Dumont, *From Mandeville to Marx: Genesis and Triumph of Economic Ideology* (Chicago: U of Chicago P, 1977) 172-73.

21. Frederick Rosen, "The Principle of Population as Political Theory: Godwin's 'Of Population' and the Malthusian Controversy," *Journal of the History of Ideas* 31 (1970): 33-48.

22. See, for example, Edmund Santurri, "Theodicy and Social Policy in Malthus' Thought," *Journal of the History of Ideas* 43 (1982): 315-30; Ezra Talmor, "Introduction," *History of European Ideas* 4 (1983): 121-22; and Patricia James's biography, *Population Malthus: His Life and Times* (London: Routledge, 1979), which depicts Malthus as a saint of moral virtue. There is even a book entitled *Homage to Malthus*.

23. Malthus and Ricardo "united in attributing the low wages and the resulting inequality to the prodigious and devastating fertility of the working classes; it was their uninhibited breeding that was the cause of their poverty" (John K. Galbraith, *The Anatomy of Power* [Boston: Houghton, 1983] 116). The English government's handling of the Irish famine of the 1840s clearly indicates the influence of Malthusian ideas; the Prime Minister quoted Adam Smith to Irish delegates seeking relief. See John Newsinger, "The Great Irish Famine," *Monthly Review* 47.11 (1996).

24. Sigmund Freud, *The Future of an Illusion*, trans. W. D. Robson-Scott, rev. and ed. James Strachey (New York: Doubleday, 1961) 48-49.

25. R. C. Tallis, "Burying Freud," *The Lancet* 347 (1996): 669. Tallis undervalues *The Interpretation of Dreams*—and Freud's many incidental insights, even apart from his theoretical constructs, especially Freud's insights into literature and imagination.

26. "*Whatever interrupts the progress of analytic work is a resistance*," as Freud suggestively puts it in *The Interpretation of Dreams* (trans. and ed. James Strachey [New York: Discus, 1965] 555. This is a reprint of the *Standard Edition*, vols. 4-5.

27. David Perkins, *Is Literary History Possible?* (Baltimore and London: Johns Hopkins UP, 1992) 167. This is what Jerome Christensen kindly calls "Bloom's paranoid scenario" (*Lord Byron's Strength: Romantic Writing and Commercial Society* [Baltimore: Johns Hopkins UP, 1993] xxiii): "freudbloomian anxieties" in Anca Vlasopolos's phrase ("When Feminists Read the Romantics," *Atlantis* 17.2 [1992] 82).

28. Sigmund Freud, *Totem and Taboo, The Basic Writings of Sigmund Freud*, trans. and ed. A. A. Brill (New York: Random, 1938) 863; my emphasis.

29. Sigmund Freud, "Some Psychical Consequences of the Anatomical Distinction between the Sexes," *Standard Edition of the Complete Psychological Works*, trans. J. Strachey [London: Hogarth, 1961] 19.253).

30. "The phallus is maleness elevated to the level of universality at the expense of the body's castration" (Charles Bernheimer, "Penile Reference in Phallic Theory," *Differences* 4.1 [1992] 130.

31. Freud's model of the psyche coheres with Object thinking, especially Newtonian physics; see Richard Lichtman, *The Production of Desire: The Integration of Psychoanalysis and Marxist Theory* (New York: Free P, 1982) 211.

32. "Its minimal unconscious notion would be to be a 'detachable object,' 'capable of being seen, exhibited, or even of circulating, of being given and received'. . . . Nevertheless this notion does not limit it to the function of a partial object [e.g. "breast, excrement, gaze, voice, transitional objects etc."] (a misunderstanding which Lacan vigorously condemned), but assigns to it, on the contrary, *the exceptional role of standard, of a privileged pole of evaluation in the chain of equivalences into which it can enter*. . . . The phallus would thus be the more or less symbolic attestation that the masculine subject (and *it is this which makes him a subject*) is entitled to enter as a taker into the circuit of the exchange of women" (Jean-Joseph Goux, "The Phallus: Masculine Identity and the 'Exchange of Women'," *Differences* 4.1 [1992]: 62-63; my emphasis).

33. See Kaja Silverman, "The Lacanian Phallus," *Differences* 4.1 (1992): 84-115, for perhaps the most lucid discussion of this subject. Lacanian psychoanalysis makes assumptions about the development of language and abstract reasoning on the basis of no empirical research to speak of.

34. Joseph H. Berke, *The Tyranny of Malice: Exploring the Dark Side of Character and Culture* (New York: Simon, 1986) 135.

35. René Girard, *Des Choses Cachées depuis la fondation du monde* (Paris: Bernard Grasset, 1978) 114: "nobody has taken *Totem and Taboo* seriously" (my translation).

36. Arbib and Hesse, *The Construction of Reality* (Cambridge: Cambridge UP, 1986) 110: "the Oedipus myth moves from ontogeny to phylogeny and is ascribed a historical reality. . . . The myth becomes first a psychological and then a historical explanation"— Freud "has created another myth: not the Genesis myth of God creating man, but the primal horde myth of men creating God." According to Stephanie Demetrakopoulos, *Listening to Our Bodies* (Boston: Beacon, 1983), the Oedipus complex allegorizes male anxiety; thus Erik Eriksen's "theory of life stages rests on Freud's theory of the Oedipus complex, as do most other life-stage theories—so much so that it seems Freud did . . . define a central source of male anxiety, perhaps more an anxiety of adult males than of the young child. This seems apparent in certain research on men's projection of Oedipal patterns onto their sons, although clinical studies of little boys do not find these patterns. As children, boys do not seem to hate their fathers, wish to usurp the mother's sexual love, or to topple the authority of the father. But as grown sons, adult males seem angry toward their fathers"—hence "often, though repressed, an anger toward fathers in many grown sons because of the relative absence of those fathers in their childhood . . . with no loving, nurturing male models or support. They then become angry in turn with their own sons for usurping the only source of love they have been able to count on, the wife as surrogate mother" (5). Hence the alienation, as if in an experiment "in which people are placed in deprivation tanks where their senses are all cut off" (6: what Mary Ingham

calls "the Laius complex" in *Men: The Male Myth Exposed* [London: Century, 1984] 234). The metaphor of mutilation—removing body-parts—seems central to this topic.

37. On Veblen's life, see Joseph Dorfman, *Thorstein Veblen and His America* (New York: Viking, 1934). Veblen's analysis of *The Higher Learning* dwells on the university's predilection for obfuscation.

38. See Jean Baudrillard, *In the Shadow of the Silent Majorities*, trans. Paul Foss et al. (New York: Semiotext[e], 1983); *Simulations*, trans. Paul Foss et al. (New York: Semiotext[e], 1983).

39. Harold Bloom, *The Anxiety of Influence: A Theory of Poetry* (New York: Oxford UP, 1973) 94-95.

40. Stanley Fish, *Is There a Text in This Class?* (Cambridge: Harvard UP, 1980) 368.

41. W. J. Bate, *The Burden of the Past and the English Poet* (Cambridge: Harvard UP, 1970) 134.

42. Qu. in Brian Easlea, *Fathering the Unthinkable: Masculinity, Scientists, and the Nuclear Bomb* (London: Pluto, 1985) 170; my emphasis.

43. Michael Vander Weele, "The Contest of Memory in 'Tintern Abbey'," *Nineteenth Century Literature* 50.1 (1995): 19.

44. I avoid the subject of de Man's Nazi background; see historian Jon Wiener, "Deconstructing de Man," *The Nation* 246.1 (Jan. 9, 1988): 22-24.

45. Paul de Man, *The Resistance to Theory* (Minneapolis: U of Minnesota P, 1986) 51.

46. Paul de Man, "Theory of Metaphor in Rousseau," *Romanticism: Vistas, Instances, Continuities*, eds. David Thorburn and Geoffrey Hartman (Ithaca: Cornell UP, 1973) 104. De Man met Derrida for the first time at the meeting where he presented this essay.

47. Paul de Man, *The Rhetoric of Romanticism* (New York: Columbia UP, 1984) 122. Cf. the ringing climax of Jerome J. McGann's *The Romantic Ideology*: "In the end Byron's poetry discovers what all Romantic poems repeatedly discover: that there is no place of refuge, not in desire, not in the mind, not in imagination. Man is in love and loves what vanishes, and this includes——finally, tragically——even his necessary angels" ([Chicago: U of Chicago P, 1983] 145). Note the impressive hyperbole.

48. Metaphysics and ideology are alike to de Man: a confusion of words with things; thus, "What we call ideology is precisely the confusion of linguistic with natural reality, of reference with phenomenalism" (*Resistance* 11).

49. One recalls Nietzsche's analysis in *The Genealogy of Morals* of the perversity of Male Envy, which views terror/cruelty as a source of pleasure, including "Thomas Aquinas, the great teacher and saint. *Beati in regno coelesti*, he says, meek as a lamb, *videbunt poenas damnatorum, ut beatitudo illis magis complaceat*" (183: "the blessed in heaven will watch the sufferings of the damned, which will be a great blessing to them" [my translation]). Nietzsche cites numerous other examples. His comments are very much in the spirit of Voltaire's *Dictionnaire Philosophique*.

50. Andrew J. McKenna, *Violence and Difference: Girard, Derrida, and Deconstruction* (Urbana: U of Illinois P, 1992) 143.

51. Paul de Man, *Resistance* 69. The fascination with death is conspicuous in de Man's comments especially on Wordsworth; for example, Lucy in Wordsworth's "A Slumber Did My Spirit Seal," "now has become a *thing* in the full sense of the word, not unlike Baudelaire's falling man who became a thing in the grip of gravity [compare the

mangled, "disfigured" body of Shelley], and, indeed, she exists beyond the touch of earthly years. . . . a grim awareness of the de-mystifying power of death, which makes all the past appear as a flight into the inauthenticity of a forgetting." Thus, for de Man, Wordsworth, a devout Christian, revealed the annihilating power of death to cancel out human desire, hence giving us what de Man calls "an eternal insight into the rocky barrenness of the human predicament prevails" (*Blindness and Insight: Essays in the Rhetoric of Contemporary Criticism* [Minneapolis: U of Minnesota P, 2d ed. rev., 1983] 224, 225). Coming from de Man's program of de-mystification, the metaphysical certainty here ("eternal") sounds very odd.

52. The final words of de Man's essay on Bakhtin illustrates the technique in a sentence: "To imitate or to apply Bakhtin, to read him by engaging him in a dialogue, betrays what is most valid in his work": Bakhtin is brilliant—but regrettably useless (*Resistance* 114).

53. "One frees the discourse on literature from naive oppositions between fiction and reality, which are themselves an offspring of an uncritically mimetic conception of art. . . . Literature is fiction not because it somehow refuses to acknowledge 'reality,' but because it is not *a priori* certain that language functions according to principles which are those, or which are *like* those, of the phenomenal world. It is therefore not *a priori* certain that literature is a reliable source of information about anything but its own language" (*Resistance* 11). Literature is self-enclosed and self-referential, unconnected to the real world, where, in any case, the ultimate authority is annihilation, nothing.

54. His *type* of theory, that is. "The polemical opposition, the systematic non-understanding and misrepresentation, the unsubstantial but eternally recurrent objections, are the displaced symptoms of a resistance inherent in the theoretical enterprise itself" (*Resistance* 12). Note the significant vocabulary: it is that of Freudian psychoanalysis: "displaced," "symptoms," "resistance".

55. See Susan A. Handelman, *The Slayers of Moses: The Emergence of Rabbinic Interpretation in Modern Literary Theory* (Albany: State U of New York P, 1982): her fascinating analysis has influenced my view of competition as the content of theory.

56. *The Wealth of Nations* 47, 51. The source of value in Smith has been the subject of years of controversy, because Smith presents a variety of contradictory formulations.

57. See my "Ricardo and the Romantic Propulsion of Time," *Nineteenth-Century Contexts* 12.2 (1988): 53-82, and "Romantic Secrets," *San José Studies* 17.3 (1991): 41-58, for the contradictions between Object thinking and the labor theory of value.

58. John Dillon, "Financial Speculation," *Canadian Perspectives* (summer 1997): 7.

59. See Michael Dawson and John Bellamy Foster, "The Political Economy of the Information Highway," *Monthly Review* 48.3 (1996): 47.

60. Daniel Singer, "Why We Need a New Manifesto," *Monthly Review* 50.1 (1998) 41.

61. The naive belief that words "represent" objects is closely paralleled in Object thinking by the notion that money "represents" objects; thus, words and money are said to be "backed" by "real" things—that is, objects in space.

62. J. Hillis Miller, "Impossible Metaphor," *Yale French Studies* 69 (1985): 155.

63. In Baudrillard's words, "This consensus around simulation is much less fragile than is commonly thought" (Jean Baudrillard, *America*, trans. Chris Turner [New York: Verso, 1988] 109.

64. Noam Chomsky, *Power and Ideology* (Montréal: Black Rose, 1987) 117.

6

Transform

For the female spirits of the dead, pining in bonds of religion,
Run from their fetters reddening, & in long drawn arches sitting,
They feel the nerves of youth renew, and desires of ancient times
Over their pale limbs, as a vine when the tender grape appears.
                                            William Blake, "America"

Modern physics screams at us that there is no ultimate material reality and that whatever it is we are describing, the human mind cannot be parted from it.
                        Physicist Roger S. Jones, *Physics as Metaphor*[1]

The virtues of competition are universally hailed, and it may be objected that "healthy competition" has not been given the veneration that it deserves here. The theory is admirable. Competition permits those who have superior qualities to exercise those qualities freely, winning over others with inferior qualities. When the best succeed, all of society benefits. As Adam Smith argues in *The Wealth of Nations*, individual self-interest is society's best interest. The greed of the individual becomes the good of society as a whole: "Private vices are public benefits," in Mandeville's phrase. But what if the ability one is superior in is the ability to sabotage and damage others? The principle of winning becomes simply rewarding aggression and deception. When asked which should be the future model for business—warfare or competition—one corporate executive responded, "What's the difference? competition *is* warfare."[2]

Given the horrors of Male Envy, it is hard to understand why it has the obsessive hold that it has. Apart from the socio-historical forces noted earlier, two factors are prominent. One is the assault on fertility, on the power of life itself, as the mythology of the evil eye indicates. It is as if Male Envy were an attack on the lifecycle in a twisted attempt to transcend the lifecycle altogether. Hence in Male-envious reasoning, destroying is creating. The other prominent factor is the self-destructiveness of Male Envy, indeed its suicidal impulse. It is as if Male Envy were an attempt to kill, not so much the self, as the creative or desiring impulse within the self, what are logically the godlike elements in us. These two factors, the assault on life and the assault on the creative self, appear to be the same compulsion but seen from two different angles.

The study of Male Envy would be incomplete without observing the resistance to it and efforts to find alternatives. Romantic narrative again offers significant "imagination experiments" for study.

One effect of feminism has been to throw Male Envy and its compulsions into relief, to make it stand out in its actual form. The compete/control hierarchy looks different from the perspective of women; in a sense, it becomes visible for the first time. But women have their own traditions of competitive struggle. And women have always invested in the compete/control system, by "backing" certain males in competition against other males. Indeed, the competitive value of a male is a standard motif in what makes a man desirable to women, as sociobiology continues to insist, with its strange business talk of "reproductive strategies" and "biological investments." The need for a woman to control her male, to be confident of his maneuvering in competitive struggles, is a commonplace element in female wisdom in respect to men under the régime of Male Envy.

By this logic, a woman must not let *anything* intervene or interfere in her access to her male—her control, if possible, over his actions, all of which affect her. Hedda Gabler clearly demonstrates this principle; controlling Tesman—making sure that the course of his ambition is unimpeded along lines she herself directs—amounts to a categorical imperative for her. Hedda's clarity about this primary concern derives from her own ambition, which requires a husband as marker or vehicle for that ambition.[3] In male-dominated society, the normal path for an ambitious woman is to act by proxy, via a male she can manipulate or direct so as to satisfy her competitive ambitions.

The emancipatory movements associated especially with gender, ethnicity, class, age, and sexual orientation are all currents that erode the logic of Male Envy, and at times confront it directly. Whatever their investment in the compete/control hierarchy, women have not been, like men, *identified* with it; their identity has not been constituted by placement in control struggles. Since they have not been on that hierarchy, traditionally, they have a potential ground for observing how it functions, and for finding other ways that might be possible. Male Envy insists that there is no other way than its own code, and to advocate another way is simply to be a loser, to rationalize losing. The full pressure of this limiting obsession has applied to men directly, and to women indirectly.

A striking illustration of this confrontation appears in Margaret Atwood's novel *Surfacing*. *Surfacing* appeared in 1972, as the recent phase of feminism began, and it has the kind of clarity often found in literary texts at the beginning of a cultural development. As I noted earlier, this clarity and prescience can be found in the Romantic writers themselves, which is why I have drawn on them so extensively. *Surfacing* is in the direct line of Romantic experimentation, with its complex rejection of Object thinking, and its attempt to formulate an alternative. For this seems to be the underlying problem of Male Envy: it is not simply a code of behavior and attitude, but the application of a worldview—what I called the Object Cosmology. Therefore, to jettison Male Envy requires a way of perceiving that is different from Object thinking and that supersedes it. In Romantic narrative this alternative is "Transform" thinking, as I referred to it earlier. "Transform" thinking assumes that (1) everything is connected, nothing is separate; (2) reality is constituted temporally, not spatially, as transformation-in-time; that is, reality is a time-unfoldment and not a static collection of separate objects. (3) Everything is part of a larger whole, and the whole is present in each of the parts: what is different is the same in another form—nothing is "other" in any metaphysical or absolute sense.

Surfacing is narrated by a young woman whose parents lived by themselves on a lake in the wilderness of northern Québec. After her mother died, her father, a botanist, continued a hermit-like existence in the woods. Then one day he mysteriously disappears. His daughter—in the manner of Lamia, we never learn her name—leaves the city where she lives and goes back to the cabin and the nearby woods in order to look for him. Her boyfriend, Joe, accompanies her, along with another couple, Anna and David.

The father's isolation suggests a wish to escape the compete/control hierarchy and its compulsions. It seems that there is something about the woods that disturbs the competitive ethos. The couples begin to break up, as the narrator has a series of perceptions that culminate in a kind of vision-quest. She finds something while diving in the lake—this something seems to be both her father's body, drowned, but also, metaphorically, her aborted fetus, from a back-alley abortion she had suffered. This "something" conflates the lifecycle, and so confronts her with her identity as a living being in a cycle of life. What follows is an intensely experienced realization that what she thought had died is alive but in another form, that all things are alive, and that life has levels as well as phases —a realization that can only be expressed metaphorically and in a way that transcends the prose of ordinary subject-space-object understanding.[4] The motif of heightened sensation closely echoes *The Ancient Mariner*; indeed it has the same prominence in *Surfacing* that it has in *The Ancient Mariner* and for very similar reasons: it is associated with exit from the alienation of Object thinking.[5] The contrast between abstract reasoning and ordinary language, on the one hand, and intense emotional and sensory experience, on the other, is emphasized.

As she is attempting to clarify the meaning of her vision and of the powers she has experienced in the wilderness, her companions, by contrast, are engaged in a complicated struggle against one another, with David emerging in the power position. The smallness and isolation of the group allows the dynamics of Male Envy to be seen as in a kind of controlled experiment. David decides he needs to have sex with the narrator and pursues her as she walks into the forest. To David, having sex with her would establish his superiority to the narrator's boyfriend, Joe—his "friend"—a matter of some urgency, since this "friend" has had sex with Anna, David's wife. Sex with the narrator would also confirm his self-importance, always remembering that to confirm self-importance in the code of Male Envy is to *inflate* self-importance. Again, in this case, the female performs a double role: demarcating male control vis-à-vis other males and providing emotional and other resources to support the male competitor's ego.

The sense that the narrator is losing her capacity to perform this double role also makes it essential that David use her sexually. In the code of Male Envy, she is becoming a Tricky Female. For the narrator has become absorbed in her own perceptions, in liberating a power of integration and understanding that is new to her and that includes a heightened sensation in which everything looks different. So intense is this experience that she can scarcely communicate with the others, and has become utterly incapable of sustaining the standard function of females in the régime of Male Envy. She has slipped away from the male compete/control hierarchy, like other women in this study (notably Hester in *The Scarlet Letter*, who is also associated with alternative perceptions of reality), and is finding a way of conceiving reality that is very unlike the model that Object thinking insists upon. This transition is so intense that she can hardly understand David when he follows her, or speak to him. David, meanwhile, is determined to absorb her power into his by sexual means, despite her excuses, including her plea that she would get pregnant. In fact, rape hangs over the scene.

Then, a means of resolving the threat comes to her, and it is simple enough. She tells him that he doesn't "turn her on." The stroke seems small, but what it does is to hit him where he is vulnerable: his vanity. She opens the emptiness that the code of Male Envy is designed to conceal. By touching his vanity, she causes his power to begin to unravel, for his vanity is a synecdoche for the whole code of Male Envy, with its fears, compulsions, inflations, and obsessions: "a bleak landscape of automatic, oversimplified ideas and definitions about how things should be—thoughts that are like judgements," as Sylvia Perera puts it. The narrator, by contrast, has "The vitality that comes through an eye that will describe and experience objectively, that can see and experience the whole."[6] She has a heightened sensation that is impossible to the obsessive routines of envy. She further saps his power position by destroying his experimental film, entitled *Random Samples*, with its scenes of aggression and death (the title is a metaphor for Object thinking: a concatenation of chaotic, separate objects). She drops it in the water, "drowning" the film. She destroys his power object, and a key signifier of his vanity and control, oddly recalling Hedda Gabler destroying the manuscript of Lövborg. The *Ancient Mariner* motif of the murdered animal is prominent in *Surfacing*. A dead heron is found, stretched out like a crucified victim. The treatment of the heron closely recalls the albatross in *The Ancient Mariner* (its picture is one of the "Random Samples" that the narrator sets free).

In *Surfacing*, the familiar configuration of character types noted earlier is in evidence. A struggling, desiring woman, is flanked by two recurring male types: an ineffectual lover (Joe in this case) and an overbearing "power male" preoccupied with nihilistic visions and power relationships (David). The narrator is the desiring woman. David's wife, Anna, meanwhile, despite her fling with Joe, is preoccupied with the standard function of women in Male Envy, to sustain the male competitor/controller, even though she obviously hates her husband. The narrator's struggle to find a different way not only results in her complete reconceiving of her earlier life and of her parents, but seems—it is hard to be certain—to have a healing effect on her boyfriend, who returns at the end of the novel to look for her, as if he had the capacity to be different, to find his identity as something that is not simply placement on the compete/control hierarchy.

The disintegrating of the compete/control hierarchy is accomplished by, in effect, deleting the "winner" position. Male Envy depends upon invidious ranking, which depends in turn on a winner. Once this position is evacuated, the principle of differential ranking itself begins to disintegrate. *Surfacing* detaches the compete/control hierarchy from its social context, where controlling others is everything, and allows it, in the context of nature, to fall apart.

* * *

The code of Male Envy precipitates out of the rise of capitalist culture, the disintegration of the Old Cosmology and its fixed social hierarchy, and the subsequent domination of consciousness by Object thinking. Romanticism is best understood as a rejection of the Object Cosmology and as a complex experiment with a different way of looking at reality, which I referred to as "Transform" thinking. Romantic narrative projects the standard figure of Male Envy: the competitor/controller, as a lone warrior, of the type found in Cooper's Hawkeye or Scott's Ivanhoe, with Milton's Satan in the background as prototype. Such figures appear as solitaries, but they are possible only as outcroppings of an assemblage of competitor-inferiors and rivals. The figure of the solitary warrior is significant because it condenses so much of the ethos of Male Envy.

This ethos assumes reality as a field of universal and unending conflict. In this field, one seizes and controls rather than creates. That is, the origin of wealth is the power to control—not the power to create. Hence a very influential belief is that the source of value is ego-power: a personal, private force of acquisition, sometimes referred to as "self-interest." In the régime of Male Envy, penetrating to the inner mechanism of self-interest is thus the key to understanding an individual's actions, the most important thing—and in a sense the only thing—there is to know about a person. Strong and weak are primal, determining categories—the capacity to get one's way regardless of others.

Male Envy can only be understood by seeing it, so to speak, from outside it; by means of an alternative model of reality against which it is possible to perceive the actual contours of Male Envy. This imaginative exit from Object thinking is not easy. Here, some guide or lead would be useful: a figure that would be opposite to the competitor/controller. The obvious candidate is the "desiring female" that has turned up off and on throughout this study, culminating in the narrator of *Surfacing*: the woman who is struggling to find freedom from the roles imposed by the compete/control hierarchy, and hence to escape the control hierarchy altogether. In other words, freedom from the roles that Male Envy imposes ultimately requires freedom from the code of Male Envy itself, and from the worldview that underwrites it. This escape clearly cannot be a total escape; it must include a mode of living with Male Envy without being at its mercy. The ideal would be to live with Male Envy by mutating it, like a beneficial virus, into something better.

What is interesting about the desiring female is the impact she has on others, especially on the males around her. It is especially interesting that this figure is typically a *healer*. Her capacity to struggle, her preoccupation with valuing desire, is associated with the ability to heal others and herself. Furthermore, the timing of this figure is interesting, for she makes her appearance in literature in Romantic narrative (along with a complex of related motifs). The same cultural forces that generated Romantic experimentation also brought the female healer figure into literature. Given the fanatical intensity of the code of Male Envy, the power of the female healer and its impact on male identity in Romantic narrative is doubly significant. One of the interesting things about Romantic narrative is that its ethos seems to be hostile toward the code of Male Envy, as the quintessential Romantic narrative, *The Rime of the Ancient Mariner*, indicates. The figure of the female healer condenses that resistance. Hence the final step in this exploration is to ponder the female healer as the focus of a counter-logic to Male Envy. Healing is an obvious point of reference, because the code of Male Envy functions as illness, as alienation, emotional sterility, and psychic distortion. It is an illness in the metaphorical sense, but it is also an actual illness in the sense that it causes extreme body tensions (what Wilhelm Reich called "character armoring"), with damaging effects on the body.

The narrator of *Surfacing* is associated with healing, perceiving, and transforming, but she is a late example in this line of character types. One of the earliest treatments of the type appears in Coleridge's Gothic poem *Christabel* (1816), which offers a paradigm for this figure in literature. *Christabel* is also a study in Male Envy, some of whose characteristic motifs, silencing and male competition, are prominent to an unexpected extent. Again, the boldness and directness of Coleridge's experimentation in *The Ancient Mariner* is evident.

Coleridge never finished *Christabel*: it seemed to have aroused anxieties too threatening for the poet to finish, as if it were encroaching upon primal taboos. For example, in the mysterious, much-discussed "Conclusion to Part II," which ends the poem as it now stands, a man becomes unaccountably enraged with his joyous child. The implication is that the inner secret of this poem is what is now called child abuse: a brutal betrayal of innocence by superior force—in short, the unbearable horror of love betrayed. In Male Envy, weakness is criminal, of course, so that the sudden attack on it is actually normative behavior: almost a paradigm of how strength treats weakness. Still, to present it openly suggests a becoming-aware that is itself threatening: the code of Male Envy works best when it is only partly conscious, as noted at the outset, when its acts of malice and aggression are rationalized as actually meritorious, necessary, or even pious.

At any rate, given the motif of child abuse which appears in the "Conclusion to Part II," it is not surprising that the father in the story, Sir Leoline, conspicuously betrays his daughter Christabel. He refuses to believe her—and thus exposes her to the monstrous Geraldine, as if he were conspiring with his daughter's deadly enemy. Indeed, in a public display, he gives his trust to this enemy, as opposed to his child. There is thus a heavy patriarchal complex in the poem, which consists of a father who is alternately sick and weak (too weak to defend the daughter he supposedly loves), and yet also tyrannical and arbitrary—hurting, indeed betraying, the child who depends upon him for protection and love.[7] The fusion which Sir Leoline embodies is typical of Male Envy—arbitrary and hostile behavior on one hand, and weakness and preoccupied self-division on the other. Hawthorne's Dimmesdale and his Chillingworth are close relatives.

One of the most striking features of *Christabel* is its *articulation of male hatred*. Ironically, what is crucial to *Christabel* has been ignored by critics, though perhaps that is to be expected, given the silencing of Male Envy. I have already noted the irrational hostility of the father to his child in the "Conclusion to Part II." Earlier in the poem, Sir Leoline believes Geraldine's story that she is the daughter of an old friend of his—a friend with whom he quarrelled, long ago—and never made up. Coleridge's description of this rupture has to be regarded as one of the most important passages from literature in this entire study, because of the clarity and precision of its vision of hostility between men.

> Alas! they had been friends in youth;
> But whispering tongues can poison truth;
> And constancy lives in realms above;
> And life is thorny: and youth is vain;
> And to be wroth with one we love
> Doth work like madness in the brain.

> And thus it chanced, as I divine,
> With Roland and Sir Leoline.
> Each spake words of high disdain
> And insult to his heart's best brother:
> They parted—ne'er to meet again!
> But never either found another
> To free the hollow heart from paining—
> They stood aloof, the scars remaining,
> Like cliffs which had been rent asunder;
> A dreary sea now flows between;—
> But neither heat, nor frost, nor thunder,
> Shall wholly do away, I ween,
> The marks of that which once hath been.   (ll. 408-426)

The anguish of male competitive hatred has never been expressed more forcefully or poignantly. Clearly, one of the central impulses of *Christabel* is to do just that, articulate the horrors of Male Envy. It is rare for these feelings to be articulated at all: the silence/silencing of Male Envy is broken in *Christabel*.

Against this backdrop of male hostility and alienation appears the figure of the vulnerable woman, trapped within the matrix of Male Envy: her vulnerability is made doubly dramatic, because the poem is unfinished. The heroine is left at the end, exposed to danger, paralyzed, virtually friendless—and silenced twice over, first by Geraldine and then by her father. She is in effect buried alive. Christabel's first act in the poem, slipping out of the castle at midnight, unseen and alone, to pray, and her deep anxiety not to disturb her ailing father, suggest the entrapment she experiences even before her disastrous meeting with the witch, Geraldine. Geraldine, meanwhile, presents herself as an innocent maiden who has been raped, in the literal sense of "carried off" if not actually sexually assaulted, by five men: her self-presentation coheres with the story's framework of the strong violating the weak. Alienation and vulnerability are merely routine.

At the same time, however, there is a contrast in the narrative to the Male-envious strand: and this is Christabel's own healing and redeeming impulse, which has led her to bring the deadly Geraldine into the castle in the first place. We are introduced to Christabel praying for her lover (a knight who is "far away"), at midnight in the woods near her father's castle. There she finds Geraldine half-fainting and rescues her; the language deliberately recalls Christ in the Gospels putting out his hand to heal: "Then Christabel stretched forth her hand, / And comforted fair Geraldine" (ll. 104-105). Christabel even carries Geraldine. Once inside the fortress, safe from the dangerous men who have assaulted Geraldine, Christabel instinctively invokes the protectress of virgins: "Praise we the Virgin all divine / Who hath rescued thee from thy distress!" (ll. 139-140). Significantly, Christabel attributes Geraldine's rescue not to her own efforts, but to the presence of the Virgin Mother. Geraldine begs off praising the Mother of God, though earlier she had thanked her lucky stars for being rescued.

Geraldine is evil enough, but Christabel innocently insists she share her bed with her this night. She also insists Geraldine partake of a healing drink:

> O weary lady, Geraldine,
> I pray you, drink this cordial wine!
> It is a wine of virtuous powers;
> My mother made it of wild flowers.   (ll. 190-93)

Christabel tells Geraldine that her mother died on the day she was born. Her long dead mother appears to act as a protective spirit, because Geraldine bluntly tells this guardian spirit to get lost, so that she can proceed to destroy Christabel unimpeded. The contrast between Christabel and Geraldine is subtle, for the two are very similar. One is an innocent maiden; the other is a witch who *looks* like an innocent maiden. The radiant, healing woman and the deceitful witch appear to be two facets of one identity, or two different ways of seeing the same figure.

What Coleridge assembles is an important group of interrelated motifs:

- maiden: an adventurous, fearless figure
- mother; female mentor; or superior female being
- special emphasis on the link between maiden and mother
- rescue: raising, carrying, protecting, serving, healing
- prayer: link between the human and the divine: grace
- the Virgin Mother: a female being of divine power linked to the maiden
- herbal flowers (a synecdoche for nature itself, as is the forest earlier in *Christabel*)
- healing words; language as healing force (as in Christabel's words of courtesy and assistance to Geraldine and her prayer to the Virgin)
- wine: drink of special power
- medicinal, healing energy
- death; life beyond death or that transcends death

The maiden embodies a power that is spiritual as well as physical: it redeems as well as heals. This power comes from nature (the drink made of herbal flowers); but it also comes from the mother, who is dead but alive as a spirit. In fact, the power derives from the Holy Mother herself in heaven, with whom the maiden has special, indeed instinctive, affinity, as expressed by her spontaneous impulse to pray and to give credit to the Virgin for saving Geraldine. The words "health," "heal," "whole"—and "holy"—are all cognate terms; healing, wholeness, and spiritual redemption seem to be inseparable. Perhaps this is why Jesus identifies healing and recovery of faith in the Gospels. The special drink here is the opposite of the blood or body fetish so characteristic of holy murder (where the victim's body parts are regarded as a power boost to the killer or his god).

Jesus often insists in the Gospels that belief heals: without belief healing is impossible. But the belief of *Christabel* does not appear to be orthodox. One recalls here what is probably the greatest scene of female healing in literature: the climax of Apuleius's *The Golden Ass*, the story of how Lucius's brutish lust and ambition cause him to be changed into a donkey by a witch's magic ointment. Finally, the goddess Isis rises from the sea to heal, and to convert, the the metamorphosed, degraded Lucius and release him from the total alienation symbolized by his donkey shape. The motifs of brutality, display, competitive struggle, and lost direction form the texture of Apuleius's narrative, a horror from which Lucius is released. *The Golden Ass* is one of the ancestral voices of Romantic narrative and makes clear that healing is itself fundamentally a *metamorphosis,* a physical transformation-in-time, so as to manifest energies that work invisibly and thus, as far as Object thinking is concerned, miraculously.

Likewise, it is not God the Father to whom Christabel turns, but the Mother of God: the divine source of the divine. In this respect, *Christabel* is very close to Coleridge's other great Romantic narrative, *The Rime of the Ancient Mariner*. *The Ancient Mariner* uses traditional religious images and motifs, but to express a kind of spirituality that is anything but protestant Christianity, as noted in Chapter 3. For example, it is not God as a male figure whom the Mariner instinctively appeals to, but the Virgin Mother. Thus, the Mariner in a moment of terror cries, "Heaven's Mother send us grace!" (l. 178, recalling Hamlet in a corresponding moment of terror, calling upon the mother of God); and after the great vision of the water snakes, when the Albatross slips from the Mariner's neck, he visualizes grace in terms of the Holy Mother. The Mariner, like Christabel, praises the Virgin:

> Oh sleep! it is a gentle thing,
> Beloved from pole to pole!
> To Mary Queen the praise be given!
> She sent the gentle sleep from Heaven,
> That slid into my soul.
>
> The silly [i.e., ordinary, everyday] buckets on the deck
> That had so long remained,
> I dreamt that they were filled with dew;
> And when I awoke, it rained.
>
> My lips were wet, my throat was cold,
> My garments all were dank;
> Sure I had drunken in my dreams,
> And still my body drank.
>
> I moved, and could not feel my limbs:
> I was so light—almost

> I thought that I had died in sleep,
> And was a blessed ghost. (ll. 292-308)

Again, the complex of motifs identified above is conspicuous: (1) the link between Heaven and Earth; (2) the praise to the Virgin; (3) the image of a healing drink; and (4) the peace associated with protection, so as to recall the protective and cradling arms of a loving mother; note also the motif of dreaming.

It would seem that the drink here and in *Christabel* is, in fact, milk—divine milk. Milk, like grace, is freely generated, freely given; it makes infants grow miraculously; milk also has healing properties, supplying antibodies to combat disease. Finally, milk bonds a vulnerable, weak being with its mother, a parent that is in practice infinitely stronger. It is no surprise, then, that the rhapsodic closing lines of Coleridge's third poetic *tour de force*, "Kubla Khan," focus on the image of a transcendent drink which is identified as milk: "close your eyes with holy dread, / For he on honey-dew hath fed, / And drunk the milk of Paradise." The closing of the eyes here signifies ecstasy—but also the protected sleep of blissful, satisfied infancy. The giving and withholding of the breast is the basis, one recalls, of Melanie Klein's entire theory of envy. Milk, as the primal gift, is the archetype for all gifts and for all dependency. In the context of this study, milk suggests not so much an exchange act that is subject to control and loss of control (as in Klein), as it is a synecdoche for a larger identity, for interconnection and dependence with a totality of which one is part. Hence it is the negation of Object thinking, with its separate/separable units struggling against one another (as we find in Klein).

In Coleridge, the figure of the inspirational maiden, who instills miraculous creative power in her listener, appears immediately before the climactic final lines of "Kubla Khan," in the form of the famous "Abyssinian Maid." The apparition of this radiant being is appropriate, for the figure of the magical maid constitutes a "source image" in Coleridge—that is, an image that stimulates a writer's ability to write and that keeps recurring in his/her work.[8] A significant number of Coleridge's poems display this figure or variants.[9] One notices that the Mariner, like Sir Leoline in *Christabel*, suffers from alienation, obsession, vulnerability, and delusions about himself and his life: the standard nightmare of Male Envy. The same contrast appears in Coleridge's "Dejection," between a numinous "Lady" associated with a healing power of life and joy, and the male speaker himself, whose feeling of futility and emptiness is the state referred to in *The Rime of the Ancient Mariner* as "Life-in-Death": to be dead while still alive. This evisceration of the creative self is typical of Male Envy; it is also the condition that needs healing, a condition for which the paralysis imposed on Christabel is also a metaphor, emblematized by the paralysis of the ship in *The Ancient Mariner* ("As idle as a painted ship / Upon a painted ocean").

* * *

Coleridge's fascination with the numinous maiden is consistent with tradition. The romance is an ancient generic formation, unlike the novel, which appears rather suddenly on the historical stage and is, like "realism," a byproduct of Object thinking. The romance carries with it a heritage of pre-Object thinking, and this heritage has made it a useful reservoir of alternative ways of perceiving; it derives from the Old Cosmology rooted in medieval and feudal civilization, with its fixed rank by birth and its subsistence agriculture. That is, the romance bears a body of suggestions or possibilities, as it were, for thinking about reality in different ways from those sanctioned by "realism," "realism" in the sense of attempting to represent reality as a collocation of physical objects in space capable of exact description and analysis.

In traditional romance, the maiden symbolizes chastity—indeed, may almost be said to *enact* chastity. Chastity, especially in the form of virginity, is a magic force, not just a matter of abstaining from sex; it is a supernatural power that links human beings with God and is analogous to an unfallen identity. As such, chastity makes miracles and great deeds possible. This is what may be called the "magic virgin" convention. Thus, it is explicitly *because he is a virgin* that Galahad achieves the quest of the Holy Grail in Malory's version of the Arthurian stories; a similar power enables the chaste maiden of the medieval romance *Pearl* to heal the paralyzing psychic debility of the narrator, with his control compulsion.

One of the standard episodes in romance is the ordeal of the virgin. This convention, in which a virgin is tested and threatened with death, is not quite as absurd as it may sound. In his study of romance, Northrop Frye explains:

> Deep within the stock convention of virgin-baiting is a vision of human integrity imprisoned in a world it is in but not of, often forced by weakness into all kinds of ruses and stratagems, yet always managing to avoid the one fate which really is worse than death, the annihilation of one's identity.

Hence "What is symbolized as a virgin is actually a human conviction, however expressed, that there is something at the core of one's infinitely fragile being which is not only immortal but has discovered the secret of invulnerability that eludes the tragic hero."[10] In Romantic narrative, which evolves out of romance, the traditional heroics of the masculine hero—the enactment of the code of Male Envy—are feeble compared to the power manifested by the innocent maiden.

The contrast between male fighter and female healer is the basis of Scott's novel *Ivanhoe* (1820), which is set in the reign of Richard the Lion-Hearted. *Ivanhoe* features one of the supreme character creations of Romantic literature, the Jewish heroine Rebecca. Rebecca endures both the siege of Front-de-Boeuf's castle (metaphorically a siege of her chastity, recalling the Castle of Alma in

Spenser's epic romance *The Faerie Queene*)—and also the literal assault of a rapist-priest who later is involved in having her burnt alive in a spectacular public display.[11] Rebecca, whose healing power is treated as supernatural, survives all these ordeals. Indeed, she survives so well that Scott has to get rid of her at the end, by means of exile, and cannot simply kill her off, any more than the rapist-priest Bois-Guilbert is able to burn her up.

The virgin is linked to the upper world: Coleridge certainly thinks of "Innocence" in these terms, as a magic force that enables one to pass through horrors without being harmed, like Marina in the brothel in Shakespeare's *Pericles*. This convention lies behind Wordsworth's elegiac poetry focused on female figures, especially "Three Years She Grew," where the maiden dies, but her death has a strangely empowering/transforming effect, an effect that coexists with the speaker's grief, as if, rather than dying, she had rejoined a mystic spiritual identity still capable of inspiring and strengthening those who knew her. One might even cite Poe here—Poe declared the death of a beautiful woman the most poetical of all subjects. The maiden's death in these cases releases a psychic power of creation and healing in the narrator; by dying, she projects a revelation of transcendent life to those who remain, healing their alienation by expanding their range of perceptions, a process that extends ideally to the reader's perceptions. It is perhaps not going too far to see this convention as the organizing framework of Goethe's *Faust* (*Ewig weibliche*, as it were). If so, the motif of the death of the maiden may not be simply sexist darkness, but a means of recognizing female power in spite of sexist darkness. A crucial point here is the reconstitution of death. Death is neither annihilation, nor the fetish of competitor/controllers, nor the humiliation of weakness, as in the code of Male Envy; death is, rather, the triumph of apparent weakness over apparent strength.

Chastity as magic agency is such a powerful convention that it persists long after the rise of Object thinking, in *Jane Eyre* and *Dracula*, for example. In *Jane Eyre*, the heroine survives not only childhood horrors, which conspicuously include disease as well as social expulsion, but also the sexual/social assault of Rochester (and later the religious mania of the fanatical priest St. John Rivers). Readers who are troubled by the bizarre coincidence of Jane's finding—by accident—her only living relatives in England, in what purportedly is a work of realism, should bear in mind that Jane has the special powers associated with the virginal heroine of romance, for whom such coincidences are really the action of a divine will, working in synchrony with the heroine's chastity. This is the metaphoric reason, too, why Jane hears the supernatural voice at the climax of her story—the Magic Virgin convention includes enlarged sensory capacity.

Hence, too, she is able to heal, in several senses, the alienated Rochester. Her return to him at the end of the story enables his physical healing and is in decorum with her identity: one who, in communion with a higher power, survives, frees—and heals. Rochester is a figure of Male Envy, for he has been demoted on the compete/control hierarchy: he was caught in the machinations of brother and father, and humiliated in a public display by his weak brother-in-law, as well as abandoned by a woman (Jane Eyre) he actually loved. His disastrous marriage is a marker of defeat in the competition and of utter alienation, despite the property advantages yielded by that marriage. In this respect, Jane Eyre's mission in the novel is one of healing the horrors of Male Envy, a mission which requires first a defiance of its control. She does this most decisively by rejecting the obsessed St. John Rivers (who corresponds closely to the obsessed rapist-priest Bois-Guilbert in *Ivanhoe*). Immediately after she rejects him, in a moment of heightened awareness, Jane hears the mystic voice calling her. Defiance of Male Envy yields a certain type of power, a power that does not operate in the predictable/controllable manner consistent with the Object model of reality.

Dracula is in many ways a very old-fashioned book, despite the emphasis on the latest, un-vampiric gadgetry (phonograph, telegraph, etc.). Nevertheless, the vampire is the epitome of the code of Male Envy, as his delight in humiliating the ambitious young man, Jonathan Harker, makes plain. Harker's fiancée (later bride), Mina, is a figure of chastity—a chastity grossly threatened by the monstrous Dracula. "Interpreting *Dracula*'s sexual substrata has become something of a cottage industry," as Kathleen Spencer notes, but the novel's obsession with gender roles, whatever it says about Stoker's sex hangups (or his VD) or about late-Victorian anxieties, is entirely in decorum with the romance genre, where chastity is literally a super-natural force. Logically, what Dracula is feeding on, in order to perpetuate himself, is not blood as such, but female chastity-energy—an energy that ultimately is the basis of reproduction in general. He is thus a parasite on the life-source embodied in women: a suggestive diagnosis of the male competitor/controller. He turns life into control: when Dracula is pierced, money comes pouring out rather than blood.[12] Dracula is not interested in anybody for sexual purposes—only for feeding purposes[13] (apart from the conspicuous pleasure he derives from humiliating his male opponents).

Dracula is full of Male Envy motifs, which are doubly conspicuous because of the female figure at the novel's center, Mina, the editor/compiler/creator of the text. Mina's chastity is spiritual in nature rather than a matter of genital behavior: his contact with her threatens her identity, her authenticity, and not merely her physical being. The other female lead in the novel is Lucy Westenra, and Lucy becomes a vampire. What one notices about Lucy is that, originally, she was one who manipulated the code of Male Envy, by playing different lovers off against each other, as if becoming a vampire were the consequence/punishment due to women who escape their assigned role in Male Envy.

Interestingly, there is a male doctor in *Dracula*—in fact, more than one—and much talk of the latest medical techniques (notably blood transfusion), all pretty useless in resisting Dracula. On the contrary, the heroic center of the novel is Mina, whose clairvoyant powers enable the *comitatus* group to track their wolfish enemy down. Mina's chastity is compromised but not destroyed by Dracula, recalling the pure Lady of Milton's play *Comus*, who is frozen but not destroyed by her enemy. Paradoxically, Mina is thereby enabled to track him and make possible his/its capture. Ultimately, she *heals* Dracula, as her own account of the peace that appears on his face, after he has been devampired, indicates: "I shall be glad as long as I live that even in that moment of final dissolution there was in the face a look of peace, such as I never could have imagined might have rested there" (377): he was dead while he was alive. Dracula, it seems, is "healed." Death here is revalued as release, not humiliation.

Stoker's novel belongs to a later phase of Romantic narrative, which was influenced by Dickens. Dickens was fascinated by the figure of the mysterious maiden with healing powers. Esther in *Bleak House* is a complex illustration[14]; but the obvious example is Lucie Manette in *A Tale of Two Cities*, especially (before she marries Charles Darnay) in her relation to her feeble father. The father, a thoroughgoing Object thinker, recalls Sir Leoline in *Christabel*. Lucie heals the father, a figure who represents calculating reason/control—and a doctor, one must note. (A parallel in French literature is the relation of Jean Valjean and Cosette/Euphrasie in Hugo's *Les Misérables*.) Dr. Manette falls into line with a series of weak male figures preoccupied with imposing and defending a self-image of control, like Sir Leoline in *Christabel* and Isaac of York, Rebecca's father, in *Ivanhoe*. They embody standard values of the code of Male Envy, like the Chillingworth/Dimmesdale complex in Hawthorne's *Scarlet Letter*. Role-reversal is conspicuous in these relationships: the female protects the male—and is often betrayed by the father. Dickens used this motif in *The Old Curiosity Shop*, where the maiden is burdened with her very disturbed grandfather and his control compulsions (he is a compulsive gambler), and again dies.

The notion that chastity links the maiden with a higher order, and that this link gives her semidivine powers of healing and protection, has its place in Romantic narrative, as these examples demonstrate. The chaste Amelia of Chateaubriand's *René* (1802), who heals the sick and is described as a higher being, is a late summing up of the Magic Virgin convention:

> From nature Amelia had received something sublime. Her soul radiated the same innocent graces as her body, the sweetness of her feelings was infinite, and there was nothing about her mentality that was not marked by a suave and dreamy texture. . . . her heart, her thoughts, and her voice made delightful music together. She took from woman her shyness and love, and from the angels, purity and melody.[15]

The ultraconservative Chateaubriand gravitated to the convention of chastity, the fusion of virginity and religion being a favorite theme of his.

But Chateaubriand's figure is also anomalous, because Romantic narrative did not simply reproduce the ancient convention of the magic virgin. On the contrary, Romantic narrative *deconstructs* the convention. For example, the female healer of Ann Radcliffe's *Romance of the Forest* (1791), Madame La Luc, is an unmarried sister, in accord with the virginity convention—but her power to heal is limited: a matter more of botany than of chastity.[16] The next step is to observe the radical de/re/constructing of the Magic Virgin convention, and what it means for the code of Male Envy.

* * *

Radcliffe's Madame La Luc is a transitional figure, for the Magic Virgin convention is effectively demolished by the Romantics. Thus, it becomes sexual *fusion* that heals and frees—not virginity. This revaluation goes beyond reversing the cultural veneration of virginity, however, for it is an attempt to identify sexual energy as in effect a divine force: a force, that is, that does more than reproduce human beings. It also enables people to grow, to heal, to perceive with greater sensory power, and to create, so that the reproductive function is synecdochic. As Sandra Shuman puts it, "the psyche registers every creative act as a birth" (67).

The reversal of chastity is clear enough in Blake, Shelley, and Keats.[17] For example, "I Stood Tip-Toe," Keats's sketch for his mythological narrative *Endymion* (1818), climaxes in an epiphany of sexual power. Here Diana, traditional goddess of untouchability and virginity—and a fanatic if ever there was one—becomes the goddess of love and sensory stimulus: the goddess who once killed those who inappropriately approached her, now indiscriminately heals. The poet invokes her as "Queen of the wide air; thou most lovely queen / Of all the brightness that mine eyes have seen!" (ll. 205-06, anticipating the invocation in the "Ode to a Nightingale").[18] Her sexual potency generates a current of energy that heals—heals not just individuals, but society itself:

> The breezes were ethereal, and pure,
> And crept through half-closed lattices to cure
> The languid sick; it cool'd their fever'd sleep,
> And soothed them into slumbers full and deep.
> Soon they awoke clear eyed: nor burnt with thirsting,
> Nor with hot fingers, nor with temples bursting:
> And springing up, they met the wond'ring sight
> Of their dear friends, nigh foolish with delight;
> Who feel their arms, and breasts, and kiss and stare,
> And on their placid foreheads part the hair.
> Young men, and maidens at each other gaz'd
> With hands held back, and motionless, amaz'd
> To see the brightness in each other's eyes;

And so they stood, fill'd with a sweet surprise,
Until their tongues were loos'd in poesy.   ("I Stood Tip-Toe" ll. 221-35)

Note the resurrection symbolism. The same complex of motifs is associated with the gracious, healing Queen of Heaven in *The Ancient Mariner*:

- coolness after parching heat
- peace: renewing sleep
- waking (transition to larger, freer phase of identity); wonder
- power of motion after paralysis
- release from obsession; startled looking
- renewed power of speech/communication ("tongues were loos'd in poesy")
- social renewal

Even the motif of the healing drink is present, subtextually: the sick wake up "clear eyed" and are no longer "burnt with *thirsting*."[19] The importance of this passage lies in Keats's cosmology. The goddess in Keats is not like the "goddess" of contemporary new age cults (a "real" deity to worship), but rather a metaphor for certain perceptions. Basic to the code of Male Envy is the Object perception of reality as nihilistic aggression ("An eternal fierce destruction," as Keats himself phrases it elsewhere). By contrast, the goddess in Keats indicates that the true substratum of reality is not nihilistic aggression but a sustaining life-energy. This primal reality is difficult to verbalize, but it is something like a continuous force of transformation-in-time (Heidegger's *Sein* as it were) that is always *in actu*, sometimes causing sudden changes but usually unfolding slowly and in all directions. Keats's poetry is full of metaphors for this sustaining-connecting power, with its implicit rejection of the subject-space-object paradigm of Object thinking, and the hostility and compulsion that it underwrites.

In this passage, the contrast of fiery heat vs. healing drink recalls *Christabel*, where one finds both the figure of the female healer—and its opposite, the disease-bringing woman, in the form of Geraldine, who is also associated with fire. (Compare the female figure "Life-in-Death" in *The Ancient Mariner*, who has the golden locks of beauty, yet is "white as leprosy.") Geraldine is an elaborate parody of the healer: she cradles Christabel in her arms, in the maternal manner characteristic of healing figures ("nurses"); she uses words in a special way, chanting a spell over her (like the vampiric "La Belle Dame sans Merci" in Keats's poem of that name); she transforms Christabel from health to helplessness, weakness, paralysis; she drains her victim of life and social identity both. Geraldine is a fallen healer; she gives death, not life; she presents herself mockingly as also a victim and unveils the "secret" of body decay as well as desire. Her sexuality suggests death, not generation: in other words, it is not really sex but bait.

Beatrice in Hawthorne's "Rappaccini's Daughter" belongs to a similar configuration: she is associated throughout with a fountain and with herbs and plants. Beatrice is poisonous, thanks to the ugly experiment of her mad-scientist father, another doctor who epitomizes both Object thinking and its negative implications. Beatrice is properly a martyr, like the martyred Miriam of *Ivanhoe*.[20] Death frees her, confounding the males who use her (like Hedda Gabler, who is also connected with the symbolism of witchcraft, fire, and reproduction). Like other female healers, she can be viewed as either a dangerous sorceress or as supernatural mother: a power to die without dying, so to speak: to span death, without being degraded by it. The reconstitution of death is a crucial motif in the complex: death not as the fetish of control-fixations, but death as *transformation*, a metamorphosis whose nature evades reason or calculating intellect.

Keats trained as a doctor, and the motif of healing is everywhere in his writing, perhaps because disease, while it is a physical ill, is also a metaphor for alienation—"The weariness, the fever, and the fret,"

> Here, where men sit and hear each other groan;
> Where palsy shakes a few, sad, last gray hairs,
> Where youth grows pale, and spectre-thin, and dies;
> Where but to think is to be full of sorrow
>   And leaden-eyed despairs,
> Where Beauty cannot keep her lustrous eyes,
> Or new Love pine at them beyond to-morrow.
>   ("Ode to a Nightingale," ll. 23-30)

Fatigue, sorrow, illness, aging—and frustration—are metonyms for one another. "Nightingale" is preoccupied with healing/transforming drinks. In Keats, disease unfolds as sexual frustration: hence sexual ecstasy heals. Frustration unfolds, like disease, as a metaphor for meaninglessness.[21]

Healing is a synecdoche for sexual union and life that transcends time; it is not only female-centered, but manifests a divine being, precisely what Cynthia in "I Stood Tip-Toe," and Diana in *Endymion*, are: divine female beings who heal, transform, inspire: like Keats's Grecian Urn, a bride who is "still unravished," but still a bride, perpetually new, as a goddess is. In undisplaced terms, the female healer is thus a goddess, a power in/over time that is inseparable from female sexual energy—the attractive/reproductive force-in-time.

As a goddess, this figure cannot be accommodated by traditional Christianity, with its split between upper/unfallen and lower/fallen worlds, presided over by an omnipotent Father. The logic of Romantic narrative implies paganism (like the Druid symbolism in *Christabel* of oak, mistletoe, and midnight prayer by female figures). More exactly, it has affinities with pre- or non-Christian religion. Again, the "goddess" here is a metaphor, not a divinity worshiped in "new age" cults.

The female healer is thus almost by definition a figure of unorthodox spirituality —though, as in *The Ancient Mariner*, traditional religious images are used to express these unorthodox perceptions, implying also the absorption of elements of Christianity within a new spiritual dispensation.

Similarly, in *The Scarlet Letter*, Hester's belief is nominally Christian, but in fact radical and speculative—unlike the sterile conformism of Dimmesdale, whose real religion is Male Envy and its compete/control hierarchy. In former times, Hawthorne indicates, she would have been what used to be called a "Wise Woman." Hester is neither chaste nor virginal, yet she has her own spiritual perception, which is not doctrinal but existential. Her power does not fit the established ecclesiastical structure: as I noted, people *voluntarily* seek her help— her authority comes from herself, not from coercion by any institution. The professional medicine of Chillingworth, her technical husband—and a doctor—is also a contrast to Hester: he is a protoscientist concerned with sadistic experimentation and the manipulation of plants.

A few years later, Hawthorne hints, both Hester and her daughter Pearl would have been denounced as witches and, like others, killed.

* * *

The greatest of these figures in Romantic narrative is Rebecca in *Ivanhoe*. Rebecca is Jewish; and Scott shows a respect for Judaism that is remarkable for his time.[22] It is equally remarkable that he allows Rebecca to upstage the action. Her personal magnetism, eloquence, and courage make every other character in the novel, including the eponymous hero, pale by comparison.

Several features about her are striking: she has no mother but is profoundly identified with a spiritual mother, Miriam, who gave her her healing skills;[23] she has a protecting relation with her father that recalls the reversal of roles in *Christabel*, where the daughter is stronger than the father in almost every respect; she has a virtually magic potion in a phial; she is associated with the forest, where she is found; and she heals the hero of the narrative, just as Coleridge planned that in the completion of his poem Christabel would save her lover.

Scott reveals Rebecca slowly. The key description comes late in the novel, as if she were too powerful to approach quickly:

> The beautiful Rebecca had been heedfully brought up in all the knowledge proper to her nation, which her apt and powerful mind had retained, arranged, and enlarged, in the course of a progress beyond her years, her sex, and even the age in which she lived. Her knowledge of medicine and of the healing art had been acquired under an aged Jewess, the daughter of one of their most celebrated doctors, who loved Rebecca as her own child, and was believed to have communicated to her secrets which had been left to herself by her sage father at

the same time, and under the same circumstances. The fate of Miriam had been to fall a sacrifice to the fanaticism of the times; but her secrets had survived in her apt pupil.[24]

It is significant that her mentor/mother (like Christabel's) is dead; indeed she is a martyr whose fate Rebecca herself barely avoids.

Scott emphasizes the fact that Rebecca is non-Christian; he goes further and associates her with semidivine beings, the saints of the Old Testament:

> Rebecca, thus endowed with knowledge as with beauty, was universally revered and admired by her own tribe, who almost regarded her as one of those gifted women mentioned in sacred history. Her father himself, out of his unbounded affection, permitted the maiden a greater liberty than was usually indulged to those of her sex by the habits of her people, and was . . . frequently guided by her opinion, even in preference to his own. (296)

Again: she is not simply Jewish—she is different from others of her own people. Scott describes her as "a beneficent being"; her words are like "the charms of a beneficent fairy" (298). The Jewish identity is not only Scott's recognition of the dignity of Judaism in an anti-Semitic society, but a metaphor for perceptions excluded by ordinary consciousness, even taboo. The fact that Rebecca heals Ivanhoe, at the very time she herself is threatened with death (and the fate worse than death), gives a sense of her power—and because of that power, her danger.

That danger is amplified by her sexual magnetism. This is the subtext of Rebecca's "healing" of Ivanhoe, namely an intense sexual passion that makes every other feeling in the novel thin, forgettable. Indeed, the erotic force between Rebecca and Ivanhoe is so potent that it intervenes in the penultimate paragraph of the novel, effectively skewing the happy ending: Ivanhoe marries the socially acceptable Rowena—and clearly never again does anything that equals his deeds before Rebecca leaves.[25] Ironically, it is Rebecca's quasi-miraculous healing power that gets her into trouble. For when she rejects the nihilistic and obsessed priest, Brian de Bois-Guilbert, he has her accused of witchcraft and threatened with ritual burning. We return to the symbolism of holy murder.

Ivanhoe appears in the nick of time to deliver her from her captors, in the climactic scene. Ivanhoe owes Rebecca a debt, the debt of life itself, as if Scott requires that this debt be paid back in order that nothing be owing to her. When no obligation to her remains, she and her erotic/healing power can be safely got rid of. Thus Rebecca mediates a dangerous supernatural energy that must be placated—treated with careful respect—even as it is being firmly rejected. Her radiant sexual force makes her all the more dangerous in an order that repudiates love for national and dynastic ambitions, requirements which, for Ivanhoe, are summed up in the word Rowena.

The female healer represents values repressed in the hegemonic culture, but that are necessary for health and sanity. Thus, Rebecca has the power to heal, *because* she embodies excluded values: what a society that is too blind to know what is good for it actually needs. The principle is that of the "shadow" in Jungian psychology: a part of the self that is repressed but ultimately vital to identity. As long as the Shadow is excluded, the self is impaired or sick, and the Shadow (like the female healer) is fearfully viewed as monstrous. The female healer thus condenses an inter-related complex:

- healing power
- erotic energy
- spontaneous sense of action, timing
- alternative (even taboo) spirituality; heightened sensation
- unorthodox, possibly forbidden and dangerous perceptions
- receptivity
- female power (power that confronts male figures)
- female lineage (special links to antecedent female figures)
- the capacity to rescue others from death
- subtle affinity with nature
- refreshing sleep; peace (metaphorically, peace of mind; self-authenticity)
- power to communicate; eloquence; prophetic insight

The context in which the female healer functions is one characterized by male competition and war, in which feelings of frustration and meaninglessness are normal: the compete/control hierarchy, in short.

* * *

What we are considering, then, is not simply the Angel in the House paradigm of Victorian culture, where the female is used as a resource for the male competitor, in other words a function of Male Envy. On the contrary, this figure is typically bold, independent, profound in thought: a figure opposed, fundamentally opposed, to the Male-envious ethos of forcing/conquering/competing/controlling, as follows:

- routine: obsessive training; automatic action; compulsive repetition
- male hierarchy; unthinking or reflex obedience
- obsession with controlling/using/owning/winning
- competition; isolation from others
- inability to rest; sickness; frustration; madness
- impermeability; sense of self as impenetrable object in space
- intense anxieties connected to feelings of vulnerability

In *Ivanhoe*, Rebecca gives Ivanhoe a healing drink that enables him to rest: it "secured the patient sound and undisturbed slumbers. In the morning his kind physician found him entirely free from feverish symptoms" (304). The motifs of special drink, healing peace, coolness after fever, and sleep are again conspicuous.[26] Rebecca's healing work and the conversations with Ivanhoe—so quiet, so private and unobtrusive—are the real heart of the novel and are in complete contrast to the panoply of Male Envy that dominate the action, the outward heroics of struggle, arguing, contests, public displays, boasting, conspiracy, disguise, pursuit, flight, fighting, and confrontation generally.

One notices in particular that Ivanhoe suffers mentally and spiritually, as well as physically. He is at the low point of his life, wounded, separated from friends, rejected by family, and could bring danger to anybody who helps him: "Thou seest, maiden, what an ill-fated wretch thou dost labour to assist; be wise, and let me go, ere the misfortunes which track my steps like slot-hounds shall involve thee also in their pursuit," he cries (304). He is not simply depressed, clearly: he resents being dependent, like the Mariner killing the Albatross, the source of his own survival; he would prefer to be abandoned and possibly die than to depend on someone else, especially a woman.

Rebecca's ministration to him is thus as much intellectual as it is bodily; more precisely, it fuses body, intellect, and spirit. Hence her healing includes a sharp critique of the values that Ivanhoe worships and that have brought him to the state he is in. She assails his despair:

> "Thy weakness and thy grief, Sir Knight, make thee miscalculate the purposes of Heaven. Thou hast been restored to thy country when it most needed the assistance of a strong hand and a true heart, and thou hast humbled the pride of thine enemies and those of thy king, when their horn was most highly exalted; and for the evil which thou hast sustained, seest thou not that Heaven has raised thee a helper and a physician, even among the most despised of the land?— Therefore, be of good courage, and trust that thou art preserved for some marvel which thine arm shall work before this people." (304)

Ironically, the Jewish female attacks the Christian male for lack of faith! Rebecca similarly assails the priest Bois-Guilbert, the personification of nihilistic ambition (502-503). A further irony is that she is what *constitutes* Ivanhoe's faith: she is the physician that Heaven has brought to save him. She even prophesies that he will accomplish some great deed in the future. Ultimately, this great deed is that of saving Rebecca herself from the flames of her obsessed captors. The true miracle is that he seeks to give back to her what she gave him: life.

Not only does Rebecca rebuke Ivanhoe's despair, she identifies its root: his total absorption in the cult of competition, "where men sit and hear each other groan," as Keats puts it: the system of Male Envy. She observes his "impatient yearning after action—this struggling with and repining at . . . present weakness." Ivanhoe angrily invokes the law of his profession: "We live not—we wish not to live—longer than while we are victorious and renowned—Such, maiden, are the laws of chivalry to which we are sworn, and to which we offer all that we hold dear." He then discloses his real god: "Glory, maiden, glory! which gilds our sepulchre and embalms our name" (317). Ivanhoe alludes unconsciously to Jesus' image of hypocrisy in the Gospels: the dazzling "whited sepulchre" of the Pharisees, spectacularly impressive on the outside, but all filth and bones inside. The allusion is apt—and ironic. Rebecca's response (317-18) is the great speech of the novel (it recalls Aholibamah in *Heaven and Earth*):

> "What is it, valiant knight, save an offering of sacrifice to a demon of vainglory, and a passing through the fire to Moloch! . . . Glory? . . . alas, is the rusted mail which hangs as a hatchment over the champion's dim and mouldering tomb—is the defaced sculpture of the inscription which the ignorant monk can hardly read to the enquiring pilgrim—are these sufficient rewards for the sacrifice of every kindly affection, for a life spent miserably that ye may make others miserable? Or is there such virtue in the rude rhymes of a wandering bard, that domestic love, kindly affection, peace, and happiness are so wildly bartered, to become the hero of those ballads which vagabond minstrels sing to drunken churls over their evening ale?"

So much for the coveted attention command of Male Envy. Note the link of "Glory"—Male Envy—with drinking. Ultimately, healing is not possible, without a healing of the social order. The healing of the psyche that is also implied is not possible without an *expanding* of the psyche. One begins to see why Ivanhoe must reject Rebecca, not simply because of her religion, but because she is too radical: her vision is too powerful for a man of Ivanhoe's conditioning and standing to contemplate—again recalling Dimmesdale's rejection of Hester in *The Scarlet Letter*. But this anxiety makes his rescue of Rebecca all the more genuinely miraculous, for it could only be accomplished by genuine perception of her value, and not performed as an act to acquire competitive advantage over other males (what Ivanhoe naively calls "Glory").

As the real center of *Ivanhoe*, Rebecca is not a figure in a historical novel, but a figure in Scott's own culture, dominated by the Object thinking that frames Male Envy. She is an index, therefore, of certain cultural perceptions that are projected on to medieval England, so that the historical novel presents Rebecca and the perceptions she figures—and at the same time safely distances them.

* * *

What Rebecca signifies, then, is not simply repressed social and psychic energies that have healing power when accepted. She represents something that, if allowed freedom, would reject the entire worldview of *Ivanhoe* and metonymically of Scott's culture itself. In short, she implies an alternative model of reality. In this respect, she recalls Hester in *The Scarlet Letter*, once more: someone whose spirituality is subversive and not just oppositional—the exemplar of another way of living and thinking, not mere rebellion against the existing power arrangements—arrangements that are psychological as well as sociopolitical in nature.

Ivanhoe's companion text is *The Talisman* (1825), which deals with similar motifs, in some ways even more profoundly. *Ivanhoe* is actually the sequel of *The Talisman*, for it deals with the period immediately before the action of *Ivanhoe*, even though it was written later. *The Talisman* takes its title from the healing power that is the centerpiece of the plot, but unlike *Ivanhoe*, *The Talisman* does not link its healing power with a female figure on the scale of Rebecca. There is nonetheless a significant connection, a connection even more important in the context of the code of Male Envy. For instead of the Jewish female healer, we find the mystic Islamic prince, wily Saladin, who employs the healing talisman as a potion for the ailing king of his Christian enemies (recalling the secret "phial" Rebecca uses to heal Ivanhoe).[27] Hence the role of Rebecca as healer is replaced in *The Talisman* with a male figure who in many respects corresponds to Rebecca: a figure who is non-Christian, even anti-Christian; royal (but neither feudal nor English); exotic; and erotic, for homoerotic energy radiates from the magnetic Saladin and his chivalrous gesture to King Richard, the enemy whose life he gallantly saves.

The union of these male competitors by a bond of love (for lack of a better word) is a remarkable feature of this novel. This love coheres with the subversive quality of the healer, a figure who does not merely heal, but embodies vital yet rejected energies. The fact that Saladin heals his competitor/enemy violates the code of Male Envy in its central point—the contempt of weakness, both in oneself and in others, that drives the competitor. In Jerome Mitchell's words, "it can be argued that Saladin is the real hero."[28] The release of love in this manner is itself a healing and implies a social order of male solidarity and mutual support, not hostility/competition. It also, necessarily, implies a social vision in which differences are not used as pretexts for controlling/using, but as the expression of life itself—life being a constantly transforming and hence genuine identity: not an object scattered among other objects, nor a mere "subject position" constructed by external or ideological forces. Perhaps the most significant feature of *The Talisman* has to do with love between males. The dismantling or weakening of Male Envy is impossible without the acceptance of love of one male for another, including homosexual love. This is not to say that all males are somehow homosexual or should be, of course. Rather, without the acceptance of this form of love, humanity cannot be freed from the more damaging aspects of the compete/control hierarchy, with its culture of hatred and contempt, in its various disguises and rationalizations.

The king whom Saladin heals in *The Talisman* is Richard the Lion-Hearted, and Richard is the true male heroic figure in *Ivanhoe*: he is also as close to a model for male identity outside the code of Male Envy as can be found in Romantic narrative and hence needs to be observed carefully. The society of *Ivanhoe* is one of civil war, a war of all against all, one ethnic group in conflict with every other ethnic group, in which the cynical Prince John rules by fraud and force. Richard enters the action secretly and in disguise and only slowly discloses his real identity. As a symbol for genuine authority, for the guiding and the authentic, Richard is not only chivalrous and kind, but capable of treating everybody he meets as a human being and not as an object to control or as an inferior to manipulate. The usurper Prince John (Richard's brother) meanwhile embodies precisely these Male-envious attitudes in the novel. Above all, what Richard represents is the reconciliation of conflicting forces: a vision of society as an array of mutually cooperating but very different peoples and individuals, not a society in which one group dominates and uses another group, a social vision not so far, really, from that of Godwin's *Political Justice*.

The interesting thing about Richard is that in *The Talisman*, Scott presents Richard as a Crusader, engaged in a bloody and futile war in a country far away from where he should be. Scott is far ahead of his time in seeing the Crusades as a quixotic horror, a ghastly mistake for which the consequences could only be misery and injustice; he does not "romanticize" the Crusades. And the Richard we meet in *The Talisman* is appropriately sick, despondent, and paralyzed, recalling the Ancient Mariner after he kills the Albatross. More to the point, Richard is in this stage very like Ivanhoe before Ivanhoe's healing encounter with Rebecca. Richard is healed by his enemy, Saladin, as noted. Afterward, he leaves Palestine, where he does not belong, and returns to England. Metaphorically, Richard is released from his Male-envious obsessions by the love of another man, and this love enables him to find his true place in human society and to leave his Male-envious obsessions behind. Male love heals, because love heals.

This love may or may not include a sexual dimension. In Male Envy, nothing is more evil than love between males, for reasons noted earlier: male love equalizes and blasphemes the sanctity of hurting and using those who are weaker, especially defeated rivals. Hence any friendship or close connection between males is suspect and regarded as possibly sexual even if it is not, by both gay males and straight males. One thinks of Raymond Chandler here, whose famous hard-boiled detective Philip Marlowe has frequently been regarded as subtextually gay, and Marlowe's friendship to Terry Lennox in *The Long Goodbye* is cited as proof. Chandler himself read this analysis of Marlowe, and he responded to it by emphatically rejecting the view "which cannot conceive of a close friendship between a couple of men as other than homosexual."[29]

The point is not whether such friendship is sexual or not: that is a distraction from the real point, which is the love that connects the two men. Male Envy already regards sex as the sensation of power over another human being, anyway; Male Envy regards heterosexual sex itself as affirmation of the competitor/controller's control power and hence identity, identity being placement in Male Envy. That is, sex is a means of self-inflation and self-enhancement; it is only accidentally a matter of pleasurable mutuality. Ironically, the Marlowe-Lennox relationship, true to the code of Male Envy, turns out to be a manipulation. Lennox deceives and takes advantage of Marlowe, who tells him off at the end in a brief but unforgettable speech of repudiation. Lennox proves disturbingly unworthy of Marlowe's regard. It is as if the anxieties of close male connection are too much even for Chandler: the taboo on male love is too great, its challenge to Male Envy too panic-inspiring to be tolerated.

Marlowe does not heal Lennox, but *The Long Good-bye* opens with Marlowe rescuing the drunken Lennox from the street. Rescue and healing are closely related motifs. Chandler's detective fiction is a late variant of Romantic narrative, and the rescuing/healing complex is a preoccupation of Romantic narrative, especially in Scott. Scott's female healer, Rebecca, also illustrates another type: the figure of the female savior. Again, this is not the sexist angel-in-the-house cliché of Victorian culture, but an aggressive, intrepid type in Romantic narrative. This figure fascinated Byron—as his *Don Juan*, canto II, and *Mazeppa* indicate, and above all in Byron's last completed tale, *The Island* (1824). *The Island* is a retelling/revision of the mutiny on the Bounty story, and its heroine is a Polynesian woman named Neuha: Neuha is both dark-skinned and non-Christian.[30] She rescues the British sailor Torquil from his own people and his own navy, metaphorically from the alienation/oppression of his culture, the brutality which encloses her white male lover. The military is a basic site of Male Envy, where comradeship is based upon conflict, not genuine affiliation. One of the descendants of Byron's poem *The Island* is Melville's *Billy Budd* (as well as, in a different tonality, *Typee*). *Billy Budd* is a study of the malice built into the code of Male Envy[31]; the difference between the two is the absence of a female figure in Melville, an absence that marks the foreclosing of alternative possibilities in the tragic régime of Male Envy. For the female acts as a symbol of independence of Male Envy, and so implies male emancipation as well as female emancipation.

Another female savior of the Neuha type appears in *Wacousta* by John Richardson (1832), a novel set on the frontier during Pontiac's conspiracy (1763) —in other words, a close contemporary of James Fenimore Cooper. Richardson is different from Cooper, in instructive ways. In *Wacousta*, the real hero is Oucanasta, a woman from the Ottawa tribe whom a British officer saved from drowning. She returns the gift by rescuing him, more than once; indeed, she saves the whole garrison of Fort Détroit from destruction by Pontiac's warriors;

and her brother delivers everyone from the curse of the deranged and obsessed character named Wacousta, who is actually a white man obsessed by Male-envious rage. The redefinition of heroism as acts of redemption rather than of aggression inevitably seeks a female figure: the male ethos of competition/control is one of alienation from which males themselves must be rescued (one thinks of Leonora in Beethoven's opera *Fidelio* here). Again, in the case of *Wacousta*, an erotic bond is noticeable: Oucanasta's love for the officer is the most potent force in the story; similarly, Neuha's love for Torquil in Byron's *Island* makes possible a genuine triumph over British imperialism at its most barbaric.[32]

The female healer and the witch may be seen as two sides of the same figure or, rather, two ways of seeing the same figure.[33] Thus, from the viewpoint of Male Envy and its compete/control hierarchy, the female healer is simply a witch (a role Hedda Gabler seems to delight in in Ibsen's play, somewhat as Miss Havisham does in Dickens's *Great Expectations*). In *Ivanhoe*, the order of the Knights Templars identifies Rebecca as an evil sorceress who needs, properly, to be burned at the stake, in the manner of Joan of Arc and other women of similar reputation. One may compare Rima, in W. H. Hudson's *Green Mansions*, who is viewed by the enclosing social order as a sorceress and is in fact burnt alive. While Hester in Hawthorne does not share this fate, the scarlet letter on her breast displaces and implies branding (a not uncommon punishment in English penal practice)—and also burning itself. Furthermore, her exposure to public scorn is a way of isolating her from society, so as to insulate society from the subversive values she embodies.

The Knights Templars of *Ivanhoe* epitomize the code of Male Envy, with their hierarchy, fanaticism, boastful pride, unquestioning obedience to the more powerful, shows of control, and, above all, obsession with competition and war against other males. The unavoidable byproduct is also evident: frustration so intense as to induce the rapist nihilism of Bois-Guilbert and the murderous bigotry of the Grand Master of the Order (an order which, via Scott's influence on the Southern states, was a model for the Ku Klux Klan). The Knights Templars and their ethos act as the cultural norm to which Ivanhoe himself is dedicated—if more naively. Again, Ivanhoe's capacity to stand outside his own conditioning and so seek to rescue Rebecca is more like real health than his life as warrior has been, in particular since he had been weak, defeated, and utterly vulnerable while in her hands.

Ironically, however, Ivanhoe is the catalyst but not the agent of Rebecca's rescue: he arrives in time to challenge Bois-Guilbert as her champion, but he is too weak to defeat his enemy, and he falls himself. When he gets up, he finds that Bois-Guilbert has also fallen, "to the astonishment of all," as Scott notes— for Ivanhoe has not hurt his enemy-rival: "As they looked on him in astonishment, the eyes opened; but they were fixed and glazed. The flush passed from his brow, and gave way to the pallid hue of death. Unscathed by the lance of his enemy, he had died a victim of the violence of his own conflicting passions" (506). Thus, the scene of single combat, which one expects to be the climax of the novel, fizzles: juxtaposed to the eloquent faith of Rebecca, it is pathetic and an anticlimax. The passage echoes Byron's "The Destruction of Sennacherib," where faith defeats military power without any actual combat, and the power of God becomes the authority of the innocent rather than the force of social control. Public display is a standard motif in the code of Male Envy—we have observed it from the outset of this exploration. In *Ivanhoe*, this display is the climax of the action and is dramatically deflated.

The perspective in which the female healer is simply a deceitful witch is, plainly, the cult of competition and control which is at the heart of Male Envy. The code of Male Envy views the powerful woman as a witch—we have seen how this works in Chapter 2, noting not only Hester in Hawthorne, but Miss Havisham, and Hedda Gabler. But this brings us once more to the other view: the Transform thinking in which the female healer emerges as female healer. Here we come to the inner logic of Romantic narrative itself, which is essentially a shift in cosmology or worldview, a complex experimentation with an alternative way of putting reality together.

* * *

This experimentation, once again, begins by rejecting the basis of Object thinking, that reality is a pile of objects in space. Instead, reality is visualized as a metamorphosis-in-time, in which all things participate. *The Ancient Mariner* is especially direct in its insistence that the human, the divine, and the natural are inextricably enfolded. Hence self-alienation inevitably flows from the compulsion to control, which the Mariner's killing of the Albatross so dramatically illustrates. If, furthermore, the human, the divine, and the natural are inseparable, it follows that self-alienation is also alienation from nature and from the divine.

Ivanhoe extends this principle in another direction, by presenting a range of individuals and groups at war with one another—Normans, Jews, Saxons, religious orders, bandits, brothers, nobles. The novel is a panorama of chaotic competitive struggle—the arena of Male Envy. In these murderous civil wars, however, the narrative is a complex revelation of interconnectedness and interdependence. The most powerful character in the social system, Prince John, is weak; the despised Isaac of York has his own power; the strong-man Front-de-Boeuf turns out to be the helpless victim of a despised old woman; the king is ally to forest thieves; the most potent knight of them all is at the mercy of a young Jewish woman; and so on. In other words, the outward form of society is the compete/control hierarchy with its Male-envious obsessions; the true form is an immense interconnection, in which those who seem weak actually have an importance that those who seem powerful lack. In Rebecca's careful intellectual discussion with Ivanhoe—one feels she is far more intelligent than her male interlocutor—her main point is that the code of Male Envy is a parasitic growth on the prior social energies and interconnections that it feeds on. Male Envy believes that it is controlling that which in fact it depends upon and cannot exist without. In a sense this is the same Veblen distinction between controlling and creating that we have observed from the outset of this exploration.

The hierarchy of total control turns out to be an illusion: an illusion that is fought and killed for, but an illusion, nonetheless. In the code of Male Envy, the substratum of reality is nihilistic aggression, but this appearance would be impossible without an underlying integration/cooperation linking all things. In the alternative model of reality that Rebecca embodies, everyone/everything is connected with everyone/everything else; the human, the natural, and the divine are aspects of a single identity, a single force. Health is ultimately an awareness of these interconnections and a respect for them, sickness the result of the compulsion to use/own/control. Ivanhoe's willingness to sacrifice himself for Rebecca thus reveals what the female healer in Romantic narrative, at the deepest level, really means, namely that society has the power to heal itself.

Notes

1. Roger S. Jones, *Physics as Metaphor* (Minneapolis: U of Minnesota P, 1982) 208.

2. See Ken Auletta, Interview with Andrew S. Grove, *The New Yorker*, October 20/27, 1997, 140-142.

3. To quote Clyde W. Franklin III again: "The adult male who is 'appropriately' socialized into masculinity is rendered incapable of forming close ties with other males. ... how does one reconcile intimate self-disclosing and being emotionally expressive with one's competitors, who may attempt to use this in future competitive games? ... *men continue to express their emotions vicariously through women in such situations and women continue to feel secure in their dependence*," hence "the extreme discomfort some women experience when their male mates attempt to establish friendships with males external to their relationship (e.g., other 'unattached' males)," friendships "perceive[d] ... as threatening" (*The Changing Definition of Masculinity* [New York: Plenum, 1984] 120). In the régime of Male Envy, the successful woman must have complete and uncontested access/control to her male partner, access/control that is threatened by the possibility of other obligations on the male competitor/controller, especially the obligations posed by the existence of friends.

4. Margaret Atwood, *Surfacing* (New York: Paperjacks, 1973) 170.

5 Compare the darting, colored, phosphorescent water creatures in *Surfacing* (142) with the water snakes in *The Ancient Mariner*.

6. Sylvia Perera, *The Scapegoat Complex* (Toronto: Inner City, 1986) 36. This kind of "eye," which sees without hostility but is not indifferent or uncaring, should be noted: it the reverse of the evil eye.

7. As noted earlier, Adam Smith sums up the logic of male behavior here, of the father to the daughter as well as of male to male: "The pride of man makes him love to domineer, and nothing mortifies him so much as to be obliged to condescend to persuade his inferiors. Wherever the law allows it, and the nature of the work can afford it, therefore, he will generally prefer the services of slaves to that of freemen" (*The Wealth of Nations*, eds. T. D. Campbell and Andrew S. Skinner (Oxford: Oxford UP, 1976) 388.

8. A "source image" is a key shape in an artist's work, one that recurs and informs artistic composition; see Sandra Shuman, *Source Imagery* (New York: Doubleday, 1989).

9. As Virgin Mother, this figure is central to Catholic Christianity, but that makes it all the more striking in a poet so determinedly Protestant as Coleridge. Some might cite Jung and his archetypal Anima figure—the belief that we share a collective unconscious that includes this figure. Anima figures ("emanation" figures, Blake would call them) are important in Romantic literature—de Quincey's female figures come to mind. But heroic women become noticeable in Romantic narrative generally, from Jeannie Deans in Scott's *Heart of Midlothian* (there are many examples in Scott) to Shelley's Beatrice in *The Cenci* and Stendhal's Duchesse Sanseverina in *La Chartreuse de Parme*.

10. Northrop Frye, *The Secular Scripture: A Study of the Structure of Romance* (Cambridge: Harvard UP, 1976) 86. Romance has always had female knights or warriors —a motif that survives in Scott, where it appears in *Count Robert of Paris*, one of many underestimated novels by Scott.

11. One of the subjects that connects with the figure of the healer in Romantic narrative is thus the psychology of ritualized murder, in particular the male serial murder of women—the holy murder discussed in Chapter 4.

12. Bram Stoker, *Dracula*, ed. A. N. Wilson (Oxford: Oxford UP, 1983) 307.

13. Kathleen Spencer, "Purity and Danger: *Dracula*, The Urban Gothic, and the Late Victorian Degeneracy Crisis," *ELH* 59 (1992): 197. The bizarre romanticizing of Dracula in recent years has distorted both the novel and the vampire itself. Dracula is a predator, not a lover; his interests fall wholly inside the compass of eating and self-replication. His breath stinks of decayed blood; his ranting speech suggests the mental vacuity of a being several centuries old, like Swift's Struldbruggs, who spends most of his/its time in a state of paralysis lying on dirt in a filthy ruin. See my "Bram Stoker: Where the Hideous Strength Came From" (*Mythlore* 19.3 [1993]: 19-23).

14. The figure of Esther is typically underrated; an exception is Michael S. Gurney, "Disease as Device: The Role of Smallpox in *Bleak House*," *Literature and Medicine* 9 (1990): 79-92.

15. Chateaubriand, *René and Atala*, trans. W. J. Cobb (New York: NAL, 1962) 110.

16. Madame La Luc helps the heroine recover, but Radcliffe treats her with gentle satire, as an Enlightenment *virtuoso*: "it was the pride of Madame to believe herself skilful in relieving the disorders of her neighbours" (*The Romance of the Forest* [London: Routledge, 1907] 249).

17. The revaluation of sex as spiritual bonding rather than as male-control-of-women is a crucial theme in Mary Wollstonecraft's *Vindication of the Rights of Woman*, which appears to be anti-sexual but is really hostile to the objectifying of women. The emphasis

on sexual energy opposes the notion of the self as an independent being manipulating objects in space, what Jacqueline Zita refers to as the "transsexual figure who is completely independent of woman's body" ("Transsexualized Origins: Reflections on Descartes's Meditations," *Genders* 5 (1989): 101)—"the social construction of masculinity as transcendence over others," as Eileen Leonard puts it ("Sexual Murder," *Gender and Society* 3 [1989]: 576), which is the object of attack in *Frankenstein*—note that both Elizabeth and Victor's mother try to heal, but fail: their powers are ineffectual, in keeping with the symbolically related repression of female reproductive power in the novel.

18. Sex is complicated in the history of ideas in the eighteenth century. As L. J. Jordanova puts it, "Generation, i.e. reproduction, was a central biological problem in the eighteenth century" (Introduction to *Languages of Nature: Critical Essays on Science and Literature*, ed. L. Jordanova [London: Free Association P, 1986] 42), because life-in-time is inherently difficult to explain with a model that visualizes reality as objects in space and society as "A form of social relations which treated persons as objects" (L. J. Jordanova, "Naturalizing the Family: Literature and the Bio-Medical Sciences in the Late Eighteenth-Century" in *Languages of Nature* 112). That is, the model of reality that is dominant in the Romantic period, as indeed in our own, is one in which reality and everything in it is essentially a mechanism. Hume's Cleanthes in *Dialogues Concerning Natural Religion* had put it thus: "You will find [nature] nothing but one great machine, subdivided into an infinite number of lesser machines, which again admit of subdivisions, to a degree beyond what human senses can trace and explain" (143). Philosopher of science Henry Margenau sums up: "Man believed there was indeed nothing in the world that was not material, nothing that failed to obey the laws of mechanics" (*Physics and Philosophy* [Dordrecht, Holland: Reidel, 1978], 276; see Carolyn Merchant, *The Death of Nature* [San Francisco: Harper, 1980], for the unexpected implications [193]; and my "The New Cosmology in Romantic Poetry," *The Wordsworth Circle* 22 [1989]: 123-31).

19. The association of magic liquid with female healer typifies the "Lady" of Coleridge's "Dejection" referred to earlier; Coleridge identifies her with "Life, and Life's effluence, cloud at once and shower, / Joy, Lady! is the spirit and the power" (ll. 66-67).

20. Compare other female figures in Romantic narrative who are burnt or otherwise martyred—Rima in *Green Mansions* (1916), Bertha in *Jane Eyre*, Ayesha in Rider Haggard's *She* (1887). All are alien or supernatural: beings whose female life-energy is threatening to the social order that encloses them. Both Rima and Haggard's She are healers who preside over their lovers' recovery (this aspect of Bertha is taken over by Jane Eyre in Charlotte Bronte's novel).

21. The notion that frustrated or betrayed love causes insanity is a key motif in Keats, as in "La Belle Dame Sans Merci," "Isabella," and *Lamia*. Shelley uses this motif in "Julian and Maddalo" (1824). Love melancholy is a very old theme, but the Romantics instinctively use it as a metaphor for alienation, for the *Weltschmerz* of meaninglessness.

22. According to Abba Rubin, *Ivanhoe* offers "the most realistically favorable portrait of a Jew that had yet appeared. . . . The sympathy evoked for Isaac of York, a Jewish usurer, and the sympathy and admiration aroused for his daughter, Rebecca, are vital elements in the amelioration of the Jew's literary images" (Abba Rubin, *Images in Transition: The English Jew in English Literature 1660-1830* [Westport: Greenwood, 1984]). Even the anti-Semitic Thackeray called her "the sweetest character in the whole range of fiction" (qu. 124).

23. The numinous mother figure achieves apotheosis in the Great Grandmother of George Macdonald's *The Princess and the Goblin* (1872), with her motifs of roses, fire, healing bath, providential guidance, moon, birds.

24. *Ivanhoe*, ed. A. N. Wilson (Harmondsworth: Penguin, 1984) 295-96.

25. "Rowena is determined to marry the man of her choice, but has otherwise few distinguishing characteristics except her blonde hair" (Frye 85).

26. *The Betrothed*, one of Scott's most underestimated novels, features a similar scene between Eveline and de Lacey. Compare the great scenes of *Don Juan* in which Haidee ministers to the shipwrecked Juan: "she bent o'er him, and he lay beneath / Hushed as the babe upon its mother's breast" (2.148.1-2), like "the Virgin Mary" (2.149.8). What follows is the most erotic writing in Byron's *oeuvre*. The motifs of: the female savior; deep sleep and miraculous waking; special drink (and food) are all noticeable. As this example shows, the female healer in Romantic narrative is a variant of the figure of the female savior, such as Neuha in Byron's *The Island* and Oucanasta in John Richardson's *Wacousta* (1832). Cooper's Leatherstocking Tales, by contrast, avoid these motifs.

27. Rebecca is visualized furthermore as a Middle Eastern noblewoman, reinforcing the "oriental" associations that connect the healers of *Ivanhoe* and of *The Talisman*. Thus the astonished Ivanhoe awakes from the faint caused by his wound: "To his great surprise, he found himself in a room magnificently furnished, but having cushions instead of chairs to rest upon, and in other respects partaking so much of Oriental costume that he began to doubt whether he had not, during his sleep, been transported back again to the land of Palestine. The impression was increased when . . . a female form, dressed in a rich habit, which partook more of the Eastern taste than that of Europe, glided through the door . . . followed by a swarthy domestic" (*Ivanhoe* 298).

28. Jerome Mitchell, *Scott, Chaucer, and Medieval Romance* (Lexington: UP of Kentucky, 1987) 178.

29. Qu. in Tom Hiney, *Raymond Chandler: A Biography* (London: Random, 1998) 246.

30. Byron's reputation as a sexist is contradicted by the variety and quality of his female figures; see Caroline Franklin, *Byron's Heroines* (Oxford: Oxford UP, 1993).

31. Joseph Berke discusses *Billy Budd* at length in his study of envy.

32. One may contrast these female figures, Oucanasta especially, with J. F. Cooper's treatment—his rejection—of this motif in the Leatherstocking Tales. Despite the heroic efforts of Dew-in-June in *The Pathfinder*, Cooper is uncomfortable with female saviors. The heroic Cora of *The Last of the Mohicans* is denied this role; in a remarkable sequence in *The Deerslayer*, three female figures in a row—Judith, Hetty, and Hist—all fail to rescue Deerslayer from torture. A related type is the "wild woman"—such as Madge Wildfire in Scott's *The Heart of Midlothian* or Crazy Jane in William B. Yeats's poems.

33. The witch uses herbs and spells to enchant, metamorphose, and transform (e.g., Keats's "La Belle Dame Sans Merci" or even Circe with her cup or the murderous Medea and her age-dissolving cauldron). On the logic of images here, see my *13 Ways of Looking at Images: Studies in the Logic of Visualization* (Los Angeles, 1999).

Index

academy (university), Male Envy in the, 9, 21, 23, 62, 154, 171-214
Adler, Alfred, 133
aggression (as virtue), 10, 18, 30-31, 33, 40-41, 75-76, 78, 105, 132-33, 137, 150, 163, 179, 181-83, 186-87, 215, 221, 231, 240, 242. *See also* code of Male Envy—Male Display; control; killing
akeda, 140
Albee, Edward, *Who's Afraid of Virginia Woolf?* 21
alienation, 26, 32, 41, 50, 107-13, 115, 121-22, 124, 147, 150, 193, 217, 220, 222-23, 225, 227, 232, 240, 242. *See also* exploitation; Life-in-Death; losing; Object thinking
Amin, Samir, 88
anger, 2, 18, 22, 67, 104, 106, 108, 110, 116, 133, 137, 139, 140, 143-44, 152, 154, 156, 158, 240; anger management courses, 18
animals, 42, 89, 91, 102, 106, 108, 118, 120, 142; abuse or killing of, 30, 75, 77, 101, 104-5, 137, 140, 143-45, 154, 156, 218
Anstensen, Ansten, 80n20
Antigone (Sophocles), 65, 187
anxiety of influence. *See* code of Male Envy
Appleby, Joyce O., 108
Apuleius, *The Golden Ass*, 19, 223-24
Aquinas, St. Thomas, 22n49
Arbib, Michael A., 190
Archer, John, 40
Arendt, Hannah, 70
Aristotle, 42n11, 65
atheism, 109, 135. *See also* Deism; God; Object thinking
attention-getting. *See* code of Male Envy—attention-getting
atomism. *See* Object thinking
Atwood, Margaret, *Surfacing*, 32, 216-20
Auletta, Ken, 244n2
Axelrod, Alan, 165n15

Bacon, Francis, 49
Bakhtin, Mikhail, 212n52
Bakker, Tammy (wife of TV evangelist), 24
Balswick, Jack, 42n9
Banks, Joseph A., 155
Bate, Walter J., 194
Baudelaire, Charles, 53, 212n51
Baudrillard, Jean, 191, 204
Beethoven, Ludwig van, *Fidelio*, 240
Bem, Sandra Lipsitz, 125n1
Bercovitch, Sacvan, 44n37
Bergson, Henri, 129n50
Berke, Joseph, 2-3, 12, 50-51, 189
Bernheimer, Charles, 210n30
Bersani, Carl A., 130n53
Bertelson, David, 79n8
Bettelheim, Bruno, 30
Bible, the, 128n32, 152, 178, 183; Abraham and Isaac, 139-40, 161; Acts, 141; Adam, 183, 156; Beatitudes, 108; Cain and Abel, 141, 144, 156; Exodus, 114, 140, 165n25; Lot's wife, 139; Nimrod, 151; Noah, 137, 147, 160; Numbers, 137-38; Proverbs, 165n22; Psalms, 150; Revelation, 85, 137; Samson and Delilah, 56; Saul, 140. *See also* Byron—*Cain*; Deism; God; Jesus Christ
Black, Joel, 164n9
Blackstone, *Commentaries on the Laws*, 188
Blake, William, 30, 137, 150, 230; *America*, 215; "Auguries of Innocence," 122; *The Marriage of Heaven & Hell*, 72, 83-85, 93, 95, 109, 143; *Milton*, 195; "The Tyger," 149; *Visions of the Daughters of*

247

Albion, 80n24
Bligh, John, 167n37
blood, 8, 28, 38, 75, 84-85, 103-4, 112, 132, 137, 140-47, 149, 156, 159, 162 223, 228, 239. *See also* code of Male Envy—Male Display; killing; magic fluids
Bloom, Harold, 185, 192-196
Bly, Robert, 43n19
boasting. *See* code of Male Envy
Boccaccio, Giovanni, 74
body, 25, 40, 77, 90-91, 101, 110, 117, 142, 154, 156, 168n41, 187-89, 195, 198, 217, 220, 223-24, 229, 231, 236; body as weapon, 35, 90, 110. *See also* blood; killing
Bogart, Humphrey (actor), 56
Bohm, David, *Wholeness and the Implicate Order*, 91
Bolan, Mac (fictional character), 35
Bowker, Pamela, 46n53
Bowlby, John, 126n11
Bowler, Peter, 180
Braudy, Leo, 164n9
Brenzo, Richard, 44n34
Bronson, Charles (actor), 35
Brontë, Charlotte, *Jane Eyre*, 227, 245n20
Brown, Charles Brockden, *Wieland, or The Transformation*, 136-37, 152-5, 157-8, 160, 167n33, 175, 183
Browning, Robert, "My Last Duchess," 151; "Porphyria's Lover," 131
Burke, Edmund, 176; *Reflections on the Revolution in France*, 175; *Thoughts on Scarcity*, 89, 177; *Treatise on the Sublime and Beautiful*, 54, 199
Burkert, Walter, 8
Burnet, Thomas, 129n41
Burns, Robert, "Holy Willie," 167n34
Byron, George Gordon, Lord, 150; *Cain*, 38-41, 136, 141-47, 149, 151, 153, 156, 159; "Darkness," 96; "The Destruction of Sennacherib," 241; *Don Juan*, 240; *Heaven and Earth*, 136, 147, 151, 159-61, 236; *The Island*, 240; *Manfred*, 169n49; *The Vision of Judgment*, 83

Calvin, John, 154
Cameron, Deborah, 164n7
capitalism (market culture), 11, 74, 87-93, 97, 106, 123, 148, 177, 187, 219. *See also* code of Male Envy; cosmology; economics; Malthus; marginal utility, theory of; Object thinking; proletarianization; self-interest; Smith
Caputi, Jane, 43n23, 164n3
Carroll, Lewis, 50
castration, castration anxiety (psychoanalysis). *See* code of Male Envy; Freud, Sigmund; losing
chance (randomness, gambling, fortune, chaos, luck), 87, 92-94, 112, 154, 190, 218. *See also* Object thinking
Chandler, Raymond, *The Long Goodbye*, 239-40
chastity. *See* Magic Virgin convention
Chateaubriand, René de, *René*, 229
Chaucer, Geoffrey, 195, 247n28
Chesnais, Jean-Claude, 165n11
Chew, S. C., 166n24
Cheyfitz, Eric, 45n58
children, 27, 30, 38, 56, 60-61, 63, 71, 83, 88, 92, 106, 131-36, 143, 145, 153-54, 158, 161-62, 194, 220, 227, 233; abuse or killing of, 4, 65, 75, 131-33, 138, 140, 153, 156-57, 220-21; children's literature, 20
Chomsky, Noam, 213n64
Christensen, Jerome, 210n27
Christianity. *See* God; Jesus Christ
circumcision, 167n36
Cixous, Hélène, 1
Clark, J. C. D., 164n10
classical economics. *See* economics—classical
Cleland, John, *Fanny Hill*, 90
Clurman, Harold, 61
code of Male Envy, 1-48 *et passim*; attention-getting, 8, 10-11, 16-17, 19, 24-25, 50, 54, 102-5, 112-13, 142,

150, 173, 183, 187, 191-93, 195-96, 200-1, 206, 227 (*see also* gaze); compete/control hierarchy, 7, 9-13, 15-18, 21-26, 27-30, 32-37, 40-41, 51-52, 54, 56, 58, 66-67, 69, 72, 76, 78, 93-97, 106, 108, 111, 132-33, 147-48, 158, 160, 162, 186-90, 192, 201, 205-6, 216-20, 227, 232, 235, 238, 240, 242 (*see also* control; hierarchy; invidious distinction; losing; winning); emotion in, 2, 6, 9, 29, 31, 37, 40, 49-50, 52-54, 57, 67-68, 72, 76, 86, 88, 96, 102, 110-11, 113-14, 117-18, 132, 135, 138-39, 152, 172, 179, 206, 217, 220 (*see also* anger; fear; hate; love); female roles in the régime of Male Envy, 26, 30, 32, 49, 55, 57-58, 63, 73-74, 185-89, 216-18, 228, 235 (*see also* desiring female; female envy; feminism); intimidation rituals, 8, 10, 17, 31, 132-33; Male Display, 5-7, 9-11, 14, 16-18, 22-24, 29-31, 36-8, 50, 52-54, 56, 68, 72, 78, 97, 104, 132-33, 142, 151, 155, 160, 162, 186, 189, 191, 193, 206, 221, 223, 226-27, 235, 241 (*see also* killing; penis; power objects; rape; sport); motif of the numerous competitors, 21, 30, 37, 61; and Object thinking, 85-86, 94-97; power-over relationships, 8, 58, 74-75, 77, 105, 115, 117, 175, 182-83. *See also* academy; aggression; alienation; death; de Man; disaster fantasies; distorted perception; Doctrine of Good Suffering; emptiness; exploitation; Freud, Sigmund; friendship; gaze; Malthus; Object thinking; obsession; rationalizing; silence; suicide; taboo; Veblen

Cohan, Steven, 42n15

Coleridge, Samuel Taylor, 135, 226; *Christabel*, 220-25, 229, 231-33; "Kubla Khan," 225; "Dejection," 225; "Religious Musings," 165n22; *The Rime of the Ancient Mariner*, 99-121, 143, 154, 158, 174, 200, 217-19, 224-25, 230-31, 236, 239, 244n5

commodity, commodification; 10, 74, 91, 182, 202, 204; commodity fetish, 96. *See also* alienation; code of Male Envy—Male Display; capitalism; Object thinking

compete/control hierarchy. *See* code of Male Envy—compete/control hierarchy

competition. *See* code of Male Envy

Conrad, Joseph, *The Heart of Darkness*, 115, 190; *The Secret Agent*, 39

conspicuous consumption. *See* code of Male Envy—Male Display

control (over objects at a distance, over emotion, over others), 7, 9-19, 22-26, 29-33, 35-40, 49-50, 55-55, 58, 60, 62-68, 70, 72, 75-78, 84, 91, 94-95, 97-98, 102-4, 106, 110-11, 113, 115-17, 120-24, 133-39, 141-43, 147-49, 151-62, 173-74, 178-81, 184-93, 195, 198-203, 206, 216, 218-19; control-without-commitment, 136, 158, 161; distinction between controlling and creating, 6, 181-82, 191, 206, 219, 225-29, 231, 235, 238-43. *See also* code of Male Envy; gravity; killing; obsession; power objects; power-over relationships; subject-space-object; suicide

Cooper, James Fenimore, 19, 34-36, 219, 246n26; *The Deerslayer*, 35, 247n33; *The Last of the Mohicans*, 34-37, 47n59; *The Pathfinder*, 35, 247n33; *The Pioneers*, 35

cosmology, 83-130, 215-42. *See also* God; hierarchy; images; Newton; Object thinking; "Transform"

Dante, 19; *The Divine Comedy*, 84, 196
Darwin, Charles, 108, 183, 209n18; *The Origin of Species*, 174, 182
Daston, Lorraine, 165n27
Davis, James, 168n40
Dawson, Michael, 213n59

death, 8, 17, 22, 67-69, 73, 75, 79, 87, 96-97, 103-5, 109, 112-15, 129n51, 135-136, 153, 197, 218, 223, 226-8, 231-32, 235; as object of fascinated veneration, 38-39, 141, 147, 154-61, 181, 199. *See also* code of Male Envy; God; healing; killing; *matanza*; Object thinking; suicide

Declaration of Independence, American, 91, 153

deconstruction, role of Male Envy in, 121, 129n51, 130n55, 185, 192-201, 203-5. *See also* academy; De Man; Derrida; Miller, J. Hillis; rhetoric

Defoe, Daniel, *Robinson Crusoe*, 102

Deism, 92-93, 108, 136, 148-49, 153, 155, 176-78. *See also* cosmology; God; Newton; Object thinking

De la Mora, Gonzalo Fernàndez, 3, 50

De Man, Paul, 184, 197-201, 205

Demetrakopoulos, Stephanie, 211n36

democracy, 93, 136, 153, 175-78

De Quincey, Thomas, 244n9

Derrida, Jacques, 192, 196, 201, 203-5; *Aporias*, 121, 129n51, 130n55, 196

desire, 24-25, 38, 55, 65, 72-75, 83-84, 95, 106, 113, 143, 158-61, 179-82, 184, 186, 191-93, 203, 207, 215, 220, 231. *See also* desiring female; "homosocial desire"

desiring female (figure accompanied by ineffectual lover and power male), 44n30, 66-68, 72, 74, 76, 80n24, 157, 218. *See also* female roles in Male Envy; ineffectual lover; power male

Dickens, Charles, *Bleak House*, 226; *A Christmas Carol*, 27; *Great Expectations*, 26-30, 77, 188, 241-2; *The Old Curiosity Shop*, 229; *A Tale of Two Cities*, 229

Diehl, Joanne, 44n37

Dijksterhuis, E. J., 109

Dillon, John, 213n58

disaster fantasies, 8, 16, 20, 41, 84, 101, 113, 148, 151, 199.

distorted perception, 8, 40, 51, 72, 77, 110, 151, 220. *See also* code of Male Envy; rationalizing

Doane, Janice, 43n26

Doctrine of Good Suffering, 8, 135, 156, 161, 166n31, 182-83. *See also* code of Male Envy

Dorfman, Joseph, 211n27

Dostoevsky, Feodor, *Crime and Punishment*, 137

Doty, William G., 31, 52

Doyle, Arthur Conan, 20

Dreiser, Theodore, 32

Dryden, John, 195

Duden, Barbara, 168n41

Dumont, Louis, 183

Dundes, Alan, 79n1

Durbach, Errol, 65

Dussinger, John, 168n40

Dyck, Sara, 130n54

Easlea, Brian, 211n42

Easton, Richard, 45n57

Eastwood, Clint (actor), 35

economics, 100, 108, 177, 181; classical, 89-90, 149, 180, 202-4; neoclassical, 174, 183, 202-4. *See also* capitalism; gravity; labor theory of value; marginal utility, theory of; Object thinking; self-interest; Smith

Edwards, Jonathan, 153

ego points (power points), 5, 7, 12-13, 15, 21, 24-25, 27, 30, 33, 36, 52, 54-55, 63, 75, 193, 196, 202, 205-7. *See also* aggression; code of Male Envy —Male Display; control; winning

Eichenbaum, Luise, 43n18

Eliot, George, *Middlemarch*, 24

Eliot, T. S., *Four Quartets*, 53; *The Waste Land*, 196

Ellison, Julie, 158

Emerson, Ralph Waldo, 149

emotion. *See* anger; code of Male Envy—emotion in; fear; hate; love

emptiness (void, waste, hollowness, boredom), 6, 40, 51-53, 58, 67, 85, 98, 109-10, 191, 193, 196, 206, 218,

225; as gap or aporia, 200. *See also* alienation; subject-space-object

Engels, Frederick, 10

envy, 1-8; as one of the seven deadly sins, 2. *See also* code of Male Envy; distorted perception; emptiness; evil eye; female envy; hate; rationalizing; silence; taboo

Eriksen, Erik, 211n36

Evans, J. Martin, 91, 126n26

evil, 2, 9, 16, 19, 26, 28, 38, 53, 60, 73, 83, 92, 94, 106-8, 131-33, 138, 142, 161, 176, 179, 222, 236, 239, 241; "banality of evil" (Arendt), 70

evil eye, 1, 4, 8, 12, 18, 22, 113, 151, 167n35, 244n6. *See also* gaze; hate

expanded awareness. *See* heightened sensation; "Transform"

exploitation, 11, 33, 78, 96, 107-8, 110, 115, 122, 150, 182

Falk, Gerhard, 169n52

Fanon, Frantz, *The Wretched of the Earth*, 27

Fatal Attraction (movie directed by Adrian Lyne), 56

Faulkner, William, *Sanctuary*, 32

Faust, David, 127n28

fear, 4, 6, 10, 12, 21, 28, 31, 40-41, 56, 64-65, 68, 84, 101, 110-11, 133, 136, 138, 148, 152, 156, 158, 161, 186, 189, 193, 196, 218, 223. *See also* code of Male Envy—emotion in

female envy, 10-11, 69, 71. *See also* code of Male Envy—female roles in

femme fatale. See Tricky Female

female healer. *See* healing

female savior. *See* healing

feminism, 11-12, 32, 58, 65, 77, 101, 104, 119, 127n22, 134, 136, 149, 153, 157, 201, 215-16

feudalism, 36, 84, 87-88, 93-94, 108, 142, 147-48, 160, 177, 225

Field, Alexander J., 176

Findley, Timothy, *Not Wanted on the Voyage*, 169n49

Firestone, Robert W., 167n28

Fish, Stanley, 193

Fitzgerald, F. Scott, 32; *The Great Gatsby*, 34, 151; *Tender Is the Night*, 34

Fliegelman, Jay, 168n39

food, eating, 53-56, 95, 131, 141-44, 180, 199, 224-25, 228. *See also* magic fluids

Formaini, Heather, 31

Forster, E. M., *A Passage to India*, 110

Forsyth, Adrian, 164n8

Foucault, Michel, 125n10, 165n11, 182, 209n19

Franklin, Caroline, 247n30

Franklin, Clyde W., 45n43

Frazer, Sir James, 190

French, Marilyn, *Beyond Power*, 74

Freud, Anna, *The Ego and the Mechanisms of Defense*, 161-62

Freud, Sigmund, 3, 14, 31, 84, 86, 100, 172, 179, 183; *The Future of an Illusion*, 157, 190; *Group Psychology and the Analysis of the Ego*, 81n27; *Interpretation of Dreams*, 42n10, 119; Oedipus Complex, 148, 161-62, 167n35, 184-91; "Some Psychical Consequences of the Anatomical Distinction between the Sexes," 187; *Totem and Taboo*, 156, 185, 189-90; "The Uncanny," 167n35

friendship, 5, 15-16, 28, 30-34, 61, 119, 157, 221, 230, 236, 239, 244n3. *See also* code of Male Envy—compete/control hierarchy; "homosocial desire"; male bonding

Frye, Northrop, *Creation and Recreation*, 92; *The Double Vision: Language and Meaning in Religion*, 169n50; *The Great Code*, 165n15; *The Secular Scripture*, 226, 246n25

Fuchs, Elinor, 79n11

Galbraith, John Kenneth, 210n23

Galileo, 88

Galton, Francis, 42n11

Ganz, Arthur, 65
Garfinkel, Perry, 31
Gay, Peter, 108
gaze, 8, 230; male gaze, 18, 22, 27, 37, 96, 103-4, 113-14, 117. *See also* code of Male Envy—attention-getting; evil eye; voyeurism
Gedankenexperimente ("thought experiments"), 6-7, 14, 20, 57-58, 99, 121, 123, 136, 172-73, 215-16, 219-20, 242. *See also* images; literature
Gessner, Abraham, *The Death of Abel*, 165n15, 167n39
Gibbon, Edward, *Decline and Fall of the Roman Empire*, 191
Gibbs, Raymond, 129n47
Girard, René, 2, 12, 25, 86, 165n15, 185, 190, 199-200
God (models of God), 24-25, 38-39, 84, 87-89, 92-93, 102, 106, 108, 109, 114, 119-20, 131-32, 135-62, 175, 177-84, 190, 226, 241; visualized in female terms, 118, 120, 144, 222-24, 232. *See also* atheism; Bible; Deism; feudalism; hierarchy; images; Jesus Christ; Object thinking; "Transform"
Godwin, William, 128n39, 149, 176, 178, 181; *Political Justice*, 107, 172, 239
Goethe, J. W. von, *Faust*, 227
Goldenberg, Naomi, 165n21
Goldweber, David E., 165n26
Goux, Jean-Joseph, 189
gravity, 13, 106, 148; analogy with self-interest, 89, 208n6. *See also* Deism; economics—classical; Newton; Object thinking; self-interest
Gray, Ronald, 66
Green, Karen, 128n31
Greenstein, Ben, 31-32
Gurney, Michael S., 245n14

Haggard, H. Rider, 19; *She*, 190, 246n20
Hammer, Mike (fictional character), 35
Hammett, Dashiell, *The Dain Curse*, 136; *The Maltese Falcon*, 56
Hammond, Dorothy, 47n59
Handelman, Susan A., 213n55
Harding, Sandra, 128n31
Hartman, Geoffrey, 201
Hartsock, Nancy, 90, 134
Harvey-Phillips, M., 209n17
hate, language of hate, 8, 17-24, 37, 41, 51, 94, 183, 186, 192, 198, 218. *See also* anger; code of Male Envy; fear
Haugen, Einar, 80n22
Hausman, Carl R., 88
Hawthorne, Nathaniel, 19; "Rappaccini's Daughter," 20-25, 29, 66-67, 76, 139, 154, 171, 188, 231; *The Scarlet Letter*, 23-26, 28-29, 54, 66-67, 97, 151, 154, 186, 218, 229, 231-32, 237, 240; "Young Goodman Brown," 22
healing, 219, 222, 224-43. *See also* heightened sensation
Hearn, Jeff, 43n19
Hegel, G. W. F., 108, 129n46, 196; *The Phenomenology of Mind*, 121, 123
Heidegger, Martin, 231
heightened sensation (expanded awareness), 117-18, 122-23, 217-18, 226, 235. *See also* healing; "Transform"
hell. *See* disaster fantasies
Hemingway, Ernest, *A Farewell to Arms*, 46n53; *For Whom the Bell Tolls*, 46n53; *The Sun Also Rises*, 32-4
Henberg, Marvin, 165n20
Hesse, Mary B., 190
hierarchy, 173, 183; fixed hierarchy, 36, 84, 87, 93-94, 142, 175, 177, 187, 219; *see also* code of Male Envy—compete/control hierarchy; feudalism
Hiney, Tom, 247n29
Hitchcock, Alfred, *Psycho*, 67
Hitler, Adolf, 134, 151, 159
Hobbes, Thomas, 186
Hoffman, E. T. A., "The Sandman," 167n36
Hogg, James, *Confessions of a Justified*

Sinner, 136, 141, 148-52, 158, 160
Holler, Linda, 128n37
Holliday, Laurel, 111
Holloway, Henry C., 45n51
Homer, Circe, 56, 247n33; *The Iliad*, 11
homophobia, 33-34, 45n47, 46n55. *See also* code of Male Envy; fear; hate; sex—homosexuality
"homosocial desire," 6, 11, 34. *See also* desire; male bonding; sex—homosexuality
Hudson, Liam, 9
Hudson, W. H., 20; *Green Mansions*, 241, 245n20
Hubert, Henri, 165n23
Hugo, Victor, *Les Misérables*, 229
Hume, David, *Dialogues Concerning Natural Religion*, 90, 92, 93-94, 168n38, 245n18; *A Treatise of Human Nature*, 3, 51, 128n33
humiliation. *See* code of Male Envy—Male Display; losing; winning
Hunt, Margaret, 168n45
Hurlbutt, Robert H., 126n13

Ibsen, Henrik, *A Doll's House*, 80n21; *Hedda Gabler*, 30, 57-74, 77, 78, 171, 215, 218, 231, 240, 242
images (mental images), logic of imaginable forms, 2-3, 6-7, 9, 11, 14-16, 18, 42n11, 50, 57-59, 62, 76, 84-90, 93, 136-37, 140, 143, 147-49, 156-57, 160, 172, 174-77, 182, 184, 188, 194, 196, 208, 215, 219, 224-26, 228-29, 232, 236. *See also* cosmology; *Gedankenexperimente*
incest, 23, 39, 76, 185, 187. *See also* aggression; Freud, Sigmund; power male; rape; silence; taboo
individualism. *See* Object thinking
ineffectual lover, 66-68, 74, 76, 160, 218. *See also* desiring female; power male
Ingham, Mary, 211n36
instinct, 2-3, 35, 50, 55, 62, 69, 89-91, 96, 121, 180, 184, 191, 222-24; instinct of workmanship (Veblen), 53, 191, 203, 206. *See also* Freud, Sigmund; Malthus; Smith
intimidation rituals. *See* code of Male Envy—intimidation rituals
invidious distinction, 6, 8, 14, 27, 37, 61, 95, 171-75, 188, 191, 219. *See also* code of Male Envy—compete/control hierarchy; Veblen

Jackson, Glenda (actor), 80n16
Jacobsen, Per Schelde, 79n11
James, M. R., 167n34
James, Patricia, 209n22
James, P. D., *A Taste for Death*, 134
Jauss, Hans Robert, 199
Jay, John, 207
Jay, Nancy, 43n25
Jeans, Sir James, *The Mysterious Universe*, 126n20
Jeffords, Susan, 11
Jesus Christ, 25, 101, 105, 108, 120, 139-141, 222-23, 236
Johnson, Christopher D., 129n49
Johnson, Mark, 125n10
Johnson, Michael, 45n42
Johnson, Samuel, 195; *The Rambler*, 191; *Rasselas*, 19
Jones, Ernest, *Oedipus and Hamlet*, 46n54
Jones, Roger S., 215
Jordanova, L. J., 95, 245n18
Jung, Carl, 234, 244n9
Justman, Stewart, 127n25

Kanth, Rajani, 149, 181
Kargon, Robert Hugh, 98
Keats, John, *Endymion*, 230-31; *Epistle to John Hamilton Reynolds*, 231; *The Fall of Hyperion*, 19; *Hyperion*, 19; "I Stood Tip-Toe," 230-31; *Isabella, or The Pot of Basil*, 74-78, 106, 117; "La Belle Dame Sans Merci," 55; *Lamia*, 15-20, 28, 66, 77, 97, 188; "Ode on a Grecian Urn," 231; "Ode

to a Nightingale," 230-31, 236
Kennedy, James, *Conversations with Lord Byron on Religion*, 165n25
Keynes, John Maynard, 203, 208n5
Kierkegaard, Soren, *Fear and Trembling*, 139, 165n16
killing, 4, 8, 12-14, 17-18, 22-24, 34-36, 39, 41, 56, 65-67, 75-77, 96, 101-6, 111-12, 114-16, 120, 131-63, 190, 218, 223, 226, 230, 233-34, 236, 239, 241-42. *See also* aggression; animals, abuse of; children, abuse of; code of Male Envy; blood; control; death
Kim, Yong Shin, 81n27
King, Stephen, *The Shining*, 131
Kipling, Rudyard, 19
Kissinger, Henry, 171
Klein, Melanie, *Envy and Gratitude*, 4, 8-9, 13-14, 225
Kling, David W., 167n33
Knox, John, 155
Kohn, Alfie, 79n6
Koyré, Alexandre, 208n7
Kriegel, Leonard, 45n55
Kristeva, Julia, 30
Kubrick, Stanley, *Dr. Strangelove*, 49-50, 102, 139, 151; *The Shining*, 131-32, 139
Kuhn, Thomas, 174
Ku Klux Klan, 241
Küng, Hans, 168n44
Kuypers, Joseph A., 125n1

labor theory of value, 96, 213n57, 202-3. *See also* economics—classical; instinct—instinct of workmanship; Smith
Lacan, Jacques, 184-85, 188, 190
language of convolution. *See* hate; rationalizing; rhetoric
Laplace, Pierre Simon de, 156
Lawrence, D. H., 35
Le Doeuff, Michèle, 43n28, 119
Lehman, Peter, 11
LeMahieu, Daniel L., 177
Leonard, Eileen, 245n17

Lévi-Strauss, Claude, 10
Lew, Joseph W., 168n40
Lewis, C. S., *The Discarded Image*, 125n6; *The Screwtape Letters*, 53, 95
Lewis, Matthew G., *The Monk*, 167n37
Lewontin, Richard C., 171, 196
Leyton, Elliott, 133-35, 151
Lichtman, Richard, 210n31
life. *See* body; death; "Transform"
Life-in-Death 112-13, 115, 225, 231. *See also* alienation; Coleridge; death
literature, 2, 6, 13-15, 20, 34, 56, 65, 106, 110, 135-36, 148, 192, 195-97, 220-23, 226, 229; social function of, 2, 7, 14, 19, 121, 170-71, 194; as thinking-in-images, 2, 9, 170-71, 173, 205. *See also* academy; children's literature; *Gedankenexperimente*; images; Romantic narrative
Livingston, Paisley, 44n29
losing, loser status, 5-6, 9, 15, 22, 24, 26, 28, 30-32, 34, 40-41, 49, 51-54, 57, 64-65, 67-72, 75-76, 94-95, 97, 111, 133, 142, 152, 181-89, 192, 216, 225. *See also* alienation; code of Male Envy—compete/control hierarchy; Freud—castration anxiety; ineffectual lover; winning
love (as control), 5, 9, 11, 13, 15-16, 21-29, 32-35, 39-40, 49-50, 56, 58, 60, 66-69, 71, 73-74, 76-77, 96, 102, 115-19, 132, 140-41, 143, 152, 154, 157, 159-60, 179, 217-18, 220-23, 227-30, 233-34, 238-40. *See also* code of Male Envy—emotion in; control; desiring female; ineffectual lover; sex; Tricky Female
Lovitt, Carl R., 164n7
Low, Lisa M., 65
Lyotard, Jean François, 12

Maccoby, Hyam, 141, 159
Macdonald, George, 19; *The Princess and the Goblin*, 246n23
Macfarlane, Alan, 179

Machiavelli, Niccolo, *The Prince*, 51
machines (mechanism paradigm), 90, 92, 98, 103, 108, 121-24, 126n20, 149, 177, 181, 219; male body as, 118. *See also* Newton; Object thinking; science
Macpherson, C. B. ("possessive individualism"), 97, 149, 178
magic fluids, 5, 8, 22, 57, 103, 117, 131, 137, 144, 222-25, 231-32, 235, 237, 246n26. *See also* blood; semen
Magic Virgin convention, 226-30; related to chastity, 34
male bonding, 31-35, 104. *See also* friendship; "homosocial desire"
Male Envy. *See* code of Male Envy
malice. *See* code of Male Envy
Malory, Thomas, *Le Morte d'Arthur*, 226
The Maltese Falcon (movie directed by John Huston), 56
Malthus, Thomas Robert, 14, 89, 97, 155; *An Essay on Population*, 95, 172, 174-91, 199, 202; *Principles of Political Economy*, 178
Mandel, Ernest, 149
Mandeville, Bernard, *The Fable of the Bees*, 215
Margenau, Henry, 245n18
marginal utility, theory of, 203
Marx, Karl, 8, 108, 129n46, 189; *Capital*, 88, 91, 123, 209n16; *Eighteenth Brumaire of Louis Napoléon*, 128n32
matanza (massacre in El Salvador), 133
materialism. *See* Object thinking
Maxwell, James Clerk, 126n23, 165n27
McDonald, Roderick, 100
McFarlane, James, 81n25
McGann, Jerome, 100, 212n49
McGill, Michael E., 45n43
McKenna, Andrew J., 199
McNay, Lois, 128n31
Medea, 64-65, 247n33
Mellor, Anne K., 168n42
Melville, Herman, *Billy Budd*, 38, 240, 247n31; *Pierre, or The Ambiguities*, 167n35; *Typee*, 240
"men's movement," 43n19
mercantilism. *See* capitalism
Merchant, Carolyn,126n18, 246n18
Merleau-Ponty, Maurice, 85
Messner, Michael A., 11, 31, 178
Meyer, Michael, 80n17
Miles, Rosalind, 133, 162-63
Miller, Alice, 161
Miller, J. Hillis, 192, 196, 204-5
Milne, Paula, 165n21
Milton, John, *Comus*, 92; *Paradise Lost*, 1, 19, 35, 37-41, 77, 86-87, 91, 93-96, 98, 105, 109, 112, 142, 149, 162, 182, 195, 219
Mitchell, Jerome, 238
Mohr, Richard D., 45n56
money. *See* capitalism; control; power objects; winning
Money-Kyrle, R., 165n13
Montcalm, Marquis de, 36
Morris, William, 19
Mose, George L., 12
movies, use of Male Envy themes in film, 35, 49-50, 56, 67, 131-32
murder, multiple murder. *See* killing; Leyton
Murdoch, Rupert, 10

Nadeau, Robert L., 122
Naiman, Joanne, 45n55
Napoléon, 109, 157; "Napoleon Complex," 163n6
Neubauer, John, 125n3
Newsinger, John, 210n23
Newton, Sir Isaac; Newtonian physics, 89, 108, 126n14, 126n20, 148, 177, 178, 183-84, 210n31. *See also* economics—classical; Deism; gravity; Object thinking
Nietzsche, Friedrich, 21, 65, 201; *Dawn of Day*, 72-73; *The Genealogy of Morals*, 13, 212n49
Nixon, Pat (wife of Richard Nixon), 24
Northam, John, 80n23
numerous competitors, motif of the. *See*

code of Male Envy—numerous competitors

Object Cosmology. *See* Object thinking
Object relations (psychology), 126n11
Object thinking, 13, 40, 83-130, 135, 141, 148-49, 153-54, 159-61, 172, 174, 176-81, 183-84, 188-89, 191, 193-95, 197-202, 204-7, 216-19, 224-25, 227-29, 231, 237, 242. *See also* code of Male Envy; cosmology; Deism; Derrida; economics—classical; gravity; machine; Newton; science
obsession (compulsion), 8-9, 14, 20, 27, 29, 37-38, 40-41, 51, 55, 66-67, 72, 77, 97, 106, 111, 113-14, 117-18, 123, 120, 122, 124, 134, 140, 147, 153, 157-58, 160, 162, 171, 173, 178, 187-90, 192-93, 196-97, 201, 215-18, 220, 225, 228-31, 235, 239, 241-43. *See also* alienation; code of Male Envy—emotion in; control; distorted perception
O'Day, Rory, 10
Oedipus, Oedipus complex. *See* Freud, Sigmund
Olsen, Stein, 64, 71
Orbach, Susie, 43n18
Orwell, George, *1984*, 115, 167n35
Owen, Wilfred, 139

Paine, Tom, 128n39, 178; *The Age of Reason*, 137, 148, 165n12; *The Rights of Man*, 149. *See also* Deism
Paley, William, *Evidences of Christianity*, 92; *Natural Theology*, 92
Pearl, 226
penis, penis envy, 12, 35, 90, 187-90. *See also* code of Male Envy
Perera, Sylvia, 218
Perkins, David, 185
phallus. *See* penis
Plato, 87, 125n4
Plutarch, 2
Poe, Edgar Allan, 19, 227; *The Narrative of Arthur Gordon Pym*, 167n37
Polanski, Roman, *Chinatown*, 67
Pope, Alexander, 195
Porter, Roy, 150
post-structuralism. *See* deconstruction
power male, 66-67, 74, 76 157, 218. *See also* desiring female
power points. *See* ego points
power objects (e.g., gun, lens, money), 7, 9, 36, 54, 57, 63, 73, 76, 91, 101, 188, 218. *See also* code of Male Envy—Male Display; control; penis
power-over relationships. *See* akeda; code of Male Envy—power-over relationships; control; money
Powers, Jonathan, 87
Praz, Mario, 56
prestige fetish. *See* academy
proletarianization, 27, 108. *See also* alienation; capitalism; Freud—castration; losing
Proudhon, Pierre Joseph, 183
psychoanalysis. *See* Freud, Sigmund
Pugh, David G., 89-90
Punter, David, 128n39

Quinones, Ricardo, 165n25

Radcliffe, Ann, *The Italian*, 167n37; *The Romance of the Forest*, 229-30
Radford, Jill, 43n21
Rajan, Tilottama, 42n
rape, 12, 23, 28, 32, 66-67, 76, 132, 187, 218, 222, 226-27, 241
rationalizing, 8-9, 67, 86, 96, 99, 107, 137, 152, 155, 174, 176, 181-83, 200-1, 216, 221, 238. *See also* code of Male Envy; control; distorted perception; hate; rhetoric
Rausky, F., 209n17
Reich, Wilhelm, 220
Remond, R., 209n17
resistance (psychoanalysis, deconstruction), 3, 185, 200. *See also* deconstruction; rationalizing

rhetoric, rhetorical devices, 3, 62, 94, 133-35, 144-45, 149, 155, 177, 197-201. *See also* killing; rationalizing
Ricardo, David, *Principles of Political Economy and Taxation*, 202-3
Richardson, John, *Wacousta*, 240
Rochefoucauld, François de la, *Maximes*, 45n54
Romanticism, as experiment in cosmology, 15, 20, 36, 85, 110, 116, 121, 123, 135, 149, 157, 216, 219-20, 242. *See also* literature; Romantic narrative; "Transform"
Romantic narrative, 13, 19-20, 36, 66, 74, 77, 98, 116, 135-36, 215, 219-20, 223-26, 229, 232-33, 238, 240, 242, 243. *See also* literature; Romanticism; "Transform"
Rooney, Phyllis, 81n26
Rosen, Frederick, 183
Ross, Marlon B., 44n31
Rotenstreich, Nathan, 129n46
Rousseau, G. S., 135
Rousseau, J.-J., 154; *The Social Contract*, 93
Rubin, Abba, 246n22
Rushdie, Salmon, 161
Ryan, Robert, 168n40
Rzepka, Charles J., 28

Sabo, Don (football player), 26
sacrifice. *See* animals, abuse of; blood; children, abuse of; killing
Santurri, Edmund, 209n22
Satan. *See* Byron—*Cain*; Milton—*Paradise Lost*
satire, 49, 82-83, 96, 196
Saussure, Ferdinand de, 204
scapegoat. *See* code of Male Envy
Schadenfreude, 6, 8, 65
Scheler, Max, 3
Schoeck, Helmut, 3, 23, 51
Schoenberg, B. Mark, 42n9
Schopenhauer, Arthur, "On Religion," 83
science (rise of science, technology), 21-23, 29, 74, 86-93, 99, 101, 109, 154, 171, 175-76, 180-83, 185, 190-91, 196, 201, 233. *See also* machines; Newton; Object thinking
Scott, Walter, *The Betrothed*, 246n26; *Count Robert of Paris*, 244n10; *The Heart of Midlothian*, 242n9, 247n32; *Ivanhoe*, 167n37, 219, 226-27, 229, 231, 233-43; *The Talisman*, 237-39
Searle, John R., 86
Sedgwick, Eve Kosofsky, 11, 14, 34, 45n55, 112
Seidler, Victor J., 32, 91
Seinfeld, Jerry (comedian), 31, 45n47
self-gratification (ego-inflation), 35, 40, 52, 78, 96, 134-35, 138, 179, 186, 194, 217, 229, 239. *See also* code of Male Envy—Male Display; ego points; winning
self-interest, 10, 35, 52-53, 69, 78, 89-90, 96-98, 109, 154, 161-62, 179, 181, 191, 215, 219. *See also* code of Male Envy—Male Display; ego points; self-gratification; winning;
self-love. *See* self-gratification
Seltzer, Mark, 90
semen, 79n1. *See also* magic fluids
sensation. *See* code of Male Envy—emotion in; heightened sensation; "Transform"
sex, sexuality, 3-6, 12, 22-24, 30, 32, 35-36, 40, 49-50, 54-56, 58, 60, 62, 66-67, 86, 89-90, 133, 160, 162, 178-82, 184-88, 216-18, 222, 226-28, 230-34, 238-40; homosexuality, 14, 16, 31, 33-35, 45n47, 46n55, 238-39; and population, 209n19. *See also* code of Male Envy—female roles in; control; love; winning
shadow (Jung), 234. *See also* Jung
Shakespeare, William, *Antony and Cleopatra*, 26; *Hamlet*, 65, 76, 169n49, 197; *Macbeth*, 4, 27, 151; *Othello*, 18; *Pericles*, 226
Shaw, George Bernard, 65
Shelley, Mary, *Frankenstein*, 35, 90,

115, 134-35, 153-62, 180
Shelley, Percy, 198, 200, 230; *The Cenci*, 23, 136, 242n9; *Defence of Poetry*, 195; "Julian and Maddalo," 246n21; "On Life," 130n57; *Prometheus Unbound*, 38, 115, 136
Sherman, Paul, 168n40
Sherned, Drury, 125n1
Shuman, Sandra, 230
silence, silencing, 2-5, 8, 11, 13, 15, 19, 28, 32, 42n9, 56, 76, 104, 107-8, 110-12, 114-15, 132, 143, 162, 192, 220-22. *See also* taboo
Silverman, Kaja, 78, 210n33
Singer, Daniel, 204
slavery, slave trade, 52, 99-100, 149, 177. *See also* capitalism
Slotkin, Richard, 45n58
Smith, Adam, 180; *Essays on Philosophical Subjects*, 125n5; "History of Ancient Physics," 87; *The Theory of Moral Sentiments*, 12n23; *The Wealth of Nations*, 42n10, 89, 106, 148, 177, 191, 202, 208n6, 209n16, 215, 244n7
Smith, Stevie, 158
sneering. *See* academy
solipsism. *See* self gratification
Spacks, Patricia, 80n18
Spencer, Kathleen, 228
Spenser, Edmund, 195; *The Faerie Queene*, 226
sports, Male Envy in, 11, 104-5, 202
Stallone, Sylvester (actor), 35
Stendhal, *La Chartreuse de Parme*, 242n9
Steurat, Sir James, 180
Stevens, Gwendolyn, 158
Stevenson, Robert Louis, 19
Stiehm, Judith, 43n20
Stoker, Bram, 19; *Dracula*, 151, 227-28
Stowe, Harriet Beecher, 19
Strindberg, August, *The Father*, 56
struggling female (figure flanked by ineffectual lover and power male). *See* desiring female
subject-space-object paradigm, 90, 98, 117, 161, 200, 217, 231. *See also* control; emptiness; Object thinking
suicide, 58, 60, 71, 73, 76, 136, 144, 151, 155, 162, 215-16. *See also* code of Male Envy; death; killing
survival of the fittest. *See* aggression
Swift, Jonathan, *Gulliver's Travels*, 196, 245n13

taboo, 1-2, 11, 33, 187, 191, 220, 234-35, 240. *See also* code of Male Envy; friendship; Freud; incest; love; sex—homosexuality; silence
Tadie, Andre, 127n30
Tallis, R. C., 185, 200
Talmor, Ezra, 209n22
Thackeray, William Makepeace, 246n22
Thatcher, Margaret, 89
Theweleit, Klaus, *Male Fantasies*, 14, 94, 97, 134, 162, 185
Thompson, E. P., *The Making of the English Working Class*, 141
Thoreau, Henry David, 149
Tillich, Paul, *The Courage to Be*, 26
Tilman, Rick, 43n27
"Transform" (experimental cosmology), 14, 121-24, 127n22, 149, 195, 215-42
Tricky Female, 20, 22, 30, 49-82, 157, 218. *See also* code of Male Envy—female roles in; sex
Tuss, Alex J., 32
Twain, Mark, *Huckleberry Finn*, 33, 136-37, 151; *Tom Sawyer*, 33, 165n22
Twitchell, James, 165n11

Vander Weele, Michael, 211n43
Veblen, Thorstein, 190-91; *The Higher Learning*, 211n37; *Imperial Germany and the Industrial Revolution*, 79n6, 129n42; *The Theory of the Leisure Class*, 4, 10, 14, 27, 53, 60, 61, 76, 88, 93, 95, 97, 104-5, 137-38, 142, 171-72, 188, 190-91, 202-3, 207
Victorian culture, 235, 240

Vitale, Marina, 169n49
Vlasopolos, Anca, 210n27
Voltaire, *Dictionnaire Philosophique*, 212n49
Vorzimmer, Peter, 208n2
voyeurism, 22, 67. *See also* control; evil eye; gaze; *Schadenfreude*

Wall Street (movie directed by Oliver Stone), 95
Wallace, Alfred Russell, 208n2
Waterman, A. M. C., 175
weapons. *See* power objects
Weigand, Herman, 80n16
Wells, H. G., 20
West, Nathanael, 32
Wetzel, James, 165n21
Whigham, Frank, 88
Wieland, C. M., *Der Gepryfte Abraham*, 165n15
Wiener, Jon, 211n44
Wilde, Oscar, 19
Williams, James G., 144
Willis, Bruce (actor), 35
Winnicott, D. W., 126n11
winning 3, 5, 9-12, 14, 18, 23-25, 27, 29-36, 38, 40, 49-54, 61, 63-69, 73, 76, 96-97, 111-12, 142-43, 147, 152-53, 156, 158, 161-62, 173, 176, 180-83, 186, 190, 192, 200, 202, 215, 219, 235. *See also* code of Male Envy—compete/control hierarchy; ego points; ineffectual lover; losing; power male
Winspear, Alban D., 125n4
Wollstonecraft, Mary, 149, 153; *The Wrongs of Woman*, 30, 80n24; *A Vindication of the Rights of Woman*, 245n17
words of hate (language as weapon). *See* academy; hate
Wordsworth, William, 123, 135, 226-27 "A Slumber Did My Spirit Seal," 212n51, "Three Years She Grew," 227
Wyly, James, 42n14

Yeats, William Butler, 247n32
Yoder, John H., 140
Yolton, John W., 127n23

Zaret, David, 90
Zita, Jacqueline, 245n17

About the Author

Mervyn Nicholson is also the author of *13 Ways of Looking at Images: Studies in the Logic of Visualization*. He is a member of the Executive of the Association of Canadian University Teachers of English, and former Chair of English and Modern Languages at University College in British Columbia, Canada. He holds a Ph.D. from the University of Toronto supervised by Northrop Frye: he was Northrop Frye's last doctoral student. He has publications in a wide range of journals, including *The Journal of the History of Ideas, Recherches Sémiotiques, LIT: Literature, Interpretation, Theory, Women's Studies, Arcadia, Canadian Review of Comparative Literature, Literature / Film Quarterly, Renascence, University of Toronto Quarterly, Ultimate Reality and Meaning: Interdisciplinary Studies in the Philosophy of Understanding, Modern Drama, Comparative Drama, Mosaic, Nineteenth-Century Contexts, Ariel, The Wallace Stevens Journal, College English, CEA Critic, The Wordsworth Circle, English Studies in Canada, Literature of the Oppressed, Children's Literature Quarterly, San José Studies, Mythlore, The Lamp-Post, The Journal of the Fantastic in the Arts*, and more.

He welcomes comment: email nicholson@cariboo.bc.ca.

OHIO UNIVERSITY LIBRARY
Please return this book as soon as you have finished with it. In order to avoid a fine it must be returned by the latest date stamped below. All books are subject to recall after two weeks or immediately if needed for reserve.

CF